Education
in America

Education in America

Fourth Edition

James Monroe Hughes

Late, Northwestern University

Frederick Marshall Schultz

The University of Akron

Harper & Row, Publishers

New York   Hagerstown   San Francisco   London

My work on the fourth edition of *Education in America*
is dedicated to Jane Petersen.

F.M.S.

Photo credits: Pp. 4, 126, 426 Mimi Forsyth, Monkmeyer; pp. 18, 240,
268, 282, 336, 366, 402, 472 Hugh Rogers, Monkmeyer; p. 44 Nancy
Hays, Monkmeyer; pp. 72, 150 Wide World; pp. 102, 388 Perry Ruben,
Monkmeyer; p. 174 German Information Center; p. 194 Culver; p. 218
Ellis Herwig, Stock, Boston; p. 314 Beckwith Studios; p. 448 Shackman,
Monkmeyer.

Sponsoring Editor: Michael E. Brown
Project Editor: Holly Detgen
Designer: Andrea C. Goodman
Production Supervisor: Will C. Jomarrón
Photo Researcher: Myra Schachne
Compositor: Bi-Comp, Incorporated
Printer and Binder: Halliday Lithograph Corporation
Art Studio: Eric G. Hieber Associates Inc.

EDUCATION IN AMERICA, Fourth Edition

Library of Congress Cataloging in Publication Data

Hughes, James Monroe, Date—
    Education in America.

    Includes bibliographies and index.
    1. Education—United States—1945–1964.   I. Schultz,
Frederick Marshall, joint author.   II. Title.
LA209.2.H8 1976   370'.973   75-43906
ISBN 0-06-042978-X

Contents

II

Educational Ideas That Have Been Influential in America / 147

III

The Schools in America / 237

IV

Aims and Methods in America / 363

Preface

This fourth edition of *Education in America* is directed, as were the previous three editions, to those who are interested in learning about the nature of education in present-day America, the development of educational institutions, and the directions in which these institutions may be heading. This volume is intended for those considering a career in professional education and for those wanting to be well informed about educational institutions, practices, and issues in America. An introductory overview of the nature and development of educational development in the United States is presented.

The fourth edition retains the overall format of the previous three editions and is once again divided into four autonomous units that can be studied in any sequence desired by teachers or readers. Professor Hughes enjoyed great success by the development of this four-unit structure because it provided great flexibility in choices of approach. Therefore, although I have modified very slightly the titles and the outlines of some chapters, the underlying principles within these units have been maintained. Teachers who use the book will note that, whatever revisions or deletions have occurred in updating and revising particular chapters, the adaptability of the text has been kept.

Every effort has been made to discuss the problems of American education in view of current social and economic conditions. Nevertheless, the sound treatment of the origins of our educational ideals has been retained. Relevant to the latter matter is the fact that Chapters 5, 7, and 8 have been almost entirely rewritten. New photographs have been included at the beginning of each chapter to reflect the diversity of American-community contexts and the educational issues of the 1970s. The end-of-chapter summaries, questions, and suggested projects are intended to give a deeper understanding of the material covered and to stimulate thought and discussion.

Since the third edition of *Education in America* appeared in 1970, the people of the United States have experienced many major dilemmas that have encouraged them to look more deeply into all aspects of their unique, culturally pluralistic heritage as a nation. As a book designed to explore the basic elements in the American educational heritage as well as to relate these events and ideas to our living present, it is particularly appropriate that the fourth edition appears in the year of the bicentennial of the American Revolution. We owe much in our educational heritage to European as well as to American intellectual and social precedents. *Education in America* seeks to broaden the awareness of readers with reference to the social and cultural foundations of contemporary American educational problems while still providing a comprehensive introduction to the specific institutional frameworks within which formal education (schooling) proceeds in the United States. This volume retains its strength as one of the best introductory overviews of educational development in the United States. Its comprehensive thematic approach to this subject will, it is hoped, contribute to its continuing vitality and relevance. Considerable updating of data has been undertaken on the basis of the latest government and private sources available.

An effort has been made to bring all sectors of the volume into harmony with the difficult economic realities in American society that challenge all segments of contemporary American educational development. But this does not mean that a pessimistic view has been taken; quite to the contrary, there is a positive line of discussion throughout in spite of the necessity to prepare prospective teachers and parents for the serious challenges ahead in building the educational future of our society.

Finally, I would like to take this opportunity to express my gratitude for the unique opportunity provided me to build on the work of so fine and dedicated an American educator as the late Professor James Monroe Hughes. It is an opportunity undertaken with a sincere respect for the depth and scope of his work. The fourth edition of *Education in America* attempts to continue the concept of the development of a sound overview approach to the study of American education.

F. M. S.

The teacher in America

Our discussion of education in America begins with a focus on the classroom teacher as an individual. After all, it is the classroom teachers who, in the last analysis, largely determine what and how effective education will be. Following the study of the teacher as an individual we shall, in later units, broaden our perspective to include many other features that influence the teacher and have a bearing on the entire educational picture.

The individual teacher in the classroom is the key to education; it is obvious, therefore, that teachers must be well informed. The most appropriate time to increase one's enlightenment about education is at the time of choosing, or considering, teaching as a career—the very time when the entire career, which may prove to be a lifetime one, lies ahead. A starting point is information about and understanding of the duties and responsibilities of a teacher, his place in the profession and in his institution, the sources and functions of his philosophy in terms of which he, as an individual teacher, will operate.

In this focus on the teacher as an individual, we consider the nature of a teacher's work, how he becomes qualified to teach, personality traits he must have, the responsibilities he assumes in accepting membership in the profession, and the rewards he may expect. How will the formulation of a personal educational philosophy help him? How does he go about building his philosophy? How does teaching in an educational institution affect what he does? How will an institution serve him?

Such questions, of course, cannot be answered categorically; indeed, they cannot even be analyzed completely. Nevertheless, questions centering around the teacher as an individual serve as a point of departure, something on which to build. Throughout the rest of the book additional information and understandings will emerge to add other insights.

In the closing unit of the book, we return to the work of classroom teachers as a professional group, emphasizing then the broader aspects of their overall instructional responsibilities.

chapter

1

Introduction

In this study of education in America we are going to look at what education has meant to the American people. In the process of doing this we are going to consider the nature of teaching as a social role as well as the ideas, institutions, and purposes that are the foundational sources of the American educational heritage.

In recent years the United States has witnessed controversies in the realm of education that have resulted directly from the deep trauma experienced by the American people since 1965. The following events have affected our estimates of the educational situation in America: the escalation of a foreign war, the beginning of the urban disturbances that were to reawaken (or awaken for the first time) most Americans to urban social and educational needs, the development of student unrest on college and high school campuses from 1964 to 1970, and the beginnings of major shifts in youth values that brought the "drug culture" and the "counterculture" not only to the college campuses but sometimes to the secondary schools and later elementary grades as well. Concern for the environment and a major

5

decrease in the projections of American population growth, which overturned the high population growth estimates of the U.S. government in the early and mid-1960s, also contributed to the need for a reassessment of education in America for prospective teachers and other citizens. American educators and others in the social service vocations have been and are striving to meet the educational problems posed by these events and the many other subsidiary ones either caused by or affected by what turned out to be probably the most divisive decade since the 1860s. The end of the decade of the 1960s and the decade of the 1970s have clearly brought a new generation of educational problems and needs to the American people. We will meet these problems best when we understand the nature of schools and of teaching in the United States and the activities and responsibilities of teachers in American society. We are engaged in the introductory study of American education within the framework of the need to solve the many unique educational problems that have been given to this generation of Americans. This book is intended to assist its readers in understanding and relating the American educational past and present so that they may be better prepared to plan for the future educational development of our nation as well as for careers as educators.

At the beginning of a study of education in America it is important to decide on the meaning of the word "education," because it has a number of meanings; they are, broadly, divided into two categories: the act or process of educating and the science of teaching and learning.

Before we choose the limited meaning of "education" that will guide subsequent discussions in this book, we should note a few of the different ways the word is commonly used. A person may be referred to as having a high school or a college education. A student may say that he is taking a course in education or that he is enrolled in a department or school or college of education. Some writers use the term to encompass all and any activities by which children learn the techniques, sentiments, and customs of the society in which they live.

In any introductory study of education in America the activities in which teachers engage in the process of educating students—that is, helping them to learn—are of central importance. Likewise, the types of educational institutions in which teachers engage in these activities ought to be examined. The vast commitment of our national resources for the education of our citizens deserves some preliminary attention at this point. (Yet in spite of the large amount of money committed to education, many argue that not nearly enough of our national resources are being used for education.)

Throughout this book the term "education" will be used to refer to the deliberate efforts undertaken by people to help other people learn, and the primary focus will be on the formal learning activities that go on in schools. As a corollary to this use of "education" in this book we must also note that only those forms of learning that are considered to have some worth by the members of the society in which a case of education occurs will be considered educative cases of teaching. People are taught to be assassins and bank robbers, but we do not consider persons who have undergone such instruction to have been educated in the arts of bank robbery or assassination. The word "education" and its adjectival form, "educative," have traditionally been reserved for cases where one person intentionally teaches another person some skill, attitude, or form of knowledge held to have some practical, intellectual, or aesthetic use to the person being taught. Practical, intellectual, or aesthetic use has traditionally been determined in terms of the values of the cultural heritage or heritages in which a particular case of education occurs.

This book is designed for readers who are either interested in gaining sound knowledge about formal education (schooling) or interested in careers in teaching or professional fields related to teaching. The word "education" is probably most often used to refer to the formal learning experiences that go on in schools. But it is also used to refer to informal learning experiences, which take place outside of schools. Examples of these would be the many types of apprenticeship and other on-the-job or family learning experiences through which many of us gain educational benefits. Most of the learning experiences we will be dealing with in this book center around those formal educational experiences people gain in schools. Whenever we refer to informal or broader uses of "education" in the discussion of the topics dealt with in this volume we will clearly note this fact.

The word "education" implies more than just one person attempting to instruct another person. It implies an unswerving devotion to truth in the act of such instruction—a devotion to the open and uncompromising love of knowledge and its free transmission to others. Education should also give the person being educated greater understanding of how what he or she is taught relates to his or her knowledge of the world. Thus one of the results of education should be that the learner comes away from the educational process with a broader perspective on the world. It is in the light of the conditions stated in this and the preceding two paragraphs that the meaning of "education" is to be understood in this volume. Most of this book is devoted to the study of formal educational development in America in terms of the development of state and local school systems and the development of the teaching profession and ideas about teaching in America. Thus throughout this book the word will be used to refer to the deliberate and formal learning that is organized and directed by the people of the United States. Most of the learning we will be concerned with in this book is that which takes place in the schools. (Whenever, as will sometimes be the case, a broader, more inclusive meaning of the word is intended, the distinction will be made clear.)

Magnitude of the Educational Undertaking

Education is one of the largest undertakings in America, and perhaps the most important. Hence it involves an immense effort. America spent more than $96 billion on education in 1973–1974, and this was far from sufficient to finance education that fully met all the requirements of every citizen. Obsolete buildings and other unmet needs attest to this. The very size of the educational establishment, one that includes almost 3 million classroom teachers at all educational levels, indicates that the problems related to educating, attracting, and supervising educational personnel are tremendous.

Every September more than 59 million people of all ages enter some kind of school, many to attend full time, some to attend part time. If we add to the full-time students at all levels the teachers, principals, and instructional specialists; the cooks, bus drivers, and custodians; and the people engaged in selling or producing something for the schools, the total is 30 percent of this country's population. In terms of numbers of persons involved, education is by far this country's chief enterprise. Other people are involved in schools in a variety of ways—parents of schoolchildren, members of school boards, school trustees, school architects, builders of school buildings, investors in school bonds. If the payers of school taxes and the voters on school matters are included, almost everyone in the United States is a participant in the vast undertaking. Whether viewed in terms of its extent or its importance, the magnitude of America's educational undertaking is immense.

When we consider that the $93 billion to $100 billion spent on education by the local, state, and federal governments in 1974 is an amount second in size only to the defense expenditures of the federal government, we can see how large the commitment of national resources is. In 1972 the total expenditures for all levels of educational development in the United States climbed to an amount greater than 8 percent of the country's total gross national product (GNP—the annual total capital productivity from all sectors of the national economy combined). Many people feel that an industrialized nation such as the United States should be spending a larger percentage of its gross national product each year on educational development, and many professional organizations are seeking to influence state and federal government educational units to work for a realignment of governmental priorities to allow for greater national and state investment in education.

The end of the decade of the 1970s might well see annual expenditures for educational development in the United States exceed 10 percent of the annual gross national product. Much more will be said about the specific dimensions of American education at the local, state and federal levels in Unit III of this book. There we will undertake a penetrating view of the nature and magnitude of the formal educational effort in the United States at each level of government. Figure 1-1 provides a vertical view of the many levels of formal educational activity in the United States. We will discuss much more about the specific dimensions of the structure of education in the United States in Unit III, where we will see how the different levels in this structure relate to schooling and to social structure in America. Likewise, Unit IV, "Aims and Methods in America," is concerned with the study of how the structure of education relates to the objectives of teachers and to society in general. In Unit IV we explore several recent issues in curriculum development.

Figure 1-1 provides a schematic design of the different levels of formal schooling activity in the United States from the nursery school level through the postdoctoral research level. Following this schematic design, beginning at the age of 3 years and progressing

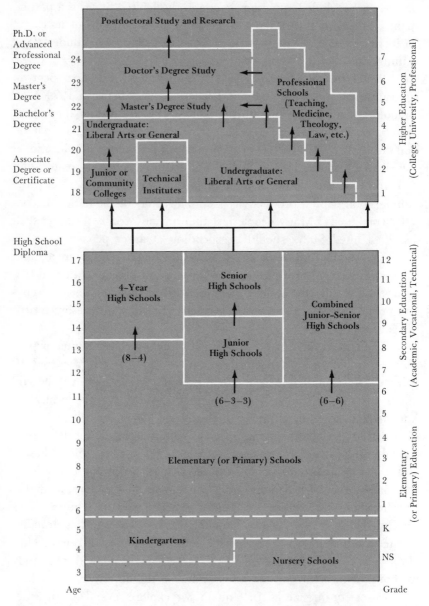

Figure 1-1 The structure of education in the United States. (From W. Vance Grant et al., *Digest of Educational Statistics for 1973*. Washington D.C.: U.S. Department of Health, Education, and Welfare, DHEW Publication No. (OE)74-11103, p. 4.)

one step up the formal educational ladder with each year in school, a very bright young person with sufficient economic and social opportunities could not reach the postdoctoral level of study and research prior to the age of 24. Figure 1-1 also provides a visual image of the different types of combinations of elementary and secondary schooling sequences that will constitute the basic concern of this text as we discuss how teachers relate to these sequences of schooling. The upper darkened square in Figure 1-1 provides a very fine visual model of what types of postsecondary educational opportunities are available to American citizens and how these levels of college education proceed from the first year of collegiate study through at least 7 years of study to reach the postdoctoral level. It is not uncommon for many people to complete more than 7 years of college work prior to receiving the doctoral degree, since many people working for doctorates will take more work than is required to gain their advanced degrees. Figure 1-1 shows only the average *minimum* times needed to complete the various stages of college studies portrayed there. On the other hand, the vast majority of successful undergraduate students do complete their 2-year or 4-year programs on schedule and sometimes ahead of schedule.

Before leaving Figure 1-1 we would like the reader to note that three basic patterns of sequencing or organizing the order of the 12 years of elementary and secondary school grades are noted there. At the left of the bottom darkened rectangular area of Figure 1-1 are the numbers 8–4, which refer to the oldest and most traditional way of dividing elementary schooling from secondary schooling, with an 8-year elementary school and a 4-year high school. In this traditional pattern there is no special kind of school for the early adolescent (such as the junior high school for grades 7 through 9) and no school for the preadolescent to early adolescent (such as the "middle schools" that now exist for this latter group that never extend beyond the eighth grade). In the middle of the bottom rectangular area you see the figures 6–3–3, which stand for 6 years of elementary school, 3 years of junior high school (grades 7 through 9), and 3 years of senior high school (grades 10 through 12). This is the sequence that most younger readers of this volume will be familiar with. Many readers will, however, have experienced some form of the third sequence, noted in the right hand of the lower darkened rectangular area of Figure 1-1, and will have elected special kinds of vocational and/or technical secondary educational programs requiring their secondary and elementary schooling to be divided in a 6–6 pattern to provide a longer and more intensified secondary schooling experience. This latter sequence is sometimes used for secondary school programs where it is not desired to retain the traditional 8–4 sequence, in which not enough types of secondary schooling experiences may be provided from the point of view of school officials in such school systems, and where a middle-level school is not desired. One form of elementary-secondary schooling sequence not noted on Figure 1-1 is the 4–4–4 sequence, where there are the first four primary school grades (grades 1 through 4), followed by a special kind of school called a middle school, which is especially designed for the learning needs of preadolescents and early adolescents (usually grades 5 through 8) and which differs greatly from the junior high school in its purposes and methods of instruction. Whenever the 4–4–4 pattern of elementary and secondary schooling is implemented, the traditional 4-year senior high school is always recreated, because the ninth grade always goes to the senior high school level. In some areas of the United States many of the readers of this book will have been graduates of middle schools and 4-year high schools. One frequent variation of the 4–4–4 pattern of elementary and secondary schooling is to create a 5–3–4 pattern, where the 4-year high school is recreated but the middle school is limited to the sixth, seventh, and eight grades and the fifth grade is kept with the primary school unit. The reasons for these different patterns of sequencing elementary and secondary schooling in the United States, the different educational aims and the different instructional purposes and methods used, as well as the reasons for their emergence in American society are discussed in following units. We have included this brief discussion of Figure 1-1 and related matters to provide the reader with a sense of the great diversity in American school settings. Understanding how teachers relate to these different types of school settings is one of the objectives of this volume.

Education
and an Enlightened Citizenry

A prerequisite to providing good education is citizens who are informed about the needs of education. Also, in the United States, where citizens control education, it is important that there be intelligent leaders who in turn will organize the citizenry for effective action. Herein lies a great challenge faced by any segment of a democratic government controlled by the public. What this implies will become clearer as we proceed.

The schools in the United States are the special responsibility of the citizens. Even privately controlled schools exist and perform a valuable function only because of public policy. Even they must meet certain regulatory standards established by the public. Placing the educational destiny of the nation in the hands of its people requires an intelligent and well-informed public.

The American people are fully cognizant of the power of education and hence are concerned that their power over education not be minimized. They are aware that education received in the schools may change a social viewpoint in a single generation. As we shall see later, the American people shrewdly exercise their power over the schools in a short, direct line by establishing their basic control over the schools from the home, the community, and the local school district, and by dictating—often through school elections—who is in charge of the schools, how much money is spent, and how that money is used. This means that it would be very difficult for any single political group in the United States to seize control over education throughout the nation. It is apparent that people who are inclined to keep their hands tightly on the reins and who insist on occupying the driver's seat should, if the schools are to achieve good results, themselves be enlightened about the needs of education and have a clear concept of the general direction education should take.

Education
and Well-informed Teachers

The public depends mainly on the trained professional teaching group for a mature and intelligent interpretation of what education in the United States should be, what its principal needs are, and what is necessary for the maintenance of an excellent system of schools. Only a well-informed, responsible teaching profession can supply this kind of information.

Furthermore, all theories of education—progressive or reactionary, liberal or conservative—assume that the classroom teacher is always in direct control. The dependence on the instructor's initiative and discretion justifies the expectation that classrooms be manned by teachers who are well informed about the entire educational venture.

While teachers play a role that requires considerable individual initiative, they also play a role that calls for a close relationship with many other persons. Throughout the day teachers are in close contact not only with the pupils in their own classrooms, but also with the pupils taught by other teachers. Further, they have personal relationships with other teachers, with principals and supervisors, with the pupils' parents, and with boards of education. In no other profession do roles interlock so intimately; maintaining good relationships in all these roles is an important factor in achieving marked teaching success. This demands that the teacher be well informed about education in general. It is not enough to know subject matter and to master methods and problems related only to the classroom. The teacher must be equipped to recognize, deal with, and influence the many forces at play in the process of education.

The Overview Approach

Research concerning the relative effectiveness of various approaches to introductory college courses in specialized fields reveals that, for most specialized fields, the overview approach is superior. "Overview" as applied to introductory courses implies that the coverage is extensive and that the topics selected are basic to later study. In many colleges students pursue 1-year or one-semester introductory courses, each of which delineates a field of study, reveals the nature of major problems included in the field, describes the methods used, and elaborates on the basic ideas. Above all, the purpose is to present the field of study so that the student obtains accurate insights into its foundational elements. The approach, then, is sweeping and general rather than technical and specialized; the treatment is simple rather than complicated; the subject matter is introductory rather than terminal. Such an approach is particularly appropriate to an introduction to the study of education.

The overview technique followed in this book is designed to meet the needs of intelligent citizens who may wish to be well informed about education in America, those who are playing a part or who expect to play a part in controlling or influencing education. The overview also will meet the needs of the college student who, as a prospective teacher, expects to become an active participant in American education. For the student the book explores basic concepts that all members of the teaching profession need to understand; further, it examines certain basic concepts that are fundamental to later professional study.

Selection of Material

Certain principles have guided the selection and rejection of both topics and materials.

First, it is assumed that the reader is taking a first systematic look at education in the United States, perhaps as a citizen who wishes to be informed enough about education to function as an intelligent parent or voter or perhaps as a taxpayer who wishes to know more about the educational venture he or she is obligated to support. The materials are selected and the discussions are fashioned with these kinds of readers in mind.

Second, those phases of education have been selected that will give students of education the information and understanding they need to assist in making a vocational choice or some related decision.

Third, in some states a general, introductory education course is required for state certification for all who enter a teacher education program. The requirement is usually imposed by the state educational authority, an agency that will be described later. Even where such a course is not required for state certification, it is assumed that every teacher will have some knowledge of the fundamental features of education as they are incorporated in the various school systems throughout America.

Fourth, the materials of the book are selected to prepare the reader for more advanced studies in professional education.

Plan of the Book

The materials of the book are organized around four aspects of education referred to as units. Each unit can be studied more or less independently of the others. Unit I focuses on classroom teachers—describing what they do, how they qualify, how they are related to their profession, how they formulate their professional philosophy, and how they are affected by being part of an institution.

Unit II focuses on ideas that have been influential in shaping the course of American education. Discussed first are the ideas that were propagated by significant European movements in educational theory and practice. This is followed by a discussion of the ideas of outstanding European thinkers and writers. Treated next are ideas that flowed from the American frontier movement. Then follows a discussion of the impact of the contemporary social scene on education. The emphasis here is on those ideas that have been and continue to be influential in shaping the course of American education.

Unit III focuses on the American school system. Five chapters are devoted to the organization of American education. These deal, respectively, with state school systems, local aspects of the organization and administration of public school systems, federal educational activity, nonpublic schools, and units of school organization.

Unit IV focuses on the pupils in the school and the processes of stimulating and guiding their learning and development. Attention is directed specifically to understanding the pupils, instructional goals, subject matter, methods of teaching, and instructional aids. Unit IV concludes with a fairly brief discussion of some future fields of study. This is designed to help the student who expects to continue in further study of education.

Summary

Many meanings are given the term "education." In the text, except where indicated otherwise, "education" refers to that aspect of learning that is deliberate and formal and is organized and directed by the people of the United States.

The schools are particularly the responsibility of American citizens. Such responsibility calls for an enlightened citizenry. Since citizens must look to the teachers in the schools for mature and intelligent interpretations of what education in the United States should be and what its principal needs are, the teaching profession also must be a well-informed body of people.

It is the purpose of this introductory study of education in the United States to provide readers with sufficient knowledge of the educational picture in America so that they can at least understand the general nature of the educational venture in the United States and can sense the needs of education and constructively advance the cause.

The plan of the book is dictated by an overview approach. Materials are organized in four units. Unit I focuses on the classroom teacher; Unit II, on the ideas that have been effective in shaping the character of American education; Unit III, on the American school system; and Unit IV, on the pupils in the school and the processes of stimulating and guiding their growth.

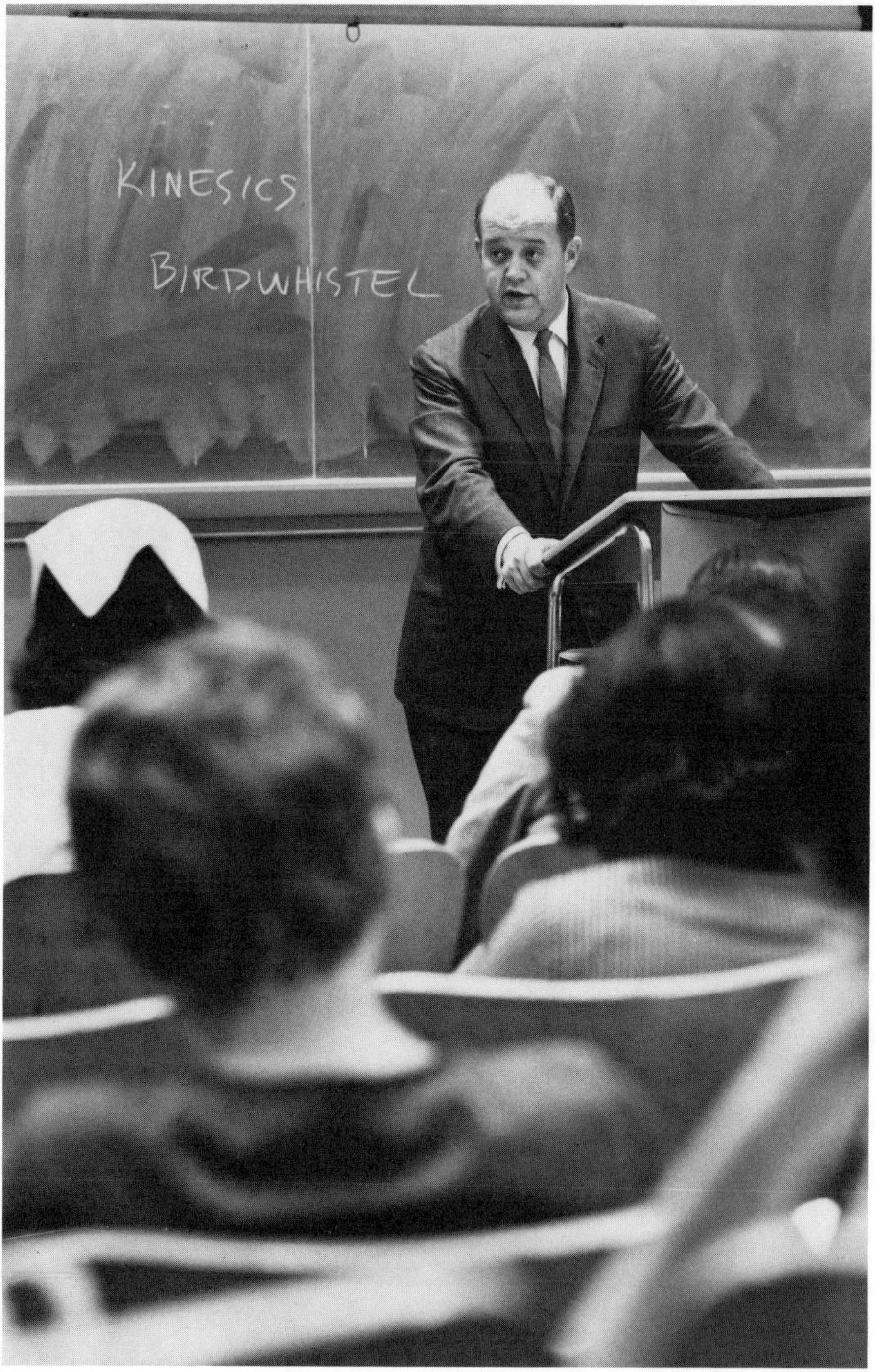
KINESICS
BIRDWHISTEL

chapter

2

What teachers do

We begin with a study of the work of the key figure in the educational picture—the teacher. In Unit I five questions about the teacher are considered. What do teachers do? How must they qualify? What are the principal characteristics of the profession to which they belong? How does a teacher formulate his professional philosophy? And how are his obligations affected by the nature of the institution in which he works? Since none of the questions lends itself to brief analysis, a chapter is devoted to each. First, what do teachers do?

The Primary Purpose of a Teacher

The primary purpose of a teacher is to help students learn those skills or subject matters that have been assigned to be taught. The learning that a teacher directs must involve the acquisition of knowledge that society considers of value. Closely related to this primary purpose of the teacher is the fact that a good teacher is also concerned with

19

integrating the knowledge being taught with the knowledge the student brings to the classroom. This means that understanding and breadth of perspective are important and are related to communicating knowledge. It is not sufficient for a teacher merely to impart isolated fragments of knowledge; the teacher must also relate what is taught in the classroom to what the student already knows. This is true no matter how young or old the teacher's client may be (and students are the clients of their teachers and as such entitled to respect and serious attention). Students are entitled to assistance and direction in the integration of past and present experience. There is no doubt that in the formal educational experiences of children or adults the teacher is the key figure in the direction of learning activities. Stimulating the desire of students to learn is a natural extension of this primary purpose of the teacher to assist and to direct; this responsibility also includes guiding students to reasoned action and the development of reasoned standards for conduct. It involves providing a foundation on which to build self-direction and the advance toward a higher level of maturity. The teacher's job is to modify the stimuli in the environment so that they have a favorable educational impact on the learners.

Complex Nature of the Work of Teachers

The work of teachers is complex. Physiologists, psychologists, and social biologists, who devote their lives to a study of the human organism and the factors that influence its growth, emphasize the intricacies involved in their searches for a fuller understanding of the human individual. Not only is the human organism complex, but the social environment that so directly influences the development of the individual also is complex and is constantly increasing in complexity. Influencing large numbers of these rapidly growing, complex systems of living energy to develop in desirable, worthwhile directions cannot be considered a simple task, to be performed satisfactorily by almost any normal person. A study of what classroom teachers do must be approached with these complexities in mind.

The complexity of the teacher's task is due not only to the complexity of the human organism as such, important as this factor is, but to the complex logical operations that teachers are called on to undertake. Teachers have many complex functions to learn, such as how to explain things so that students will learn most easily and well, how to communicate basic skills of reasoning, how to design coherently structured and interrelated learning tasks for their students, how to develop long-range and short-range instructional goals, and how to do many other complex cognitive (intellectual) tasks. In Unit IV there are chapters on goals and methods of instruction; in those chapters the problem of instructional goals and their development and the structural design tasks in the learning process to which teachers must be attentive will be considered in greater depth.

Limitations on Interpretations of Teachers' Work

Gaps in Knowledge About the Human Organism

One factor that limits our interpretation of what teachers do and should do is a lack of fundamental knowledge about the nature of the human organism. It is significant, for instance, that those who work in the fields referred to as the life sciences have never adequately defined what life is. Their efforts to measure the amount of life an organism possesses have been unsatisfactory. They are resigned to describing life and sometimes to measuring some of its manifestations. Life and death, cell growth, and the nature of individuality and emotions can be cited as only a few of the many unknowns. Furthermore, complete explanations of such processes as learning, perceiving, reasoning, and imagining are not available to the educator.

There is, however, sufficient knowledge accumulated from the past 2000 years (and particularly from the work of scholars in the twentieth century) to state that we now know a great deal more about the human organism and the motivations of human behavior than was true a generation ago. All our actions in our roles as teachers must stand the ancient test of the British common law: Would a reasonable and prudent person do the same thing under the same or very similar circumstances? Our knowledge of human perception and reasoning has grown with each decade of the twentieth century, and we can now assert with some degree of confidence that there is a body of reliable research and writing to help teachers in their efforts to improve the perception and reasoning of their students. We have also learned much about the problems of creative students and the possible ways to create learning environments in which the creative potential of students can flourish. We still have much to learn about the nature of creativity itself, but we have much more knowledge of the nature of creative processes now than at any previous time in human history.

Voids in knowledge are, of course, common to all fields of study. For example, when Newton stated the laws of gravitation, he exempted certain natural phenomena such as light, electricity, and magnetism from his interpretation. What gravitation is remains an unknown. The whole field of cosmology, the general science of the universe, involves much that is unexplained. Since such gaps exist in our knowledge of the physical aspects of human environment—aspects that can be measured—it is not surprising that so many gaps exist in our knowledge of human organisms, an area that does not lend itself to experimentation and quantification.

Despite the gaps and the many obstacles to narrowing them, useful knowledge of human behavior has been accumulated. The gaps are stressed here because students are sometimes disturbed when final answers cannot be given to some educational problems. Beginning teachers particularly are apt to be confused by the tendency among those who teach education courses to reason along theoretical lines. Where one does not have facts and the principles or "laws" abstracted from facts, one must turn to theories. Yet it is the presence of unsolved problems that helps make teaching such an intriguing occupation.

Influence of Past Experience

The individual's interpretation of what he reads about education and the generalizations he makes about the teacher's work are inevitably influenced by his own past school experiences. This fact both helps and limits an attempt to understand what a teacher does or should do. Personal school experiences provide only a partial view of all that a teacher does. In addition, any individual has been taught by a sampling of teachers that would not be considered statistically representative. Furthermore, from decade to decade, the role of the teacher is modified because of various continuing changes. Nevertheless, because certain more or less persistent attitudes of the student toward teachers and teaching, favorable and unfavorable, have been acquired through an individual's own experiences in school, we necessarily begin our study of what teachers do with certain varied, individual predispositions. It is important to be aware of these predispositions in our study of the work of a teacher.

Tendency to Oversimplify

The student is taught to rely on the *simplicity postulate* when working on a problem in the field of physics. This postulate asserts that of two alternatives the one that can be more simply stated is likely to be more acceptable. The principle of simplicity is often applied to our thinking about problems of teaching. When two educational theories are proposed, we tend to accept the one that is simpler, that more nearly accords with our previous experiences, and that promises to be more fruitful in its application. The simplicity postulate holds in education as it does in other fields of learning, but oversimplification sometimes presents the teaching profession with its most frustrating situations. Simplification is desirable only when it follows careful and expert analysis. The tendency generally leads to good habits of thinking. In interpreting the work of the teacher, however, it can be unwisely used and lead to harmful results.

Often influential citizens who are relatively uninformed about education will make statements such as, "I am opposed to federal aid to education" or "Teachers should fail more pupils in the interest of higher achievement standards." Their statements appeal to many partly because they are simple, positive, direct answers about what schools should be and what teachers should do. Those who have diligently studied the problems, however, are not always sure of the solutions. They wish to weigh various alternatives with care.

Such generalizations as those just noted require reasoned qualification or refutation as they stand. Teachers often have to respond to such overextended and oversimplified assertions about "education," the schools, or the teaching profession. One of the things that really competent teachers do is to learn some basic reasoned ways of responding to such oversimplified assertions. In the early and mid-1970s teachers were called on to become more accountable for their own behavior in the classroom and to answer directly the public's challenge to verify publicly their professional competencies. Teachers must learn the skills of synthesis and analysis of educational ideas and policies. They function in the classroom and this is where their primary responsibility lies. However, teachers also function as members of a profession with other concerns relating to broader professional commitments to school and community relationships. We examine in depth in Units II and IV how contemporary teachers are called on to demonstrate their skills in determining and achieving educational objectives of various sorts. The tendency to oversimplify our goals or our statements of belief or our claims to knowledge can be avoided. Teachers who are aware of the problem and who have developed some basic principles of procedure for clarifying their ideas can avoid the temptation to oversimplify or to overextend their points of view in conversation. Since most teaching activities involve some form of verbal behavior on the part of the teacher, this is a most important point.

Unobservable Elements

Not all activities in the work of a teacher can be clearly revealed simply by seeing a teacher at work. Much of the work of teachers involves such activities as clarifying ideas (concepts), finding evidence to support a point of view in the literature of the subject matter being taught (or verifying that evidence), and demonstrating (proving) why statements are true or false. These sorts of activities relate to what has been called the "qualitative factor" in teaching. The qualitative factor has to do with the insight, perception, and understanding of what is being taught, which are qualities exhibited by excellent teachers. We not only have to observe what teachers do, we have to study how good teachers communicate ideas and what sorts of learning strategies they use in classroom situations to help students learn. The qualitative factor also involves the commitment of a good teacher to the idea that a teacher should not be satisfied if students have only learned facts, for they need to understand how what they learn relates to the problems of life.

Classifying Teachers' Duties

Need for Classification

Classification is a basic method used for studying the similarities and differences among objects in the universe. Those objects that have similar characteristics are assigned to the same category. This is perhaps the oldest and simplest method for arriving at order in the world of knowledge. By noting similarities among the activities in which teachers engage, we can in some measure reduce many of them to a class and then speak of them as a single activity. Thus we can discuss guidance as a single activity even though we know that guidance actually includes a large number of individual activities.

Exactness in classification of a teacher's duties would be helpful but does not seem possible. Educational terminology is not fully standardized, and, even more important, teaching activities do not fall into readily classifiable categories. Lines of demarcation between classifications are often blurred. They frequently overlap. No classification is, therefore, to be considered final or authoritative.

If we had generally accepted definitions of educational terms, more uniform classifications of activities would be possible. In an effort to promote a kind of standardization of terms to be helpful not only in classification but in education generally, a dictionary of the specialized vocabulary of professional education has been written.[1] Such standardization is particularly important to the student who needs to know that professional writers and instructors in education use the same words to convey like meanings. More work is needed in this area of standardization. There is, however, more or less general agreement with respect to some of the classifications of teacher activities.

Classifications

In general, teacher functions have been broadly grouped into five classifications: (1) classroom instruction, (2) guidance, (3) staff functions, (4) community duties, and (5) professional activities. The classifications are, of course, arbitrary. Everything a teacher does might be classified as related to classroom instruction or to guidance.

Classroom instruction is the foremost duty of the teacher; it comprises the bulk of his or her activities. It involves all the duties that the teacher performs in directing group and individual learning. Teachers direct discussions, make assignments, listen to reports and recitations, direct reading, show films, check workbooks, and plan and check work, often at home in the evenings. This most important function is discharged in a great variety of ways, and the reader can appreciate better now that it reflects most accurately the philosophy of the teacher and of the school and that it is most readily modified by the social environment of the teacher and by the available physical resources. Extended observation of classroom instruction is necessary if one is to get a complete picture that reflects this aspect of the total school situation.

I. CLASSROOM INSTRUCTION

The instructional activities of teachers in classroom settings involve two basic categories of activities to facilitate the learning of

[1] Carter V. Good, *Dictionary of Education*, Second Edition. New York: McGraw-Hill, 1959, 704 pp.

students: (1) formal rational activities involved in helping students reason about that which is to be learned and (2) those planned activities, behaviors, or attitudes intended to facilitate such learning. The formal rational activities of instruction deal with providing evidence for or against claims made in text materials, films, or other instructional materials. The rational activities of instruction also involve the teacher in providing valid, understandable explanations of ideas or concepts as well as in providing examples of why certain points of view are true or useful and others not and of why certain skills and techniques for doing certain kinds of activities are the best ways to get those activities accomplished. These rational activities (activities based on relevant reasons) involve a teacher in developing sound examples of points to make clear to students, demonstrations of skills or ideas, or comparisons and contrasts of different ideas to be related in teaching any subject matter. The second major category of instructional activities deals with such helping activities as sound and understandable planning of the sequential order of presentation of information and motivating student interest through frequent encouragement of students and the use of such instructional aids as films, recordings, and visual diagrams. This second order of facilitating activities also involves diagnosing student abilities and needs as well as individual counseling sessions with students (however brief or long these may be) to sustain student interest.

We will have more to say in greater depth about the rational and the facilitating activities of teachers in later discussion in this volume on the subjects of the institutional roles of teachers and their strategic commitments to achieving success in classroom instruction, on the one hand, and the subject of the teacher as designer and controller of the instructional process, on the other hand.

2. GUIDANCE

Every teacher is a counselor to pupils. Duties in this classification consume much time and energy. Often they are incidental to instruction. Sometimes they are definitely scheduled (perhaps weekly conferences with an individual pupil over a period of time). The teacher may find it necessary to counsel pupils outside of school hours. Counseling may also involve parent conferences, home visits, or interviews with supervisors, principals, or other teachers. The teacher must be adept at group guidance, too, and almost every day must assist the entire class, a committee group, or some other group in making choices and decisions.

In some schools teachers devote a number of periods a week to counseling. Some schools provide special help for teachers in the performance of this function—deans, social caseworkers, school psychologists, testing departments, and others.

Regardless of the organizational plan, however, most guidance is directed by the classroom teacher. It is the teacher who must work with the specialist in helping a pupil make an adjustment. It is the teacher who must utilize what the specialists supply to help guide and counsel a pupil. It is the teacher who does most of the investigating, testing, interviewing, followup, and record making that are involved. But the satisfactions that accrue to the teacher as a result of success in pupil guidance are commensurate with the effort involved.

Teaching and guidance are inseparable functions. When the teacher directs a pupil in developing a chemistry project for a contest, he or she instructs the pupil in the necessary chemistry and provides guidance in making a mature approach to a competitive situation, in independently completing self-assigned work, and in developing good study habits. The distinction between instruction and guidance cannot be a sharp one. When a teacher reprimands a pupil for discourteous behavior, is classroom instruction or guidance involved? Much guidance is incidental. No guidance is unimportant.

Some teachers find that a basic guidance or counseling approach is helpful in dealing with any student's behavioral problems as well as with any other problems of students in classroom settings. Brief private counseling episodes where the teacher can speak in private with a student are often helpful in making students aware that a teacher cares about them on a personal basis. One of the authors always uses private counseling episodes in the hall, the school cafeteria, the school grounds, or the classroom when other students are busy with other learning activities (as well as any other school or informal after-school setting) to build strong student-teacher trust and mutual respect. It is always possible to find a time mutually agreeable to both student and teacher to discuss problems of concern to either or both parties either in or out of the classroom setting. In such brief counseling sessions neither party need fear "losing face" and each can take on the attitude or position of "the other." One may have several such meetings with each of one's students over the course of a school year; this informal, face-to-face communication of teacher trust and concern is the most viable way to build strong student-teacher relationships. In such a way a teacher builds a reputation for reasonable conduct and genuine dialogue with students. Many good teachers do all their instructional planning and grading at nights and on weekends so that they will be free during the entire school day to do their instructional activities and to counsel and interact with students in their classes so as to build sound human relationships both in and out of the classroom.

3. STAFF FUNCTIONS

The classroom teachers, collectively, are responsible for the greatest part of the administration of a school. The classroom is the administrative unit in the school, and the teacher is primarily responsible for the administration of its affairs. But classrooms are not isolated independent units of school administration. The school is the larger unit, an organization with a principal who is responsible for achieving a reasonable measure of coordination of the staff members' efforts. Teachers are organized into a system to work as a unit and to plan together.

As a member of an organized staff the teacher is obliged to attend faculty, departmental, or grade-level meetings; to work on curriculum committees; and to assist with such school functions as plays, parties, and concerts. The teacher must make announcements, issue bulletins, collect fees. In schools that do not have modern data-processing equipment, the teacher must still keep attendance records, make monthly enrollment reports, prepare report cards, and record health, behavior, and achievement data. The teacher must make inventories; order, distribute, and collect supplies; and assign lockers. In addition, play periods and lunchrooms must be supervised and children must be proctored in the halls. These are just examples of the kinds of duties added to the teacher's work because the classroom is the unit of administration and the teacher is a member of a staff whose work must be coordinated. Many of the duties are routine and mechanical. All are time-consuming.

It is in the area of these auxiliary activities that teachers tend to be most vocal in their complaints. The complaints arise not because the importance of the work is unrecognized but because the duties tend to be numerous and exceedingly time-consuming. Usually they must be made to fit into a rigid schedule. Sometimes the teacher cannot see that certain records are utilized sufficiently to warrant the time they take to make them out. Often meetings are held after school hours and seem unduly prolonged to a tired teacher. At times responsibilities such as lunchroom supervision and hall proctoring seem to be unfairly distributed.

Parents or mature students are sometimes used to assist the teacher with such duties. Lay readers, paraprofessionals, and student teachers often relieve the teacher of doing some paper work, recording, collecting fees, setting up teaching aids, and so on. Teachers have more time for classroom instruction and guidance functions when the load of other duties is lightened.

4. COMMUNITY DUTIES

The typical elementary or secondary school in the United States is a community institution, whose teachers are valued members of the community. The responsibility for the education of the pupils is shared by the school with the community. The community largely controls the school. It decides who is to be educated. By controlling the purse strings it determines, for instance, whether there will be summer schools, nursery schools, and classes for various atypical children. The community influences what the schools can attempt to do. For instance, if community mores are opposed to social dancing, the school cannot offer instruction in it. The people connected with the school can, of course, by exerting influence on the Parent-Teacher Association and other community groups, work to change community attitudes.

As we have said before, all the classifications of duties overlap. Perhaps producing the concert is the music teacher's job because he or she is a faculty member, but perhaps it is because he or she is a member of a community of interested lay people. Certain teaching duties, such as participating in the Parent-Teacher Association, seem to be related to the teacher's community membership. In many communities the teacher is expected to have a church affiliation. The teacher might very well have many of the community relationships anyway, but the point is that the teacher is *expected* to have them, to be a community participant. Free choice is somewhat curtailed.

Besides the responsibility for contributing to the community, the teacher usually has the opportunity and privilege of using various community resources. Individuals with unique skills, special talents, or interesting backgrounds of experience can, at appropriate times, be enlisted to supplement the regular work of the classroom or to contribute to some professional activity, perhaps curriculum planning. Museums, historical societies, courts, and industrial organizations are examples of another kind of community resource that can also be used. Teachers feel free to use suitable and available human and material community resources because they, as well as their schools, are a part of the community.

5. PROFESSIONAL ACTIVITIES

Certain other tasks fall to teachers because they are affiliated with various local, regional, state, and national professional organizations—organizations dedicated to promoting good education and to advancing teacher welfare. Teachers may add markedly to their work load by sharing in the preparation of a study of salaries and a faculty salary schedule for the local board of education; by participating in the development of a state convention program for English teachers; by writing an article for a professional journal describing success in the classroom with some novel approach or device; or by serving as a discussion member on a program for a local professional organization. This kind of work is usually assumed voluntarily, and the extent of an individual's time and energy invested varies with that person's interest, zeal, and ability. Even those who take no responsibility for leadership devote considerable time to attending meetings and reading professional publications. All teachers are interested in aspects of their own welfare related to teaching load, retirement, pensions, salaries, certification, and tenure.

As a rule, teachers also are expected to advance professionally by participating in various kinds of workshops or by pursuing college study, either after school hours during the year or during the summer vacation period. A master's degree is not a terminal point. In some places advancement on a salary scale depends on the accumulation of specified hours of additional college credit.

Allocation of Time

To a teacher each school day is a challenge, not only because of the constancy of important and varied activity, but also because of the element referred to earlier as the unobservable, but nevertheless real, qualitative factor. A teacher must learn many things about each pupil and, in terms of these, formulate daily aims, select subject matter, decide on procedures to follow, and choose appropriate teaching aids. One who teaches effectively with a free and easy grace has expended considerable time and energy in achieving the background that makes such a performance possible.

No two-days' work is precisely the same for any teacher, nor is a day's work for any two teachers ever identical. This is evident from the descriptions on pages 34–37 of the work of six different teachers. Certain broad classifications of duties are, however, common to most teachers.

That teachers have a short working day is a myth. Teachers are required to be at school before the pupils arrive and must remain for stated periods after the pupils leave. Statistical estimates vary regarding how much time teachers spend on various teaching activities during any average work week. But we know that many good teachers spend a great deal of time after school, in their evenings, and on weekends doing long-range and short-range instructional planning and either designing student learning tasks or evaluating students' responses to such tasks. Teachers vary greatly as to how much time they put into such out-of-school but classroom-related planning and evaluation activities.

We know that the amount of time provided for such facilitative planning activities during the school day is never sufficient for the amount of facilitative instructional activities required in most elementary or secondary school classroom teaching assignments. It is not unusual for a teacher to work 55 to 60 or more hours a week during the school year even though the teacher is only required to be in school about 36 to 40 hours a week in most school districts in the United States. Moreover, the teaching assignments of most elementary school or secondary school teachers vary considerably in the types of instruction required as well as in differences in the numbers of students assigned to each teacher and the numbers of instructional preparations and the variety of instructional preparations required of each. The work responsibilities of most teachers are such that more than 63 percent of the work week in school is spent directly with students. The teacher's school responsibilities relating to student activities and to such tasks as supervising study halls or cafeteria areas, serving on faculty committees, and counseling students will usually absorb most of the rest of the in-school work week.

One other point must be mentioned that relates to the allocation of teachers' time or their commitment of their own time to the teaching profession. Not only is it a myth that good teachers have a short working day, but teaching is also hard physical labor. An active, energetic teacher is often tired at the end of an average school day. The demands on personal physical reserves of strength and energy from having tried for more than 5 to 7 hours to instruct, motivate, and sustain the attention of the students are *enormous*. Five days a week for 36 to 40 school weeks a year this process goes on. By the end of an average school year the average teacher has, combining the 36- to 40-hour school week with out-of-school or after-school classroom-related work, put in as many work hours as the average American industrial worker or "middle-management" executive who works a straight 37- to 40-hour work week for 12 months of the year. Few conscientious teachers need ever feel apologetic about the "summer break." To teach well is to be a very active person during the 36 to 40 weeks of an average academic year. Even during the "summer break" some teachers teach summer school classes and many others advance their own education by taking advanced graduate courses, doing independent reading, and making long-range plans for the coming school year. Teachers may also have summer jobs while they do these things.

We believe that dedicated, conscientious teachers are among the hardest-working people in America. It is often assumed that teaching is an "easy job"; others observe teachers going to school in nice clothes and doing a lot of talking and counseling but not doing as much obvious physical labor as some other workers. However, the appearance is deceiving. The drain on personal strength required to sustain the rational and the facilitative activities of teaching and to fulfill the institutional responsibilities of teachers during the school year is as exacting of physical strength as most jobs requiring obvious physical labor. Good teachers stay in teaching because they like the daily contact with young people, the opportunity to exercise their own independent intellectual judgment in teaching and helping others, the opportunity to achieve a wondrous sense of personal autonomy as they independently chart and direct the course of learning in their own classroom settings, and the thrill of seeing other people learn and knowing that they had something to do with it.

Such practices as lengthening the school day, requiring additional study by teachers for promotional credit, enlarging class size, increasing pupils' home study, and expecting teachers to share more in formulating administrative policies that closely concern them have inevitably added to the teacher's work day; this is true in spite of attempts to alleviate the situation by providing such help as expert supervision, paraprofessional aides, lay readers, special classes for slow learners, and opportunity rooms for the handicapped. There is little evidence to indicate that the teacher's working day will be lighter in the future. Indeed, recent teacher strikes reflect a growing concern among teachers about teacher loads.

Study of Teachers' Work

There are two approaches to studying the work of teachers. The first is an intensive study of the work of one teacher or of a few teachers. This approach has certain advantages. It enables one to study the work of a highly skilled teacher who works at a given level of education, who teaches a special subject, or who works in a particular kind of environmental setting. The second approach is an extensive study of the work of a large sampling of teachers teaching at several levels of education and in many kinds of situations. This approach also has certain advantages. It gives breadth to the findings, reveals the possible range of duties, and gives perhaps a more accurate picture of the kinds of duties performed by teachers. A more realistic and complete account of what teachers do results from a combination of both methods of study. Therefore we shall first note the results of studying the work of individual teachers and then follow with the more extensive findings of a wider sampling.

Studying Individuals

Two procedures may be followed in studying the work performed by a selected individual or individuals: (1) directly observing what they do and (2) obtaining from the teachers themselves verbal descriptions of what they have done over a definite period of time. The two procedures lead to slightly different conclusions. Both methods contribute useful information.

I. DIRECT OBSERVATION

By observing a teacher at work for several successive days, one may secure a more vivid and realistic picture of what a teacher does than by any other method. This is especially true if many activities are observed.

It is important to realize that this method has its limitations. In learning about the work done by one teacher, we may not directly observe all that is done, such as preparing for the day's teaching, counseling with pupils or parents, or reading the written assignments handed in by pupils. Also the value of the observation is related to the maturity, the insights, and the understandings of the observer. What an experienced teacher concludes from an observation tends to be quite different from what a novice or a layman concludes.

However, this method is especially helpful to the beginning student, who can thus learn what and how to observe. The student learns to discriminate, to get a feeling for what the teacher's job is in a particular subject, at a given level of teaching, or in a single aspect of his work.

2. VERBAL DESCRIPTION

Some of the shortcomings of direct observation are overcome by having teachers describe their work in simple, direct statements. They can accurately describe their own work and are more likely to select what is most important. A description of the work of individual teachers tends also to emphasize the many differences in the work that various teachers do. Descriptions also are valuable in revealing some of the subtle, more qualitative aspects of the teacher's work. The following examples illustrate some of the features of teaching.

A first-grade teacher says:

> There are 38 children in my room. It would take 38 pages of typewritten material to describe the work I do. [A lengthy, although condensed, description of classroom work then follows, closing with this statement.]
>
> Now a few words about the "extras." I attend faculty meetings, committee meetings, meetings of the Parent-Teacher Association, district meetings and, well, just meetings. These are always held during school time.
>
> I operate the movie projector, the slide projector, and the hectograph machine. I prepare the seat work by hand and run it off on the hectograph, and sometimes I make drawings from typewritten material which I prepare. I keep records of daily attendance, daily work, test grades, and monies collected. I prepare monthly summary sheets of attendance, monthly supply orders, lists of supplies to be put away, and book inventories. I fill out health records, quarterly report cards, cumulative records, and other office records required at the end of the semester and, occasionally, make special reports. I also prepare plan books for the work of each day.

A third-grade teacher writes:

> No two days of work are ever alike. I view my job as that of working with children—all kinds of children—striving to help them make worthwhile progress each day. In order to do this I try to understand each child and try to find ways of helping him adjust to me and to his many classmates. I try also to know all of the

parents, to find out how they live and what their interests are. Yes, I even enjoy talking to Mrs. Hill, who insists that her son has a right to break other children's crayons whenever his heart desires. It is only by being able to talk to her that I have hopes of showing her what our common problems are. Teaching is such a natural, easy way of living, in spite of the many things there are to teach and do, like making impromptu talks to parents, selling taffy apples, growing a community garden, and learning about the insects that are garden pests. . . .

A junior high school teacher says:

My functions are to teach music to four classes on the sixth-, seventh-, and eighth-grade levels. Each of these music classes meets twice a week, eight periods of music in all. The remainder of the teaching week is spent with my homeroom, the eighth grade. I teach the following subjects in my homeroom: arithmetic, social studies, reading, composition and related language arts, and health. The school day begins at 8:30 and runs until 3:15. Sometimes it merely creeps. The genuine teaching duties are stimulating and highly rewarding, for the most part. The numerous nonteaching duties and clerical duties definitely take the edge off the pleasure of being a teacher. . . .

A physical education teacher writes:

I teach physical education to boys and girls, 8 to 14 years of age. I teach 35 class periods a week, 28 of which are devoted to regular physical education activities, four to co-recreational programs for the seventh- and eighth-grade pupils, one to a gymnastics class, one to the school safety patrol which I sponsor, and one to keeping my records and equipment in good order. In addition I assist with the annual paper drive, present an assembly program once a year, direct the color guard, take charge of the boys' entrance, and serve as a member of the audiovisual aids committee, as cochairman of the community resources committee, as chairman of the standards of achievement committee, and as instructor at our school's after-school social center. I also serve as recording secretary and member of the executive board of the teachers' union. My listing of duties might leave the impression that teachers do quite a bit. They do!

Another teacher says:

I am a teacher of industrial arts in an industrial arts department in a high school of 2,600 pupils. I teach two classes of industrial arts pupils. The shop is general shop, each experience extending over six weeks. The two classes alternate experiences. I also teach two classes of sophomore printing of 22 pupils each. There are some juniors and seniors in these two groups. The pupils are of all kinds of abilities and offer all kinds of reasons for being in the class—from an intense interest to nothing-else-to-take. I also have an advanced vocational class which does much of the production printing of the school. . . .

The linotypes and presses require repair and maintenance that must be done by the teacher. The costs of jobs must be figured, charged, and recorded. Supplies of paper, ink, and other materials must be replenished as needed. Telephone calls on the status of the newspaper and other jobs frequently interrupt the work of the classes. Club sponsors and office personnel come into the shop often. Copy is handed in late, and finished jobs are expected overnight.

I like printing and I like teaching. There are no boring moments. . . . Each week I take home some work—papers to be corrected, orders to write, costs to be figured, jobs and projects to be planned. Each week I return to the school for an average of three hours to keep abreast of the work at the school shop that cannot be done during the day and, of course, cannot be taken home.

Before entering college I worked at the printing trade and I still do during the summer months. I keep in touch with the trade, earn additional income, and have the assurance that I can tell the principal "good-by" tonight and go out tomorrow and take my pick of 10 jobs which pay more than teaching and require less work. But, then, I wouldn't be helping young people! I'd just be helping myself!

A team teacher writes:

As a member of a seventh-grade teaching team charged with fulfilling curriculum requirements in social studies, language arts, and mathematics on an interdisciplinary basis, my teaching week includes a significant allocation of time for team planning. Even so, I meet with the group regularly and frequently during the lunch period, carrying a tray to a vacant classroom. Every week I share in drawing up a weekly schedule in terms of activities planned for each of the fields. Some weeks I am responsible for presenting a large group lesson related to the social studies curriculum. This involves a 30-minute presentation four times to groups of 60 or 90 children. Before the lesson I prepare appropriate transparencies for use on the overhead projector, locate and have on hand maps, film strips, or other visual aids, and prepare follow-up textbook, study, and enrichment material to be used when I, and others on the team, meet with boys and girls in smaller groups. I also decide on such related language arts activities as paragraph writing, outlining, and reading biographies or poetry.

Inasmuch as team teaching seems to mean something different wherever it is used, I have had to make certain decisions in terms ot trial and error and to spend time individually and in group meetings evaluating procedures and materials. In addition to large group presentations, at certain times I work with small groups in subject-matter areas and also for group guidance and enrichment activities. Of course, I have the regular responsibilities for attendance, collecting fees, etc. I have individual pupil conferences, team-teacher group conferences with pupils, and team-teacher group conferences with nonteam teachers who teach seventh-graders in nonteam areas like foreign language or science. I share in regular parent conferences where the parent meets with the child and the three teachers who have the main responsibility for the child's instruction in language arts, social studies, and mathematics. In addition, I hold other parent conferences as they are requested by the parent or as I decide they would be helpful. From my experience I conclude that a team teacher's day is a full one, and that all of the team teacher's work cannot be done in the "required" hours of the school day.

Personal description of a teacher's duties shows that the work of an individual teacher is unique. Instead of emphasizing similarities in the work of teachers, such descriptions tend to bring out the differences. Even when the same activity is reported, the approach, the time invested, and the manner of performing it tend to vary. One teacher, as a result of his interests, may emphasize some activities far more than others. The teacher's philosophy, interests, and abilities are related to the proportion of time invested in any activity. Usually the more favored activities are more efficiently performed.

A carefully written and fairly complete description of the work of a single teacher sets forth what the teacher believes important to report, not what the investigator thinks is important to observe. It gives a reasonably accurate picture of each teacher's work, but does not afford as definite a summation of duties as some of the other methods of study.

Studying Large Samplings by the Method of Vocational Analysis

The method of vocational analysis has been borrowed from industry and the armed services, where it has been used as a sort of measuring stick to select individuals who, in terms of personality and training, have the greatest promise of success with certain kinds of work.

In general, the method consists of three steps: (1) the duties involved in a particular vocation are itemized; (2) the relative difficulty of performing each of the duties is determined; and (3) the knowledge, skills, and habits necessary to a successful pursuit of the vocation are ascertained. Appropriate instructional materials can then be prepared to teach an individual to meet successfully the demands of the job. Each of the steps calls for considerable interpretative skill. The method has proved very valuable for providing information about all the vocations—information that has been especially useful to those who formulate training programs.

The method should be used, however, with full recognition of its limitations. One shortcoming can be illustrated from the findings of one vocational analysis project. This project analyzed reports from over 6,000 classroom teachers who enumerated what they did while on their jobs. The activities reported numbered around 200,000! Those activities considered to be most significant were selected for more intensive study. They still numbered 1,001 items. They could not be further reduced and still give a realistic picture of the work of teachers. The list of duties is so extensive that it is of little value in providing a typical picture.

Although largely inappropriate for studying the work of any given teacher, the vocational analysis method has revealed certain general features of the work of teachers as a group. It has shown that the range of activities teachers engage in is enormous and that many of these activities are difficult and time-consuming. It has made clear why teachers, if they desire to become expertly proficient, must continue to study throughout their professional careers. Competence is not quickly developed. There is a continuously mounting hierarchy among the skills to be acquired. One competence becomes the foundation for building another, higher level of competence. Skills, however, are not accumulated as one fits bricks into a rising wall.

Incidentally, educators have applied the vocational analysis method to the activities in which adults generally engage. These activities have then been classified and the results made the basis for planning the school curriculum. In Unit IV, in the study of aims, this approach is examined in more detail.

In enlarging the sampling, the various investigators have not found it practicable to make a complete vocational analysis. The various studies have used certain specialized techniques, each of which gives an incomplete but nevertheless helpful picture of the teacher's work. The more common techniques include the questionnaire, direct observation, verbal description, and time analysis.

1. THE QUESTIONNAIRE

The questionnaire is a device frequently used in the analysis of teaching. Many carefully selected and skillfully phrased questions are directed to the teacher. Each question can be answered simply, sometimes with a single word, such as "yes" or a number. The questions are prepared in advance by the investigator and cover those aspects of the teacher's work that the investigator selects for study.

Questionnaire studies are convenient to tabulate, record, and summarize. The questionnaire is especially appropriate in determining what practices are current. Because of this, studies of teacher activities based on questionnaires are often called *status* studies. They have been helpful in revealing what activities give most difficulty, recur most often, and seem to persist over long periods of time. They are well adapted to showing what problems are peculiar to teaching a given subject or to teaching at a given grade level. The English teacher, the shop teacher, the kindergarten teacher, and the eighth-grade teacher all encounter a range of problems. Even when the problems are approximately the same at different educational levels, dealing with each of them involves a different kind of teacher activity.

Questionnaires, like each of the other techniques, have certain weaknesses of which one must be aware when interpreting the information they provide. For example, if a teacher has a behavior problem in the classroom he or she cannot by a simple answer tell how it was solved. The teacher may report how many behavior problems he or she has had, but his or her answer gives no indication of how serious each of them has been or how much time and energy have been given to the solution of each. If an English teacher makes a vivid presentation of a beautiful poem and gives it a striking interpretation, it is impossible to report on a questionnaire precisely what was done. Nor can the teacher accurately report all the time spent in preparation. The findings of a good questionnaire are revealing, but the picture provided is never complete.

2. DIRECT OBSERVATION

Direct observation can be applied to a group of teachers in much the same way that it is applied to an individual teacher. In this case an observer may extend the number of direct observations, or a team of observers may observe teachers working at different levels and in varying situations. Direct observation of the group has the same limitations as direct observation of the individual. As a method of mass study it suffers further because it is exceedingly time-consuming.

3. VERBAL DESCRIPTION

The method of obtaining individual descriptions can be expanded to include any number of teachers teaching at any level of education or teaching any given subject. It is somewhat difficult to summarize verbal descriptions, and the interpretation of the results presents a special problem. The sampling, however, can be as wide as the investigator wishes to make it.

4. TIME ANALYSIS

The time analysis of activities can be used as an extension of the questionnaire, direct observation, or the analysis of individual descriptions. The time given to the performance of a certain activity is recorded. As an observer notes what activity a teacher engages in, for instance, he or she also uses a stop watch and makes a record of the exact time spent on the activity. Or teachers may report on questionnaires their estimates of time they devote to the various activities they perform.

The Qualitative Element

Each of the techniques of discovering and reporting what a teacher does gives a picture of the work from a somewhat different perspective. In all the information gathered, however, one important element of the teacher's work, perhaps the most important feature, is more or less omitted; in fact, it is almost simplified out of existence. This is the qualitative factor mentioned earlier. It is the one element that is in large part responsible for the great differences in what teachers do. Two teachers covering the same subject may make identical assignments, but the two assignments are not qualitatively the same and may have differing effects on how the pupils feel and what they learn. The same is true of giving tests, assigning marks, or any other activity.

Through observation we may sense this qualitative characteristic, or teachers' descriptions may reveal its presence; but no statistical tabulation, classification, or report can completely capture it. In making conclusions about what teachers do, using all the sources of information, we must recognize the importance of this factor and avoid oversimplification.

Qualitative differences stem from many factors, some of which do not lend themselves to ready analysis. The freedom that teachers in American schools have to use their own judgment about what is taught, how it is taught, and how the classroom is managed is but one example. Teachers differ greatly in personality and in the kind of personal and professional philosophy that guides their teaching. They differ in social background, in education, and in many other ways. They teach in vastly different situations. All such factors contribute to the encouragement of the qualitative differences so characteristic of teaching. As we discuss such topics as the philosophy and aims of the teacher, subject matter, methods, and other aspects of teaching, we will become increasingly conscious of the causes and effects of

---

From earliest times to the present, great thinkers have directed their thinking toward the education of children. In 1416, a renowned discoverer of ancient learning, Poggio, found the complete text of Quintilian's On the Training of an Orator in a dump heap in one of the abbey towers at a Swiss monastery. This great work, written in the first century A.D., was in form a manual on the training of a public speaker, but it was actually the outline of a liberal education. It came to be viewed as summarizing all the pedagogical wisdom of the ancients. The following quotation from Quintilian shows the trend of his thinking about the successful qualities of the good teacher.

Let him therefore adopt a parental attitude to his pupils, and regard himself as the representative of those who have committed their children to his charge. Let him be free from vice himself and refuse to tolerate it in others. Let him be strict but not austere, genial but not too familiar: for austerity will make him unpopular, while familiarity breeds contempt. Let his discourse continually turn on what is good and honorable; the more he admonishes, the less he will have to punish. He must control his temper without however shutting his eyes to faults requiring correction: his instruction must be free from affectation, his industry great, his demands on his class continuous but not extravagant.*

* Marcus Fabius Quintilianus, *The Institutio Oratoria of Quintilian*, with English translation by H. E. Butler. Cambridge, Mass.: Harvard University Press, 1921, vol. I, book II, ii, paragraph 5, p. 213.

the ever-present qualitative differences that are characteristic of teachers' work.

Summary

What knowledge of the work of the teacher has Chapter 2 revealed? In commencing our overview of education in the United States, what details about what school teachers do can we now fill in?

In seeking to discover what teachers do, studies that use the method of vocational analysis are one source of information. We get a picture with a different perspective by turning to teachers' own descriptions of what they do. Another readily available source of fruitful information is direct observation, which allows us to capture some of the "feel" of the teaching, to get an appreciation of the essence of the pupil-teacher relationship and other classroom relationships that elude tabulation and reporting, and to focus our study on a single teacher or particular factor.

From the many studies made we discover that the work of the teacher is highly complex and that his duties cover a great range. For convenience we group teacher activities into five classifications: (1) classroom instruction, (2) guidance, (3) staff functions, (4) community duties, and (5) professional activities. Such classifications are neither definite nor rigid in their boundaries. They are made in order to facilitate our thinking and to simplify our understanding.

It is evident that in reporting what teachers do it has not been possible to include the qualitative difference that marks the activities of any two or more teachers. This elusive and intangible element is present in all features of the entire school picture. It is influenced most dramatically by the teacher's philosophy, personality, training, and experience as manifest in his or her values, beliefs, and ideals. Because this factor is elusive and because perhaps the current tendency in many subject-matter fields is to stress quantification, many studies that bear on education have omitted this subjective element entirely.

In conclusion, then, we recognize that teaching involves many kinds of work and many kinds of activities. Describing the work that teachers do is somewhat analogous to analyzing the ingredients in a soup. The soup is a mixture of a large number of ingredients, which are separate but also heterogeneous. Each ingredient changes its original characteristic when it becomes part of the final dish. The ingredients that make up teaching are numerous, and, like the ingredients in the soup, are heterogeneous. The work of the teacher, then, does not lend itself to a simple description of the kind that would suffice in telling how a cook bakes a cake or how a machinist uses a lathe.

This study of what teachers do in American schools can be no more than preliminary—preliminary to further study, to a more detailed analysis, and to a broadening of interpretation that will continue throughout the book. (In Unit IV, "Aims and Methods in America," teacher responsibilities are explored from another angle.)

QUESTIONS

1. What are some reasons why the work of one teacher is never exactly like the work of another?
2. How do your own experiences in school contribute to or limit your better understanding of the work of a classroom teacher? In what respects are your experiences probably atypical?
3. In describing a teacher's work, how can one give due recognition to the factor of excellence of performance?
4. What attitude should a beginning teacher assume toward the performance of routine duties?
5. What are some purposes served by classifying all that teachers do into broad categories? What undesirable effects may also result?
6. In the school, what are the functions of such specialists as the supervisor, guidance director, and school psychologist? How is the teacher's work affected by specialists in the school?
7. What has caused recent tendencies to increase the work load of classroom teachers?

PROJECTS

1. Interview a classroom teacher concerning the kind and amount of work done over a period of 1 week.
2. Observe a teacher teaching a single class and describe the kind of preparation you think was made before teaching the class.
3. Write an essay of not more than 500 words explaining why most teachers find teaching school an interesting and challenging occupation.
4. Write a letter to some highly successful teacher inquiring about the aspects of teaching he or she finds most challenging and those that are least challenging. Ask what advice this teacher would like to give to one seriously considering entering the teaching profession.

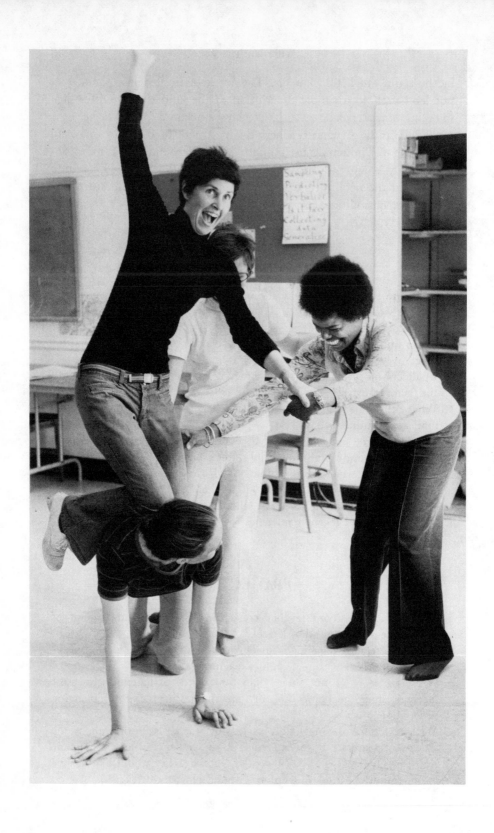

chapter

3

What it takes to become a teacher

This chapter is about the things people do to become teachers. Teachers are expected to meet certain general personal requirements and some specific professional requirements, some of which developed as a matter of social custom or tradition and some of which were specifically established by the governments of the respective states. We are going to involve ourselves in an exploratory introduction to these matters. In doing this we will review (1) the basic societal expectations that influence teachers' behavior, (2) the sorts of requirements teacher education institutions generally expect of people preparing to become teachers, and (3) the sorts of skills one should acquire if one is to become a successful teacher at any age level.

Societal Expectations

The American people make possible the various private and public school systems in the United States either through their tax payments or through their voluntary tuition payments to private schools. Americans differ among themselves on what they expect from their schools (whether public or private). They have had major disagreements from time to time on what the full range of specific educational aims ought to be for providing the core "general education" of a citizen. But they do share certain common expectations about their schools, and these will be examined in this volume. We need to point out here, however, some of the basic qualifications expected of teachers in America.

It is important to begin this introductory statement of public expectations about teachers with a brief explanation of how the American people obtained local control over their community schools. When the people who wrote the Constitution drafted that document and submitted it for ratification by the original 13 states they did not include any reference to education in it. In the debates in each of the original 13 states regarding whether or not to adopt the Constitution there was concern (to put it mildly) that the central government not become too powerful. (Nine of the 13 original states had to ratify the federal Constitution before it could be considered ratified; this number was agreed to by the members of the Constitutional Convention.) Thus the first 10 amendments to the Constitution were drafted and proposed as a block of amendments to be immediately adopted and made part of the Constitution upon its ratification by the requisite number of states. Each of the first 10 amendments was designed either to guarantee certain specifically stated individual rights or to limit the interpretive construction of the Constitution such that any right or power not referred to or listed in the Constitution would still be reserved *to the individual citizen, the state governments, or the people generally and not to the federal government.* Thus these first 10 amendments became known as the Bill of Rights. The Ninth and Tenth Amendments were to cover all human rights not specifically mentioned in the Constitution:

> AMENDMENT 9: The enumeration in the Constitution, of certain rights, shall not be construed to deny or disparage others retained by the people.
> AMENDMENT 10: The powers not delegated to the United States by the Constitution, nor prohibited by it to the states, are reserved to the states respectively, or to the people.

Education, as noted above, not being a topic dealt with in the body of the Constitution, thus became a matter for the individual state legislatures and the state constitutional conventions to debate. The legislatures of the respective states developed their own provisions for education in their states. Thus was born in the meaning of the wording of the Ninth and Tenth Amendments to the Constitution a great concept of ultimate popular control of education and all other rights and services not dealt with in the federal Constitution. As a "reserved power," and as many would now argue (including the present authors) a right retained by the people, education must be zealously controlled by the citizens of the respective states. Education in basic literacy skills is a minimum need for the citizens of a democratic state; this was recognized as early as 1769 by Thomas Jefferson and others. As America became more and more industrialized through the decades of the nineteenth century and into the twentieth century and as the American economy became more and more technologically oriented there grew ever more complex educational needs to meet the demands of a high state of technology and industrialization. Throughout the nineteenth and twentieth centuries there was evident in the more industrialized states of the Union the need to provide more complex and more extended educational opportunities to American citizens. By the middle of the second decade of the twentieth century the need for such extended educational opportunities was apparent to the legislatures of most of the agrarian states of the Union as well. As the nation came of age with an ever-advancing agricultural technology as well as an industrial technology the teaching profession began to organize and to develop its purposes and standards. (These matters will be dealt with in terms of their relevance to today's American teacher and the sources of American educational development in Units II, III, and IV.) Our educational present was forged in large measure as part of the forging and development of a new and unique national experience.

We want to make clear at the outset of our study of American education how and on what constitutional premises the unique decentralization of control over education to the people of the respective states began. In Unit III of this volume we will demonstrate further how our great constitutional tradition worked in the twentieth century (starting in 1954 and earlier) also to guarantee the personal civil rights of students in the schools through applying the equal-protection-of-the-laws clause of the Fourteenth Amendment to the rights of students. But that is a matter to be taken up later in this volume; it is referred to here to note further one of the basic elements in the American constitutional tradition that works to safeguard the educational rights of parents, students, and teachers. Teachers are supported by all the citizens of the republic, as noted earlier; consequently, citizens come to expect certain qualities of teachers.

Society imposes certain minimum qualifications that individuals must meet before they are admitted to teaching. This policy of control over teachers is exercised in part because society recognizes that the schools are vital to its welfare. Society depends on the schools for the transmission of many of the essentials of our culture. Many indispensable beliefs and skills and techniques are taught to children through the schools. Without such transmission and preservation our culture could not survive. Society is aware that the responsibility is so important that it should be entrusted only to competent individuals, and it is to this end that society sets up some qualifications for teachers that it believes will assure a degree of teaching competence.

Society exercises a measure of control over teacher qualifications also in part because the public is determined to do what it can to insure that the huge amount of money invested in the schools is spent wisely. Society requires that the great single item in school costs— salaries for school personnel—be paid only to individuals who have met minimum requirements. It hopes thereby to assure an adequate return for the money invested.

By imposing standards for admission to teaching, society also provides teachers with a measure of security and stability. It thereby adds to the attractiveness of teaching for capable people. By adding rewards of status and financial advantages to those within the profession who meet more exacting or more specialized professional requirements, encouragement is provided for development along lines that society considers desirable.

The state is the unit of government generally responsible for safeguarding minimum educational standards. Naturally, details of control over the qualifications of teachers vary from state to state. But by and large, state control is accomplished through two practices: certification of the teachers and accreditation of the institutions that educate the teachers. Certification brings the individual under the scrutiny of the state, whereas accreditation gives the state an opportunity to influence the nature and quality of education the teacher receives. Control over teacher qualifications is the end sought in both cases.

Certification

In frontier times, when local school boards certified teachers, the standards were, of course, almost nonexistent. Later, district and county boards or their designated school authority took over the task of licensing teachers. In some states, by the end of the century the county superintendent of schools periodically administered competitive examinations covering the various subjects taught in the elementary and high schools and issued certificates only to those who "passed" the examinations. Little or no emphasis was placed on college attendance, and in some states graduation from the eighth grade was the only prerequisite. Since the beginning of the century upgrading the teaching profession has been a continuing policy, and controlling entrance to the profession through licensing has been one means of accomplishing this. In line with the principle that the state is the unit of school administration, local licensing of teachers has been discontinued, and now in all 50 states the state authority assumes this function.

Although an improvement over licensing teachers by local school authorities, centralizing licensing of teachers in the state educational authority has not eliminated the perplexing problems caused by lack of uniformity in standards among the states. Despite a great variation, however, there is general agreement about the following:

1. Authority for the certification of teachers is centralized in the state department of education.
2. Certificates are issued for definite subject fields or a specified grade level.
3. Certificates must be renewed periodically.
4. A bachelor's degree is a minimum requirement for a teaching certificate.
5. Specific courses in education and a definite number of semester hours in a subject-matter teaching field or fields are required.

There has been a tendency to increase the subject-matter requirements for teaching at all grade levels. In fact, judging from present trends in certification, the standards of competence demanded for entrance to the teaching profession will continue to rise, though perhaps slowly.

There are usually several levels of teaching certificates awarded in the respective states. The initial teaching certificate that a teacher receives is often referred to as a "provisional certificate," which is a beginning teaching certificate requiring that a certain amount of postbaccalaureate academic study and a specified number of years of teaching experience be completed within a specified number of years before the teacher can obtain one of the more advanced professional certificates. Provisional teaching certificates are usually renewable once. Although each state legislature, acting on the advice of its state department of education (or state department of public instruction), has the sole ultimate authority over what qualifications teachers will be required to meet in each state, there are some general similarities in requirements for first or initial teaching certificates among several states. Usually a beginning elementary teacher will have had to take at least 29 semester hours or 44 quarter hours in professional education courses. They will also have had to take at least 60 semester credit hours or 90 quarter credit hours in "general education," or courses in the arts and sciences that relate to the sorts of cultural background or teaching skills required of elementary school teachers in their respective states.

A beginning secondary school teacher will generally have to take a minimum of 21 semester hours or 32 quarter hours in professional education courses such as courses in the relationships of school to society, understanding learning theory or basic behavioral foundations of education, secondary school curriculum and/or teaching methods, and possibly graphics or the use of audiovisual aids; in addition, student teaching for 8 to 10 weeks is required. Elementary and secondary school teachers' basic preparatory ("preservice") professional course work in the behavioral and the social foundations of education is often taken in classes in which both prospective elementary and secondary teachers are students together. Usually the social foundations and behavioral foundations course work is "heterogeneously grouped," since all teachers need the same sorts of background knowledge in these areas, or at least very similar general knowledge. Where elementary and secondary teachers do not take the same educational foundations courses they take very similar ones taught by people who approach these areas of knowledge from either an elementary school or secondary school point of view. However, the course work in curriculum, methods of instruction, and student teaching and any other courses that specialize in their emphasis based on different developmental stages of different age groups leads to separate courses for prospective elementary and secondary school teachers. Usually we find that schools, colleges, and departments of education at the university or college level find it necessary to place prospective elementary teachers and prospective secondary teachers in different courses to teach the specialized areas of professional preparation. The secondary teacher also takes a large block of course work in "general education," or arts and sciences areas, which may or may not be related to chosen teaching fields. Then the prospective secondary school teacher takes a large block of credit hours (approximately 45 semester hours or

68 quarter hours) in a "comprehensive" teaching field, or he or she takes a "major" of about 30 to 40 semester hours or 45 to 60 quarter hours in a particular academic subject area and a "minor" of about 24 semester hours or 36 quarter hours in a second academic or vocational field.

One can develop as many certification endorsements on one's teaching certificate as one wishes by continuing to take course work in teaching areas where one thinks one might wish to teach. Many teachers do this and add very much to their flexibility in their teaching assignments; they achieve greater "lateral mobility" in the profession by enlarging the range of possible teaching positions potentially open to them.

In some states, such as Ohio, there are listed "comprehensive" secondary teaching areas as described above or "specific high school teaching fields." These "teaching fields" correspond to the academic and the vocational and technical subject matters taught in the particular state in question and range in credit hour requirements from at least 30 semester hours or 45 quarter hours to at least 20 semester hours or 30 quarter hours. The number of credit hours in a teaching field required by a particular state is usually based on the state department of education's estimate of the nature and complexity of the subject matter to be taught and a reasoned value judgment as to just how much college or university study in a teaching field a person ought to have to be considered competent to teach that particular subject matter at the grade levels for which the prospective teacher is seeking certification.

Certification of teachers is but one avenue to upgrading teaching competence. As the following discussion shows, accreditation of institutions preparing teachers is another. A third is for the profession itself, through its own professional organizations, to assume responsibility for guaranteeing the public adequate standards of competence. A fourth is for the individual institutions that train teachers to assume a greater degree of responsibility for improving their teacher education programs.

Accreditation

In exerting control over the qualifications of teachers by a process of accreditation of teacher education institutions, the state authority requires that a college or university, to be accredited, offer an acceptable program for teacher education. This is actually an extension of control by certification. After setting up training qualifications for teaching, the state requires that the teacher education institutions provide the facilities and curricula that will permit students to achieve the stipulated qualifications.

Some college staff members resent state accrediting policies. They argue that the state has encroached on functions that belong to the institutions, that formulating a program for teacher education should be left to the discretion of the institutions, that the state's dictation of the program shows a lack of confidence in the ability of those who administer higher institutions. They do not maintain that the final control of the education of teachers in the state is not a proper function of the state. Rather, the argument is over whether the state makes wise use of its accrediting authority.

The accreditation of institutions seems to be peculiar to American higher education and is perhaps an outgrowth of our system of government. Teaching is only one of many fields subject to accreditation, and the official state authority is not the only agency to accredit or pass on whether a teacher-training institution is fully qualified to prepare teachers. Different criteria are used by various agencies. Although, except for a state department of education, each of the accreditation agencies is an extralegal authority, the lists they prepare of acceptable institutions are usually accepted by legal bodies as equivalent to the lists prepared by legal authorities.

Among the many agencies outside the state authority that make decisions with a bearing on the qualifications of teachers, two influential associations are selected as illustrative; one is regional and the other is national.

The North Central Association of Colleges and Secondary Schools is an example of a *voluntary* regional accrediting organization that influences standards in a multistate region. Rigid standards, often higher than those set by the states, must be met by any school before it can become a member of this association. So influential has the association become that, to the general public, a school that does not hold membership is an inferior educational organization. The association has also tried to guard against the efforts of some organized groups to lower teacher qualifications.

The association has not concerned itself with standards for elementary education; these standards have remained completely under state control. Since the North Central Association and similar regional associations include colleges and secondary schools only, their accreditation practices have tended to add to the prestige of high school teachers and thus, to some extent, to lower the prestige of elementary teachers. In general, however, the effect of accrediting associations of this kind has been salutary. They have not attempted to infringe on the states' rights to set standards. They have sought only to raise the standards of education given in public and nonpublic schools.

In 1949 the presidents of a number of colleges and universities became concerned about the growing number of accrediting agencies for higher institutions and they established the National Commission on Accrediting. In the words of the executive secretary, "the commission is serving as a coordinating agency through the labyrinth of accreditation; it is continually making suggestions for improvement in this frequently misunderstood educational activity. . . ." In 1968 the members of the commission included more than 1200 colleges and universities located in many sections of the United States and seven national organizations, such as the Association of American Universities. Serving as a coordinating agent, the commission recognizes six regional associations and 23 professional associations.

When one state accepts the undergraduate teacher education program of another state for purposes of hiring and certifying teachers from that other state, it is said that the two states have a "reciprocal" agreement in teacher certification. The process of one state's department of education or public instruction accepting for certification graduates of teacher education programs in other states is referred to in professional educational circles as "reciprocity." Many states have entered into such reciprocity agreements with the state departments of other states. Campus offices of teacher placement or career development offices can provide data on which other states have such "reciprocity" agreements. These agreements are developed as a result of cooperative negotiation and consultation among leaders of state departments of education or state departments of public instruction. The National Education Association (NEA) is very concerned to see unified national standards developed for teacher education. To this end the NEA is working in conjunction with other national professional organizations to achieve consensus among the 50 states on basic requirements for initial teacher certification that will allow graduates of teacher education programs to teach in any state. The National Council for Accreditation of Teacher Education (NCATE) is also supportive of such a possibility, and other organizations, such as the Education Commission of the States, seek greater uniformity and quality in basic teacher education programs. There is an interstate organizational agreement whereby those state departments of education that are parties to the agreement accept teacher education graduates of the other states for initial certification. This agreement is known as the *Interstate Certification Reciprocity Compact*. In its 1973–1974 "Annual List" NCATE reported that 31 states had an official policy of approving, under most circumstances, graduates of teacher education programs approved by NCATE. Thirty-one states had passed enabling legislation to allow such reciprocity agreements by mid-1974. The State Directors of Teacher Education and Certification (NASDTEC) has obtained the support of 22 states for reciprocity agreements for initial certification of graduates of teacher education programs in those 22 states.

Among the professional associations recognized is the influential National Council for Accreditation of Teacher Education (usually called the NCATE), which was established by the NEA in 1952. In 1967, 28 states had reciprocity accreditation through the NCATE. Currently, more than 450 of America's foremost teacher education institutions, the prime source of the new supply of teachers each year, are members. In 1956 the National Commission on Accrediting officially recognized the NCATE as most directly responsible for determining the accreditation procedures for teacher education programs. The plan is to have this association evaluate and accredit each qualified teacher education program. The states would then automatically license all graduates who successfully complete an accredited program.

All the problems of accreditation have not been solved, nor can a complete analysis of the issues be made here. For example, why is a plan of accreditation that is successful for secondary schools not logically extended to the elementary schools? Efforts are being made on a broad scale to discover proper ways to guarantee academic standards, to encourage, even coerce, institutions to maintain certain minimum standards in the education of teachers, and to coordinate and approve the activities of the many voluntary agencies involved in accreditation of teacher education programs.

The National Council for Accreditation of Teacher Education (NCATE) sets up eight specific standards to govern the qualitative development of basic preservice teacher education programs. We earlier noted the "general studies" component of such programs and the general types and amounts of course work within baccalaureate degree programs taken by prospective elementary or secondary school teachers. We will now briefly describe the categories of study recom-

mended by NCATE; every college or university that is accredited
by the National Council for Accreditation of Teacher Education has
to submit to a comprehensive and in-depth evaluation by an NCATE
visitation team once every 10 years according to current NCATE
guidelines. The year before the NCATE team arrives on a college
or university campus the members of the professional education faculty
of the institution develop a major in-depth "self-study" in which the
faculty and administration of the college to be evaluated who are
responsible for teacher education describe in detail all the college's
present and anticipated efforts to meet NCATE's accreditation standards. This self-study includes a complete and detailed listing of all
courses in professional education subjects taught with course objectives
and content fully described, complete data on each faculty member
involved in teaching the courses, budgetary support for the teacher
preparation program, library and office as well as classroom facilities
and equipment available to the teacher preparation program as well
as reports on faculty research, publications, student enrollments, and
other relevant matters. The "general studies" component of teacher
preparation programs consists of courses designed to assist teachers
in developing a broader cultural perspective on life so as (1) to be
better able to impart general educational ideals in broad perspective
to their own future students as well as (2) to serve as models of educated people themselves. The NCATE standards refer to general education rather obliquely as the "studies most widely generalizable," by
which they mean arts and science courses that will foster the preceding
points 1 and 2. In some cases a college student's work in his general
studies component will relate to or be a part of a secondary "comprehensive," "major," or "minor" teaching field or the general studies
course work will relate and add to elementary grade-level teaching
areas. The content of the "professional studies component" of
NCATE-accredited basic teacher education programs is divided into
(1) the study of the subject matter content area that the prospective
teacher plans to teach; (2) the study of the basic behavioral and
humanistic foundational studies in education (which deal with behavioral theory and psychology of education as well as historical, philosophical, or social foundations of educational theory and practice);
(3) "the teaching of learning theory with laboratory and clinical experience" (where students are taught the theoretical bases of teaching
practice and given opportunity to practice the application of teaching
methods based on such teaching and learning theory); and (4) a

"practicum" or student teaching experience in an actual school setting under professional supervision.[1]

One recent and powerful trend in the development of teacher preparatory programs in recent years has been to provide undergraduate students considering the possibility of careers in teaching with the opportunity to have limited and closely supervised "practicum" or "mini-teaching" experiences in the sophomore and junior years of their undergraduate studies prior to the senior-year "student teaching" experience. This trend has been encouraged by NCATE. There have been several experimental efforts to set up "student intern" programs that would either run longer than current student teaching programs or be designed to occur under closely supervised and limited teaching circumstances the year before student teaching to relate better the knowledge students gain in their classes at the college level to the problems of teaching at the elementary or secondary teaching levels. Classroom teachers are always included as members of NCATE visitation teams and they are usually most interested in the efforts of colleges or universities to provide more field experience or practicum experiences for undergraduates in preservice preparation programs for teachers.

Teacher Preparation

For years all the states have attempted to improve the quality of education by improving the programs of teacher training, by assuming the authority for accrediting teacher education institutions, and by imposing more demanding certificate requirements. A college degree has, in most states, become a requirement for entrance to teaching. Furthermore, degree candidates must take specific courses deemed essential for teacher preparation.

Since 1952 the degrees in education awarded by American colleges have far exceeded in number the degrees conferred in other areas of concentration. One might conclude from this that there is a surplus of teachers. That is not true, however, partly because of the rapid attrition during the early years.

Although there is some difference of opinion concerning the details of a desirable program of teacher education, there is general

---

[1] See *Standards for Accreditation of Teacher Education,* adopted January 1970 by the National Council for Accreditation of Teacher Education, 1750 Pennsylvania Avenue, N.W., Suite 411, Washington, D.C. 20006.

agreement that it should be at least four years in length and that an ideal length would be 5 years. There is also general agreement that the program should be *balanced*—made up of three broad classifications of subject matter: (1) background education—the broad cultural setting, (2) specialized subject matter, and (3) courses in professional education.

Background Education

There is no disagreement about the fact that a prospective teacher should pursue a program designed to give him a broad cultural background—contribute to making him a "cultured person." There are, however, different schools of thought as to how this may be best achieved.

Until about 1940 the teacher in preparation typically pursued traditional courses in subject-matter fields and planned his study around required majors and minors. Since then, early specialization has become progressively more generally required. More recently, the necessity for mastering skills of quantification has been extended beyond such fields as mathematics, chemistry, and physics to such areas as economics, geography, and biology. Emphasis on study in depth in an area necessarily limits the possibilities for study in breadth. For instance, it may be assumed now by a college that courses in chemistry, physics, calculus, and statistics are prerequisites to a first course in biology, to provide a necessary background for a biologist. Are such requirements, however, necessary for a good biology teacher who must also have that first course in biology?

Most colleges recognize the weaknesses of the traditional approach and are attempting through different kinds of courses to provide students with a broad cultural background. It is agreed that the enlightenment and refinement of taste acquired through formal intellectual and esthetic training can be cultivated in more than a single pattern of education. The experimental, new courses are based on the belief that the desired cultural background can be achieved through courses that are general rather than specialized. For instance, often a course is offered that encompasses subject matter from a group of closely related fields. The professors from these related fields combine their talents in a kind of team teaching, utilizing the resources of their individual departments—visual aids, laboratories, and the like. An Introduction to the Behavioral Sciences, Modern Society, Basic Science, The Use of English are examples of courses offered where the broader approach is followed. In some colleges this kind of course is given for all beginning students, except for those who specialize immediately. A student is expected to achieve an understanding of the basic concepts common to all the subject-matter fields included.

It is not possible to evalute accurately the success of colleges in providing the broad cultural background necessary for the prospective teacher. Obviously, however, regardless of the approach, the teacher to be will profit most when taught by highly skilled teachers in all college-level courses. Furthermore, as students plan their programs with advisers, they too may influence the quality of their own learning situations. Most colleges allow the student considerable leeway in choice in this background education.

Specialized Subject Matter

For prospective high school teachers, specialization in a particular field is obligatory. The state usually requires from 24 to 36 semester hours of work in a given subject or field for certification. Leaders concerned with improving present high school programs urge states to require that teachers prepare themselves in broad fields corresponding to the major areas taught in secondary schools. Some colleges have responded to such requests. Some of them, for instance, permit students to complete majors in such areas as general science and social studies. These subjects harmonize with the classifications of subject matter found in secondary and elementary schools. Some offer such courses as Mathematics for the Intermediate Teacher or Basic Mathematics, Physics for Teachers, Chemistry for Teachers, and the like. They are taught by specialists, but not for the purpose of preparing specialists. Often the subject matter is designed to complete the education received by the teacher-in-training, to fill in gaps. The aim of the courses is vocational but not for the preparation of professional mathematicians, physicists, chemists, or biologists. Such courses may carry graduate credit in a graduate school for those who are in the teaching profession but not for specialists following other programs in the graduate school. Vocational need is one criterion for the selection of the subject matter taught.

Deciding on the best type of specialized preparation for elementary teachers presents special difficulties to the colleges. School officials frequently expect an elementary teacher to be prepared in every basic and special field of the elementary curriculum, besides being competent in the areas of child growth and development and human relations.

Some state authorities have made the elementary school certification requirements so specific that the curriculum of the colleges has been practically dictated by a state educational authority.

Whatever the final answer to the question of required specialized training, there is wide agreement that the fields included in the teacher education program should be carefully selected for the purpose of improving potential teaching competence. In other words, although the specialized content of the teacher education program should be balanced in relation to the broad cultural courses and the professional courses, it should also be designed to give the teacher professional competence in those special fields of study in which he or she intends to teach.

Professional Preparation

Although the academic education of a teacher, including general and specialized courses, is basic, it is not the whole of his essential preparation. Much of the professional knowledge and skill necessary for starting to teach must be acquired in professional courses given in college. These courses are, in many states, specified in state regulations; thus some uniformity in this portion of the prospective teacher's program is assured. However, there is much difference of opinion about what part of the total time of training should be devoted to professional education and whether courses should begin with the freshman year or at some later stage in the program. Professional courses are sometimes considered to be so theoretical as to make them more suitable for graduate than undergraduate study.

The Commission on Teacher Education recommends that "strictly professional elements should be allocated from one-eighth to one-sixth of the time available in a 4- or 5-year program of teacher preparation." Most colleges accept this division of time. Usually out of the total of 120 semester hours of college work required for graduation, from 15 to 20 semester hours of professional courses, including special methods and student teaching, are required for high school teachers and from 20 to 30 hours for elementary school teachers. Colleges differ, however, in their specific requirements and in the nature of the content and organization of professional courses.

In the area of teacher preparation perhaps the greatest agreement is in the matter of practical experience. It is uniformly agreed that the individual and class assignments of prospective teachers should include observation in classrooms, that prospective teachers should participate in a wealth of activities with children in both school and community situations, and that they should engage in actual student teaching. It is only through supervised full-time work with pupils over a period of time that students gain a "feel" for the teacher's task and can assess their own potentialities in relation to the task. Despite agreement that teaching should be included in a prospective teacher's program, there is no general agreement on how much time students should spend teaching, in which fields they should teach, and when they should begin teaching. (Usually, however, student teaching starts during the senior year.)

Sometimes, usually during a fifth year of preparation and as a part of graduate study, a program of teaching internship is offered. This is teaching, full or part time, in a regular public school classroom with the approval and under the close supervision of the teacher education institution. The program provides an opportunity to combine theoretical with practical work while completing requirements for a master's degree. Some feel, however, that beginning teachers who have complete teaching responsibility for a group of children need to give all their time to teaching during their initial years and that the effort to combine teaching with graduate study and seminar attendance works to the disadvantage of both the practical and theoretical phases of an internship plan. Whether an internship plan is a part of the teacher education program or not, the trend is toward planning the total teacher preparation program in terms of five years' work.

Selection of Prospective Teachers

In the long run, the number of capable people who will be attracted to teaching will increase only if teaching standards are high enough to win respect and if the prestige, security, and financial rewards are attractive to qualified people.

Unfortunately, research has provided neither the measures for making predictions of success nor a scientific basis for deciding how selections should be made. We cannot, for instance, with accuracy define what successful teaching is, or specifically identify the personality traits that are the attributes of the successful teacher. Our selection must therefore be largely subjective and must be based on such sources of information as interviews, letters of recommendation, standard tests, physical examinations, marks in college courses, and the like. Even with data concerning scholastic achievement, special aptitudes, attitude toward teaching, and experience with youth groups, we cannot with assurance predict what teaching ability an individual possesses. Subjective judgments are liable to considerable error. This does not mean, however, that we cannot recognize that some factors are more favorable to producing teaching success than others.

Perhaps the most important qualifying factor in determining success is the individual's interest in teaching. Unfortunately, it cannot be measured. A student who has an interest in teaching, ideally founded on some kind of firsthand experience in working with children and youth, will be motivated to plan wisely with his advisers in selecting the most fruitful teacher education program. He will be alert to the opportunities to develop necessary basic abilities appropriate to the field of his choice. If his institution does not offer the necessary opportunities, he will discover them in some other institution.

The selection of students to pursue the teaching profession is a process that continues during the entire period of preparation. It is not one act completed when the student is admitted to college. Continuous study *by* the student is accompanied with continuous study *of* the student so that a redirection of the student's program can be made at any time when warranted. The student's welfare is kept in mind but so is the welfare of all those whom he may teach. Counseling by the professional staff is an important aspect of selection. An attempt is made to aid the student in matching his potentialities with his choice of teaching field and to eliminate only those who obviously possess disabling qualifications such as, for instance, emotional instability or low ability to succeed in academic work. In selection, the college staff emphasizes positive factors related to the growth and education of the student rather than the negative factor of denial of the right to continue.

Although all higher institutions have admissions officers, the process of making a reasonable selection of potential teachers is a responsibility of the staffs that actually prepare them. In this way the professors themselves influence the standards applied to the selection of those who will qualify for and enter teaching.

Placement of Teachers

After completing the teacher preparation program and qualifying for certification, the prospective teacher faces the important step of placement. All teacher education institutions counsel their students about placement and recommend them for positions. Most of them maintain placement bureaus. Graduates are assisted in writing letters of application and in making personal applications. It is, however, the superintendent of a local school system, a school trustee, or someone else officially charged by a local school system with the responsibility of employing the staff who makes the final offer.

Commercial teachers' agencies, organizations that make a business of placing teachers and that charge a commission for their services, also may be utilized by the student. If a candidate wishes to teach in a certain school system, it is considered ethical to write a letter of inquiry that includes information about the candidate's training, experience, and interests.

Personal Qualifications

Problem of Generalization

We have indicated that it is impossible to define in detail the personality characteristics of the successful teacher. One must use terms that are general, that call for considerable subjective interpretation, and that are related more or less to standard virtues about which there can be little disagreement. We can, for instance, agree that a sympathetic personality is desirable. Can we define a sympathetic personality? Can we agree on the specific traits that must always, or generally, be identified with such a personality? Numerous studies of what constitutes first-rate teaching have resulted in a list of virtues expressing more of a hope than an expectation.

The difficulty of defining personal qualifications necessary to teaching success is further compounded because, strictly speaking, teaching is not a single occupation. It is a large family of occupations. Opportunities for specialization in teaching are numerous. Obviously the requirements for a third-grade teacher will not be identical with those for a teacher at the graduate school level, for a teacher-librarian, or for a teacher of physically handicapped children. Even positions that appear, at first, to be the same may make widely varying demands, depending on variations in total school responsibilities and the composition of the pupil enrollment.

Minimum personal qualifications required are influenced, too, by the times. In one generation, one set of qualifications is deemed sufficient, whereas in another, such qualifications are considered inadequate. Radio, television, films, new electronic aids, maps, globes, improved textbooks—all help to change the character of teaching and to modify teacher requirements. New knowledge about such matters as individual differences, special abilities, or the nature of growth changes the nature of teaching, modifies the standards of successful teaching, and influences the personal qualifications needed.

Studies

Despite the difficulties, numerous studies have been made in an effort to shed some light on our understanding of what characteristics, in general, seem to be related to teaching success. The studies have been principally of two kinds—those that approach the problem by asking pupils to report the characteristics of the teachers they considered most successful and those that base conclusions on reports from school administrators and professors of school administration.

One early investigator analyzed the opinions of a total of 30,000 pupils.[2] He discovered that those characteristics most persistently cherished by pupils were fairness, cheerfulness, businesslike procedures when teaching, ability to obtain pupil response, and skillful methods of teaching. Under the classification of fairness, for example, the pupils hoped that praise and criticism would be based on fact, that the teacher would show no favoritism, that grading would be fair, that the opinions of pupils would be respected, and that the teacher would reveal at all times a willingness to help pupils. Pupils did not like teachers who consistently found fault, nagged, scolded, used sarcasm, and otherwise reacted negatively to what the pupils were attempting to do. They seemed greatly to appreciate the teacher who had what they thought to be a wholesome sense of humor.

Studies based on reports from school administrators and professors of school administration are legion. In general, the most impressive fact emphasized by the findings is that only a very low correlation between any single personality trait and teaching success can be discovered.

Studies by psychologists have been devoted to the relation of personality traits to success in various lines of endeavor. They have emphasized that a combination of traits is vitally related to performance. However, it is not always possible to state what this combination actually is. Indeed, many different combinations may be equally suc-

---

[2] Dwight E. Beecher, *The Evaluation of Teaching.* Syracuse, N.Y.: Syracuse University Press, 1949, pp. 41–63.

Applying for a Teaching Post
1871

"Want to be a school-master, do you? You? Well what would you do in Flat Crick deestrick, *I'd* like to know? Why, the boys have driv off the last two, and licked the one afore them like blazes. You might teach a summer school, when nothin' but children come. But I 'low it takes a right smart *man* to be a school-master in Flat Crick in the winter. They'd pitch you out of doors, sonny, neck and heels, afore Christmas."

. . . The impression made by these ominous remarks was emphasized by the glances which he received from Jack Means' two sons. The older one eyed him from the top of his brawny shoulders with that amiable look which a big dog turns on a little one before shaking him. Ralph Hartsook had never thought of being measured by the standard of muscle. This notion of beating education into young savages in spite of themselves dashed his ardor.*

Today

While the policies with respect to employment vary considerably from district to district, the following practices are not uncommon:

1. Most teacher education institutions now help the student to obtain his initial appointment. Many colleges have placement offices that specialize in teacher placement. They collect information about the student, counsel him, and direct him in his attempts to obtain his first teaching position.

2. Some superintendents of schools visit the colleges and personally seek out and employ the student. Many administrators look upon this as their best opportunity to improve the quality of teaching in their school systems.

3. Many school systems print attractive brochures about the schools and the community that are sent to all applicants for teaching positions. The administrative policies of the school system are plainly set forth.

* Edward Eggleston, *The Hoosier Schoolmaster: A Story of Backwoods Life in Indiana.* New York: Orange Judd, 1871.

cessful. A weakness in one trait may be compensated for by strength in another. In focusing attention on the individual it is easy to forget this and to overemphasize the importance of some one outstanding personality trait.

Classification of Qualities

Because it is impossible to identify any single ability or trait that is principally responsible for success or to determine whether training will lead to the development of some required combination of abilities, our discussion of personal qualifications is developed in terms of five broad classifications of qualities: (1) ability and willingness to learn, (2) social intelligence, (3) facility of expression, (4) special abilities, and (5) physical stamina. These are obviously not the only traits required of successful teachers, but they are representative of the personal qualities often said to be required to teach well.

I. ABILITY AND WILLINGNESS TO LEARN

A teacher has to be a person who enjoys learning and who is capable of learning well. It is doubtful that a teacher who has often had difficulty in learning would continuously seek to learn in the future. Teaching is a process of communicating knowledge, learning, and relearning, which requires a personality able and ready to engage voluntarily in the learning process without being pressured to do so. For as paradoxical or puzzling as it may seem to some, one of the basic characteristics of a "master teacher" is that he is a person who wants to be a good learner and to share his learning with others. Therefore what Hughes called "native intelligence" or the capacity and the desire to learn well must be counted as the most essential personal characteristic of a person with the qualities to become a good teacher. This is a quality that goes well beyond personal I.Q. scores or intelligence test scores, for a teacher must desire and seek to learn more each year about life and those segments of it that compose his or her subject matter teaching areas.

There is a myth in America that the famous American historian Richard Hofstadter condemned in his famous prize-winning study *Anti-intellectualism in American Life.*[3] The myth, put simply, is that bright, inquisitive people are to be distrusted. A person who wishes

[3] Richard Hofstadter, *Anti-intellectualism in American Life.* New York: Random House, 1962.

Many studies have been made to discover what traits or personal qualities pupils consider characteristic of the teachers they like best and those they like least. A pioneering investigation by Professor Frank William Hart (1881–1968) of the responses of 10,000 high school seniors is summarized as follows:

Highest Ranking Traits of the "Best Liked" Teachers

1. Is helpful with school work, explains lessons and assignments clearly and thoroughly, and uses examples in teaching.
2. Cheerful, happy, good-natured, jolly, has a sense of humor and can take a joke.
3. Human, friendly, companionable, "one of us."
4. Interested in and understands pupils.
5. Makes work interesting, creates a desire to work, makes class work a pleasure.
6. Strict, has control of the class, commands respect.
7. Impartial, shows no favoritism, has no "pets."
8. Not cross, crabby, grouchy, nagging, or sarcastic.
9. "We learned the subject."
10. A pleasing personality.

Highest Ranking Traits of the "Least Liked" Teachers

1. Too cross, crabby, grouchy, never smiles, nagging, sarcastic, loses temper, "flies off the handle."
2. Not helpful with school work, does not explain lessons and assignments, not clear, work not planned.
3. Partial, has "pets" of favored students, and "picks on" certain pupils.
4. Superior, aloof, haughty, "snooty," overbearing, does not know you out of class.
5. Mean, unreasonable, "hard boiled," intolerant, ill mannered, too strict.
6. Unfair in marking and grading, unfair in tests and examinations.
7. Inconsiderate of pupils' feelings, bawls out pupils in the presence of classmates, pupils are afraid and ill at ease and dread class.
8. Not interested in pupils and does not understand them.
9. Unreasonable assignments and home work.
10. Too loose in discipline, no control of class, does not command respect.*

* F. W. Hart, *Teachers and Teaching*. New York: Macmillan, 1934, pp. 131, 250–251.

to be a teacher should be able to engage in the rational analysis, appraisal, and evaluation of information and of the concepts of the subject matter. There is another myth that creative people somehow cannot get along with other people well and that they are to be distrusted. Part of the characteristic of possessing a willingness to learn involves fostering and encouraging others (one's students) to learn not only what the teacher knows and plans to teach but also relevant alternative knowledge in the teacher's field that the teacher may not know about. In other words, teachers must be willing to have students explore even those areas of their teaching fields with which they are not familiar. Teachers should respect and encourage creative students; there is a body of sociological research that has indicated that some teachers often fear or distrust and/or resent highly creative students. Teachers ought to have sufficient confidence in their own learning capacities that they will not resent creativity when they see it in the behavior of students. As Richard Hofstadter once stated with resounding effect, an intellectual should "enjoy the play of ideas" and he or she should be the sort of person who lives for ideas and not off of them. Hofstadter's attitude on this point is one that all teachers should share.

Obviously the many different sorts of teaching assignments given in school systems require varying degrees of intellectual skill; teaching drivers' training classes is not the same as teaching an honor's physics class. Both teaching assignments are very important, but they require different sorts of skills, and this distinction must be kept in mind when we discuss the talents of teachers. Whatever their teaching assignments, teachers should want to learn and have the capacity to learn well those subject matters or skills they hope to teach. Underlying the discussion in the preceding paragraphs is a fact that most experienced teachers understand well: most students, even very young ones and even those considered by some to be "slow" learners, know when a teacher is bored or unprepared.

2. SOCIAL INTELLIGENCE

Teaching is always concerned with helping people to grow in maturity and develop desirable responses to various social situations. Behavior is primarily social. The one who teaches others must himself, to a reasonable degree, possess what the psychologists call social intelligence. He must exhibit social competence. Social intelligence cannot, of course, be separated from native intelligence or from any of the other personality traits.

The social competences associated with successful teaching include capacity for leadership, tactfulness in working closely with others, sensitivity to the needs and wants of those with whom one works. There are no techniques to measure the degree to which an individual possesses social intelligence. Only through intimate personal acquaintance can one make a subjective appraisal of what the effectiveness of training and experience in developing this qualification might be.

3. FACILITY OF EXPRESSION

Regardless of the field or the level of a teacher's work, he or she is always aided by fluency in the use of symbols, or what is sometimes called verbal ability. The demand for this ability is almost constant, although some teaching positions place a higher premium on it than others. Explaining, expressing original thought, interpreting, advising, giving directions—the effectiveness of these and many other activities depends, in part, on the teacher's facility of expression. This is an ability that can be developed, largely through training and persistent practice. The teacher who is apt in choice of words and phrases, who gives vivid illustrations, who speaks "trippingly on the tongue" is one who has a quality that is valuable indeed.

4. SPECIAL ABILITIES

It is not difficult to recognize individuals who have unusual artistic ability, musical ability, mathematical ability, mechanical ability, or some other similar special ability. Certain people, for example, delight in working with numbers and develop mathematical skills with ease. Obviously, a special ability would enhance an individual's interest and success in teaching any subject related to this ability.

5. PHYSICAL TRAITS

Because teaching taxes physical strength, it is generally accepted that physical vigor and good health are necessary to teaching effectiveness. Supply of energy, appearance, and quality of voice are all believed to have some bearing on the quality of teaching. There is little evidence, however, that any particular type of physical structure or amount of physical vigor is essential to success in teaching. As is true with all the other traits, various physical traits must all be considered in relation to each other and to the entire personality.

Many people who are not teachers fail to realize the amount of physical energy expended by teachers, which we have already noted.

Many student teachers and first-year teachers have been surprised at the extent of the demands on their physical energy as they began their teaching careers.

COMBINATION OF ABILITIES

None of the abilities classified previously and designated basic in teaching is an entity. Success in teaching seems to be related to all of them, but the degree of relationship for all teachers can only be guessed. The relationship undoubtedly varies with the entire teaching situation, including the teaching field and the grade level. In some teaching situations a woman of small stature and great intelligence would have less chance of success than a less intelligent man built like a professional heavyweight boxer. Situation makes a difference. The concept of what a skilled teacher is continuously takes on new meaning in different times and places.

Predicting Teaching Success

In considering whether it would be wise for an interested individual to enter teaching, it is well to consider all the qualities—native intelligence, social intelligence, facility of expression, special abilities, and physical traits. Four years of college study, carefully planned to meet the individual's particular needs and earnestly pursued, can contribute significantly to improving the combination of traits that characterize the student when he first enters the program.

The most accurate way to predict success in teaching and to test abilities and combinations of abilities is through experience in student teaching or in activities closely related to teaching—working with children in clubs, teaching Sunday school, or counseling in boys' or girls' camps. How one works in the classroom and shoulders teaching responsibility will, in say 3 years' time, establish whether one possesses the basic abilities needed for successful teaching. Even here, however, an initial failure does not prove that success is impossible. Some great teachers have failed in their initial attempts.

Summary

By setting standards for teachers as a condition for granting teaching certificates, the state attempts to protect the public against substandard education and the teaching profession from infiltration by the inferior and the poorly prepared. States also control the quality of teaching through their accreditation policies for teacher education institutions. In addition, schools themselves have banded into voluntary associations that cut across state lines and that have established standards for the schools to meet as conditions to membership. Their standards do not apply to levels of education below the high school.

In qualifying, the prospective teacher receives his college education through three classifications of subject matter. One is referred to as courses for background education. Another is made up of specialized courses that are related to what the teacher will teach. In the third are professional courses that point directly to the vocation of teaching. Although progress has been made toward improving courses pursued by prospective teachers, marked agreement as to what the curriculum should be has yet to be reached.

Ability and willingness to learn, social intelligence, facility of expression, special abilities, and physical traits seem to be positively related to success in teaching. There is, however, no stereotype of the successful teacher. The key to success is not found in one or several personality traits but in the combination of all the traits in a total personality.

QUESTIONS

1. What advantages may accrue to the teaching profession from the imposition of minimum standards of qualification by society?
2. When may minimum standards of qualification be inimical to the cause of good education?
3. In what ways may a state legislature misuse its authority to establish minimum standards of qualification for teachers?
4. How can the legislatures of the various states deal with the problem of encouraging a free interflow of teachers between states?
5. Why have voluntary accrediting agencies arisen in the different geographical sections of the country?
6. Why have voluntary accrediting agencies concerned themselves mainly with standards at the high school and college levels? How has the teaching profession been affected by this policy?
7. Why have the colleges in America not agreed on what constitutes a satisfactory background education?
8. What are some of the difficulties colleges face in offering suitable content courses for elementary teachers? For junior high school teachers? For, say, teachers of social studies in senior high schools?

9. What are the principal differences between the content of a professional education course and a specialized content course?
10. How can stricter selective policies be made effective in the occupational field of teaching?
11. What is the responsibility of American society in upgrading its teaching profession?
12. In view of the fact that there are more than 2.7 million teachers in the teaching profession, how selective, in your opinion, can teacher education institutions become?
13. Considering the number of teachers in the teaching profession, what responsibilities do college teachers need to assume for the development of outstanding teaching skills?

PROJECTS

1. Study the official certification requirements for teaching in your state. Give your personal evaluation of the requirements in (a) background education, (b) specialized subject matter, (c) professional subject matter.
2. Describe an outstanding teacher you have known in terms of his personal qualifications for teaching.
3. For 1 week note your own speech inadequacies. Outline for yourself a speech improvement program. Follow this program for 1 week and make a note of the results. You may substitute another qualification if you desire.
4. Write your reactions to the Conant recommendation, which reads as follows:

> For certification purposes the state should require only (a) that a candidate hold a baccalaureate degree from a legitimate college or university . . . ; (b) that he hold a specially endorsed teaching certificate from a college or university which, in issuing the official document, attests that the institution as a whole considers the person adequately prepared to teach in a designated field and grade level.

5. a. Explain how a graduate of an institution holding membership in NCATE would qualify for a teaching certificate in any one of the participating states.
   b. Explain how he would qualify if the institution from which he had been graduated was not accredited by NCATE.
   c. State how you believe the problem of reciprocity in certification among the states should be resolved.
6. How are required standards of competence and a surplus of teachers related? Explain what is involved in any practical solution.

chapter

4

Teaching as a profession

It is always important to know the sorts of responsibilities involved in a vocation. A commitment to teaching is a commitment that involves many fundamental value choices on the part of the person making the commitment. Teaching is a vocation that those of us who are proud to be a part of it consider to be a profession. To outline what it means to refer to a particular vocation and its membership as a profession is part of the task of this chapter. In this chapter we will attempt to familiarize the reader with those organizational frameworks and relative social status relationships within which teachers tend to carry out their activities.

Most American parents demonstrate great faith in the idea of the necessity of schooling for the development of a democratic social order. They insist that the teaching profession can improve its services to the nation's population. Americans tend to see teaching as a very necessary social function and teaching in schools as the best way to guarantee systematically some minimal degree of equality of opportunity to gain knowledge for all citizens. There have been many severe criticisms of the schools in American society in the 1970s, with some scholars maintaining that the American public schools have worked more to maintain the social status quo and to prevent maximum opportunity for minority groups in America than to facilitate upward social mobility for minority groups. The 1970s have seen renewed evaluation of the nature and aims of the teaching profession both by the members of the teaching profession and by the public. However, as of the writing of the present edition of this work the formal educational institutions of the country are viewed by most citizens as an essential aspect in the process of guaranteeing some degree of equality of educational opportunity to all citizens.

As we look forward to the continued development of the teaching profession in the next several years we need to know where we have been and where we are as professional educators. In terms of current demands that the teaching profession become more accountable for achieving a high qualitative standard in student learning there is widespread debate regarding what actions to take to improve the outcomes of schooling. Such matters as the following ones are well worth considering: (1) the nature of teaching considered as a profession and how it differs from other professions, (2) the size of the teaching profession and the great variety of professional roles within it or related to it, (3) the relative social status of teachers in American society, and (4) the provisions made for the professional and economic security of teachers.

The teaching profession in America is always economically and socially dependent on the tax-paying public it serves. Teachers are taxpayers and citizens as well as people who attempt formally to "educate" their clients; they are, however, totally dependent on the good will of the general public for improved teaching and learning conditions in the schools and for the improvement of their own socioeconomic positions in society. This economic and social power of the general public to express its feelings about the content and the quality of schooling has been a powerful force for guaranteeing professional educators' sensitivity to the needs and feelings of the general public. There is thus a working "partnership" between the teaching profession and the general public that must be continually developed and protected. Schools will operate best to enhance the values of a democratic society if those who teach in them have the rights and best interests of all their students at heart. As teachers must be aware of the implications of membership in their profession, so the public must recognize the impact that the profession has on the general welfare. Together they must work toward policies that strengthen both.

There is still a vast reservoir of public confidence in the American public school. According to the Sixth Annual Gallup Poll of "Public Attitudes Toward Education" reported in the September, 1974, issue of the *Phi Delta Kappan,* parents of children attending American public schools constitute the segment of the population that rates them most favorably. In the same survey only 9 percent of the high school juniors and seniors reporting gave their public schools an "A" grade, but a striking 41 percent of the high school juniors and seniors gave their public schools a "B," and another 35 percent gave their public schools a "C." Thus 85 percent of the high school students surveyed in that poll rated their public school experiences average to excellent. However, only one in two of the student respondents rated their public school in the good-to-excellent range. There is no scientific way of knowing how such responses correspond with the feelings of previous generations of parents or students toward their public school educations, although we do now have available much data on student and parental feelings about education in the past decade.

What Is a Profession?

Difficulties of Definition

In attempting to define a profession, to set up criteria to distinguish a profession from other occupational groups, significant difficulties are encountered. The word "profession" is loosely used. Even in a college textbook in sociology, for instance, the gambling "profession" and other illicit "professions" are mentioned. When we speak of certain professions as "full-fledged," we imply that some are more professional than others. Many vocational groups claim professional status, and the number continues to increase. The oldest of the professions—medicine, law, and the ministry—have been joined by other groups seeking and achieving, in varying degrees, recognition as professions: teachers, engineers, pharmacists, dentists, nurses, social workers, architects, and, more recently, scientists, journalists, accountants, and others. The boundary between professional and nonprofessional occupational groups is, in fact, so hazy that the Bureau of the Census has refrained from defining the term "profession."[1]

The attitudes of the American people toward a vocational group,

---

[1] For an able explanation of the elements common to professions and other leading occupations, see Talcott Parsons, *Essays in Sociological Theory,* Revised Edition. New York: Macmillan, 1954, chap. 2, "The Professions and Social Structure."

such as the journalists, for instance, determine whether the desires and efforts of the group to be accorded professional status will be successful. If the public recognizes the importance of the group; has an uncommon regard for the training, knowledge, and skill that membership in the group requires; and highly respects the relatively few people who engage in the occupation, then they may consider that occupation a profession.

Despite the confusion over the meaning of the word "profession," there are certain characteristics typical of, and more or less unique to, professions.

Certainly for a group to be considered a profession, comparable to the professions of medicine and law, the members of the group in question must have occupational functions that require a broad cognitive (intellectual) perspective. These functions must require frequent use of interpretive judgment by the persons who practice these functions. In terms of defining teaching as a profession, teaching must be held to be a vocation requiring some form of general or "liberal" knowledge of the arts and sciences as well as of the "practical arts" of facilitating student learning in the activities of teaching. The practice of teaching must, as in the case of medicine, be based on certain scientific and theoretical bodies of knowledge concerning how people learn as well as the most humane and effective ways to achieve human learning. The study and practice of teaching as a profession are based on such bodies of knowledge as (1) the behavioral sciences, with emphasis on learning theory and knowledge of human development; (2) the history of the efforts of human beings to educate one another and related "teaching" practices that have emerged; and (3) the study of the philosophical beliefs about the purposes of education, the values and ways of valuing that educators have developed as well as conceptions of the nature of knowledge and methods of acquiring knowledge.

Teaching becomes a learned profession because teachers are called on to exercise what traditionally has been called practical judgment. Teachers have to interpret or diagnose students' learning needs as well as their abilities. They have to make ethical decisions about what activities or courses of action they ought to pursue with individual students. This practical judgment is exercised by the teacher on the basis of knowledge of those foundational studies that make teaching a learned profession in ways similar to the foundational studies required for more traditionally accepted professions such as medicine and law. In summary, then, the practical judgment of the teacher requires that he or she engage in the following activities:

1. Development and retention of knowledge of how people learn.
2. Development of interpretive skills in finding out what students know at a given time and being able to provide a prognosis of students' learning requirements as well as of projected sequences of instructional efforts to meet their learning requirements.
3. Development of philosophical skills in the interpretation of values and in the art of making morally defensible value judgments in planning learning activities for students.

Plumbers and carpenters exercise interpretive judgment, but they do not base the practice of their trade on an abstract theoretical knowledge of the physics of the materials they use in doing their work, as does the architect who designs what the plumber or carpenter or mason or plasterer builds or services. The architect is a professional person in the classic sense, but the skilled craftsmen who put up what he designs are not. So also the teacher is a professional, for he or she is an architect of the learning process of students, a process that requires great interpretive judgment on the part of the teacher because of the vast range of differences in the abilities of individual persons. The well-prepared teacher is a professional person, for he or she possesses all the qualities traditionally associated with members of learned professions: the interpretive application of basic principles of reasoning to the day-to-day practice of a vocation involving sophisticated cognitive judgments.

Organization

In this discussion we think of education as a learned profession, defined in the dictionary as "any profession in the preparation for or practice of which academic learning is held to play an important part." Historically, professions have been initiated when those practicing a technique or craft that required special training desired to be set apart and identified as the persons so specially equipped. For this purpose they formed associations, limiting membership to individuals with minimum qualifications. By excluding the unqualified, they guaranteed their own competence and secured public recognition of their competence. In addition, they set up standards of conduct required for continued membership. In this way they sought to guarantee honor and exclude not only the incompetent but also the unscrupulous. Having established their membership, the professions sought next to improve the status of their members. Since the relation between status and remuneration is a close one, the professions gave attention to remuneration, among other factors.

In the teaching profession members exert their powers over standards for membership and influence over benefits through various organizations, mainly the national organizations AFT and NEA. Today one may be a member of a profession without the organizational affiliation. To exercise the historical prerogatives of the profession, however, a member of the teaching profession acts through the national organization just as, for instance, a doctor works through the AMA to influence controls and standards in the medical profession.

Nature of Work

Persons in a profession are engaged in work that involves special mental and other attainments. In general, a profession is related to a vocation that appeals to those who enter because they recognize the social importance of the work to be done. This recognition helps them to do the work better and to get satisfaction from doing it well. We see that the line between a profession and another vocational group need not be clear-cut. Certainly a vocational group may also be social-minded; on the other hand, a professional group may deemphasize its social responsibility. In general, however, it is the professional group that gives greatest deliberate stress to its opportunities and responsibilities to render services that contribute to the public welfare.

The teacher-to-be is willing to devote much time and thought and money to adequate preparation partly because he or she recognizes that the work of the teaching profession is socially significant. A profession should seek improvements of benefit to the public as zealously as it seeks improvements of benefit only to the profession or to individuals within the profession. A profession is distinguished from other vocational groups in this stress on social perspective, in its emphasis on the dedication of its members to public service.

A profession is somewhat distinguished also because it involves work that is generally more mental than manual. Members of a profession must seek a constant flow of ideas from the seminar, from the laboratory, from communication within the profession. Such intellectual demands call for a liberal education as a part of the preservice preparation. Teachers and those in other professions, too, must have broad and basic understandings. Every teacher should strive to secure a broad cultural education, not only in order to live a rich, meaningful personal life, but also in order to be intellectually prepared for professional membership.

Entrance Requirements

Certain standards must be met by those who seek entrance to a profession. In licensed vocational groups and in the professions, including the teaching profession, standards for entrance are, in the final phase, established by the state and embodied in certification laws. In determining admission to the teaching profession, the state educational authority works closely with leaders in the profession and with those in higher institutions responsible for administering teacher education programs.

How Is the Teaching Profession Different?

Although all the professions have some features in common, they differ in the amounts and kinds of preparation required, in personnel, remuneration, security provisions, and the like. The teaching profession has certain unique characteristics related to function, control, support, size, and the sex of its membership. These differences necessitate a special approach by the profession to the attainment of a higher level of professionalization.

Function

The primary function of the teaching profession is, of course, teaching. The schools of the nation are structured to encourage good teaching. Teachers are selected for their potential ability to perform well, school buildings are planned to encourage expert teaching, and citizens devote much time and spend much money to promote and encourage the best possible discharge of this function.

Good teaching necessarily involves both the guidance of student behavior and the competent effort by the teacher to achieve development of learning of the subject matter taught on the part of the student being taught. Good teaching is a very broad concept and means different things to different teachers. Some discussion of the meaning of "education" took place in earlier sections of this volume. In later parts of this volume we will focus in greater depth on the meaning of the term "good teaching" when we discuss educational aims and methods in modern American education.

Control

The legal control of education lies *outside* the profession, in the hands of the public. What the teaching profession is, therefore, and what it develops into depend partly on what those in control want it to be or, to put this a little more strongly, on what the public will permit it to be. That the American public firmly holds the reins is evidence that it has a deep and abiding concern for education. It also means, however, that teachers must continually strive to keep the public intelligently informed about their problems and needs. Public control over the schools is continuing and extensive. Hence teachers, as a group, must interact with the public in a more direct and vigorous manner than is necessary for other groups.

Support

Closely linked with control is the matter of financial support. He who holds the purse strings wields the power. Public education in the United States is financed through public taxes. Private education is privately financed, largely by fees and tuition. Those who establish the policies of school support determine the status of members of the teaching profession. Adequacy or inadequacy of support, for example, has a bearing on the number of applicants for entrance to the profession and thereby affects selection policies. It influences teachers' living conditions, affects the amount and kind of education that can be required, and raises or lowers prestige. A generation of citizens that places a low priority on teaching and that wishes to get good teaching but does not wish it strongly enough to pay well for it is a generation that will impede the progress of the teaching profession toward desirable professional goals. Generally speaking, a narrow-minded community, whose support of its schools is reluctant, is likely also to be reluctant in granting the degree of freedom that is necessary to good teaching. The result is professional regression rather than progression.

Size

The teaching profession has far more members than any other profession. Its instructional membership numbers almost 3 million people when we include all teachers at the elementary, secondary, and higher educational institutions, both public and nonpublic.

However, the current oversupply of teachers in almost all teaching areas in the United States has forced prospective teachers to consider very carefully the areas in which they hope to teach. No one knows how long the current tight market conditions will last for teachers seeking their first or a new teaching post in the United States. The current difficult job situation for teachers is expected by some to last at least into 1980 or 1981 and possibly longer. More optimistic observers of the state of the teaching profession today generally note that the present situation will continue until about 1979. In the autumn of 1973 it was estimated that the number of teachers teaching at the elementary and secondary school levels was about 2.336 million. There are reasons, however, for young persons sincerely wishing to enter the teaching profession not to jump to the conclusion that there are no places for them. Some teachers retire each year and others leave the profession each year for other reasons.

The negative data on the current employment situation for teachers in America should certainly not be viewed too dismally. There are a number of things prospective teachers and in-service teachers can do to improve their chances of finding employment as teachers. Prospective elementary or secondary teachers should seek professional counseling in the teacher education departments or colleges of the colleges or universities they are attending so as to choose prospective teaching areas in which there is more current demand than in others. The prospective teacher can also choose as part of his or her undergraduate education to complete work in two comprehensive teaching areas rather than one, or to develop a teaching minor in an area where there is higher demand than in others and in which he or she is interested. Also, given the current employment situation for teachers, a teacher should be willing to relocate geographically. Another very important point for the undergraduate student considering teaching as a career is that in the present competitive job market in teaching, school systems can demand higher academic and social standards from the people they hire as teachers. Therefore it is most important to develop the best undergraduate grade point average possible. A high undergraduate grade point average can be very useful to young persons seeking their first positions as teachers in the present circumstances. It may also help if a prospective teacher can qualify for any academic distinctions, such as getting on one's college Dean's List and qualifying for any honor society in professional education, such as Kappa Delta Pi (a society open to juniors and seniors who achieve high academic averages and who are highly recommended by the faculty of education at their colleges or universities). There are other honorary organizations in other disciplines as well as other honorary organizations in professional educational studies. Any evidence of summer or part-time experience as a tutor for elementary or secondary school students or of youth work in summer camps or for the Boy Scouts or the Girl Scouts may also assist a prospective teacher in building a set of undergraduate learning experiences that will be attractive to hiring school systems.

Some observers have noted that part of the current "teacher surplus" is caused by the fact that some school systems have increased class sizes and have not replaced teachers who have retired. We have seen in the years since 1970 in some school systems a reversal of trends evident in the 1960s to reduce steadily the size of classes in the public schools (in professional terms, to reduce "teacher-student" ratios). The effort on the part of some school systems not to replace some retiring teachers has been a stopgap effort, and these sorts of actions are responses to the devastating effects of the inflationary trends in the American economy over the past eight years. The size of the teaching profession has continued to grow since 1970, but there may be some reduction in the rate of growth. A prospective teacher should also bear in mind that there are many new sorts of secondary and postsecondary educational careers opening up in the 1970s. There is in many states a rapid extension of specialized vocational and technical teaching fields developing in response to the demand of the American public that young people be given the opportunity as part of their secondary schooling to learn certain skilled vocations or technical trades well. There are also many teaching opportunities that could be created if our country were ever to make a real commitment to the concept of continuing adult education in general educational studies, in vocational and technical fields, and in the use of the public schools to teach skills in the use of leisure time and the creative arts. One can also usually qualify to teach in a 2-year community or technical college if one has earned a master's degree in the areas in which one would teach. But even at the community and technical college levels one must choose one's teaching field carefully. There are a number of types of positions involving working with children or adolescents that can be used to gain experience and skills and thereby increase one's attractiveness to prospective school employers. There are, as well, several educational and instructional services required in business corporations and the military services.

Young people should not give up hoping for happy careers as teachers. There is some (although less than in the 1960s) "natural attrition" from school systems each year resulting from such phenomena as those referred to earlier, such as retirement of teachers and the decision by some people to leave the profession each year. However, it is believed by many that the percentage of people leaving the teaching profession annually and not planning to return to the teaching profession has dropped steadily since 1970. Firm and accurate empirical figures on this phenomenon have been difficult to find and it is most difficult to generalize at this time as to the exact percentage of annual "drop-out" rates of teachers from teaching. But it is reasonable to suggest that the generally tighter job market in the entire American economy since 1970 is having its effect in terms of fewer people planning to leave the profession permanently each year. Therefore young persons planning or hoping to teach should follow as many of the preceding suggestions as possible to make themselves competitive in the job market. The size of the teaching profession in terms of the overall number of people in it will probably not shrink much in the next decade, and possibly not at all. There may be shifts in the numbers of people in different teaching specialties as public demand for different types of educational services may require in the next decade. There may be more demand for early childhood education or for early childhood day-care services, for example. Another possibility is continued sophistication in and development of special educational services for exceptional children. We are in a new era in American education, and flexibility and foresight in preparing for change in the profession and in the practice of the teaching profession must be our watchwords.

Whenever there is an upward turn in the American economy (with inflationary trends under control, one hopes), then the next period of American prosperity will probably bring another mild upturn in the professional possibilities of professional educators. The American public will then once again feel free to demand and to get more and different educational services. But this future educational development will probably take different forms from past American experiences in extension of educational opportunities to all citizens. Note the fantastic rise in the numbers of 2-year community and technical colleges referred to earlier; this has been a major educational development in the past decade from modest beginnings in the early decades of this century. No one can firmly predict with accuracy what the nature of future educational trends will be, but the teaching profession in the United States is stronger today than it ever has been in the past to meet future challenges.

Ratio of the Sexes

In 1971 it was estimated that 34.2 percent of all public school teachers in the United States were men and 65.7 percent were women. These figures change from year to year, with the percentage of men teachers rising in recent years. There are still many more women than men teaching in public elementary schools, but the numbers of men entering elementary school teaching as a career appear to be rising. However, job market conditions for teachers are such that no accurate predictions can be made about whether this particular mild trend in the increase in the number of male elementary school teachers will continue. Differences between men and women are being deemphasized in all areas of work in America, and the issue of the numbers of women as opposed to men in the teaching profession should not be viewed with great concern. We as a people have been committed by our national government, through fair employment policies laws passed in recent years, to the concept of total equalization of the work opportunities of women and men. This is a process long overdue. In the past, vast numbers of women chose careers in teaching because most other professional opportunities were limited for women. Now that technical schools, colleges, and employers can no longer limit the numbers of women in various trades and professions we may begin to see in future years a more realistic ratio of men and women in the teaching profession as well as fairer opportunities for women to rise to positions of authority in schools, school systems, and universities.

In the past, most men teachers tended to enter junior high school or senior high school teaching areas, although in recent years more men teachers have entered the teaching ranks in the middle elementary grades and in "middle schools."[2] Still, we look forward to the continued equalization of the professional roles of men and women in the teaching profession. As women achieve equalization of their career options and as the recent federal laws prohibiting discrimination by sex are enforced ever more rigorously, there will develop a more natural balance between the numbers of men and women in teaching.

The predominance of women does differentiate the teaching profession from most other professions. It is both a result and a cause of some basic economic and social factors. Traditionally, in America, women have constituted the most important economic minority group. There has always been an unwritten policy in the United States to pay women less than men and to deny them those positions that are most lucrative. In the past, women elementary teachers typically received less salary than men elementary teachers. The effect of artificial barriers resulting from deeply embedded social attitudes toward

---

[2] A "middle school" is one specifically designed to replace the junior high school. The middle school is usually composed of either the sixth, seventh, and eighth grades or the fifth, sixth, seventh, and eighth grades. In a school system where there are middle schools the ninth grade always goes to the senior high school, thus creating again the old 4-year high school concept of ninth, tenth, eleventh, and twelfth grades in the high school. More will be said about the "middle school" concept in later sections of this volume.

women in the other professions is also significant. Restrictions on the entry of women to some fields, e.g., law and medicine, have led to a disproportionate representation of women in others, e.g., teaching and nursing.

In summary, then, the teaching profession differs from other professions in its primary function, in the nature of its control and support, in size, and in the ratio of men to women in its membership. Any program of improvement initiated by the public or by the profession must be planned with these differences in mind. They have a bearing on procedures used in the selection of members for the profession, on the specialized training that is required, and on other qualifications for admission.

The Prestige Factor

When an individual assumes membership in the teaching profession, he not only accepts the obligation to render certain services and to play a certain role according to established rules but he also accepts the social status associated with people who fulfill that role. Prestige is the distinction or reputation that people attach to individuals or groups. It has a great deal to do with determining those who will be attracted to a profession and how long they stay in it.

Does the public regard teachers highly? Does it value intellectual endeavor highly? Do the positive and sympathetic features of the social climate in the United States assure the kind of prestige status for teachers that will encourage a desire to enter the profession?

The Scale of Social Prestige

Prestige is, of course, related to income and education. It is determined also by a combination of other factors, including what the public thinks of the kind of service rendered to humanity; the special training, intelligence, and ability needed; and the morality of the group.

Prestige ratings of selected vocations obtained through public opinion polls give a picture of the average of comparative ranks only. Such a rank does not reveal the level of public acceptance in any specifically designated public elementary or secondary school district. In those districts where the citizens give a low priority to public education, the prestige of teachers usually suffers accordingly. In other districts where education is more highly respected, the community probably will accord its teachers a higher degree of respect. Although ratings do not tell the whole story, they are significant enough to justify a critical self-examination by the profession.

Most human societies have developed in such a manner that the members of each society develop certain criteria for evaluating the relative importance of the various sorts of work performed by the society's members. Teaching as a form of work and as a profession is much more highly regarded than it was several decades ago. There are no firm empirical research studies so rigorous that we could state unequivocally the exact rank-order rating the average American citizen would give to teachers. However, the improved social image of the teacher is largely due to the hard work of certain national organizations, to be discussed later. The general social status of the teaching profession has also risen as the standards for entry into the profession have risen.

There was a time not too many decades ago when few teachers ventured into politics and when the general social status of the teaching profession at the elementary school and secondary school levels was low. But in recent decades many teachers have been elected to public offices and have been encouraged to serve on public bodies. This was achieved largely through the efforts of such national professional organizations as the National Education Association and the American Federation of Teachers.

Social status is gained by a professional group as it demonstrates to the members of the society in which it exists certain competencies and qualities considered to be both desirable and necessary to the members of that society. Today the personal and professional interests of teachers are well represented before the state legislatures, Congress, and local school boards. Prestige is the regard in which people are held by those who know and relate to them. Some teachers relate to students and parents much more effectively than others and consequently enjoy more social prestige in their community than do other teachers. The status or prestige of the teaching profession occurs at three levels of development: (1) the national social image of the profession projected by the leadership of national and state professional organizations for teachers; (2) the development of local school districts' citizens' impressions of the quality and worth of the teaching profession in their local communities; and (3) the informal evaluation of the worth of individual teachers by school boards, parents, students, neighbors, and friends at the local community level. Whatever the generalized image of the members of a particular professional group, Americans still tend to evaluate people as individuals in terms of how they see an individual's competencies or personal qualities. This is not to say, however, that some Americans do not evaluate people on the basis of certain stereotypes (racial, religious, ethnic, or sexual). But the teaching profession has emerged in the 1970s as one that has committed itself to increased personal professional competence and to the elimination of all forms of discrimination in America.

Social status is not a fixed idea; the social status of particular groups in a society frequently changes because of the fact that "status" or "prestige" are products of the qualitative and evaluative interaction of people with one another, as noted earlier. Status is not a purely vertical (up and down) social idea; one can achieve some degree of social movement or mobility of a lateral sort. For instance, although at any particular time a society may have some general ideas about the status of the teaching profession, within this system of general ideas concerning the status of teachers individual teachers may achieve higher social status than others, because of competence, successful interpersonal relationships, and other related factors. (Note the third level of development of teacher status referred to previously.)

The prestige of the teaching profession is influenced also by the fact that two large, highly influential but competitive associations represent the profession—the American Federation of Teachers and the National Education Association. The prestige of the profession probably would become higher if the strengths of these two organizations were combined. At the present writing there is only scant evidence that such an amalgamation may be achieved some time in the future. Once the profession becomes organizationally united and so organized within itself as to have a greater degree of unity among its three levels—local, state, and national—than is now apparent, the public image of the profession will be improved.

Security Provisions

Security Defined

Security is a basic personality need, a frame of mind, an attitude defined by psychologists as a persistent state of readiness to use the self for motive satisfaction. All attitudes have an emotional core. They are related to the affective aspects of our lives. A teacher with a sense of security feels protected, is free from fear of unfair dismissal or unjust and unwarranted treatment. But security does not imply complacency. Rather, it builds confidence. The teacher becomes more sure of his or her own personal and professional adequacy, is encouraged to improve, to become more proficient. Insecurity has the opposite effect.

The teacher who is insecure tends to feel inadequate to meet his assignments and lacks confidence in his ability to achieve.

State and local school systems and the teaching profession strive to provide teachers with a suitable degree of security. Certain security features, such as tenure, retirement, and salary scales, are illustrative of the provisions intended to avoid the ill effects of insecurity. Also, it is now true (as it was not in earlier years) that most of America's teachers, both men and women, are or have been married. Many, of course, have children of their own. Married or not, they expect to maintain a manner and standard of living appropriate to their status as professionals. Thus their homes or apartments, distance of residence from place of employment, and other aspects of their way of life are much the same as for other career people. These facts naturally influence their attitude toward the number and type of security provisions they wish and need to have.

Associations

So numerous and so influential are associations in this country that the United States is sometimes described as an "associational" society. Organizations of both private and public employees have become accepted as an important phase of American life. As many as 340 different kinds of local teachers' organizations have been identified. Some are entirely local, some are affiliated with a statewide group, and many are units in an organization of national scope, the NEA or the AFT.

The fact that school teachers are prolific organizers may be an indication of their deep-seated desire for greater personal security. Their numerous organizations indicate confidence in affiliation and association. The relationship between the individual teachers and the profession may be better understood by a brief look at some of these associations.

I. NATIONAL EDUCATION ASSOCIATION

Founded in 1857, the National Education Association of the United States (NEA) is now the world's largest professional association. Its headquarters is an eight-story building in the nation's capital, with a full-time staff of more than 300 people. It has members, from all types of schools, in all types of educational positions, and at all levels in the educational program; by far the largest group is composed of classroom teachers (about 92 percent, or approximately 1.6 million teachers). The NEA states its purpose thus: "to elevate the character and advance the interests of the profession of teaching, and to promote the cause of education in the United States." In seeking to achieve this purpose, the NEA engages in such activities as issuing reports dealing with important issues, making the results of research available in popular form, holding conferences, providing consultative and other field services, working with members of Congress and federal agencies to promote and protect the interests of children, working for higher standards for the teaching profession and for more reciprocal certification requirements, aiding school systems with salary problems, seeking improved personnel practices, and promoting working professional relationships in the profession and between the profession and the public. The NEA states that it urges the improvement of the quality of teachers in order that the public will be well served. Likewise, it protects members of the teaching profession in the discharge of their duties, and it urges that only proper dismissal procedures be employed if teachers are found unworthy.

At its annual convention in the summer of 1967, the NEA passed this resolution about teacher strikes:

> The NEA recognizes that under conditions of severe stress, causing deterioration of the educational program, and when good-faith attempts at resolution have been rejected, strikes have occurred and may occur in the future. In such instances, the NEA will offer all of the services at its command to the affiliate concerned to help resolve the impasse.

However, the resolution gave major attention to a series of steps which "should make the strike unnecessary." These were mediation, fact-finding, arbitration, political action, and sanctions. It was made clear that every effort should be made to avoid a strike.

In the late 1960s and during the 1970s the National Education Association became increasingly militant in its efforts to defend the interests of teachers in the United States. It developed the DuShane Fund to defend the legal interests of teachers in need of legal assistance to defend themselves against arbitrary dismissal from their positions or against interference with their academic freedom. Further, the NEA adopted many of the principles for organization of the common interests of a "united teaching profession." The NEA found it necessary to adopt the principle of collective bargaining and to train representatives of local NEA affiliate organizations in the skills of formal collective bargaining procedures to protect the interests of teachers and to foster continued efforts to achieve the highest-quality educational programs possible. The NEA found itself in the position of having to adopt the organizational skills required to support strikes by local NEA affiliates when all other measures in the collective bargaining process had failed. Although fiercely refusing to ally itself formally with large organized labor unions, the NEA found it necessary, in order to attain professional goals, to adopt the procedures for collective negotiations of teachers' associations with school boards and the arbitration procedures usually associated in the public's mind with labor union procedures. The NEA has steadfastly insisted that it is a professional "association" in that it seeks to defend the interests of students and teachers. The National Education Association and the American Federation of Teachers (AFT) have engaged in a semantic debate for years over the terms "association" and "union." What is clear is that the NEA has had to adopt a much more militant position in recent years. Although it has adopted many of the methods of union organization and bargaining, the NEA has tried to remain a "professional association." It has been often sympathetic to legitimate demands of local labor unions in local disputes, but it has sought to maintain, as much as possible, its own unique "professional" identity.

2. STATE TEACHERS' ASSOCIATIONS

The NEA has 59 state and territory and 8264 local affiliated associations. The state organizations, sometimes referred to as the state education associations, are among the most effective of all organized teachers' groups. Each enrolls a majority of the teachers in the state. Generally, each has a well-paid executive secretary who is an able and experienced professional educator. Most state associations have well-equipped offices and able personnel. Many of them publish a monthly journal that compares well with the best professional magazines.

State teachers' organizations are generally effective in their relationship with the state education authority and with the state legislatures. It is through the state organization that local groups or individuals can make known the specific nature of the security provisions needed to improve education in a particular state. Teachers indicate confidence in this kind of association through their financial support and their participation.

Teachers in fields such as English or social studies, those working at a particular educational level such as nursery or elementary, and educators in special fields such as guidance or administration have their own associations. Typically, these comprise local or regional units that are part of state organizations that, in turn, hold membership in a national unit more or less directly affiliated with the parent organization, the NEA.

3. LOCAL OR CITYWIDE TEACHERS' ORGANIZATIONS

Local teachers' organizations are the oldest, the most numerous, and the most varied of all teachers' organizations. Their number attests to general confidence in their worth. They provide most individual teachers with an opportunity for participation in the affairs of the profession that is not possible in the groups covering a broader geographical area. The individual teacher, through the local organization, has the opportunity to experience the satisfaction of actively helping to protect his own and his profession's security. Local organizations also serve a significant social function in some communities by providing a common meeting place for teachers.

Local organizations have a variety of patterns. Some admit all the teachers in a system; some admit only those working in a given field or at a specific level or those discharging a common specialized function, such as guidance or administration. The aims are always broader than that of providing security for the members, but security for the members is an implied complement to all the other stated aims. Local associations strengthen group loyalty and reinforce the members' efforts to protect the organization's and the profession's reputation for the benefit of the membership.

Local associations enable teachers to become better acquainted with each other, with their school systems, and with their more urgent local problems. Thus they can learn more directly what the community is like and what the attitudes of its citizens are toward the maintenance of good schools. Local organizations open paths of communication by functioning as liaison between teachers, teachers and the public, and teachers and school administrators.

The NEA is encouraging a trend toward unification of local, state, and national organizations. Oregon is an example of a state that has achieved this through unification of dues. Instead of allowing a teacher to choose among the organizations at the three levels, membership has been made mandatory, and a single collection of dues pays for membership in all three. Such unification markedly increases organizational strength and effectiveness while eliminating waste in collecting dues for separate organizations. It is through their organizations—local, state, and national—that the teachers claim their rights to professional autonomy like that granted to other professions.

4. AMERICAN FEDERATION OF TEACHERS

The organization that competes with the NEA for the privilege of representing teachers is the American Federation of Teachers, a national union of classroom teachers affiliated with the American Federation of Labor-Congress of Industrial Organizations. The AFT limits its membership to classroom teachers because it believes that classroom teachers can and should speak for themselves and that school superintendents, principals, and other administrators therefore should not be admitted. Within the AFT organization are local, state, and national affiliates. Dues in each local union of the AFT are determined by its members and depend on the demands of the local's program, which is also member-determined. As its brochure "Questions and Answers About AFT" states, "Because the AFT believes in action—in 'getting things done' rather than issuing reports, letting someone else do the 'doing'—a powerful, cohesive structure is necessary." The AFT includes more than 650 local unions of teachers, has state federations in most of the states, and maintains a national headquarters in Washington. The AFT is currently working for improved teacher salaries; recognition of the rights of teachers everywhere to organize, negotiate, and bargain collectively; a "more effective schools" program; state tenure laws; elimination of overcrowding in classrooms, excessive class interruptions, and the use of students as teacher substitutes; state laws requiring free and uninterrupted lunch periods for all teachers; better teacher pensions; adequate, cumulative sick leave pay; and hospitalization and medical insurance paid from school funds. The organization states that strikes should be a last resort when all other means to bring about a fair settlement of a serious controversy have failed.

A president of AFT has written in its official publication:

> The days ahead will present many additional occasions to test the integrity, the selflessness, the devotion to a common cause, of the two teacher organization giants. There is no use denying that the AFT and the NEA are engaged in dire competition for the membership of the teachers of America. But we must do this without giving aid and power to the governmental authorities, boards of education, and superintendents with whom we are contending. And then, let us keep the door open; let us look forward to the day when AFT-NEA unity may become a reality. Heaven knows, we badly need a strong, unified, militant, and labor-oriented teachers' union to fight the great battles that lie ahead. Teacher welfare, a sound educational system, and the good of society as a whole require nothing less.[3]

---

[3] Charles Cogen, "Teacher Militancy: Bridge to AFT-NEA Unity?" *American Teacher,* 52 (No. 7), March, 1968.

5. NATIONAL CONGRESS OF PARENTS AND TEACHERS

The largest organization connected with education in the United States is the National Congress of Parents and Teachers, with a membership of more than 11 million. As the name implies, members are both lay and professional, with the lay membership far outnumbering the professional. This organization represents one of the greatest educational movements in history. It operates largely through state congresses, which in turn reach down into the local community through local parent-teacher associations. It is influential and provides for active, direct participation at local, state, and national levels. The state and national congresses speak with authority to legislatures. The National Congress of Parents and Teachers, recognizing that security is linked with the other aims of the organization, has consistently and effectively advocated policies favorable to improving teacher security.

The Teacher and Teacher Associations

Teacher associations reflect the collective judgment of school teachers as to the goals of education. The large number of unrelated organizations is partial evidence that the teaching profession, nationally, is not fully unified to achieve these goals.

A well-informed profession is one safeguard to education. The individual teacher becomes informed about current educational needs through periodicals and yearbooks that are issued by most state, regional, and national organizations. Speakers and consultants are sent out from headquarters to local groups. Many of the organizations have regular state or regional and national conventions. Often teachers are released from teaching in order to attend meetings, e.g., the annual convention of the National Council of Teachers of English. Frequently, planning and executing a program for special days called "institute days" is delegated to a regional or state organization.

Through associations teachers gain a reasonable degree of autonomy of action that would otherwise be denied them. This is essential to securing and maintaining a satisfactory degree of professional solidarity. Because control of the schools lies outside the profession this is especially important to classroom teachers. Teachers, unless well organized, are vulnerable to all kinds of external influences, some of them inimical to the cause of education and threats to the individual teacher. Influential groups throughout the United States consistently oppose state and community efforts to improve education and to improve the welfare of teachers. For instance, an organized group may be dedicated to reducing taxes. Such an aim will usually lead to opposition to any teacher association program that requires tax money for the improvement of teacher welfare. Individual teachers cannot be alert to all such organizations and pressure groups in the community or in the state, but teacher association officers are trained to recognize and to recommend action to deal with such situations.

Security Policies in School Administration

Local policies of educational administration, especially those related to security provisions for teachers, vary strikingly throughout the United States. Not all state school authorities agree on what security provisions are appropriate. Policies toward contracts, promotion, tenure, retirement, pensions, and salary scales illustrate rather vividly some of the concrete problems in procuring reasonable security provisions.

I. CONTRACTS

"Contract" is the legal term for a binding agreement between two parties A teacher's contract is prepared by the local school district and is a statement of terms and conditions of employment. It generally stipulates that the teacher receive a certain salary for a period of time. Contracts vary all the way from a simple, oral agreement to extended technical statements of terms. What is said in the contract is a fairly good expression of the attitude of the school officers toward the individual teacher.

The present trend is greatly to simplify teachers' contracts. Frequently school policies, as they pertain to teachers, are worked out with the help of the teachers' associations. The school system may publish the policies, including specific statements relating to teacher welfare, in a handbook. When the teacher accepts a position he or she then knows precisely the commitments of the school system. Large school systems, and most smaller ones, make the community's commitments to its teachers unmistakably clear and binding on the community.

2. TENURE

Tenure refers specifically to the period of time a teacher is entitled to hold a position—the length of the term of appointment. A teacher beginning in a school system ordinarily serves a probationary period before receiving what are called continuing contracts, indefinite contracts, or permanent contracts. Tenure provisions, as they are stated in official pronouncements of school district policy, vary from community to community and from state to state, and there is some disagreement within the profession about what constitutes the best manner of stating the terms of tenure. In most states the circumstances under which teachers are entitled to permanent tenure are defined by law.

Tenure is an important security provision. Free from any fear of unfair dismissal, the teacher is relieved of a strain that might impair teaching effectiveness. This means, however, that three steps in the selection of teachers are especially important.

The initial selection comes when application is made for admission to teacher training. It is impossible to state definitely the qualifications of a successful teacher, much less to assess an individual's possession of potential powers for good teaching. It is possible, however, at the time of original application to eliminate some individuals who because of intellectual, physical, or social factors seem poor prospects for teaching. Some institutions select again when students apply for the privilege of student teaching.

After a student has completed the training requirements and has received his or her college degree, an employing official, perhaps a superintendent of schools, makes another evaluation of potential success. If the applicant is given a teaching position, the initial contract is typically for 1 year. Sometimes a teacher beginning in a system has three of these 1-year contracts. During the period of the 1-year contracts he or she is "on probation." At the end of each year, often in joint conference with an administrator, the teacher's work is reviewed and direction and advice given. At the end of any year a teacher's contract may not be renewed.

The most important point of selection comes at the close of the probationary period. At this time the teacher is eligible for a permanent contract—for tenure—and is eligible for an extension of the probationary period, or may be dismissed. The employing official faces a significant responsibility. If only those of proven competence are allowed to have permanent contracts, the virtue of the tenure provisions for teachers will not be questioned and most future dissatisfaction with the tenure laws will be avoided.

When a teacher has passed the selection barriers and has permanent tenure, tenure then is for *a* position in the school system, not for the position that he holds at any particular time. For instance, a principal could, without loss of salary, be shifted to a classroom teaching position without any violation of his or her tenure privileges, although this would be most unusual.

The burden of the proof of incompetence or misbehavior rests with the school officials. A teacher who is "on tenure," who has permanent employment in a school district, cannot be dismissed because of the personal whim of an administrator, school board member, or political manipulator. The protection of tenure, however, as well as any of the other security provisions provided teachers, does not relieve the teacher of responsibility to fulfill obligations to the school system. The teacher has been judged the kind of individual who has the qualifications for professional membership and must merit this confidence. The tenure laws are not intended to protect the incompetent.

3. PROMOTION

In joining the profession and in affiliating with a local school district it is important to know what lies ahead, what the avenues for advancement are. One may decide advancement lies in leaving classroom teaching and entering some specialized educational field. There are many such opportunities—e.g., special teaching, supervision, and school administration. Outside-the-classroom positions often offer such rewards that the individual decides early in his career to prepare for one of them. Unfortunately, a skillful teacher is all too frequently rewarded with an appointment to such a position rather than to a position that fully utilizes his or her teaching skill. *This policy reflects a tendency in the profession itself to depreciate the importance of teaching, to attach greater significance to nonteaching functions.* It would seem logical that an outstanding teacher who prefers to remain in the classroom should be given the same recognition and salary that would be his in an administrative or supervisory post. But practice within the profession itself does not encourage this.

Many excellent teachers who, at considerable sacrifice, have stayed with classroom teaching have been resourceful in supplementing their salaries with other employment. Part-time services of teachers have always been in great demand. The poorer the school district, the more likely it is that the more competent classroom teachers will be encouraged to move up to other positions or to seek other teaching positions that offer financial inducements. Partly as a result of policies of this kind, teaching is an excessively mobile profession. And for this, education in the United States pays an enormous price. Preparing prospective teachers and orienting new teachers are expensive operations. Too rapid personnel turnover results in diminished returns from this investment. The turnover also is educationally wasteful, not only from the viewpoint of the pupils who suffer from lack of educational continuity over a period of years, but also from the viewpoint of a personnel handicapped in its long-term plans and frustrated in carrying on activities designed to be built up over the years. Rapid turnover is costly in terms of group morale and is detrimental to teacher prestige because a transient group usually does not command the respect afforded a stable, continuing, professional group.

4. RETIREMENT

Admission to the teaching profession assumes the candidate intends to serve the profession and attempt to improve it. At the age of 70, or thereabouts, the teacher will be expected to retire. The problem of income for the rest of his or her life must be solved. Because education is a state function, each state has the responsibility of establishing laws covering public school teacher retirement policies. All the states have done this with characteristic variations consistent with differing points of view about educational policy.

In general, retirement provisions are developed in terms of three plans. The state may establish its own system—define its own policy toward retirement and retirement pay. When this plan is followed, the teacher usually contributes a share toward retirement pay. By basing the plan on actuarial predictions, the system adopted tends to be sound. In some cases special provisions are made for survivors' benefits to protect a teacher's dependents, as well as for those becoming disabled before retirement age and for those who for personal reasons desire to retire at an earlier age.

The second plan is for the state to join the federal government in providing for old-age benefits. It conforms to the current tendency to shift state and local financial burdens to the national government. Teachers' associations, however, are generally opposed to this. A pension plan set up within a state for teachers is usually also a savings plan. A teacher may withdraw funds invested at any time he or she leaves teaching, regardless of age. The plan provides some flexibility in that the age of retirement is determined partly in terms of years of service and is not set at a chronological age point. Teachers' associations contend also that a pension fund worked out for them specifically is unifying for the teachers and is more within their own control. For a career teacher, the benefits of a state teacher retirement plan tend to be much more generous than those offered under a federal plan for old-age security.

The third general plan is for the local school district to gain state permission to administer its own pension program. A few larger cities continue to support local teacher retirement plans established years ago. New adoptions of this plan are rare.

Programs of retirement have some weaknesses. Differing state policies make it difficult for a teacher to transfer to another state without sacrificing some accrued pension benefits. The question of what percentage teachers should contribute to the costs is difficult to decide. What to do about disability insurance and what the age of retirement should be are points of disagreement. Survivors' benefits have not always been made clear. But improvements in retirement provisions are gradually being made. The NEA, the AFT, state teachers' associations, local teachers' unions, and other organizations are working on the problem.

5. LEAVES OF ABSENCE

Teachers who have some good reason for enforced absence, who may become ill, are given further security through a policy providing sick leaves. It is usual for a school system to grant 2 weeks' leave a year for enforced absence, to permit these leaves of absence to be cumulative, and to inflict no loss of pay. Such a policy does not jeopardize the teacher's pension status. Some systems grant extended leaves on full- or part-time pay or without pay. These leaves may be for a semester or more to be devoted to study or travel or something else that will enhance a teacher's worth to the community.[4]

6. SALARY

Two factors in a teacher's situation do much to influence the feeling of satisfaction that he derives from a conscientious discharge of responsibilities: the salary structure and scale and the teaching load. An excessively heavy teaching load either leads a teacher to work beyond his or her strength or forces adjustments in the interest of self-protection that are, from an educational standpoint, undesirable. Substandard salaries limit the number of capable people attracted to teaching and the number willing to stay in the profession. With inadequate salaries, those dedicated to teaching are forced into "moonlighting" and summer employment in other lines of work in order to maintain a comfortable standard of living. In better communities, therefore, much thought is given to establishing a salary *structure* and a salary *scale* that provide incentive and encouragement for a satisfied and relatively stable professional corps of teachers.

The salary situation among the more than 16,000 school districts

[4] For an overall picture of this aspect of security provisions, see NEA Research Report 1967-R5, *Leaves of Absence for Classroom Teachers, 1965–66.*

in the United States is perhaps of more immediate personal importance to the individual seriously considering entering the profession. After all, the teacher will probably be employed by an independent school district, and the policy of that district toward paying teachers will have much to do with future satisfactions in teaching.

Local salary policy is reflected in the salary structure and in the salary scale for a given year. Since the salary structure and salary scale are developed and formulated to attract and retain capable teachers, taken together they constitute a fairly reliable criterion for judging the value a given school district places upon good teaching.

The salary structure, usually printed or mimeographed, is a written statement of the policies that govern salaries in a given school district. The policies adopted by the board of education include salary differentials for preparation and experience—and sometimes for so-called merit differences—allowances for sick leave, for dependents, for health insurance, sabbaticals, pensions, extra pay for extra work such as coaching, and other matters related to teacher welfare.

Both the NEA and the AFT view the formulation of a salary structure as a matter for mutual consideration by both the teaching personnel and the school board. Research studies are made regularly by the NEA, and the results are disseminated throughout the profession.[5] In their report on the economic status of teachers in 1966–1967, the NEA's research staff said, "It can be concluded from the data presented here that teachers' salaries, though much improved in recent years, are still far below the levels of compensation attainable by college graduates in other professional occupations." The NEA and the AFT provide expert help to local organizations in formulating salary scales. By using an "index" system, allotting a value of 1.0 to the salary paid beginning teachers with a bachelor's degree and no experience and assigning value increases in terms of training and years of experience, the entire scale is geared to the amount that must be paid to the beginning teacher in the competitive market.

Summary

Membership in a social group has striking effects on the individual. Assuming membership in a professional group implies acceptance of standards of behavior adopted by the group. The standards not only

[5] See, for example, NEA Research Report 1967-R8, *Economic Status of Teachers*.

protect the teachers but also guarantee children a satisfactory quality of education.

Opportunity to improve the profession is afforded teachers through membership in teacher associations that influence both local and state governments. The status of the profession will not rise perceptibly unless the profession itself exerts its energies to bring this about. The problem of improvement is different from other professions because of the differences in functions, control, support, and the ratio of the sexes in the teaching profession, and also because teaching is a tax-supported profession.

The prestige status of teachers is well above the average. A measure of the value placed on education by a state or by a community is reflected in the security provisions made for teachers. Salary scales are especially important. Often teachers, through their associations, participate in determining their security provisions.

An NEA research publication shows that most teachers would enter the teaching profession again if they had to make the choice once more. The professional features of teaching help to make it very desirable work.

QUESTIONS

1. What sorts of things can you do to make yourself as competent and as employable as possible in the present difficult job market in teaching?
2. What are your views on strikes by teachers to achieve their professional goals?
3. What is the local salary structure and salary scale for teachers in your home town or in any two or three towns in the state where you are attending college? Is the structure of the salary system in your home town or other towns you check on composed of just one scale for teachers with baccalaureate degrees and one scale for teachers with master's degrees? Are there salary scales for 30 or 60 hours of college credit beyond the master's degree level or for the doctoral level of preparation or its equivalent? What are the differences between the baccalaureate and master's degree level scales? In how many years does a teacher reach the top of the salary scale?
4. How many years does a teacher have to teach in a school system in the state where you reside before he or she becomes eligible to receive "tenure"? Under what circumstances can a tenured teacher be dismissed in your state?

5. What considerations would be most important to you if you had to decide between joining the NEA or the AFT? Why?
6. How do you perceive the status of the teaching profession? What do you believe to be the most important personal and professional characteristics teachers should possess if they wish to have as much respect and status as possible in the community in which they teach?
7. What role should be provided for the teachers of a state in determining certification requirements for teachers in that state?
8. If you were asked to demonstrate why teaching is a profession what sorts of reasons would you give and how would you try to back them up?

PROJECTS

1. Develop a report of the sequence of events and issues involved in a recent teachers' strike somewhere in the United States.
2. What recent research can you find on the economic or the social status of teachers in the United States? Report on this.
3. Although this topic is not directly dealt with in this chapter (it is considered in a later section of this volume where the historical development of American education is discussed), how would you develop a report on the now established trend of using labor negotiation, or collective bargaining, methods to achieve teachers' professional goals? Develop a project report on this as you see it relating to the nature and status of teaching as a profession in the United States. (Refer to both NEA and AFT research sources on collective bargaining in recent years in doing this, and relate your views as to how and why the NEA and AFT now agree that such methods are appropriate ways for teachers to meet their professional goals.)
4. Review some of the issues of *Education Today,* the journal of the National Education Association, for a 6-month period or for a year of publication. Report the main themes and points of view evident in these issues. Do the same for a publication of the American Federation of Teachers.
5. Do a brief study of retirement provisions for teachers in your state. Do teachers in your state get both federal Social Security and a pension from a state pension fund, or do they just get a pension from the state agency set up to provide for teacher retirement? Considering all retirement benefits, including both state and federal benefits and any major medical coverages, if applicable, how well off are your state's teachers in terms of retirement benefits when you compare them with the retirement benefits of teachers in neighboring states?

chapter

5

The teacher's philosophy

Every teacher develops a set of beliefs regarding the knowledge and skills that should be taught in his or her subject or grade-level areas. Likewise, every teacher develops a set of standards for determining how the teacher should treat students and colleagues as well as parents. Every teacher's views on such matters are subject to continuing review and reexamination throughout his or her career as a teacher. Some of one's basic beliefs regarding what to value in life and how to examine values may be traced back to one's basic assumptions regarding reality or human nature. A teacher's philosophy of education rests on three major concerns: (1) the nature of human and physical reality, especially human nature and the nature of human development and learning; (2) the nature of human values and what standards for interaction with other people are most defensible; and (3) the nature of knowledge and the methods for getting reliable knowledge. A teacher's decisions in the classroom and as a member of the teaching profession can be influenced by any one or all of these concerns. One thing is certain, if it has not already become evident in reading this volume, teachers are called upon to make many decisions; and the quality of those decisions is directly related to the quality of thought they apply to their problems as teachers.

Students preparing to become teachers receive advice from many sources on how to approach the challenges they will face as teachers. We are influenced by many factors in our efforts to develop reasoned beliefs about our lives as teachers. We are influenced by the books we read, by our family backgrounds and experiences, and by our cultural backgrounds; some of our behaviors and beliefs are influenced by our socioeconomic status and possibly our perception of our social class background if we perceive it as relevant. These all call for careful examination in framing our basic or "core" beliefs about how we ought to behave as teachers. We need to examine these aspects of our experience and to compare our views on these matters with those of people who come from different backgrounds from our own so that we can develop better understanding of the "core" beliefs of others. A teacher works with people, and all of a teacher's professional activities are designed to help other people. In order to help other people a teacher has to seek understanding about the beliefs of other people as well as the skills of inquiry into the subject matters he or she teaches to be able to relate that subject matter to the experience of the learners to whom the teacher is responsible. A teacher's philosophy of education is relevant to all the preceding concerns. All teachers find it necessary to develop standards for determining what their beliefs ought to be as well as beliefs about what counts as reliable knowledge and what does not; a conscientious teacher improves in the ability to develop further a philosophy of education with every year that he or she remains a teacher.

It is not the intent of this chapter to attempt a comprehensive treatment of the subject at hand; that could take an entire course in itself. Instead, the purpose of this chapter is simply to assist the beginning student in educational studies to become aware of a few of the overarching concerns regarding a teacher's philosophy of education. If the reader should pursue a desire to become a teacher, he or she will have the opportunity in the later undergraduate courses or in studies for the master's degree in education to take a course in philosophy of education. This chapter is intended to open a large range of fundamentally relevant concerns regarding how teachers define and deal with educational issues that involve value conflicts and that any practicing teacher can encounter.

Education is one of those areas in which people tend to think that they know a great deal. The study of education is, however, much more complex than most people realize. Perhaps the reason for this phenomenon is that every American has been exposed to the schooling process to some extent. Students planning to teach face contradictory views regarding educational policies and beliefs from the people with whom they come in contact. Therefore they need some preliminary conceptions of how to define and deal with educational issues. Teaching is a value-laden enterprise because teachers must always decide how they should behave as teachers.

Some of the questions that confront the teacher are the center of public debates about education: What should the role of the federal government be in improving education? Traditionally, the role of the states has been relatively clear, but is the federal government causing a modification in the states' role? How can educational leadership be improved, be divorced from the machinations of professional politicians? What subject matter should be taught in the elementary and secondary curriculums? How can America's schools meet the challenges of rapidly advancing technology throughout the world? On all such questions the classroom teacher is expected to have a well-formulated point of view.

Other questions that the teacher faces are of more immediate and direct personal concern. Teachers ask themselves: What kinds of rewards and positive incentives can I use in the classroom to encourage desirable forms of behavior? How shall I take into account the special problems of the pupils? Shall I judge the work of each pupil relative to the achievements of the rest of the class or in terms of the pupil's individual efforts? How do I determine a reasonable standard to apply in judging the work of pupils? How much weight should I give to the differences in learning ability of my pupils?

There are also questions of another kind that the teacher must answer. These center around the relationships of a teacher with the community, the parents of the pupils, fellow teachers, and administrators. A teacher must answer such questions as: What responsibility should I take in the total program of the school? What should my relationships be with my fellow teachers and with school administrators? If there is a teachers' union in my city, should I belong? In what ways should I participate in the administration of my school? In the programs of the PTA?

The answers teachers give to these questions and to others like them are reflected in classroom teaching. Great variation in teaching methods and procedures stems from varying answers.

Differences on an Educational Issue

An issue always involves a controversy, for an issue requires two or more points of view on a particular matter. There obviously could never be an issue if there were only one point of view. When people hold different points of view on a matter we have to examine the reasons for the different points of view in the controversy and we have to examine the kinds of reasons offered by the adherents to each point of view in the controversy. We also have to ask what sorts of evidence the adherents might have to support their reasons for their positions in the controversy, and we have to check the reasons given and the evidence offered by the adherents to each of the points of view in the controversy. People develop different points of view on educational issues often because they fail to communicate their positions clearly, and misunderstandings arise. In addition, different people often have goals so different that conflicting points of view necessarily follow. There are many other reasons why issues arise that are not easily settled and that require teachers to exercise independent judgment in developing their own positions. When one segment of a faculty wants only very traditional, classical humanist values, represented in a very traditional classical curriculum, and another segment of that faculty wishes to adopt more flexible existentialist concepts emphasizing the freedom of individual students to search for their best interests and their "best" or "deep" selves without being in competition with their fellow students, a controversy must develop. There are workable compromises that could be developed in such a controversy, but such compromises would involve the faculty in making intensively reflective personal decisions about the best qualities of the two philosophies in conflict and the best means to implement these qualities in an atmosphere in which students would compete with themselves rather than with other students.

Differences in the amount and variety of life experience can contribute to misunderstandings regarding the merits of different points of view on an issue, as can differences in age or cultural background. People coming from different socioeconomic backgrounds often find themselves having different points of view on their educational needs and the role of the educational system in meeting them. There can thus be both quantitative and qualitative differences in the experiential backgrounds of participants to particular educational controversies; in fact, this is usually the case. Major educational issues in the United States in recent years have centered around such matters as the following: (1) how to provide equal educational opportunities to all citizens; (2) how to provide racial balance in the schools of racially pluralistic neighborhoods or cities; (3) whether busing students to achieve racial balance in schools is defensible; (4) regarding how teaching *about* religion in the public schools, which the *Schempp* case before the United States Supreme Court in 1963 involved and which the Court ruled was constitutional, should be implemented; (5) how and under what circumstances neighborhood control of urban neighborhood schools can be achieved; (6) the legal rights of students in the schools (such as the right to privacy and freedom from unlawful search); (7) how best to finance schools in an inflationary period; and (8) how to define the limits of the freedom and responsibility of teachers and how to secure academic freedom for teachers. These and many other matters could be enumerated as issues still to be resolved by the American public and the nation's professional educators.

Educational issues arise concerning curricular matters, student-teacher relationships, teacher-administrator relationships, and community-school relationships. Controversy has arisen in recent years over how federal aid to local school systems should be distributed and how much independence local schools should have in using that aid. All educational issues have their origins in the needs of society for the educational services provided by a nation's schools or other educational agencies and in the way these educational services should be distributed and managed.

As a controversy develops over an educational matter and it becomes recognized as an issue by the participant groups to the controversy each point of view regarding the matter must be considered carefully. We try to find out what the main points of contention are and we try to see if we can identify the differences in perception of the situation that may have led to the controversy. The basic reasons for each point of view in the controversy are examined. We sometimes find that more than one issue is involved in a particular controversy; for instance, if a large city's central board of education chooses for what it believes to be the soundest educational reasons to abandon its neighborhood schools and to build "educational parks" on large campuses at each end of the city, we have a controversy involving the following other issues:

1. The "neighborhood school" concept, since some parents might oppose the educational park concept because they do not want their children going to school in a distant part of the city, which relates to (among other matters that could be mentioned)
2. Busing, for when an educational park is built in a city everyone is bused to the park (or the nearest park if there is more than one), and this issue relates in turn to
3. The matter of ethnic and racial integration of schools, for an educational park would involve all children of a city in going to school in the same place, so that the children would be in classes together; and finally,
4. The location of the park, the large costs involved in the construction of one or more educational parks, and the means of financing such an undertaking would all be issues related to such a controversy.

Very strong arguments could be made for future savings in costs by the consolidation of all educational services in cohesive campus situations, but people on all sides of the four related issues would base their judgments on their positions on all of the matters related to the proposal. Indeed, the city of Pittsburgh, Pennsylvania, went through such a controversy recently; other cities have considered the many educational, social, and economic ramifications such educational controversies generate. (The preceding hypothetical controversy does not describe any particular city's controversy over the educational park issue, but it is representative of the kinds of educational issues frequently related to this one when such a proposal is offered. There are many other issues that could be related to such a proposal, such as the costs involved in transporting pupils to the park, the amount of time students are on school buses, and safety factors.) As in many complex educational issues teachers must examine carefully their reasons and their values in taking stands on such matters, as, indeed, must all citizens. The preceding issue, referred to as the "educational park" issue, has an even wider range of effects than what has been briefly described here, but the preceding account should be sufficient to help the reader understand how more than one issue can be related to an educational controversy.

We always have to consider the effects of our actions on others and we need to see what might be the underlying beliefs of a person for a stand or a position he or she takes on a particular matter. Try to consider what might be the underlying rationales or sets of beliefs or reasons of each of the three examples of attitudes toward motivation of students suggested below.

The variations among answers given to questions revolving around an educational issue may be illustrated by analyzing the use of motivation in classroom teaching. Practices related to motivation are selected as illustrative because there are few subjects in the field of teaching that lead to more heated controversy than pupil motivation. From the following descriptions of the practices of three conscientious and intelligent teachers, it is apparent that each teacher has asked and answered in radically different ways such questions as: What teaching methods will motivate pupils to learn what I think they should learn? What degree of coercion is appropriate to motivate children to learn? What kinds of coercion are most likely to lead to the best results? Are grades, examinations, credits, graduation requirements, and the like, the most promising tools for motivating learning? To move to a set of broader and, in the long run, more significant questions: How can I motivate pupils to be strong and self-respecting? To have wholesome relationships with their classmates? To resist exploitation? To avoid gullibility in the face of constant streams of propaganda? To put the questions in still more comprehensive terms: How can I so motivate pupils that my whole educative influence will be oriented toward encouraging pupil growth—growth toward what the psychologists call self-actualization of the pupil?

Teacher A exacts strict obedience from his pupils. He tells the pupils all they need to know and expects them to be able to repeat what he has told them. He makes daily assignments to be completed before the next class meeting. He gives frequent tests based on the assignments; they are objective and rigorously graded. His methods of teaching are founded on the principle of authority. Pupils are trained to "behave" and to study "because the teacher says so." Teacher A relies heavily on coercion, rewards for merit, definite assignments, and the like, to motivate the pupils to learn what he expects them to learn.

In Teacher B's class the pupils all study the same assignment. Learning is a contest. Pupils compete with one another, with the awards and approval consistently going to the winners. Pupils are graded on a curve of probability. The highest grade is awarded to the pupil at the top, with the lowest going to the pupil at the bottom. In the minds of the pupils, certain children are consistently "good," others are habitually "bad." The teacher believes that motivation stems from rivalry and that the race for mastery is a fair one even though those who are required to compete are unequally endowed. The teacher acts as a referee, making and enforcing the rules of the game. The strong survive. The weak fail, "as in life," Teacher B observes. Success and failure, as measured against classmates' performances, are the primary sanctions.

Teacher C emphasizes group accomplishments and tries to build confidence in each pupil and good will among all of them. He or she encourages each pupil to contribute to class projects. There is an exchange of ideas among pupils and between pupils and teacher there is a sharing of responsibility. The theme of class work is cooperation. Grading is considered to be of minor importance. The teacher strives to encourage each pupil to develop along lines that are in accordance with his or her natural talents, to build confidence and self-respect, to develop a feeling of responsibility, and to resist exploitation. Sanctions lie in the success of the group and in the individual's acceptance by the group. Methods that motivate the pupils to learn allow the pupils considerable freedom of choice.

Let us assume that the three teachers are equally capable of being effective teachers. Why do they differ so markedly in their procedures? Fundamentally, they have different educational philosophies that lead them to teach differently. They give different answers to the question of what is good education. An analysis of their teaching reveals several kinds of disagreement. There is, of course, the initial disagreement about the most successful way of motivating pupils—to put it briefly, whether authority, rivalry, or cooperation can best stimulate pupils to achieve the desired ends. But there are also disagreements about the ends themselves—whether, for example, learning academic subjects is more worthwhile than learning to compete with others, or learning to get along with others, and whether all are desirable goals for the teacher in the classroom. There are also disagreements about the justice of judging pupils according to a single standard. There are disagreements about the relative value of directed and nondirected inquiry. Further, among teachers who might agree that cooperation is the most desirable basis for motivation, there will be many differences about what cooperation means in practice, and to what extent the restrictions of a classroom situation allow cooperation to be put into practice at all. There are just as many disagreements about the meaning and practicability of authority and rivalry.

Sources of Differences

The kind of wide differences discerned in the examples illustrating questions related to motivation may be discovered in many educational situations. Why are there such differences? What differences are typical? Where do differences originate?

We must not be led into the error of thinking that the differences that teachers have in answers to questions of an educational nature can be explained in terms of differences in intelligence or sincerity. Wide differences on many issues and problems may be expected of teachers who are all fully capable and all deeply concerned for the welfare of their pupils. If a teacher is not intelligent or interested, the decisions he makes may be wrong; but for a teacher to make what others conclude is a wrong decision does not necessarily imply that he *is* dull or insensitive.

That teachers cannot turn to a single unquestioned authority for established answers to their questions explains in part the variations in their responses. If psychologists, for instance, knew a great deal more than they now know about the behavior of human beings, they might develop an authoritative theory that would be an accepted guide to teaching practice and thereby encourage uniformity.

What Is Philosophy?

Every human being develops a philosophy, however adequate or inadequate it may turn out to be when subjected to close scrutiny by others. Philosophy is based, as noted at the outset of this chapter, on the human quest for understanding of the nature of reality, knowledge, and value. The problems of human existence, taken collectively as a subcategory of the study of the structure of reality, is a major component in any person's efforts to develop clear thoughts about the dimensions of life and the universe, the sources of knowledge and methods of knowing, and the sources of values and methods of valuing. Philosophy can also be said to be a product of systematic thought about these matters as well as a process for "getting at" or inquiring into these matters in the ongoing examination of one's own life experience and goals. A person's philosophy consists of two major sets of components: (1) the search for understanding from one's experience and study of such factors as the nature, sources, and meanings of the universe; humanity as a part of that universe; knowledge; and the sources and standards of human valuation (valuing); and (2) coherent, rational methods for the achievement of reliable knowledge about these matters. There is both substance and process to any person's philosophy of life.

  · Philosophers often try to help us to understand the search for reliable knowledge about these two levels of concerns by showing us ways to clarify concepts or ideas and to clarify the values we either cherish or wish to compare with our own cherished values. People wonder about the ultimate nature of reality, the ways in which people claim to "know" or to ascertain the truth of statements, and kinds of values and assumptions about what is worthwhile and what is not. Philosophy is relevant to teachers for a variety of reasons: (1) all the activities of teaching center around the task of teaching knowledge or ways of knowing or skills that require knowledge of principles of thought or action (cognition); (2) teachers cannot carry on the activities of teaching without having to evaluate the relative importance and the sequence of the knowledge they must teach; (3) teaching is a value-laden activity in that teachers are always evaluating instructional materials, student behavior, student learning, and their own opinions on professional and academic issues; (4) teachers are expected to guide student conduct and to have coherent and clearly communicated goals or objectives in terms of careful planning of student learning, and this requires considerable interpretive judgment and evaluation of the instructional process on the part of teachers; (5) teachers usually cannot be exposed to students for extended periods of time without intentionally or unintentionally letting some of their own values and methods of valuing be communicated to their students; and (6) teachers all wonder about the ultimate goals of their lives as teachers.

There are coherent, organized systems and types of systems of philosophy, and there are ways of thinking or clarifying thought about philosophical concerns. Teachers need to think clearly about these two dimensions to their own philosophy of life because they are all influenced throughout their teaching careers by each of the six reasons for the relevance of philosophy to teaching just noted. "Philosophy" literally means "love of wisdom," and "wisdom" has traditionally been considered to encompass the characteristics of deep insight into and understanding of knowledge coupled with the prudent use of knowledge of the preceding factors.

What Is Philosophy of Education?

From what we have said in providing a brief general description of the nature of philosophy it follows that we need to define "philosophy of education." Philosophy of education deals with the same basic concerns as does philosophy itself, but it directs philosophic inquiry into these concerns to the analysis and the clarification of issues and values affecting the educational process. A teacher's philosophy of education develops around his or her ideas about the nature and the function of knowledge in school curricula and in classroom instruction. Teachers are particularly concerned about the ways in which statements are proved to be true or false. Teachers are concerned to help students learn to reason for themselves; and a central, the central, concern of philosophy is the study of verifiable and accurate methods of reasoning. Thus philosophy of education should be a central concern to every teacher. Every teacher's philosophy of education centers around the teacher's efforts to develop logical methods of gaining knowledge, methods of knowing and valuing that can stand the tests of debate.

The study of standards of conduct and the standards or principles on which conduct is to be evaluated are known as ethics, and these concerns are basic to any teacher's philosophy of education. There is, for instance, a set of standards for teacher conduct accepted by all members of the National Education Association (NEA) in 1968; it is known as the "Code of Ethics of the Education Profession." All teachers develop their own standards of behavior with regard to students, co-workers, superiors, subordinates, and parents. The study of values and ethical standards is, or ought to be, part of every teacher's thought throughout his or her teaching career.

A philosophy of education should involve the identification and clarification of a person's goals as an educator. Attempting to learn how the knowledge and skills with which a teacher works relate to the lives of students and the problems of society is a continuing task. A sensitivity to the cherished beliefs of others and knowledge of ways to clarify one's own values and to assist students to identify and clarify theirs are most important. Another objective should be to help one's students appreciate and enjoy the knowledge one teaches and to enable them to relate that knowledge to their understanding of their own existence in relation to others.

Sources of a Teacher's Philosophy

Experience—The Roots of Individuality

Every human being is born into the world in association with other human beings. As an infant proceeds through life he or she selectively responds to the reactions of certain significant other human beings with whom he or she comes in contact. One's parents, siblings, relatives, friends, teachers, and other members of the community in which one grows up influence the development of thought and behavior. All human beings are involved in a continuous process of evaluating and reconstructing their experiences from birth to death. Indeed, John Dewey was so impressed with this fact that he believed education to consist entirely of the continuous reconstruction of experience. There have been hundreds of volumes and thousands of learned papers and articles on the topic of the social origins of human personality and the stages of human development. We only comment briefly on this matter to sensitize the reader to the fact that when one is in the process of building one's own philosophy of education one should consider very carefully the matter of the influence of people's experiences upon their activities.

Ideological Bases of a Philosophy of Education

All readers of this volume have had sufficient life experience to be aware of the fact that they have been influenced by certain systems of ideas about government, society, religion, and social conduct. An ideology is a formally organized system of ideas about some set of concerns in the world. We have all been influenced by ideologies; every human culture produces out of the historic experience of the members of the cultural group certain organized systems of ideas to govern at least partially the behavior of the members of the group. Further, in technologically advanced democratic societies, such as the United States, there frequently exists a plurality of formally organized systems of ideas (ideologies) that compete for the allegiance or sympathy of citizens. All teachers should, as part of the development of their own philosophy of education, develop some understanding of the systems of ideas that have influenced the development of their thought about the sources of knowledge, their values, and their personal priorities or goals. For instance, in evaluating what one thinks should constitute defensible criteria of teacher behavior in the classroom, one should understand why it can be socially destructive for teachers to indoctrinate students with their own system of ideas rather than instructing them in such a way that students will learn the rational skills of examination of their own ideas and the systems of ideas that have influenced them. Very much more could be said about how one would go about doing this, but this is an introductory text in educational studies, not a text in philosophy of education. Only a single brief chapter can be devoted to this topic in this volume. Nevertheless, every human being in the world has been influenced by at least one culturally evolved ideology, and most have been influenced by more than one. Every formal educational system in the world is organized on some set of ideological grounds. In thinking about and beginning to build one's philosophy of education it is very important to consider what formally organized systems of ideas have influenced one's life and to begin to evaluate more consciously one's thoughts about them.

The Influence of Sociocultural Patterns of Belief and Behavior

Every person lives in a social setting, and every person is exposed to one or more cultural heritages with which he or she will identify. This is as much a fact of social life as the facts of birth and death. One's cultural heritage does not in itself possess the power to determine one's behavior totally, but one's cultural heritage does influence how one reacts to the social environment(s) in which he or she lives. Culture can be viewed as involving two sorts of social phenomena: (1) the qualitative or aesthetic tastes and standards of a person in art, music, letters, thought, and so on, and (2) more broadly speaking, the total evolved past and present laws, customs, and patterns of living of a human group that would also include the factors noted in item 1. When we speak of culture in education with reference to such matters as the teaching of multicultural populations, we usually have the second, all-encompassing conception of culture in mind. It is important to note that a person's philosophy of education is always developed at least in part as a response to the sociocultural realities with which that person has interacted.

People's perceptions of the social structure of the community and social order in which they reside can influence their values with reference to that social structure; and these values usually have some bearing, however directly or indirectly, on the substantive development of their philosophy of education. People view phenomena such as social class and social status relationships within a society differently and apply differing criteria to their personal evaluations of the functions of institutions within a society. They evaluate the desirability of different social relationships differently, and since one of the purposes of the schools in any society is to prepare people for intelligent fulfillment of their responsibilities as citizens, teachers should be aware of and sensitive to such matters.

There are several ways in which sociocultural contexts can be perceived. These ways of defining sociocultural contexts are often referred to as metacultural assumptions. Whether people relate their sociocultural perspectives to a religious ideology or whether they refuse to do so can make a significant difference in how they define the roles of such formal institutions as schools. Whether we think of the sociocultural contexts of education in terms of purely personal aesthetic conceptions of personal "culture" in the letters, arts, or sciences or whether we think of these contexts in terms of broader anthropological conceptions can make a significant difference in determining what sorts of concerns are most important in the development of our philosophies of education.

Three Great American Philosophers:
Introductory Sketches

This brief section is comprised essentially of three very brief biographical sketches of the work of three great American philosophers whose ideas have had great impact on twentieth-century philosophy of education. This is true even though one of these three scholars, Charles Sanders Peirce, never wrote an essay on education. He was, nevertheless, the first truly great American philosopher, and his philosophical insights into the natural order of the universe and his version of "pragmatic" philosophy greatly influenced American philosophical and educational thought. This influence derived from the effects his writings had on the work of William James and John Dewey, two very influential persons in the history of American educational thought. Peirce, James, and Dewey will be briefly described and then some of the influences their work had on American educational thought will be noted.

Charles Sanders Peirce

Charles Sanders Peirce (1839–1914) was born the son of a famous American mathematician, Benjamin Peirce, who was a professor at Harvard University. Charles was a graduate of Harvard University in the class of 1859, and he later received a degree in chemistry from the Lawrence Scientific School *summa cum laude*. It is not necessary here to trace in detail the growth of his philosophy. He developed four systems of thought, which we will describe in the following paragraph. It is necessary to point out that he became one of the most unique innovators in the area of philosophical logic in his time. Although not accorded international acclaim during his own life, he is now internationally recognized as possibly the most original and gifted philosopher America has ever produced. He created the earliest version of the philosophical system known as pragmatism, which was based on a purely naturalistic (nontheistic) conception of the nature of the universe and the social emergence of the human self. Moreover, he achieved true greatness for his unique conceptions of human knowledge as being based on experience and differing categories of perception of human experience. He did not come to the development of an original philosophical system quickly.

As noted, Peirce's philosophical insights took shape in four unique systems. The first system was developed after his graduation from Harvard, from 1859 to 1861; it was strongly influenced by some of the logical views of the great German philosopher Immanuel Kant's views of reality and the sources of human knowledge. Peirce then immersed himself in the study of logic (systems for developing correct methods of reasoning and for determining the truth or falsity of claims to having knowledge). He came to believe, unlike Kant, that there were new methods of inquiry into the nature of logic to be developed; and his greatness as a philosopher rests in large part on his unique contributions to logical inquiry and to the general field of epistemology (theory of knowledge). His second system of philosophy emerged in the period 1866–1870 as he continued to develop his philosophical thought and to build upon his studies in logic. The third system was developed in the period from 1870 to 1884. The fourth and final philosophical system was in development from 1885 until his death in 1914. Each successive system represented a continuation of his attempts to respond to new discoveries of his own and others in the areas of mathematical logic and differing systems of logical inquiry that were emerging at that time.

Peirce's thought greatly influenced the philosophical systems of James and Dewey. It is now generally recognized, however, that the philosophical system known as pragmatism, which he created, also received original interpretations from William James and John Dewey. (It was in the year 1878 that Peirce published a paper that referred to the idea of pragmatism as a systematic philosophical view.) Although James was greatly influenced by Peirce, he went on to develop his own original version of pragmatism. Peirce's greatness as a philosopher stands in its own right; however, many philosophers of education also recognize him for the impact his views had on such other great American philosophers and educators as George Herbert Mead, William James, and John Dewey.

Peirce believed that all human thought (cognition) moved through logical categories of processes in which logical inquiry proceeded through a critical examination of all the actual consequences of human action. He championed the use of the best mathematical and scientific knowledge available in the conduct of human inquiry. His four philosophical systems are much too complex to describe in the space allowed here, but his work deserves mention here because his was a unique contribution to American thought that was to affect, however indirectly, two of the major philosophers of learning and education in twentieth-century America—William James and John Dewey.

William James

William James (1842–1910) was a contemporary of Charles Sanders Peirce. In 1898 James presented a lecture at the University of California in which he discussed pragmatism and referred to the 1878 paper by Peirce, which was entitled "How to Make Our Ideas Clear." James was responsible for reviving interest (and for creating the first widespread national interest) in pragmatism as a philosophical position. William James carefully avoided trying to create his own unique comprehensive philosophical "system"; however, in effect, he did create his own unique version of pragmatism as a philosophy of life and education. John Dewey, on the other hand, although influenced greatly by Peirce's ideas, did proceed to build his own comprehensive version of a pragmatic philosophical system also based upon a commitment to new methods of logical scientific inquiry, the social origins of the human self and intelligence, the continuity of human experience, and the belief that all human learning is and thus should be perceived as the continuous, rational *reconstruction of experience.* (We will briefly note some major themes in Dewey's philosophy after we have had some more to say about William James.) Peirce was to take issue with James's interpretation of pragmatism; indeed, John Dewey was not in agreement with all aspects of James's position. But it is correct to say that each of these three philosophers did share some beliefs; they represent the three most original exponents of pragmatic philosophy in America, the only totally new philosophical system to come out of the American culture. All of our other philosophical perspectives regarding education had their origins in Europe. Pragmatism was a unique American response to post-Darwinian social thought after 1859. Moreover, it was a specific reaction to extreme forms of social Darwinist thought, which emphasized the desirability of a highly competitive, "survival-of-the-fittest" view of life and learning. Pragmatic social philosophy was, under Dewey's leadership, to champion social reform and to emphasize human cooperation and the reconstruction of our social values in harmony with the needs of people.

William James (1842–1910) was the son of a prominent theologian and the brother of Henry James, who was to become a famous American novelist. He was educated privately at home and in various private European and American schools. He graduated from Harvard University with an M.D. degree in 1870. From 1872 until his death in 1910 he taught various subjects, including philosophy, at Harvard University. His family was wealthy, and he had the best education available in his time. He involved himself in the study of psychology for many years, and his two-volume *Principles of Psychology,* published in 1890, is considered a classic. He had many original insights into the psychological theories of his day far too complex to go into here. His most famous book in philosophy is a collection of essays entitled *Pragmatism: A New Name for Some Old Ways of Thinking.*

In a series of eight lectures given at Columbia University in December of 1906 and January of 1907 he set forth his basic views on pragmatic philosophy. James, as did Peirce and Dewey in their own philosophical styles of argumentation, set forth the principles that all knowledge and inquiry are the results of processes and are best perceived as dynamic, changing processes rather than as entities themselves. He believed that we evaluate our conduct and the outcomes of human inquiry in terms of the consequences of our conduct and inquiry and the relative harmony of those consequences or outcomes of inquiry with what we already know from our experience as thinking, rational organisms capable of reflective judgment.

After 1900 most of William James's writing was done in the areas of philosophy and religion. He, unlike Peirce and Dewey, had a mystical dimension to his philosophical perspective that led him to be interested in many varieties of religious experience. He was a complex person, capable of great concern, great wit, and great compassion, as Ralph Barton Perry (another great modern American philosopher, but of a different, more "scientific realist" persuasion) has noted so well in his book *The Thought and Character of William James.*

John Dewey

John Dewey (1859–1952) was born in the year of the publication of Charles Darwin's *Origin of Species* and the year, it will be recalled, of Charles Sanders Peirce's graduation from Harvard University. It was to be John Dewey who would create out of pragmatic philosophy a powerful and dynamic, however controversial, philosophy of education. His philosophical position was also based on a commitment to arouse the social consciousness of people to the need to view democracy as a moral way of life and not just as a form of government. In his articles in *The New Republic* in the 1920s he spoke out for creative social reform and against what he considered to be selfish, competitive influences in American society. He based his philosophy of education on a revisionist view of Jeffersonian democracy and a faith in the power of an informed and critical public to transform society into a "Great Community." He believed that educators and educational institutions should teach the skills of critical inquiry and discussion that would allow people to develop more fully the kinds of democratic institutions they wished to create. He was always a nonconformist in politics; a democratic socialist, he consistently sponsored liberal reform efforts. He encouraged teachers to organize their efforts more formally to meet the educational needs of society by forming a strong union movement centered on principles of collective bargaining. He believed that teachers should have the right to encourage students to engage in inquiry into controversial matters and that teachers should take on the role of directors of inquiry into the processes of learning the subject matters being taught to their students. He asserted a commitment to the principle of free and open public debate and discussion of all sensitive matters relevant to the life of the local community or the nation. His contributions to American social thought were highly original and courageous. He based his philosophy of education on the principle that students need to learn how to do well-reasoned inquiry into the problems of people and to relate such inquiry to the life of the community and nation. He emphasized logical inquiry into human interaction and the social origins of the human self based on unique experience and in-depth reflection concerning that experience.

In *The Public and Its Problems* (1927), his most important book in social philosophy, he referred to a book by the famous early-twentieth-century social critic Graham Wallas, entitled *The Great Society* (London, 1913). One of the central themes to emerge out of Dewey's faith in the educative power of enlightened democratic communities was his belief that the "Great Society" of twentieth-century industrial civilization must be transformed into a "Great Community." His social and educational thought was far more enlightened than some of his present-day critics appreciate. His views on social reform were too advanced for many to accept. Dewey did not have all the answers to America's social problems, nor did he pretend to have them; but he was committed to the idea that if people could be taught processes of scientific, logical inquiry into human problems, they would be able to create a more humane and just society. He was fearless in his attacks on public greed and excessive conformity in social life. He believed that all, including teachers and students, should have total freedom of inquiry.

John Dewey wrote many other books, but the one that has attained the greatest social recognition was *Democracy and Education*.[1] In this book he called for the reorganization of our conceptions of

[1] John Dewey, *Democracy and Education*. New York: Macmillan, 1916.

the social purposes of schools and school curricula, so that, as noted earlier in this biographical sketch, students would learn how to reconstruct their experience continuously and relate it to the problems of communities and cultures. He challenged traditional theories of human nature and conduct and called for the schools to function as centers of inquiry and for teachers to develop instruction in such a way that they could relate the subject matters they taught to the perceived problems of society.

In *The Public and Its Problems* Dewey raised this fundamental question: "What are the conditions under which it is possible for the Great Society to approach more closely and vitally the status of a Great Community, and thus take form in genuinely democratic societies and state?"[2] Almost 50 years after it was first raised, his question has yet to be fully answered. It is a challenge to which each generation of Americans must seek to develop its own unique response based upon its own unique requirements. John Dewey's philosophy of education was an attempt, born out of faith in the power of human reason and rational inquiry, to contribute to the fulfillment of the promise of the American heritage. Anyone who reads *The Public and Its Problems* realizes that the concept of a "Great Society" was not first forged in the mid-1960s.

Dewey wrote three famous volumes on pragmatic approaches to logical inquiry that had great impact on educators' ideas about his conception of the nature of human thought and critical thinking: *How We Think* (1910), *Essays in Experimental Logic* (1916), and *Logic: The Theory of Inquiry* (1938). *Democracy and Education* was probably the most widely read of his books on education, although a little volume published in 1938 and entitled *Experience and Education* probably represents the best brief (93 pages) summary of his educational views.

Born in Vermont and a graduate of the University of Vermont, Dewey received his graduate education at Johns Hopkins University in Baltimore. He taught at the University of Minnesota (1888–1889), the University of Michigan (1889–1894), the University of Chicago (1894–1904), and Columbia University (1904 until his retirement in 1930 and thereafter as professor emeritus of philosophy in residence). To close this all too brief biographical outline of the nature of John Dewey's contribution to American education and the concept of free-

---

[2] John Dewey, *The Public and Its Problems*. Chicago: Swallow, 1927, p. 157.

dom of thought and action in American society, let us quote from Richard Hofstadter:

> Dewey repeatedly denied that pragmatism, with its interest in what James had called the "cash-value" of ideas, was an intellectual equivalent of American commercialism or an abject apology for the acquisitive spirit of a business culture. He reminded its critics that it was James who protested against the excessive American worship of the bitch-goddess SUCCESS! Hostile to all absolutist social rationalizations, conservative or radical, instrumentalism [Hofstadter's designation for Dewey's form of "pragmatism"] has varied in social content from the Progressive era to the days of the New Deal; but what is most important in its history is its association with social consciousness and its susceptibility to change.[3]

and, later,

> If Dewey's belief in the efficacy of intelligence and education in social change was justified, his own philosophy was more than a passive reflection of the transformation in American thought. The sight of a distinguished philosopher occupied with the activities of third parties, reform organizations, and labor unions provided a measure of some of the changes that have taken place on the American intellectual stage since the days when Fiske and Youmans were dramatizing Spencer for an enchanted audience.[4]

Such a comment represents the determination of John Dewey to oppose social Darwinism's ultraconservative "survival-of-the-fittest" conceptions of social life. It also clearly suggests that Dewey was not merely trying to get students to "adjust" to American society; Dewey said that he was not sufficiently satisfied with the existing industrial organization of society to be content with mere social adjustment. He wanted the schools to foster and perfect the skills for teaching critical intelligence and inquiry; because, as he often noted, a people cannot maximize its potential unless it is totally informed and able to pursue avenues of inquiry freely. Hofstadter's comments suggest a rebuttal to some recent criticisms of Dewey's point of view. Whatever one may believe about John Dewey's social views, anyone who studies them closely realizes that this was a philosopher and educator of fierce courage and devotion to his beliefs.

[3] Richard Hofstadter, *Social Darwinism in American Thought*. Philadelphia: University of Pennsylvania Press, 1944, p. 141.
[4] Ibid., p. 142.

Summary

In this brief overview of the concerns with which one must deal in any philosophy of education we have had to discuss in broad terms the sorts of concerns to be dealt with by teachers in development of their personal philosophies of education. Given the fact that only a single chapter in this introductory volume can be devoted to this subject, it seemed imperative to take a synoptic overview of the types of concerns to consider rather than attempt to discuss established "systems" of philosophy of education or specific analytic approaches to the topic. The reading list at the end of Unit I contains a few sources that can assist readers who wish to explore philosophical concerns in education in greater depth.

We noted that a teacher's conception of the nature of reality, knowledge, and values is basic to the development of any coherent philosophy of education. Reasons were given as to why this is the case. The ways in which people can differ in discussing educational issues were suggested, and the influence of socioeconomic and sociocultural backgrounds in shaping or conditioning views on the role of the schools in society was discussed. It was asserted that a teacher will continue to develop (or at least ought to continue to develop) his or her philosophy of education throughout his or her teaching career. The point was made that most educational issues are highly complex and not as clear-cut as they might appear on the surface; this fact underscores the necessity for precision of point of view and comprehensiveness of view on the part of teachers, students, parents, and other citizens. We briefly noted, as well, why philosophical concerns are highly relevant to any teacher's activities.

QUESTIONS

1. Why should the development of a person's philosophy of education be an activity that should continue throughout his or her teaching career?
2. How might socioeconomic or sociocultural factors influence the development of a person's philosophy of education?
3. What are sound reasons for identifying clearly the ideas and systems of ideas that have influenced one's own philosophy of life?

4. How might the development of a coherent and specific understanding of the effects of one's actions as a teacher on one's students and colleagues influence the revision of one's philosophy of education?
5. Why should teachers especially share many of the concerns of philosophy in their capacity as teachers?
6. What does it mean to refer to a set of standards or criteria for evaluating what is true or false? For what kinds of reasons might something be "more desirable" or "less desirable"?

PROJECTS

1. Identify the ideological, social, and cultural influences that are most likely to influence the types of substantive assumptions you now make in your personal philosophy of education.
2. Identify what you believe to be a major issue in American education. Define the issue and identify the several complex questions related to it. Identify and discuss the different assumptions being used to form the bases for the different points of view to the controversy. What would be a good strategy for resolving the issue?

chapter

6

The teacher and the institution

We have examined what teachers do, how they qualify, what their relationships to the profession are, and why their individual philosophies are important. It is also important to interpret what they do and should do in terms of reciprocal relations with the total personnel of a school or a school system. For an accurate picture of the total work of teachers we must take into account the institutional character of the school and recognize the impact of the school as an institution on what teachers do and how they do it.

When a teacher accepts a teaching position, he or she joins forces with an institution that will affect his or her life in professional and personal ways. At the time of one's first appointment, one will ask, "What should I expect the institution to do for me?" There is a difference among institutions regarding opportunity for personal growth and advancement offered, standing of the institution in the community, morale among the personnel, fringe benefits such as sick leaves and hospital insurance. One will want to know if the teaching load is reasonable so that there will be time to confer with pupils and parents, if meetings are held after or during school time, if the teachers are represented by and have an opportunity to participate in an effective organization. The school board employs a teacher to render services to the institution; the institution is also expected to contribute to the teacher.

Schools As Institutions

What an Institution Is

In order to understand how the institutionalization of education dictates to a considerable degree what education will be and conditions somewhat the work of teachers, we turn to the question of what an institution is and then discuss some of its effects.

"Institution" is defined with slightly different emphasis by the social philosopher, the social psychologist, and the sociologist. We turn to the definitions of the last because it is the sociologists who deal with the fundamental laws of social relations and institutions and who concern themselves with basic social phenomena.

One sociologist writes:

> More commonly the term *institution* is applied to those features of social life which outlast biological generations or survive drastic changes that might have been expected to bring them to an end. . . . Institutions are the established forms of procedure by which group activity is carried on.[1]

Another sociologist states:

> Institutions . . . are patterns governing behavior in social relationships which have become interwoven with a system of common moral sentiments which in turn define what one has a "right to expect" of a person in a certain position.
> . . . the essential aspect of social structure lies in a system of patterned expectations defining the *proper* behavior of persons playing certain roles, enforced both by the incumbent's own positive motives for conformity and by the sanctions of others. Such systems of patterned expectations, seen in the perspective of their place in a total social system and sufficiently thoroughly established in action to be taken for granted as legitimate, are conveniently called "institutions."[2]

[1] R. M. MacIver, *Society: A Textbook of Sociology.* New York: Holt, Rinehart and Winston, 1937, pp. 14, 15–16.
[2] Talcott Parsons, *Essays in Sociological Theory,* Revised Edition. New York: Macmillan, 1954, pp. 143, 231.

Another sociologist gives still a slightly different emphasis in his definition of "institution."

> The real component units of culture which have a considerable degree of permanence, universality and independence are the organized systems of human activities called institutions. Every institution centers around a fundamental need, permanently unites a group of people in a cooperative task and has its particular body of doctrine and its technique or craft. . . . But institutions show a pronounced amalgamation of functions and have a synthetic character. Each of them satisfies a variety of needs.[3]

From these general definitions it is not difficult to identify the characteristics of a school that qualify the school and various features of the school as an institution. As society felt the need for ordered, systematic fulfillment of the educational requirements of children, the school evolved. As it acquired the qualities of permanence, universality, and independence, the institution emerged.

We note that an institution possesses the characteristic of persistence. Even if some technical advance were invented that might achieve a desired end, the institution and its established practices of achieving the end would tend to persist.

The definitions also stress continuity in conscious forms of group behavior. The history of the school is, in one sense, a history of a continuous form of collective behavior. When we think of the school, just as when we think of the family or the church, we immediately summon certain images of definite forms of collective behavior that are characteristic of the institution—forms of behavior continuous from generation to generation. Individuals within the school realize that the institution is older than they are and is expected to outlive them. They fit into the stream of continuity and expect to behave, within limits, as have their predecessors.

Another idea carried by the definitions is that the institution exercises a degree of restraint on the individual. Participants are subjected to a degree of control. The school, for instance, furnishes the pupils, personnel, and, to an extent, the parents with a routine of life, with patterns of expected behavior by which they will be judged, and with objectives and ambitions toward which they may strive. The school encompasses recognized rules, formal procedures for their application,

---

[3] Bronislaw Malinowski, "Culture," in *Encyclopedia of the Social Sciences,* ed. E. R. Seligman. New York: Macmillan, 1931, p. 626.

and a structure consisting of persons acting officially. The school and all other institutions are subject in some measure to the common mores. In addition, the school is a vehicle of conscious and formal control over the years when children are enrolled (whether the enrollment is compulsory or voluntary). School personnel often attempt to bring to explicit formulation matters that have been subject to the mores, and to apply to them the formal procedures of the school. Insofar as teachers and other school personnel successfully set themselves up as the proper persons to define and enforce the mores, these take on the qualities of the law. Identification with the established rights and duties growing out of society's deliberate organization of knowledge and techniques to fulfill the need for education is part of the process by which a teacher becomes a person with a social identity.

Institutionalization embraces the concept that human relationships within an organization are structured, that they are consistent with a fairly well-defined pattern. A school—an institution—has a basic structure, and one who functions within the school fulfills a fairly definite role—a role that fits into the total pattern of roles played by all the participants. As Parsons expresses it, "His role is defined by the normative expectations of the members of the group as formulated in its social traditions."[4]

On a wider perspective we see the school as a social institution playing its part in a total pattern of institutions and contributing to a total system of social integration of which it is a part. Along with other institutions the school contributes to uniting human beings in a stable system. It shares in regulating and establishing the rules that determine the relations of individuals to one another. Also, in common with the other social institutions, schools make such adaptations to the environment and such internal adjustments as seem necessary to advance social life.

The school shares in the fulfillment of unique and significant functions. It is vitally responsible for teaching children the techniques and rules of society, the particular ways of doing all the things society cherishes. The school is interrelated with other institutions, for example, the family. It is also interrelated with informal parts of our culture, such as community attitudes. The school's functions are to be understood only in relation to the total social system. The same is true of any institution.

[4] Parsons, op. cit., p. 230.

Why Education Is Institutionalized

The education of the young in any country could, conceivably, be carried on without the establishment of schools. It could be left, for example, to the family or to the church or to industry, or it could be shared by all these. Why have various societies chosen to institutionalize education? Why do the schools in the United States have a kind of organization, rules, regulations, customs, traditions, and practices that are now associated with them? How do these common understandings among many people about the functions of the schools influence the work of the teachers in the schools?

Basically, the reason for the institutionalization of education is the same as the reason for the institutionalization of other large group interests. There has been first of all a perceived need. Driving on the right side of the street became an institution in the United States because of a widely recognized need for traffic order. Institutionalization was the solution to a perplexing social problem. When enough people desired that children be educated in a deliberate fashion, their common response was the organized school, eventually with the rules, organization, and customs that are attached to it.

The school was established for particular purposes. Eventually a pattern, conforming in general to the broad outlines of what most people desired, was evolved. In time the pattern became standardized and ultimately the word "school" meant approximately the same thing to everyone. The school had become an institution as the result of a degree of unity of beliefs about what it should be and should do. Once established, the school served to further the degree of unanimity of belief.

Effects of Institutionalization

The institutionalization of education brings many benefits to the individual pupil and to the individual teacher. It preserves cultural values in customs and traditions. As an institution the school has qualities of endurance and stability. Continuance of accepted practices results in universal familiarity and encourages understanding and sharing.

The characteristic of continuity in educational institutions may sometimes have adverse effects. When practices, customs, and traditions become deeply ingrained, pressure is exerted on schools to maintain what people have come to regard as almost sacred or, at least, a revered part of the status quo. Under such conditions originality

Institutions are viewed in their educative effect:—with reference to the type of individuals they foster. The interest in individual moral improvement and the social interest in objective reform of economic and political conditions are identified. And inquiry into the meaning of social arrangements gets definite point and direction. We are led to ask what the specific stimulating, fostering, and nurturing power of each specific social arrangement may be. . . . Just what response does this social arrangement, political or economic, evoke, and what effect does it have upon the disposition of those who engage in it? Does it release capacity? If so, how widely? Among a few, with a corresponding depression in others, or in an extensive and equitable way? Is the capacity which is set free also directed in some coherent way, so that it becomes a power, or is its manifestation spasmodic and capricious? Since responses are of an indefinite diversity of kind, these inquiries have to be detailed and specific. Are man's senses rendered more delicately sensitive and appreciative, or are they blunted and dulled by this and that form of social organization? Are their minds trained so that the hands are more deft and cunning? Is curiosity awakened or blunted? What is its quality: is it merely aesthetic, dwelling on the forms and surfaces of things, or is it also an intellectual searching into their meaning? Such questions as these . . . become the starting-points of inquiries about every institution of the community when it is recognized that individuality is not originally given but is created under the influences of associated life.*

* John Dewey, *Reconstruction in Philosophy*. New York: Holt, Rinehart and Winston, 1920, pp. 196–198.

may be curbed, wholesome freedom for creativeness may be restricted, and expertly planned innovations may encounter serious obstacles, some, even, from within the profession itself. For example, older school buildings, designed somewhat like boxes, have proved obstacles to changing class size and deterrents to wise use of teaching aids, to services from resource centers, to some changes in kinds of subject matter taught, to such innovations as team teaching. Later discussions will focus on causes and kinds of changes desired. What we wish to emphasize here is that institutions, including schools, have not always encouraged or been friendly to change. The school is an institution based on cultural values, and therefore functions in part to preserve these values. As a result schools, in some measure, tend to resist change.

As the story of education in the United States unfolds, we become conscious that so-called cultural lag and institutional lag apply to education. For example, technological advances may indicate the desirability of changing techniques in teaching science and mathematics. Certain well-established traditions, however, may be a bulwark sufficiently strong to perpetuate techniques inconsistent with the contemporary life picture or inadequate in terms of current social demands. Sometimes practices in the schools lag behind those in other institutions or do not keep pace with the needs of pupils. There is a tendency for the school, since it is a social institution with the characteristics of permanence and continuity, to lag behind the point of advancement indicated by social understanding and professional theory. The degree of lag varies with communities, with states, and with sections of the country.

It is important that a teacher be conscious that he functions as part of an institution. He makes decisions and acts in terms of a superstructure that has both a regulatory and a protective effect on everything he does. The institution is embedded in customs and traditions that have origins historically remote. However, it is also currently dynamic, an organization that contributes to a teacher in many ways and, conversely, to which a teacher contributes in many ways.

Ideas and the Institution

The current pattern of American schools and school systems and the contemporary traditions in educational practices have resulted from a recombination of ideas and from institutional accommodations to ideas some of which have been influencing social institutions for thousands of years and some of which are very recent. Obviously, no adequate interpretation of education can be made if regulations, rules, customs, and typical practices are considered apart from the ideas and social values they are supposed to reflect.

The Teacher As a Group Member

Variety of Memberships

In studying the work of the teacher we indicated certain duties and responsibilities that were added because the teacher is a member of an organized group that shares certain common tasks and whose work has to be coordinated with the work of others. Besides being associated in an institution established for the education of the young, a teacher is part of a variety of other groups also, by virtue of his employment in the school.

The overall, organized group is, of course, the faculty group, which may be a districtwide group or a schoolwide group. Whether the group is an interschool or intraschool group, membership is implied with employment and the duties assigned the teacher always include certain tasks that are related to coordinating work within both kinds of groups. Often the meetings of the districtwide group are annual or semiannual, coming perhaps before the opening of school in the fall and at some designated time during the year when the pupils are dismissed. Frequently the districtwide meeting is enlarged to include a number of school districts in some geographical unit, perhaps a county. Often local teacher groups cooperate with school administrators in planning and conducting meetings.

In the local school the number and kind of professional groups to which the teacher belongs will be determined partly by the size of the school and partly by the philosophy of the school. If the school is large and the policy is to encourage cooperation and participation, the teacher may belong to several professional groups, in addition to the general faculty group. These might include, for instance, all the social studies teachers in the system, all the freshman homeroom teachers, or a group made up of the teachers new to the system.

In addition to the groups to which the teacher is probably required to belong and that are directly related to his professional work, the teacher belongs to numerous groups that may be quite nebulous in their purpose and indefinite in their membership boundaries but that usually, nevertheless, have a significant bearing on the teacher's happiness on the job.

When a number of people are together for any length of time, they tend to form small cohesive groups based on some shared purpose, common interest, or other factor that draws individuals together. For instance, a teacher may be a member of a married teachers' group. The group probably will not be related to any school activities; it may get together only after school hours. But the fact remains that it *is* a group and members talk things over and present a more or less common front on many matters, often matters pertaining to the school. The group may be comprised of those interested in a particular hobby. The golfers, for instance, may get together for dinner and golf or for weekend outings. Perhaps the teachers who live in a particular area have a car pool and discuss and develop a measure of unity as they share time spent in transportation. Perhaps a difference of opinion over some school policy divides the teachers into opposing groups. Those in an elementary school who believe, for instance, in traditional report cards and letter grading oppose those who advocate written messages and parent conferences. They may form a group, a kind of clique, and sit together at faculty meetings and vote alike even on issues entirely unrelated to the report card matter.

The possibilities of group membership for the teacher, even in his school associations, are many and exceedingly varied. A point to remember is that such memberships may be a powerful factor in the teacher's satisfaction with his work. A teacher's pleasure in helping Johnny advance to sixth-grade reading level may be diminished by the knowledge that some other teachers are having a weekly card game to which he has not been invited.

A teacher, and especially a new teacher, should be conscious that it is possible to make errors of lasting effect by hastily affiliating with some social group or other. Groups cannot usually be judged at their face value; they may be in conflict with one another; potent feelings of security and respect may be involved. Social groups within the faculty represent a challenge to human relations, a problem requiring tact and consideration.

Evaluating a Teacher Membership Group

In evaluating the effectiveness of a school as an institution contributing to the requirements of its personnel for group membership, what criteria should be used? What should participation in a school group contribute to the members? For just as each individual is expected to contribute to the institution so should the institution be expected to contribute to the individual.

First, participation in the school group should entail fulfilling a clearly designated role that, when successfully and efficiently performed, brings to the individual a feeling of being respected and considered important by those with whom he or she has institutional connections. It is particularly important for individuals to know that their superiors respect them and value their work.

An individual's work in the institution should net a financial reward high enough to insure physical health and the fulfillment of reasonable desires with respect to food, clothes, housing, travel, transportation, and hobbies. The institution is responsible for meeting this need.

The school should not unduly inhibit the desire of individual teachers to make their own decisions, shape the course of their own lives, and direct the course of their own actions.

It is important that the institution makes it possible for individuals to contribute their abilities to the fullest. Where, because of the narrowness of an assigned role, only a portion of a teacher's capabilities is permitted to function, both the school and the teacher lose.

The individual's desire for and achievement of a well-integrated personality and wholesome morale among members of the group can be encouraged or discouraged by the institution. These will be discouraged in a situation where an excellent teacher is assigned unreasonable responsibilities—an unduly heavy teaching load, numerous extraclass and extraschool responsibilities, regular classes with a number of emotionally disturbed children in them. Where efforts of the personnel are thoughtfully and skillfully coordinated and teaching loads and school responsibilities wisely and equitably distributed, individual teachers tend to be satisfied.

Adjustments Within the Group

What adjustments must teachers make because they are guided in their actions by the goals of an institution and are thus subject to institutional restraints?

Institutional behavior is, to a considerable degree, regulated behavior. The school legislates this behavior through a social superstructure consisting of traditions, rules, regulations, school laws, and the like. In addition, a complex pattern of school administration is set up in every community to guarantee that the laws, rules, and regulations all operate effectively. The individual in this structural pattern, then, must make certain accommodations or adjustments. For example, the school has its institutional goals, which, in certain instances, may be at variance with those of the individual teacher. Since the individual cannot very well change the institutional goals, he must adjust to them. Occasionally the goals of the individual may be so completely out of harmony with those of the institution that the adjustment required is especially difficult and is accompanied by heightened tension. Likewise, an individual teacher may be out of harmony with certain administrative policies in the school, and this also may cause a serious problem of adjustment.

The most desirable and fortunate situation is, of course, one in which the individual finds his personal goals in harmony with institutional goals and administrative policies. However, complete harmony is not usually possible; consequently, we must ask how the tensions of personal adjustment can be reduced. Some social psychologists suggest that participatory action should be the basis of institutional patterns of behavior that are determined by rules, regulations, laws, and other structurized elements in the institution. For example, a school policy toward any and all of a school system's teacher security provisions should grow out of the thinking of all the personnel. This is one reason for teacher negotiations with school boards—teachers are participants in making decisions that affect their welfare. It should be noted that those who advocate participation in making school policy are not arguing that the resulting rules and regulations will be wiser because of the participatory procedure or that group judgment will be any wiser than the judgment of a single expert. What they argue is that participation in and of itself is a value wherever action within a group must be uniform or patterned. It should be fostered in every institutional situation because it contributes to better-adjusted personalities and is an essential element in the maintenance and improvement of a satisfactory level of group morale. Although participation does not provide the entire solution to the problem of tension in individual adjustment, it is a significant factor.

Through various group memberships the individual seeks to promote security and insure respect. How can the individual adjust to the group and within the group? How may he or she attempt to influence the adaptation of the group?

Each group—faculty group, departmental group, or even bridge-playing or golf-playing group—has more or less definite goals. In the case of the organized, professional group, goals may be stated, perhaps broadly and generally, or may not be expressly stated. There may be long-term or short-term goals.

In addition to the goals of the group, members also have their own short- and long-term goals. Individual and group goals may not always be in harmony. The individual may belong to a number of groups whose goals conflict. The teacher's problem, then, is to establish a proper relationship between personal goals and those of the groups to which he or she belongs. New teachers who join a faculty group whose goals conflict with their own, whose ways of doing things are different, will make a temporary adjustment. Eventually, through interaction and discussion within the group, they may expect to achieve a degree of integration with the group that will lead to satisfaction and effectiveness in functioning through the school organization.

1. INTERACTION

Interaction within the group provides members with the opportunity to influence others and to be influenced by them. Two teachers may begin with conflicting goals, disparate views, or divergent opinions. In their direct relationships, afforded by the school, they have the opportunity for interaction. Each has the chance to learn about and evaluate the other's views, an opportunity to exert mutual influence for mutual change. Interaction may not result in unanimous agreement, but it may lead to a modification of views that will result in substantial agreement either in terms of one view or another or in terms of a compromise. The agreement, on the other hand, may be something new and different. Through the process of group interaction not only is agreement reached, but, through the process itself, enrichment of personal satisfactions is achieved.

2. DISCUSSION

Discussion is the basic procedure of group action, the tool of interaction that leads to integration. Discussion is the method of group deliberation. It is an observable manifestation of a group studying and learning together, a group thinking out loud, a group whose members interact. The success of discussion in any school group in promoting interaction and achieving integration depends somewhat on the discussion leaders.

Discussion may degenerate into a kind of "bull session." Sometimes individuals turn a faculty meeting into an unproductive kind of parliamentary debate. Or it may be merely a meeting of listeners receiving institutional pronouncements or decisions and directions from a school authority. To insure facultywide participation in a discussion, it is usually necessary that the topics be well selected, pertinent to the interests of the members of the group, and appropriate to the time available. Usually they should be announced in advance so that the members are prepared. The discussion leader—the school administrator, the teacher chairman—at the faculty meeting, like any other discussion leader, has the responsibility of keeping discussion "on the track," encouraging effective participation, summarizing the main points, and directing the group toward sound conclusions.

In all group relationships, but especially in a faculty group and particularly during discussion, tact is of great importance. Tact does not imply weakness or lack of standards. It means, rather, treating other people in such a way that their self-respect and one's own are preserved. The desire for prestige and importance is universal. In using tact in discussion, one is consciously sparing pride, developing confidence, and assuring the other person a sense of importance. Ridicule and sarcasm are anathemas to effective discussion.

The new teacher who is intolerant of experienced faculty members must realize that anything different from what he anticipated is not necessarily bad. It is only after one has become intimately acquainted with a specific school situation that one is in a position to evaluate policies and practices. What might at first seem undesirable may, after careful examination in the light of a specific situation, appear very desirable. A new teacher from another school should not be tactless in references made to his previous employment. Both the experienced and the inexperienced teacher in group discussion, in personal conversations, and in other institutional relationships should be alert to the danger of appearing to feel superior, seeming to believe that it is his or her business to enlighten and to point the way. By failing to understand the merits of the institution in which he works and to recognize the importance of respect for the staff members' achievements, a teacher retards his or her own integration and cannot achieve the climate most favorable for maximum success.

3. INTEGRATION

The goal of group action is integration. Integration is achieved when all members of the group are completely identified with it, when individual pleasures and satisfactions accrue from the successes and achievements of the group as a whole. An integrated faculty group exhibits *esprit de corps.*

Integration is particularly desirable in the school faculty group because a teacher's role is interlocking, never individual and independent. It is especially important that a teacher be completely identified with the institution. The goals of the school and the teacher's own goals should be harmonious and to some extent identical. If a teacher has been a participant in discussion that led to the agreement on matters related to these goals, he or she will probably have a sense of personal responsibility for the contribution. This will facilitate acceptance of the goals and identification with them.

Integration is essential because even teachers with superior teaching skill cannot make their best contribution to the institution's program unless they see their jobs in relation to the services of other staff members. The success of the school is determined by its total performance. Teachers integrated within the group will perform as members of the group and will not seek exclusive limelight apart from their contributions to the institution's goals.

In many schools an effort is made to acquaint the entire faculty with what is being done throughout the school and within the system. This is done not only to increase understanding and cooperation but also to promote mutual respect among all staff members, which leads to an appreciation that many diverse tasks are performed by members of the school group and that the tasks are coordinate in importance. It also may contribute to confidence in one's ability to contribute successfully to the school's program.

4. FUNCTIONING THROUGH ORGANIZATION

Interaction, discussion, and integration can be promoted more effectively where there are local professional organizations. In the chapter on the teacher and the teacher's profession, teachers' organizations were discussed. Where there is a strong local teachers' organization there are broad opportunities for participation and avenues for channeling constructive suggestions and for airing grievances. In studying problems, suggesting solutions, and proposing plans for implementing change, the organization is, of course, more potent than an individual. As we have mentioned, in many large districts teacher organizations employ a full-time salaried executive who is available to receive individual complaints, use professional skill to study the problems, and see that they receive appropriate action.

Functioning through a teachers' organization, however, places a responsibility on the teacher, who must help build a justifiably strong organization and then must learn when and how to act through the organization. Once a problem is referred to an association, its solution should be worked out through organizational channels. Sometimes an individual, dissatisfied with a policy of the local association, works individually and at cross-purposes with the organization to achieve personal ends. If a policy of the organization is not acceptable, then the correct procedure is to work wholeheartedly to have the organization change that policy. Since it is the product of many different persons, no professional organization is ever perfect. Nevertheless, the association that makes it possible for its members to share in an effective professional organization is providing them with important opportunities.

Induction of New Teachers

How are new teachers to be directed and aided in fulfilling their roles in the school personnel group? What steps are taken to "induct" them into a school system, a school group, a classroom group? This is a problem that has been gaining more and more attention from school administrators.

Handbooks

In many school systems, particularly the larger ones, handbooks are issued to all teachers. They are especially helpful to teachers new to the system. This is an effective way of eliminating indiscretions, uncertainties, and disappointments that grow out of ignorance about what is expected of the new teacher, what is available, and what the teacher can expect to receive in the way of advancement. The handbook speaks for the institution. It usually tells something about the community, its location, transportation facilities, resources, and so forth. It describes the history and location of the schools and the policies concerning salary, tenure, and sick leave. It gives the calendar of events and holidays. Usually the handbook is very helpful. In some cases, however, it is so detailed that the teacher tends to be overwhelmed. Ideally, it is not considered the final word but rather the basis for personal discussions with the teacher, whether old or new.

Presession Workshops

Sometimes a new teacher attends a presession workshop, an orientation week, a get-acquainted period in advance of the regular opening of the school session. Often the teacher receives extra compensation for this work, especially in those cases where it takes as much as a week. Customarily, the principals, supervisors, and certain others of the regular staff work with the new teachers during this period. The activities include tours of the community and discussions of school policies. The teacher is given an opportunity to become acquainted with his classroom, with the resources of the school—audiovisual aids, library, art facilities, and so forth—and also with community resources. He is given an opportunity to ask questions that would be inappropriate in a larger faculty meeting scheduled after the opening of school. Such minor questions as "Does the teacher lead his children in line to the lunchroom?" "With whom should I communicate when I am forced to be absent from school?" "Are children allowed to go to their lockers at any time?" would be a waste of time in a faculty meeting and would seem so petty in that setting that they would never be raised. Knowing the right answers to such seemingly insignificant questions might, however, be important to the teacher's initial adjustment.

Faculty Adviser

In some communities it is common for one experienced teacher to be assigned to advise an incoming teacher. This arrangement continues throughout the school year. The incoming teacher knows where to go for directions and information, and the experienced teacher feels a responsibility for giving the newcomer hints, suggestions, and directions that may be helpful.

Other Plans for Induction

Perhaps fortified with a handbook of information, the experience of a presession workshop, and the name of a faculty member to whom he or she may turn for advice, the new teacher arrives at school on the opening day. Typically the session opens with meetings, district-wide and schoolwide, and then perhaps at the department or grade level. The new teacher is introduced to the groups and meets most of his or her colleagues for the first time. He or she is informed of the plans for the opening of school and is supplied with details of his or her assignment, textbooks, and information about pupils. At once, the duties of checking, organizing, reporting, and accounting begin.

Summary

The institutional aspects of a school have a bearing on what teachers do and how they do it. Good schools in good communities contribute to the welfare, to the feeling of well-being, of teachers. The opportunities provided for participation in a group influence the total adjustment of individual teachers. The program of induction is important to new teachers. Their feelings of security and pleasure in their work may be directly related to knowledge about what is expected of them and what traditions they should respect. There are important, continuing relationships that they will have with other members of the personnel on a social and professional basis that are exceedingly important to success in teaching.

Teachers are likely to work more efficiently and discharge their duties with greater satisfaction if, at all times, they are conscious that the nature of the institution is an influence on both them and their work. The institution contributes to the teacher while the teacher is contributing to the institution.

The school must be viewed as a group enterprise. Teachers' attitudes about their own role in relation to all other roles influence group morale, personal satisfaction, and even the school's educational achievement. Although teachers have assignments that are largely individual and a great deal depends on their individual initiative, they also must perform as members of a group. This means that they see their own achievement partially in the light of the total achievements of the group and recognize that the group has contributed to their achievements, that they are part of a system characterized by interlocking roles, and that they have groupwide, institutional responsibilities.

The group, in order to have wholesome group relations, must be characterized by a high degree of mutual respect on the part of all staff members. Teachers must appreciate that all tasks contribute to the whole and that each contribution is different and must be so because functions and needs are different and also because individuals cannot follow stereotyped patterns in carrying out any educational assignment.

In working in an institution, one works within a framework that must permit adaptation to change. Institutional membership requires that teachers possess flexibility to adjust to institutional change.

Being a member of a teaching group implies the responsibility of adaptation leading to general understanding and a common acceptance of satisfactory goals. Adaptation depends on interaction within the group. Discussion is the important group method of communication leading to integration. Developing skill in discussion is a sure path to effective performance in one's institutional relationships.

QUESTIONS

1. How are American schools affected by the attitudes of the people?
2. What are some of the principal effects on the individual teacher that result from the institutionalization of education?
3. What are the principal ways in which institutionalization influences educational progress?
4. When may a school be said to be progressive? conservative? reactionary? stereotyped?
5. Assuming that institutional changes should be made, how can the direction for desirable change be discovered?

PROJECTS

1. Explain the ways a school represents the common response of the people of a community.
2. Describe some of the adjustments that individual members of the teaching profession must make by virtue of membership in a group because they work in an institution.

unit

I

Suggested Readings

DORROS, SIDNEY, *Teaching As a Profession*. Columbus, Ohio: Charles E. Merrill Publishing Co., 1968. This small, readable book gives an overview of the teaching profession. Chapters 7, 8, 9, 10, and 11 deal, respectively, with selection and orientation, certification, economic welfare, work climate, and professional organizations. This is an excellent supplement to the topics discussed in Unit I of this book.

EDELFELT, ROY A., "The Reform of Teacher Education," *Today's Education*, 62 (No. 4): 20–22, 52, April, 1973. This is a very interesting account of one educator's views of the goals and strategies that ought to be involved in reforming teacher education.

FRANKEL, CHARLES, "Philosophy," *NEA Journal*, 51: 50–53, December, 1962. A scholarly review by a professional philosopher of what the study of philosophy is about. Prepared expressly for classroom teachers.

GALLUP, GEORGE H., "Fifth Annual Poll of Public Attitudes Toward Education," *Phi Delta Kappan*, LV (No. 1): 38–51, September, 1973. This annual poll of public attitudes toward education is an excellent summary sampling of the perceptions of parents, students, teachers, and other citizens toward current issues and problems in education.

GREEN, THOMAS F., *The Activities of Teaching*. New York: McGraw-Hill Book Company, 1971, pp. 1–39. This is the best discussion of the nature of the activities in which teachers are engaged and of the different "modes" or types of teaching activities in which teachers engage to be published in recent years. The author clarifies the concept of "teaching" in these two chapters in such a way as to distinguish clearly between "instructing" and "indoctrinating," on the one hand, and "conditioning" and "training," on the other hand.

GRIMM, ROBERT R., "The Fears and the Joys of the Beginning Teacher," *Ohio Schools*, LII (No. 12): 19–22, 33–34, October 11, 1974. This is a short but most interesting account of beginning teachers' reflections on their first-year experiences as teachers and their ideas about teacher education.

HODGKINSON, HAROLD L., *Education, Interaction, and Social Change*. Englewood Cliffs, N.J.: Prentice-Hall, Inc., 1967. 228 pp. This is an excellent summary of major sociological concerns regarding the problems of education and educational change in social perspective. It provides strong supplemental reading not only for Unit I, but also relates to the concerns of Units III and IV.

HUGHES, MARIE M., "What Teachers Do and the Way They Do It," *NEA Journal,* 53 (No. 6): 11–13, September, 1964. Discusses some of the ways of doing things in the classroom that can make a difference in the overall quality of teaching.

HUTCHINS, ROBERT MAYNARD, "The Role of Public Education," *Today's Education,* 63 (No. 7): 80–83, November–December, 1973. This is a perceptive account of the valuable role played by public schools in preparing young people for responsible citizenship in a democratic society. The author responds to some of the major criticisms of the public schools in recent years.

KNELLER, GEORGE, *Introduction to the Philosophy of Education,* Second Edition. New York: John Wiley & Sons, Inc., 1971. 118 pp. This is a short and readable elementary introduction to major approaches to philosophy of education. Like all such brief syntheses of complex topics, this book does not engage in intricate discussion of some of the issues it raises; but it provides the general reader with a good overview of the topic with which it deals. It is strongly recommended.

MEAD, GEORGE H., *Mind, Self and Society.* Chicago: University of Chicago Press, 1934. A distinguished social philosopher explains the theory behind the establishment of social institutions. Pages 260 to 273 afford an insight into the relationship between the community and the institutions it establishes. This is an early but still quite relevant development of the theory of social institutions.

NATIONAL EDUCATION ASSOCIATION, "Code of Ethics of the Education Profession." Washington, D.C.: NEA Publications, 1968. This is the basic set of ethical standards for professional conduct adopted by the membership of the NEA in 1968. The NEA is the largest professional organization for educators in the United States. Every prospective teacher should read this document.

New York Times. Contains articles on education along with advertisements by colleges for students and a section advertising teaching opportunities in Section 4 of the Sunday edition.

ROSS, LILLIAN, "Dancers on the Green," *New Yorker,* pp. 35–90, July 18, 1964. A description of the work of a fifth-grade public school teacher in New York City. This is a rather long, but highly readable, photographic-style picture of the work of a dedicated teacher, with some sidelights on what she was paid, how she lived, and the like.

SHANKER, ALBERT, *New York Times,* Sunday Edition, Section 4. Weekly comment on educational issues by Albert Shanker, president of the American Federation of Teachers. The column is a paid advertisement presenting union views on major educational issues and is most interesting.

Today's Education. This is the official magazine of the National Education Association; it is one of the most informative and well-written professional journals in the field of education. The articles are always highly relevant and very readable. Readers can find this magazine in college libraries and in most public libraries. It is a valuable resource for anyone interested in the problems of education or trends in educational development. Several special feature columns or articles are published in every volume.

II

Educational ideas that have been influential in America

All of our ideas about what "education" is, what it ought to be, and what we hope it will be have developed out of a rich fabric of cultural heritages which constitutes our inheritance as human beings. In Unit II of this volume we are going to draw upon some of the rich and influential aspects of our inheritance as human beings to summarize briefly a few of the ideas which have influenced the course of educational development in the West in the past and present. This part of the present volume is thus an attempt to give a broad overview of some of the key concepts and movements which have particularly affected education in America; it cannot be an exhaustive treatment of the sources of our educational heritage, but then an exhaustive treatment of that heritage is not necessary in a volume oriented toward an introductory approach to its topic.

The American educational heritage was greatly influenced by European cultural development. This is not surprising since the dominant groups in American society in its formative years were of European descent. It was not until the very late nineteenth century that any truly original American educational theories or practices were developed, and even late in the twentieth century the deep influence of European cultural and teaching traditions continues to affect us. Therefore in this section we are going to examine a few of the European and American ideas that have influenced our views as to what education is and what it ought to be. The brief list of readings at the end of Unit II refers readers to standard sources on the history of Western education and American education, for those who want to study the history of education in Europe and America further.

Each of us needs to remember that every formal social institution with which we are familiar is the product of cultural evolution. No one is the product of the present alone, and no one can understand fully his or her living present without some general understanding of the past. What is true of the need for historical perspective in understanding the development and functions of formal social institutions is true of human beings as well, for it is human beings acting in social contexts who create and change institutions as they live and contribute to their cultural heritages. Indeed, the problem of understanding the American educational heritage and how that educational heritage ought to be modified and directed in the future requires at least a basic sense of historical perspective, for we are one of the most culturally pluralistic and religiously diverse national social orders in the world. To achieve justice for all Americans in the realm of educational opportunity, we need to reflect on the basic ideas that have affected the development of our educational institutions. For it is within these institutions that young citizens and their parents are required by laws of the states to place their trust and hopes for academic and vocational education.

Chapter 7 deals with major European influences on American education. Chapter 8 deals with great ideas in educational thought from both the European and the American historical experiences. Chapter 9 deals with the American educational heritage exclusively, and Chapter 10 explores briefly a few major social issues and conditions to which American educators, as well as all other citizens, should be attentive and about which they should be informed. If past promises and goals of the educational system are to be fulfilled in the future, then we must relate past to present and examine the nature of certain contemporary social conditions in America that affect the lives and education of children and youth.

chapter

7

The social origins of educational ideals

Ideas are always the products of human thought; institutions are always the products of the collective thought of particular groups of people developing their own particular means for guiding and controlling the behavior and beliefs of group members. The process of institution development takes time; consequently, traditions of a group of people possessed of a unique identity are an important component in the development of both ideas and institutions. An institution cannot develop unless a people has experienced some idea or set of ideas it wants to see formulated and acted on in some formalized way. All patterns of living, such as a group's ideas about law, religion, marriage, child care, or education, are expressed through the language and customs of the group. Educational ideas and the forms and purposes of educational institutions, such as schools, are developed and modified over time as particular groups of people create them to achieve their perceived social needs.

It is also true that we sometimes develop our ideas about a particular matter of concern through the influence of other people or other groups of people. The history of the development of European and American educational ideas is such a case, where the ideas of many nations and peoples have contributed to what is known as the Western educational heritage. We can only summarize some of the most important types of factors that have influenced the development of educational ideas in Europe and America in this brief chapter; although our treatment will be brief, it will help in the effort to understand how certain institutions and ideas that came from the European historical experience have influenced the development of educational ideas in America.

Sources of Ideas About Education

The educational ideas and institutions that emerged in the United States were derived from European social settings. Every people wonders about how to initiate its younger members into the life of their social group in a manner that will best prepare them to ensure the survival and continued development of the group. Western European and American civilizations owe the beginnings of formal education as we know it in the West to classical Greek civilization (starting from about the sixth century B.C. to about 338 B.C.). We particularly owe a debt to Hellenistic civilization (approximately 338 B.C. to 146 B.C.). In the classical and Hellenistic periods of Greek civilization our earliest conception of a formal "liberal education" took form. Greek civilization and later Roman civilization, which would adopt and spread Greek educational ideals all over the Mediterranean world and western Europe, greatly emphasized the importance of the individual citizen. We will discuss a few of the aspects of Greek and Roman conceptions of education in this chapter, but first let us complete our brief discussion of the sources of educational ideals. One source of educational ideals can be the influence of great cultures with which other peoples identify or from which they borrow, as Europe and America borrowed some ideas about the importance of the individual in their conceptions of education. But there are other factors as important as that of borrowing educational concepts from other peoples. What are some of these?

One of the other factors in the life of any culture that almost always affects the types of educational ideals adopted by the people of any particular society is the religious factor, where religious thought and practice are encouraged or at least tolerated by the state. The reverse of a religious factor might operate if a country's government is trying to reduce the influence of religion on the country's population. But clearly in western Europe and the United States the religious factor has been most important in terms of the efforts by religious groups to influence the types of values taught in the schools, even though the First Amendment to the Constitution clearly forbids any legal connection between formal religious bodies and public institutions. Nevertheless, religion has influenced American values and the expectations of a majority of Americans about the kinds of values their public institutions are supposed to represent. So, because of the importance of the religious factor in American civilization to date, we will briefly discuss the ways in which religious values have influenced educational values in Europe and America and the different assumptions often made about the significance of the religious factor.

Other factors to be noted in our discussion of the social origins of educational ideals are nationalism and economic structures or ideals. Both nationalism and different sorts of economic assumptions greatly influence the educational development of any country. Finally, we will briefly note the factor of cultural pluralism as having had great impact upon the development of American society and American education, particularly since the United States is inhabited by people whose ancestors came from Africa, Asia, and every part of Europe. However, in this chapter we will define the idea of cultural pluralism and describe briefly its effects on American society; in Chapter 10 this factor will be discussed further.

Since this volume is designed only to provide students with an introductory overview of American education, it cannot deal in depth with the history of Western education per se. That task is difficult to accomplish even if one can devote an entire volume to this topic. We are concerned in this chapter with the discussion of some very broad themes and types of factors that continue to influence American education and that have their roots in our cultural past.

Classical Greek Contributions to the Development of Critical Thinking

There emerged in the intellectual and political life of the ancient Greek city of Athens in the sixth through the fourth centuries B.C. a series of great teachers, writers, orators, and scholars whose thoughts provided the foundations for Western civilization's quest for clarity in thought and expression. There emerged great intellectual leaders, thinkers, and teachers whose contributions to human thought and knowledge are respected and closely studied in our own time as much as in earlier times. Although many of the great leaders of classical Athenian civilization did not spend their entire lives in the city of Athens, it was in Athens as the center of Greek intellectual culture that many of them lived and worked, exchanging their ideas about knowledge and values with others.

We will not in a brief chapter be able to examine in depth all aspects of classical Athenian culture as it continues to be reflected in present-day conceptions of teaching and learning. But we would be remiss if, prior to summarizing our ideas about the Greek contribution to education, we did not pause to discuss briefly the educational ideals of three of the greatest teachers of all time: Socrates (469?–399 B.C.), Isocrates (436–388 B.C.), and Plato (427–348 B.C.). Only a brief summary of their great contributions to our ideas about the "educated person" and the quest for development of critical thinking skills can be offered here. Their efforts in providing motivation for people to think more interpretively and evaluatively about ideas and social issues contributed greatly to the human pursuit of truth.

Critical thinking involves the attempt to define ideas and issues accurately, to identify the assumptions that form the basis for statements claimed to be true, the effort to amass relevant evidence to support such statements, and the capacity to construct valid arguments and counterarguments to the points of view of others. The Socratic tradition in critical discussion, or "dialogue," about controversial issues created a new force in human thought so powerful in its influence that reasonable people are more and more indebted to it with every passing generation. Before we look at the contributions of Socrates, Isocrates, and Plato to the quest for reasoned critical thinking as it affects our thoughts about teaching, let us examine very briefly the social context of the "Athenian movement" in Western educational thought.

In the fourth and fifth centuries B.C. in Athens, an idea gained ascendence in Athenian culture that was literally to transform Western civilization in later centuries. It was the idea that human affairs should be guided by reason and not solely by tradition. It was the idea of reasoned debate and discourse into all aspects of human life and the universe in which that life exists. It was an idea that became a moral commitment to all well-educated persons of that and later times in the European educational heritage. The need to examine critically and to reconcile on the basis of the best reasoned arguments available the needs and best interests of people was proposed in opposition to the traditional method of making personal and public decisions by appealing to traditional authorities, myths, and political tyrants. Later the Western world was to experience many instances of tyranny and injustice, but the light created by the Athenian movement in Western intellectual thought was never entirely extinguished. It has given hope to people everywhere for the rule of justice and reason in human affairs. The ideas of Socrates, Plato, Isocrates, and Aristotle were to forge a new faith in the transforming power of human reason.

Before the beginning of this commitment to the development of methods of critical analysis and thought in human affairs, any attempt to criticize traditional civic myths and beliefs was usually suppressed. Athens became one of the great centers of aesthetic culture and commercial trade in this period, and under the leadership of Pericles it entered a period of true greatness. The city had a population of just over 100,000 persons during the "Golden Age of Pericles" (500–400 B.C.), when the intellectual movement to which we are referring in this chapter reached the height of its development. It had always been dangerous to challenge established authorities or groups in ancient Greek cities, and it was especially dangerous to challenge traditionally accepted religious beliefs or literary myths. People were subject to trial for offending traditional customs and persons could be exiled from their native city or put to death if convicted of "impious" acts or expressions of disbelief regarding the sacred myths of a city-state or of an established religious point of view. Socrates was executed in 399 B.C. for supposedly having taught students "impious" thoughts and attitudes when his chief accomplishment had been to teach them how to think critically and incisively about human affairs. Such teaching was seen as a threat to the security of the Athenian state.

It took great courage for the great teachers of Athens such as Socrates, Plato, and Aristotle to stand firm in their commitments to the value of reasoned oratory and debate and of verified knowledge or truth as the sole basis for human decisions. In fact, late in his life Aristotle had to flee Athens to avoid a fate similar to that of Socrates. Plato knew the historical Socrates well and learned much from him; he established his own school in Athens, which was called the Academy. He wrote several scholarly dialogues in which he related his ideas on the nature of human nature, virtue, knowledge, and the ideal social state and its laws. Aristotle had been taught in Plato's school where he came for a time under the strong influence of the mathematician and astronomer Eudoxus of Cnidus, among others.

We find that Plato's own ideas were unpopular for a time after the execution of his friend and teacher, Socrates (who had been forced to drink a cup of hemlock as his death sentence). Thus the idea of "critical thinking" was one that required great courage to support. The world is indebted to these great philosophers and teachers who championed the skills of critical argument (*eristic*) and dialogue (critically rational open debate and discussion).

CRITICAL THINKING IN THE EDUCATION
OF A CITIZEN

The Greek development of the critical thinking skills to which we have been referring reached its peak in the middle of the fifth century B.C. under the influence of a new group of professional teachers called Sophists. They were the teachers who developed the skills of critical argument and debate to which we have referred. Socrates and Plato reacted vehemently to some of the Sophists who seemed intent only on "convincing" or winning arguments. Socrates and Plato believed that the search for truth, the quest for certain knowledge and virtue should be the only motivation for debate. They disagreed with those Sophists who only taught their students techniques for "convincing" others. They held that the search for truth must be the only basis for morally sound conduct as a citizen. The Sophists greatly changed the lives of the people of Athens; however, not all Sophists were content merely to teach people how to "win" arguments. Sophists such as Protagoras (481–411 B.C.), the first Sophist, and Isocrates (436–388 B.C.), who was probably the greatest of all the Sophist teachers, contributed much to the process of helping Athenian citizens examine their civic affairs more critically. The Sophists, through their skills in rhetoric and logic, contributed to Plato's sharpening the lines of argument in his *Republic* and other dialogues.

Plato wrote several famous dialogues, which were discussions in which various points of view were taken on such major philosophical issues as, the nature of virtue and of human nature and knowledge. In some of Plato's dialogues, such as the *Republic, Protagoras,* and *Meno,* he portrays in depth the character of Socrates, his teacher and friend, involved in critical thought and searching questions about such problems as whether and how people can learn, what virtue is, what the ideal state is, and so on. The name of Socrates became synonymous with excellence in teaching.

Socrates always had a devoted group of friends and students with him when he taught in Athens, and after his death, Plato immortalized him in his dialogues. Socrates reacted to many Sophist teachings. Although some say he was a Sophist of sorts himself, he was different from the main body of Sophists in that he believed in the search for truth and the nature of human virtue or excellence above all else. Socrates was not content merely to "convince" a person; he wanted him to understand why a statement was true or false. Thus he taught through a question-and-answer discussion technique, which has been described as the Socratic method of teaching ever since his time. No greater tribute could have been paid to his skills as a teacher; his whole object in instruction was to get his student actively involved in critical reasoning about what was being discussed. To do this he would ask leading questions and then demand clarifications and definitions in an effort to force the student to examine critically and incisively all aspects of a topic under discussion. He believed, as did most of the Sophists, that "man is the measure of all things," but he also believed that the "unexamined life is not worth living."

Plato's *Republic* emphasized the concept that the civil state should exist to provide justice for all individuals; in fact, throughout the *Republic* the question is asked, "What is justice?" Henceforth the struggle of human beings for truth and justice in their lives as citizens would ring with this question. Plato recommended a very sophisticated and long-term program of literary, logical, and mathematical studies that all who would become rulers of his ideal state would have to complete successfully. However people may today react to the political structure recommended in the *Republic*, there can be no doubt that in his concept that only philosopher kings (the best and most able who could pass through a required program of studies) were fit to rule a free people Plato was concerned with the problem of justice. He suggested procedures for selecting and educating the guardians (civil servants) and the rulers (philosopher kings) of his ideal "polis," or state.

Early in the *Republic* a very interesting turn of events occurs in the dialogue; it is decided that one cannot determine what is just for the state until one can determine what is just for an individual citizen of that state. This is a historic moment in Western literature. Plato was building on philosophical foundations laid by the Sophists and others yet the formulations of his thought and his ideas themselves were very original.

In the Athens of Plato's time it was considered imperative that each boy be educated to become a good citizen. What constituted a good citizen and what constituted virtuous conduct were matters of great concern. Plato's concept of the philosopher king was of great significance in emphasizing the need to stress the necessity of searching for truth and moral virtue in the education of those who would lead the state.

Equally important is the Platonic emphasis on the responsibility of the individual citizen for seeking justice for himself and others. Thus it was argued that the search for the wise use of knowledge and the consideration of the rights and legitimate interests of all citizens must become a major part of the moral code of any responsible citizen. Plato believed that citizens should study the problems of life philosophically, to develop skills in critical and interpretive reasoning for the purposes of seeking truth and virtue. Athenian civilization reached its peak and made its finest contribution to Western educational thought in its commitment to this ideal. Plato emphasizes the importance of the preceding points in an allegorical comment in the *Republic:*

> Unless either philosophers become kings in their countries or those who are now called kings and rulers come to be sufficiently inspired with a genuine desire for wisdom; unless, that is to say, political power and philosophy meet together, while the many natures who now go their several ways in the one or the other direction are forcibly debarred from doing so, there can be no rest from troubles, my dear Glaucon, for states, nor yet, as I believe, for all mankind; nor can this commonwealth which we have imagined ever till then see the light of day and grow to its full stature.[1]

With this telling comment from Plato's *Republic,* we conclude this section. The next section of this chapter deals with further dimensions of the Greek contribution to our thought about the education of persons for excellence and virtue.

The Greek Contribution

Some of our most fundamental educational ideals, as we know them, can safely be said to have received their most eloquent initial development in ancient Greece from the seventh century B.C. to the first century B.C. There were several ancient civilizations in the distant past

[1] *The Republic of Plato,* translated with introduction and notes by Francis MacDonald Cornford. New York: Oxford University Press, 1965, pp. 178–179.

that contributed to the development of our Western educational traditions, but we will discuss only briefly the classical Greek contributions to our educational thought. Some of the sources listed as suggested readings at the end of Unit II can provide a comprehensive view of ancient Greek and other civilizations' contributions to our educational heritage. We are here going to encapsulate briefly a few of the major types of ideas about education that Greek civilization has contributed to our view on this topic.

When formal education was first developed in ancient Greece and other early Western civilizations it was restricted to only a small percentage of the population. Not everyone was allowed what was then the privilege rather than the right (as it now is in the United States) to go to school. Yet in the formulation of the classical Greek educational ideal and its later development in the Hellenistic period (approximately 338 B.C. to 146 B.C.) there arose a deep commitment to the idea that formal education should lead to the perfection of individuals. Classical education, at least in terms of education in the more advanced academic studies, was usually limited to the education of boys. However, in the Hellenistic period this sexual discrimination was modified and some girls did earn the right to formal education.

After the Hellenistic age there were centuries of sexual discrimination in Western educational systems during which girls were denied equal educational opportunities. Yet with the educational emancipation of women in modern times, especially in the nineteenth and twentieth centuries, the classical ideals of educating the individual human being to maximum standards of personal perfection finally applied to both sexes in most Western nations, including the United States.

Without going into detail concerning the several different forms and stages that classical Greek education took, such as the differences between the earlier and the later forms of Athenian and Spartan educational systems, we need to consider those few overarching, universal goals of Greek education that have inspired the world. They are summed up in two concepts. The concepts of *arete* (roughly defined preliminarily here as "consummate personal excellence") and *paideia* (personal culture, representing the highest aesthetic ideal of personal cultural achievement) are at the heart of what we mean when we refer to a person as educated. We will consider the meaning of these ideas and how they have affected our views about living and learning. These two ideas were finally perfected into their presently understood meanings in the Hellenistic period of Greek civilization.

Arete, a concept that evolved and developed its meaning from early Homeric times in Greece to the Hellenistic period, has as its central meaning the achievement of utmost personal perfection, the development of the best possible qualities in a person's life, taking into account his or her unique individual capacities. In different periods of Greek civilization people had different ideas as to what these best personal qualities were. But one thing is certain; as an educational ideal *arete* came to stand for the maximization of whatever unique gifts a particular person might possess. Also certain is that this concept referred to more than academic excellence. A person's *arete* could refer to maximum and creative use of the talents or resources available to him, to courage and resourcefulness, to great skill in personal expression of one's views. In its earlier usages, *arete* did not necessarily refer to academic excellence; it had to do with personal virtue of any sort. However, by Hellenistic times it did come to be associated with the concept of total personal excellence in virtue, honor, maximization of one's intellectual talents, and the product of having been educated with an emphasis on perfection of character as well as learning. Every person could develop some aspects of *arete,* and each of two different persons might possess different kinds of *arete.* Nevertheless, education for total personal virtue and excellence became the standard for the achievement of a person's ultimate educational goal, *paideia. Paideia* involved the achievement of a personal culture embodying the highest standards and traits of excellence in human thought and conduct known at the time.

Let us consider further, but briefly, the meanings of these two ideas. H. I. Marrou and E. B. Castle are two historians of education who have had very pertinent things to say about the concepts of *arete* and *paideia.* Marrou and Castle each note that the particular kinds of personal excellence suggested by *arete* changed through Greek history until the term came finally to stand for all the highest forms of personal excellence, as noted earlier. Marrou asserts that *arete* is impossible to translate literally, but that a rough translation of the term would be "valor."[2] As the Greek cultural experience unfolded over the centuries, *arete* came to stand for both a form of personal virtue and forms of excellent human achievement. The object of education became a personal one, the making of human beings. Marrou notes that, "The object was the whole man, but man as man, not

---

[2] H. I. Marrou, *A History of Education in Antiquity.* New York: Sheed and Ward, 1956; a Mentor paperback that is a translation of the third French edition. (See p. 32 for this reference and the index of the book for references to the later development of the concept of *arete.*)

in any special form or any special part."[3] He also asserts that during the Hellenistic period sexual discrimination between boys and girls in the schools "tended to disappear." Medieval Europe (and before that the Roman Empire) revived sexual discrimination in schools. It was not until the late nineteenth century that women would again make great strides in achieving equality of educational opportunity with men. E. B. Castle has noted the Greek emphasis on humane education in the following statement: "It is on the main theme that we must concentrate—on the idea that education is the making of men, not training men to make things."[4]

The quest for *arete* led in the Hellenistic period of Greek civilization in the Mediterranean world to such an emphasis on the high quality of a person's critical thinking abilities and personal virtues that a concept of educating the whole personality emerged that had profound effects upon the Western world. That concept is the idea of *paideia,* briefly referred to earlier. It led to the firm establishment of what came to be known as the seven liberal arts of Greece and Rome. When the idea of *paideia* was related to the concept of liberal arts (or those studies that have a liberating effect on the personality) there emerged the basic foundation for Western humanistic studies in the Roman period and in medieval and renaissance Europe as well. We shall note a few of the comments of Marrou and Castle on this topic before concluding this section. Marrou asserts that in the Hellenistic period of Greek civilization:

> Henceforth the norm and justification of all existence are to be found in man—man considered as an autonomous personality in his own right, achieving the realization of his being—beyond the self, and without ever renouncing his own individuality. To a greater extent than any who went before him, Greek man had regarded himself as the centre and measure of all things, and in Hellenistic times this humanism became conscious of its personalist claims. For Hellenistic man the sole aim of human existence was the achievement of the fullest and most perfect development of the personality.[5]

This development is summed up and expressed in the Hellenistic conception of *paideia.* Our generation has been conditioned to think that the idea of "educating the whole person"—or, to use the current edu-

---

[3] Ibid., p. 302.

[4] E. B. Castle, *Ancient Education and Today.* Baltimore, Md.: Penguin Books, 1961, p. 102.

[5] Marrou, op. cit., p. 141.

cational cliché, of "educating the whole child"—was an original twentieth-century concept conjured up by "progressive" educators. We ought to reflect about why we always seem to be "rediscovering the wheel" in the field of education. We see that we are not the first civilization to value the education of the total personality, and we do not live in the first century in which such effort was made. Roman scholars were later to translate the word *paideia* as *humanitas;*[6] and therein we have the beginnings of those studies that we know as the humanities. In a time in which there is much talk of "humanistic education" in educational circles we might take note of this fact.

We can now consider a bit more closely the concept of *paideia.* Marrou says, referring to the significance of *paideia* in Hellenistic times, that this word is of such significance that had he to describe or define the special character of the Hellenistic period he would refer to it as the "civilization of *paideia.*"[7] E. B. Castle has said that,

> The Greek conception of educating for 'wholeness' is summed up in the word *paideia,* which Plato defines as: "the education in *arete* from youth onwards, which makes men passionately desire to become perfect citizens, knowing both how to rule and how to be ruled on a basis of justice."[8]

Castle goes on to note that,

> Plato defined *paideia* as a form of education. The word is derived from *pais,* a child, and originally referred to what we describe as education, the preparation of young people for adult life. In Hellenistic times, by an interesting transference of idea from the means of producing a desired end to the end itself, the word came to signify 'culture', the end to be achieved.[9]

Finally, Castle synthesizes what all this means in these words:

> We become educated, cultured, by continuous searching. The personal culture thus attained is a man's *paideia,* the thing for which he is born, the sum of intellectual, moral, and aesthetic qualities that make him a complete man. This was the pearl of great price for which the true seeker of *paideia* was willing to yield up all else.[10]

[6] Ibid., p. 142.
[7] Ibid., p. 143.
[8] Castle, op. cit., p. 103. Castle is quoting here from Plato's *Laws,* 643e.
[9] Ibid.
[10] Ibid., p. 104.

This was the essence of the great intellectual and moral treasure we inherited from Greek civilization as it was to be transmitted throughout the Western world, first by the legions and proconsuls of Rome and later by the explorations and transcontinental migrations of the European peoples.

The Roman Mission

The Roman republic, and later the Roman Empire, inherited from Greek civilization the "seven liberal arts" that the Greeks had modified and developed over the centuries and that Roman and early Christian educators continued to modify to meet their own educational requirements. These seven liberal arts were divided into two sets of studies: (1) the *trivium,* which consisted of grammar, rhetoric, and logic and constituted the first course of study of young citizens; and (2) the *quadrivium,* which consisted of studies in geometry, arithmetic, astronomy, and theory of music (which often related basically to the theoretical and mathematical laws that formed the basis of music and harmony). The Romans built on this tradition of liberal studies and developed their own schools, including their own forms of secondary and higher learning. It is not our purpose to describe these here, but to point out that the Greek quest for *paideia* was continued in the Roman culture's quest for *humanitas.* (Readers wishing a detailed account of Roman educational development are referred to the standard historical sources included in the list of suggested readings for Unit II.)

In the Roman educational tradition greater and greater emphasis was placed on literary and especially rhetorical skills as Rome grew from a sturdy young republic to be the master of the Western world in the fourth century A.D. An emphasis upon the quest for *humanitas* (*paideia*) through development of personal excellence in spoken and written expression became important to those privileged Roman citizens and subjects of the Empire who were destined to rule the Mediterranean world and Europe and to carry the inheritance of Hellenistic civilization.

Two famous Roman intellectual leaders were particularly important in the development of Roman educational ideals. Marcus Tullius Cicero (ca. 106–43 B.C.) was a great Roman senator and essayist whose speeches and essays became standards of excellence to Roman and later European students of the Latin language. Many other Latin authors were studied as eloquence and aesthetic style became dominant themes in preparing young Roman citizens to adopt and to champion the strong values and close personal ties and obligations of Roman family and civic life. Marcus Fabius Quintilianus (A.D. 35–95), known widely as Quintilian in the history of educational thought, became a very famous Latin scholar and teacher. He raised the rhetorical tradition in advanced Roman education to a very high point and is best remembered for his collection of essays entitled *Institutes of Oratory*. Quintilian's work had great effect upon the development of later Roman education.

H. I. Marrou sums up well the Roman mission in education. He points out eloquently that many modern historians have been unjust in their appraisals of Rome's educational achievement. Since Rome adopted the basic educational structure and content of Greek education many historians have criticized Rome's educational system as merely a degenerate copy of the original Hellenistic model. Marrou points out how unfair this assessment is, in that, as he asserts, it misses the point regarding Rome's true contribution in the field of education. He also points out that Hellenistic civilization's educational efforts have been similarly attacked[11] for not rejecting its cultural inheritance and not creating a totally new educational theory. Marrou then asserts his view of the Roman mission in education:

> Rome's historic function was not to create a new civilization, but to take the Hellenistic civilization which had conquered her and establish it firmly on the whole of the Mediterranean world.[12]
>
> . . .
>
> And if Greek civilization in its turn had remained the jealously guarded preserve of a few Aegean cities, it too would have disappeared long ago, without renewing, as it has, the face of the earth.
>
> And the fact that it thus fulfilled its destiny is largely due to Rome. Rome's historic function was to complete the work begun by Alexander [Alexander the Great, 356–323 B.C.], and plant Hellenistic civilization from the Sahara to the lochs of Scotland, from the Euphrates to the Atlantic; and to give it such deep roots that it could withstand the storms of Teuton and Slav invasions, and the Arab invasion, if not that of the Turks. It is this profound labour, ensuring the renaissance of the future, that constitutes Rome's real honour and imperishable glory.[13]

---

[11] Marrou, op. cit., p. 391.

[12] Ibid.

[13] Ibid., p. 393.

What more could be said of the Roman cultural and educational mission? We take our stand with Marrou in his assessment of the Roman contribution to Western education.

The Religious Factor

Another factor to be noted briefly for its relationship to the social origins of educational ideals is the religious factor. The cherished systems of belief about reality and the standards of human behavior that have been taught by the major religions of the world have often influenced the educational ideals of their adherents. We will not discuss in detail the history of the relationship of religion to education; that story is available in standard histories of education. What we want to provide here is an overview of the effect of religious values on the educational ideals of religious people.

The Roman Empire found it difficult to tolerate Christian religious beliefs prior to the fourth century A.D., when (approximately A.D. 325) it officially tolerated the Christian religion. It declared Christianity the official religion of the Empire very late in that century. The Christian church then developed its organizational structure patterned after the units of Roman law and civil administration, so that when Rome finally collapsed in the West and Europe was thrust into the medieval period, there was a structure to maintain order and Latin culture. The Judeo-Christian tradition in European religious thought had great impact upon the restructuring of the classical liberal arts to meet the social, cultural, and religious needs of medieval and Renaissance Europe. The standard histories of Western education document this story well. The American colonies and republic reflected well this Judeo-Christian reinterpretation and extension of classical views about the means and ends of education. Medieval and, to a lesser extent, Renaissance intellectual cultures were still dominated by the classical Greek and Roman languages.

The polytheistic belief in several gods was characteristic of the Greeks and Romans. The Romans found it difficult to tolerate the Jewish belief in one god when they occupied Palestine. Christians and Jews found it very difficult to tolerate each other's different views about one god; and the Christians were to have particular difficulty comprehending the Moslem view of God's nature when the Moslem faith was established in the seventh century A.D. Christians engaged in many bloody holocausts with Moslems and with one another before the relatively firm establishment of more peaceful ways of reconciling, or at least tolerating, differences of religious belief in the eighteenth and nineteenth centuries. And in the 1930s and 1940s another holocaust was inflicted on Europe's Jewish population when religious hatred developed again. The social origins of educational ideals are rooted in the total cultural life of a people. Where there are two or more widely accepted religious traditions in a society, citizens, especially parents and teachers, have a moral obligation to encourage children to accept people as individuals regardless of their religious beliefs.

However devoutly people may ascribe to their belief in the divine and absolute truth of a religious faith to which they adhere, they practice that faith in society. Their practice of their religious faith affects their relationship with all the established institutions of that society. Therefore all teachers should try to understand what religious values a community may have with reference to student or teacher conduct or human conduct in general. We are not going to compare different religions here, but we emphasize the need to be aware of the social ethics championed by the members of communities in which one teaches.

As noted in the introductory comments at the beginning of this chapter, the First Amendment to the Constitution prohibits any "establishment of religion" as the state religion of the United States. There have been several federal court cases in recent years about reading Scripture and saying prayers in schools. Although the Supreme Court has ruled that prayer and partisan Scripture reading are unconstitutional, it ruled in the *Schempp* case in 1963 that "teaching about" religion in the public schools is constitutional so long as the following conditions are met: (1) a comparative approach to the study of religion is taken; (2) the teacher does not attempt in any way to convert students to his or her religious point of view; and (3) students are voluntarily enrolled in such a course. In other words, God was not "kicked out" of the public schools by the Supreme Court as some right-wing groups have maintained. Partisan prayer and Scripture reading were the only things denied access to our public schools. The real underlying question in this whole controversy is whether people are really willing to allow in-depth comparison of the theological beliefs of different religions in the public school classroom and whether they can agree on how this should be done or what the qualifications of those teaching such classes should be. What was the background of so complex a chain of events in America in the 1960s as the issue of prayer and Bible reading in the public schools? This issue has deep roots, not only in American constitutional history but in the history of the entire Western world. One of the things we ought to be sensitive to as teachers is the right of a person to have any religion or no religion under our constitutional form of government. The right to freedom of belief is now enforced rigorously, but it was not always so.

Where religious creeds are important in the life of a people the general ethical standards upheld by these religions often tend to influence, to some degree at least, some of the kinds of educational ideals for social behavior adopted by the society in question. The great degree of pluralism in types of theistic and nontheistic points of view about life has necessitated acceptance of the principle of toleration of all types of ethical codes in the United States. However, as well established as the constitutional guarantee of freedom of belief was in the United States, various forms of Protestant belief tended to dominate American religious and social thought prior to the latter half of the nineteenth century, when millions of immigrants from predominantly Roman Catholic and Orthodox nations of Europe came to the United States.

The Factor of Nationalism

With the development of nation states after the collapse of the Western Roman Empire in the late sixth century A.D. European civilization underwent changes of such magnitude that any description of them, particularly in such a brief commentary as this, falls short. Charles the Great (Charlemagne) forged a great empire in western Europe in the late eighth century A.D. until his death in A.D. 814. From then on nationalism and the struggles among feudal lords became factors in European life in spite of the fact that hundreds of autonomous states developed, merged, or disappeared in the ensuing thirteen centuries. The story of the development of nationalism in Western civilization would be a vast one to tell. Several important but short-lived kingdoms had existed in Europe between the final fall of the Western Roman Empire in A.D. 576 and A.D. 800, when the Pope crowned Charlemagne (Charles the Great) "Roman Emperor" on Christmas day of that year.

It is important to note that the social origins of educational ideals have always been influenced by the forms of government under which people have had to live. Many nations have been composed of more than one people, and where this has been the case human history is full of examples where one people has tried to dominate another people living within the same nation state or a neighboring nation state. Not all "nations" have their own completely autonomous states. National goals and policies always influence the types of formal educational goals established in any nation state. America was settled by people who came from many parts of the world seeking greater control over their own affairs.

Influence of Classical Languages on Modes of Thought

All books and legal documents in Italy at the time of the Renaissance were written in classical Latin, although the common people spoke regional Italian dialects. The learned teachers delivered their lectures in Latin. In time, skill in the use of classical Latin became the badge of the educated man. It separated him from the uneducated, gave him membership in a distinguished prestige group. Latin was the means for international communication.

Because of his mastery of classical Latin, the educated man was able to study the great works produced before the Renaissance. Many an educated man also mastered classical Greek. Through his command of Greek he had access to the works of the Athenian scholars—to their drama, philosophy, oratory, poetry, and great literature. To the Italian scholars of this period there was no source of learning so rich in quality, so universal in application as that handed down by the Greeks.

The effects of this emphasis on Latin and veneration for the works of the Greek scholars have been far-reaching and long-lasting. The Italian scholars believed that the works produced by the Athenian scholars were unsurpassable, well-nigh perfect, sufficient for exclusive study, and applicable to every aspect of human conduct. The knowledge of the ancients became the authoritative guide for man's every endeavor. In the books of the ancients were found all the answers to man's esthetic, ethical, and political problems. Thus a knowledge of Latin and Greek was the key to all the answers. The man with the key was in a position of intellectual power and consequently had social prestige.

Naturally, classical Latin became the core of the educational curriculum. Methods of teaching it were developed into highly refined techniques that had the psychological advantages of being both logical and definite.

The effects of these methods on teaching in general seem fairly clear. A definiteness was given to teaching methods. The selection and management of subject matter were made more logical. The effects were felt long after the classical languages ceased to serve as the official language of communication. Latin continued to hold the central place in the curriculum. Methods of teaching Latin were deemed suitable for teaching the subjects in most other fields.

The predominance of Latin also served to perpetuate the separation of scholars into a class apart from the practical affairs of life. Even after newer subjects came into the curriculum, teachers of the older subjects retained special prestige, were considered more erudite, and were ascribed higher social status.

The Role of Economic Structures and Goals

Whether the country is primarily agrarian, dependent on an agricultural economic base for its development, or industrialized affects its economic development. There are various stages of industrial development among nations. The United States has one of the most advanced industrial technologies in the world. It also produces huge quantities of agricultural commodities. Although only about 6 percent of the American population is involved in agricultural production, the United States possesses both the most advanced agricultural technology in the world and large areas of fertile land. The local schools in the United States tend to reflect in their social goals and values either the needs of an agricultural economy or those of an industrial-commercial one, depending on the area in which they are located. This is not to say that the economic base of a local school district totally determines the goals of local schools; there are certain universal educational goals shared by all American schools. Some of these shared universal goals involve the need for a sound education in basic literacy skills or "general education," as well as the need for citizens in all areas of the country to achieve the goal of a sound understanding of the history of the country and its political traditions.

Different philosophies of economic life lead to different social structures for the allocation and use of a country's resources. Whether a nation is primarily capitalist or socialist affects the allocation and use of its economic and natural resources. The United States has an economic structure based on a capitalist, private enterprise conception of economic activity and productivity in which there is a public sector of the national economy to meet certain social welfare and defense requirements. The public sector of the American economy coexists with and is controlled by the private sector through coordination of national economic policies at the national, or federal government, level of policy development. Thus American economists often refer to the American economy as a mixed private enterprise economy.

The financing of schools was left totally to the states under the United States Constitution. This occurred because control of education was one of those powers not mentioned in the Constitution. The "elastic clause" of the Tenth Amendment to the Constitution gave all those powers not mentioned in the Constitution to the respective states or the people. Thus the financing and governance of local school systems was totally dependent on state and local funds, although the federal government has provided various forms of aid to education in the history of the republic. The federal government's relationship to educational development in the United States is discussed in Chapter 13 and referred to in other sections of later chapters.

Cultural Pluralism and the American Educational Experience

Cultural pluralism is a concept that refers to a series of positions regarding what people think ought to be the attitudes and types of social relationships among different cultures or peoples living in the same society. The idea of cultural pluralism has been used in two different ways: (1) merely to describe the fact of cultural diversity in a nation state such as the United States and (2) to refer to a philosophical position claiming to recommend how different cultures within the same society ought to interact where there is a desire to maintain the basic cultural identity of each cultural group in the nation. The issue centers around the question of whether cultural diversity in a nation's population is a great asset to the development of national character, and hence highly desirable, or whether it is best for all ethnic groups in a society to blend into a new one. Those who champion a philosophy of cultural pluralism (position 2 above) are concerned with the basic question of how to preserve each cultural group's identity and heritage within a national unity. There has been considerable discussion of the idea of cultural pluralism as this phenomenon may relate to culturally diverse populations such as that of the United States. Those who believe that there should be a strong commitment to equal treatment of all cultural groups and to preservation of the respective cultural identities of peoples within a national unity (national "polity" as some political scientists and philosophers say) are aware of the importance of educational institutions in achieving such ends.

The United States has one of the most culturally diverse populations of any nation state in the world. This has had profound effects on American school systems and American teachers. This is particularly true since it is one of our most fundamental constitutional principles that every American citizen is equal under the law and entitled to the "equal protection of the laws" guaranteed by the Fourteenth Amendment. As a result of some famous federal court decisions regarding human rights and education, this guarantee of equal protection as it relates to what should count as true equality of opportunity has profoundly affected American school systems, particularly in the past twenty-five years.

Cultural pluralism as a philosophical position relates to what its adherents believe ought to be the preservation of the cultural diversity and richness of American life because they believe that each cultural group in America has its own unique contribution to make to American civilization. America has been inhabited by peoples from all over the world; the remnants of its first inhabitants, the American Indian tribes, have been here for thousands of years. People of African descent have lived here since at least 1619. Between 1820 and 1927 about 37-million people from all parts of Europe migrated to the United States. The fact that Americans have come from many different cultures and practice many religions has greatly influenced the development of American institutions. The current demand that young Americans be taught the contributions of all cultural groups to American civilization requires our attention. We will have more to say about cultural pluralism and American education in Chapter 10.

Summary

In this chapter we have focused on some of the most significant social origins of American educational ideals. The origins of our most fundamental educational ideals in the culture of classical Greece were discussed, as was the Roman extension of these ideals, with modifications, to the rest of Europe. The significance of the religious factor in Western educational history was briefly noted. Nationalism was discussed as a powerful conditioning factor in the development of school systems. The influence of classical languages in Western educational thought was described. We discussed the relative influence of different types of economic structures and noted the factor of cultural pluralism and the importance of cultural diversity to the American educational experience. In this chapter the contribution of seven major types of social factors to the development of our educational ideals was discussed. In Chapter 10 we will discuss the factor of cultural pluralism in America when we discuss the contemporary American social scene and current problems in American education.

This chapter has been designed to provide a basic overview, rather than an in-depth treatment, of some of the types of socially originated factors that tend to influence the development of educational values and goals. A definitive treatment of the topic of this chapter would require an extended volume on the intellectual and social history of Western educational thought. What the authors have tried to do here is to choose for consideration some of the most important types of social factors that affect formal educational development.

QUESTIONS

1. Describe how religious or economic factors have influenced the development of the public or private local school system(s) you attended.
2. How have the ideas discussed in this chapter enabled you to see the significance of nationalism and economic structures as influencing a society's educational goals?
3. Is the education of the "whole person" a new educational idea? How do you feel about a school's responsibility to educate the whole personality? Compare the educational ideas of *arete* and *paideia* with your own educational values or goals.
4. What is the significance of the idea of cultural pluralism in relation to the problem of guaranteeing "equality of educational opportunity" for all citizens?
5. What comparisons can you make between classical Greek educational ideals and current American educational values and practices?

PROJECTS

1. Try to find out, if you do not already know, the precise ethnic (national and cultural) composition of the community in which you were raised.

2. Review some of the literature on the aims of education and values in education in educational or general "trade" journals during the past 20 years or local schools' statements of purposes for any reference to educating the "whole child" or the "whole person." Are these statements of educational aims or values specific enough from your point of view? List the sorts of educational aims or values you think a teacher should have.

3. Identify three present-day social movements that have an influence on current education. What conflicting points of view have arisen regarding these movements?

4. Develop a rationale (a statement of purpose with reasons given for your position and an effort to support the logic of your reasons with evidence for them) for the view that teachers should be concerned to develop in their students such characteristics as courage, character, or resourcefulness as well as academic learning.

chapter

8

Some great contributions to educational thought

The brief overview of some of the social origins of our educational ideals given in the previous chapter had as it major theme the proposition that all our values, including our educational values, have their origins in the experience and thought of people living in society. In the present chapter we examine briefly a few of the major concepts about knowledge and education that have had a major influence on European and American educational thought. When we refer to "educational thought" in this chapter we mean more than just thought about the conduct of teaching and schooling, although these concerns dominate the major portion of this chapter. We also mean thought about the nature and relative importance of different ways of ordering or structuring knowledge that indirectly influenced the emergence of the disciplines of knowledge and of different ideas about what ought to be the priorities of importance placed on different types of studies at different stages of human development. The discussion of people and ideas in this chapter is necessarily limited. As in the previous chapter, we refer readers wishing to study these particular concerns further to the histories of Western educational thought listed at the end of Unit II.

We consider selectively some of the major educational thinkers' ideas about teaching and learning, and then we examine briefly some major thematic concerns in past and present educational thought. Some conspicuously significant European writers whose ideas about education greatly influenced educational development in America and who we discuss briefly in the present chapter are John Amos Comenius (1592–1670), Jean Jacques Rousseau (1712–1778), Johann Heinrich Pestalozzi (1746–1827), Friedrich Wilhelm Froebel (1782–1852), Johann Friedrich Herbart (1776–1841).

Comenius

John Amos Comenius was a Moravian bishop who was severely persecuted for his Moravian Protestant religious beliefs, as were most Moravian Protestants in the seventeenth century. He held deep spiritual beliefs and was also deeply interested in formal education. He was interested in teaching and schooling because he held to the advanced belief for his time that the social and cultural environment of a person greatly influences that person's development. Comenius was convinced that if formal education (schooling) could be reformed, it might be possible to reform society. He believed in toleration of religious freedom, and he believed that children not only should be taught about the spiritual dimensions of life, but should be prepared for all their responsibilities as human beings. Therefore he saw the schools as having a civil function as well as a spiritual one.

In his time most thought that the primary aim of education, if not its sole aim, was to prepare people for their spiritual destinies. Comenius did believe that all truth was revealed by God, but he also believed that children learn best from experience (a very advanced view for that time). He believed that knowledge, virtue, and piety were the primary goals of education and that, further, these could best be taught in an atmosphere in which students learned from their senses and from reflection on their experience and in which they would be encouraged to make reasoned judgments of their own. Comenius did not believe that it was either proper or effective to teach students in ways that only required them to memorize or that did not encourage them to develop the skills of independent judgment. Students would, he argued, grow to learn how to control themselves if they were shown how to think independently and how to gain knowledge, practice in virtuous conduct, and sound religious beliefs.

Comenius believed that a teacher must develop insight into the relationships between the substance taught (subject matter) and the methods used to teach it. He was one of the first educators to see the necessity, not just the desirability, of relating the manner or method of teaching to the type of subject matter taught. He was very critical of educational development in Europe in his own time and developed his ideas on teaching and learning in textbooks that he wrote, some for teachers and some as classroom texts. His book *Didactica Magna* (*The Great Didactic*), published in 1632, is considered by many to have been centuries ahead of its time in its concern for the integration of teaching substance and method and for the types of teacher-pupil relationships it encouraged. He noted in that book that for more than 100 years before the publication of the *Great Didactic* people had been complaining about the lack of coherent method in the conduct of teaching and the unmethodical ways in which schools were conducted. He noted that it had only been in the previous 30 years that any serious efforts had been made to reform the conduct of schooling, and that, in his view, these efforts were not suitable. (The rules for teaching developed by the Society of Jesus, or the Jesuit Order, had been established in 1599 after much experimentation and modification. However, Comenius did not approve of them, for they tended to be in disagreement with his own philosophy of teaching. The 1599 Jesuit document was called the *Ratio Studiorum;* it called for and specified a very orderly and disciplined method of instruction, but it did not allow students the degrees of freedom Comenius thought they needed, nor was it based on sense experience or the life experience of the learner, as was the system of Comenius. *Ratio Studiorum* was the Latin designation for the Jesuit "plan or rationale for studies.") Comenius stated the main object of *The Great Didactic* as follows: "Let the main object of this, our Didactic, be as follows: To seek and to find a method of instruction, by which teachers may teach less, but learners learn more; by which schools may be the scene of less noise, aversion, and useless labour, but of more leisure, enjoyment, and solid progress. . . ." Comenius is considered by many to have been the first educator to develop a systematic conception of instruction that embodied throughout a commitment to the acquisition of knowledge and virtue in an atmosphere in which students could enjoy learning and learn from experience.

Comenius started with the organization and selection of subject matter, which he decided must progress step by step from the familiar to the less familiar. He wrote textbooks in which, as he said, he aimed to give an "accurate anatomy of the universe, dissecting the veins and limbs of all things in such a way that there shall be nothing

---

The Great Didactic, or *Didactica Magna,* was a theoretical treatise on education that contained all the views of Comenius on education. It laid the foundation for educational development for all the succeeding centuries. Examples from the Table of Contents illustrate the nature of the educational topics he discussed:

6. If man is to be produced, it is necessary that he be formed by education.
7. A man can be most easily formed in early youth, and cannot be formed properly except at this age.
8. The young must be educated in common, and for this schools are necessary.
9. All the young of both sexes should be sent to school.
10. The instruction given in schools should be universal.
11. Hitherto there have been no perfect schools.
12. It is possible to reform schools.
13. The basis of school reform must be exact order in all things.
14. The exact order of instruction must be borrowed from nature.
16. The universal requirements of teaching and of learning; that is to say, a method of teaching and of learning with such certainty that the desired result must of necessity follow.
17. The principles of facility in teaching and in learning.
18. The principles of thoroughness in teaching and in learning.
19. The principles of consciousness and rapidity in teaching.
20. The method of the sciences, specifically.
21. The method of the arts.
22. The method of languages.
23. The method of morals.
26. Of school discipline.
27. Of the fourfold division of schools, based on age and requirements.*

* As quoted in Paul Monroe, *A Brief Course in the History of Education.* New York: Macmillan, 1907, pp. 247–248.

that is not seen and that each part shall appear in its proper place and without confusion." The textbooks, instead of presenting a collection of facts, presented material arranged so that study could proceed step by step from what is best known to what is less familiar. Each chapter and each paragraph led to the next. Comenius stressed the soundness of connecting words with the objects for which they stand, of learning a language the natural way—that is, by topical conversation—of making generous use of pictures and natural objects as classroom aids to instruction, and of including singing, economics, world

A New Method

Comenius considered subject matter and method to be inseparable aspects of teaching. The nine principles of teaching method that Comenius stated reflect his devotion to the inductive method, his long experience as a teacher, and his sensitiveness to logical and psychological relationships:

1. Whatever is to be known must be taught by presenting the object or the idea directly to the child, not merely through its form or symbol.
2. Whatever is taught should be taught as being of practical application in everyday life and of some definite use.
3. Whatever is taught should be taught straightforwardly, and not in a complicated manner.
4. Whatever is taught must be taught with reference to its true nature and its origin; that is to say, through its causes.
5. If anything is to be learned, its general principles must first be explained. Its details may then be considered, and not till then.
6. All parts of an object (or subject), even the smallest, without a single exception, must be learned with reference to their order, their position, and their connection with one another.
7. All things must be taught in due succession, and not more than one thing should be taught at one time.
8. We should not leave any subject until it is thoroughly understood.
9. Stress should be laid on the differences which exist between things, in order that what knowledge of them is acquired may be clear and distinct.*

* As quoted in Paul Monroe, *A Brief Course in the History of Education.* New York: Macmillan, 1907, p. 242.

history, geography, science, politics, art, and handicrafts as everyday parts of the subject matter of classroom instruction.

The most remarkable and most successful of all the Comenian textbooks for children was *Orbis sensualium pictus* ("The World of Visible Things Pictured"). Its method of dealing with things was that of leading by inductive process to a generalized knowledge. It was also the first textbook for children that utilized illustrations.

Students were to engage in a process of inquiry wherein they were encouraged to develop logical skills in evaluating sense experience, knowledge derived from the human senses such as sight, sound, and touch. Students were to be taught how to reason inductively from particular truths to more general truths as well as the traditional forms of deductive reasoning from general truths to particular truths.

Comenius's views on teaching seem quite familiar when they are described to present-day elementary schoolteachers. He believed that objects or ideas to be taught should be presented directly to students and that skills to be taught should be demonstrated so that students could practice them having seen them performed. Teachers were to use the simplest, most direct explanations possible, and they were to teach only those ideas or skills that students were ready to learn. The subject matter to be taught was to be ordered in the sequence that would make it easiest to learn. No new subject was to be introduced until the students had mastered their previous lessons. Thorough learning and stress on being able to make distinctions and see relationships were basic points in his philosophy of teaching. Students were to be able to apply in their lives what they learned in school, and academic subjects were to be taught with this as a continuing objective; this latter point was a revolutionary educational idea for the seventeenth century. No more than one idea, object, or skill was to be taught in any one lesson, according to Comenius, and the causes of things and the methods of reasoning with ideas were to be emphasized.

Besides improvements in subject matter and method, Comenius proposed improvements in the organization of the schools so that they might also be more consistent with his basic philosophy. He proposed an organization of schools providing four levels of education based on the growth and development of children. Each level was to be a different kind of school, and each school was to encompass six years. This is basically the pattern of organization that we follow today. The system proposed a single program applying to all classes. He rejected the idea of one school system for upper-class children and another, poorer one for the children of the lower classes. The first level,

More than 300 years ago Comenius helped to lay the foundations of what we now think of as modern education. He was a teacher of teachers. He stressed methods of instruction that have since been embodied in the thinking of the teaching profession. He was both a great educational theorist and a practical reformer who was accorded international recognition in his time and who is still recognized as one of the earliest innovators, a forerunner of modern education. Comenius believed in universal peace, and he believed that proper education of the young was an avenue to the advancement of peace and the elevation of society. Like some other advanced social thinkers, Comenius was severely persecuted. He suffered greatly in the religious persecutions that were inflicted on him and his fellow Moravians during the Thirty Years' War. His wife and children were murdered. His home was twice plundered, and his books and manuscripts were burned. He was exiled from his native land and then worked as an educational reformer successively in Poland, Sweden, England, Sweden a second time, Hungary, and Poland again, where he was severely persecuted and was again exiled. He finally found refuge and support in Amsterdam, where he spent the later years of his life.

for infancy, should be at the mother's knee; the second, for children at the vernacular school; the third, for boyhood at the Latin school or gymnasium; and the fourth, for youth at the university or in travel.

Other educators who were the contemporaries of Comenius seem to have been unaffected by his practices and by his educational philosophy. He was, however, without doubt the greatest educator of his century. Many of his ideas are incorporated in our present educational system. All his ideals have not as yet been attained in the countries where he lived and worked. The ideas of Comenius, especially his application of the technique of induction to teaching, are important because of their profound effects on the formulation of subsequent educational theory.

Rousseau: Education in Accordance with Nature

Jean Jacques Rousseau became extraordinarily prominent in the field of educational thought through his writings on the general theme of educating the child according to, or in harmony with, nature. He discussed what he meant by this in several writings, the most famous of which was a book entitled *Émile*. *Émile* was published in 1762, and it immediately became one of the most controversial essays on education ever to have been published. It deals with the ideal education of a boy, Émile, according to the dictates of nature, and with the aid of a tutor. The book follows Émile from infancy to young manhood, and it even describes the character and training of Émile's future wife, Sophie. Rousseau's ideas about education relate to his basic social philosophy, which was rooted in the French Enlightenment conception of the natural rights of man. The thesis that runs throughout *Émile* is that human beings are good in a state of nature but that society tends to corrupt them. "Everything is good as it comes from the hand of the author of Nature, but everything degenerates in the hand of man." He is credited by some as having been the first educational theorist to conceive of childhood as consisting of developmental stages, although his categorization of the stages of childhood and youth was not in any way based on psychological and biological research in the patterns of human development as we now know them. The five stages of childhood and youth discussed in *Émile* were infancy, childhood, preadolescence, adolescence, and youth. Rousseau argued that young people should not be taught any subject until they are ready to learn it; he discussed his theory of education in terms of these stages of development in *Émile*.

Rousseau believed that education of the young should be based on their natural interests and readiness to learn. All education should be based on the natural development of the human organism. "Present interest: that is the great motive impulse," he asserted in the section of the *Émile* dealing with boyhood. However, his educational ideas and writings are quite complex. Émile grows up in a natural environment that is based on one student's encounter with one tutor, whereas in Rousseau's later essay on "Considerations on the Government of Poland" in 1773 he recommends an education based on building national pride and patriotism. But even in the latter essay Rousseau says that education ought to be "negative," keeping children from encountering vices, and that teachers ought to instruct students "with exercises which give them pleasure by satisfying the needs of the growing body, and in other ways besides." Rousseau's great contribution to educational thought was that he encouraged us always to consider the relationships among students' social environments and their physical environments and to relate instruction to the natural capacities of the learner.

Pestalozzi: Experimenting to Discover Effective Teaching Methods

The Experimental Movement

To state the principle that education should be in accordance with nature gives no indication of how to incorporate that principle into classroom teaching. How that principle can be connected with concrete teaching realities and made a part of teaching in a specific school setting with a whole set of customs and traditions remained a problem.

Following Rousseau's enunciation and elaboration of his principle, experiments in teaching were undertaken to discover the most promising methods for interpreting the principle through practice. Rousseau's ideas appealed to numerous European teachers, but it was Pestalozzi who established the first of the European experimental schools. Pestalozzi was a Swiss schoolteacher, the ablest of the advocates of Rousseau's ideas. Because his experiments with Rousseau's ideas set a pattern and his conclusions and theories had a wide circulation, the educational trend became known as the Pestalozzian movement.

The First Experimental School

Pestalozzi's first experimental school (he conducted several) was at Neuhof, near Zurich, Switzerland. He moved to a farm and combined the teaching of children of poor parents with work at agriculture. He failed financially and was thereby forced to discontinue his experiment. He had, however, made a beginning that strengthened his faith in experimentation in education. He had gained some insights into educational method appropriate for implementing the naturalistic principle. He began to publish his educational ideas, and his influence spread. The conclusions Pestalozzi arrived at as a result of these 'first experiments in teaching were consistent with Rousseau's principles. In *The Evening Hour of a Hermit* he wrote:

> Man driven by his needs can find the road to truth nowhere but in his own nature. . . . Man, if you seek the truth in this way of Nature, you will find it as you need it according to your station and your career. . . . Whoever departs from this natural order and lays artificial emphasis on class and vocational education, or training

for rule or for service, leads men aside from the enjoyment of the most natural blessings to a sea of hidden dangers.[1]

He also said:

Man can, at best, do no more than assist the child's nature in the effort which it makes for its own development; and to do this, so that the impressions made upon the child may always be commensurate, and in harmony, with the measure and character of the powers already unfolded in him, is the great secret of education.[2]

Basic Theory and Later Experimentation

Pestalozzi and his followers continued with their experiments to discover better methods of teaching and to work out practical applications of the naturalistic educational principle. Pestalozzi, teaching without pay, experimented with various school subjects. His most productive period was from 1799 to 1804, when government and private financial assistance enabled him to conduct an experimental school in Burgdorf, Switzerland, an industrial community near Berne. The experimental school enrolled 72 pupils and employed 10 teachers. Here he participated also in a program for the training of teachers. In 1802 he had 102 teachers studying in his institute, among them a number of foreigners who were studying in order to take ideas about teaching methods back to their homelands. Thus experimentation in methods of teaching and the training of teachers were related through a single program.

The Pestalozzian movement was a direct continuation of the strivings for social reforms stimulated by Rousseau's revolutionary books. At first Pestalozzi's endeavors were directed toward an improvement of the social condition of the lower classes through industrial education. It was in later experiments that he attempted to determine the psychologically soundest methods of teaching subjects in the elementary school. He protested vigorously against teaching children words and phrases that they did not understand, and insisted on the substitution of firsthand experience with natural objects as the fundamental starting point of instruction. He believed that the primary purpose in teaching through observation and concrete experience was to have

[1] As quoted in Robert Ulich, *History of Educational Thought*. New York: American Book Company, 1945, pp. 259, 261. Translation is by Ulich.
[2] As quoted in H. Holman, *Pestalozzi, His Life and Work*. New York: McKay, 1908, p. 172.

Pestalozzi was a Swiss educational reformer whose principles of teaching found manifold application in the United States. The principles of teaching that he developed in his experimental schools were especially influential in teaching such elementary school subjects as language, science, domestic geography, and primary arithmetic. Partly as a result of Pestalozzi's influence, the methods of instruction that were developed in America in these subjects represented an enormous improvement over the methods prevalent in the schools before 1800—methods that were highly routinized, mechanical, and flagrantly wasteful.

Following the French invasion of Switzerland in 1798, Pestalozzi collected in a deserted convent a number of children made homeless by the invasion and spent his energies reclaiming them. In 1781 he had written his educational masterpiece *Leonard and Gertrude,* and the indigent and forsaken children under his care now gave him an opportunity to test his educational theories.

In his later years he was visited and consulted by many political and educational leaders who recognized him as one who had demonstrated the worth of his educational ideas.

Around 1860 Edward A. Sheldon of the Oswego, New York, Normal School introduced the new Pestalozzian procedures to American teachers. The school was visited by leading educators from all parts of the United States, and it has been said that within 20 years the "Oswego movement" had completely reshaped instruction in the better elementary schools throughout America.

the children get real and clear ideas instead of mere words and hazy notions. The teacher became an active instructor of groups of children instead of a hearer of individual recitations. Children were freed from the dominance of textbooks and given training in oral expression. In all subjects—geography, science, arithmetic—emphasis on training in oral expression was prominent.

Froebel: Emphasis on Social Participation and Self-activity

Friedrich Wilhelm Froebel was also influenced by Rousseau's educational ideas; he was attracted to the idea of educating children in harmony with their natural development. However, he was also greatly influenced by major "absolute idealist" philosophers of his time, who developed theories of life based on the idea that each person must seek some mystical union with the "Absolute" power (Idea) that they claimed governed the world and the universe. Thus Froebel, very unlike Rousseau, was a mystic; his theory of education emphasized the need for the student to seek cooperation with others and spiritual union with the powers that he believed governed the universe. Froebel believed, as did Rousseau and Pestalozzi, that formal education should begin as early in life as possible. He developed a new type of school for very young children that emphasized the self-activity of the young child in seeking to discover his or her own unique relationships to other people and to the world of which he or she was a part. Froebel's new type of school became known as the kindergarten, which in the original German meant literally "children's garden." Children were to grow, through teacher-coordinated self-activities, into a relationship of self-discovery and cooperative union with others. Since he had learned to teach under Pestalozzi's guidance, it is not surprising that Froebel emphasized the individuality of the student and the basic principle that all learning proceeds out of the individual's self-initiated activities. He believed that students should be given opportunities to engage in learning activities desgned to teach them the skills of social participation. He maintained that socal interaction as well as cognitive (intellectual) skills should be taught. Students needed freedom, individual attention, and opportunity to initiate (under the teacher's guidance) activities that would lead to knowledge and skill development.

Froebel always believed that his thoughts on education were as pertinent to the education of older students as they were to the education of younger ones. However, his views found their strongest audience with the teachers of very young students; thus his name is usually associated with early elementary-level forms of schooling.

Froebel thought that children naturally desire freedom of social interaction and that they learned best in situations or activities wherein they had the opportunity to initiate interaction with objects, ideas, or other people. He believed that children are inherently good. Self-initiated cognitive (intellectual) and psychomotor behavioral activity was for him the way a person achieved not only a sense of identity but all knowledge as well. In teaching preschool children he emphasized rhythms, music, singing, creative dramatics, handicrafts, drawing, painting, modeling with clay, collecting art specimens or objects of nature, growing plants, bringing animals to school, and suitably equipped playgrounds. Children were to learn through teacher-designed and teacher-coordinated activities that were specifically developed to enhance intellectual, emotional, and psychomotor development. His most famous book is *The Education of Man.*

When Froebel's ideas were applied by American educators they used all his forms of teaching activity, but they eliminated from those activities the mysticism that Froebel had built into them. His views on teaching had great impact on the conduct of elementary schooling in America.

Herbart: Education in How to Think

Johann Friedrich Herbart was a German philosopher who became one of the greatest pedagogical theorists and practitioners of all time. He is most famous in educational thought for two great contributions: an original psychology of learning (which is, of course, now dated but which was a great contribution in nineteenth-century thought) and the development of a system of instruction that enabled teachers to draw systematically on and to relate to the experiences of their students.

Herbart was born in 1776 and died in 1841, having received his doctoral degree in 1802 at the University of Göttingen in Germany. In 1809 he was invited to take the professorial chair in philosophy and pedagogy at the University of Königsberg, a position that had once been held by the illustrious philosopher Immanuel Kant. In 1833 he returned to the University of Göttingen, where he remained until his death in 1841. He first became interested in psychology and then, as a natural related interest, in pedagogy (the theory of teaching and learning). Earlier in his career he had been for about 2 years a private tutor to the three sons of the governor of Interlaken in Switzerland. Some have said that this experience was a major factor in Herbart's later fascination with the problems of teaching and learning.

His psychology of learning was based on the idea that from infancy onward each person receives and develops percepts (perceived experience or sense-data) of ideas and objects that become translated, via the vehicle of human language, in a person's consciousness into concepts, each of which is composed of these percepts. As a person perceives reality and develops percepts of what he observes these percepts become the bases for all the ideas or concepts learned by the person. Herbart then hypothesized that the mind categorizes different types of percepts and concepts into differing masses of related ideas or associations. The mind then was thought to apperceive, or to understand fully, ideas by comparing these ideas to related ones. These clusters of related ideas in one's consciousness drawn from the perceived experience of a person were then referred to as "apperceptive masses." His psychology of apperception, as it was called, was based on an effort to explain human learning through the phenomena of perception and experience. All human concepts or ideas, Herbart maintained, are the result of human perception of the environment and the attempt to find relationships and differences between the phenomena of experience. Herbart's psychology of learning (apperception) was very popular in America in the very late nineteenth century and the early twentieth century. It was taught in most American teacher education institutions in the 1890s and the first decade of this century until more advanced behavioral theories of learning were developed. Charles De Garmo, Charles A. McMurray, and Frank M. McMurray were the leading American exponents of Herbartian theories of learning and teaching.

The indirect influence of Herbart's educational thought on American education continues to the present, as will be evident in our discussion of his theory of teaching. Herbart's ideas led to the first development of the sorts of systematic lesson plans that we know today, based on clearly designated steps of instruction and on the experience of the learner. Herbart and his European and American interpreters were also the major developers of the concept of the unit of instruction in a course of study. (A unit of study is a series of interrelated but sequentially arranged lessons on one particular topic.) Thus Herbart's ideas and writings on the problems of teaching, especially as they were interpreted and modified by his European and American interpreters, constituted one of the most significant contributions to thought about the theory and practice of teaching.

Herbart's model of instruction was designed to move learners beyond memorization to interpretation of perceived objects and experiences and to encourage students to attempt to make defensible, reasoned judgments or generalizations. It was based on the idea that the teacher would decide what was to be taught and the conclusions to be arrived at, but the teacher would lead students through certain stages of instruction in which they would have to reason on their own and relate the new knowledge being taught to their own experiences. His theory of the classroom recitation did not consist merely of random questions from the teacher and student responses to them. Instead he broke the instructional process into four stages: (1) preparation, (2) presentation, (3) comparison, and (4) conclusion or generalization. His interpreters extended his model to include a fifth step, which was (5) application. Herbart's goal was to encourage reflection and conceptual analysis in the classroom in addition to any necessary memorization or association of ideas. His followers did not always achieve his goals, but his intent was clear.

In the "five formal steps of instruction," as they came to be known to American teachers, the emphasis was on reasoning with and understanding ideas and objects, on apperceiving their meaning and significance. Students were to be prepared for a new lesson by the teacher trying to get them to think of experiences they had had that could be related to the new knowledge and/or skills about to be taught. Next a statement of the purpose of the new material to be learned was formulated by the class. Then followed the steps of presentation of new ideas, objects, or skills to be taught and the comparison of the new knowledge with that which had already been learned. Whenever possible, students were required to develop some defensible general statement on the significance of what had been learned and then to apply it as best they could to situations or problems with which they had had some experience.

One additional point about the five formal steps of the recitation should be emphasized. The steps applied to the teacher's preparatory work as well as to the actual manner in which the recitation would be conducted. The teacher had not only previously gained a mastery of the subject matter, but had also, through careful advance work, arranged an approach that would enable him to conduct the recitation in a manner best suited to cultivating thought. The teacher would carefully prepare by thinking through what might be done in each of the five steps. He or she would need to review: What do my pupils already know? What questions shall I ask in order to bring out what they know and think? What aids shall I use? What incidents shall I relate? What are the difficulties some of the pupils may have? What conclusions should be reached?

Through preparation the teacher was freed from any necessity of further study during the recitation and was able to focus entirely on skillfully conducting the recitation. The teacher could be flexible, teach as the occasion demanded, and still end with some order and organization in what had been learned by the pupils. He or she did not intend blindly to formalize the recitation into a pattern of five steps. Rather, it could be modified as needed by a teacher alert to the opportunities for stimulating pupil thought. In interpreting Herbart's principle this point should always be kept in mind.

Herbart's efforts have had a great and wholesome influence. For the first time, trained schoolteachers generally realized the importance of turning periods for reciting into periods for stimulating and directing reflection. In fact, in the modern school, perhaps because of Herbart's emphasis on thinking as an important part of teaching, the very word "recitation" has disappeared from current educational vocabulary.

Learning from Experience

The educational views of the famous educators discussed in this chapter encouraged the idea that learning is most effective when it is related to the experience of the learner. Each of these writers had a different approach to this theme, but this is an important element in their views nonetheless. The educational thoughts of the authors whose views were discussed in this chapter represent major attitudes toward the education of children and adolescents that were to be modified and developed in twentieth-century American educational thought.

John Dewey was to write in 1916 that,

> We thus reach a technical definition of education: It is that reconstruction or reorganization of experience which adds to the meaning of experience, and which increases ability to direct the course of subsequent experience.[3]

Dewey was to call for a much more open-ended form of inquiry than that advocated by Herbart, one in which the teacher would not predetermine the conclusions of student inquiry and one in which a greater degree of democratic social consciousness would be called for than Herbart advocated. Nonetheless, Herbart's conception of instruction was a major breakthrough in advancing thought about instruction. There were other major differences between John Dewey and the authors discussed in this chapter regarding the nature of interest and "effort" in education and regarding the specific social uses toward which inquiry in classroom settings should be aimed. But the basic idea that learning proceeds best when related to the experience of the learner became a dominant theme in twentieth-century American education.

[3] John Dewey, *Democracy and Education*. New York: Macmillan, 1916, pp. 89–90.

Humanistic Views of Childhood

There are several conceptions of humanism in Western culture, some of the basic origins of which in classical educational traditions we explored in Chapter 7. However, it can be said that from the time of Comenius on there was a slow but steady recognition among major educational theorists of the need for a more humane conception of the nature of childhood. Progress in the reform of education seems to be relatively slow. Most schools remained harsh places in which to learn, or at least places where student concerns often were not dealt with as the authors discussed in the present chapter would have recommended. Relatively few educators hastened to adopt Comenius's educational recommendations in his own time. Yet as at least a partial result of the educational thoughts of the authors discussed in the present chapter, there developed an awareness of the idea of educating children and adolescents with more attention to their needs, interests, experience, and stages of development. This set the foundations for more scientific and humane views regarding the conduct of schooling in America in the twentieth century. This is not to say that all schools in America are humane places in which to learn; this is clearly not true, and some schools are more pleasant or more harsh places in which to be a student than others. But the conception of childhood and adolescence as developmental stages took root in the ideas of the authors whose views we have considered.

Differing Ways of Structuring Knowledge

Out of the development of the seven liberal arts of Greece and Rome, European civilization developed in the medieval, Renaissance, and early modern periods the basic disciplines of knowledge we know today. Such disciplines as history, literature, law, theology, medicine, biology, chemistry, physics, and so on, emerged as well-respected areas of study with their own methodologies of inquiry by the end of the nineteenth century. Centuries of development of schooling along classical literary lines made it difficult for the newer social sciences, such as sociology, economics, and anthropology, to find places in the curricula of American secondary schools in the twentieth century. Thus renewed interest has developed in recent years in alternative ways to develop interdisciplinary studies in elementary and secondary schools in America to make some room for all the disciplines of knowledge that might be relevant to becoming an educated person in a technologically and industrially advanced society.

It is difficult for us to imagine now, but true nonetheless, that the social sciences as we know them are basically the products of renewed scientific interest in the problems of humanity in society in the mid- and late nineteenth century. The social sciences were not well established in American universities until the late nineteenth century and, as noted, are relatively recent additions to secondary school curricula.

From the time of Aristotle onward philosophers and other scholars have disputed what ought to be the sequence and structure of school studies. Each of the authors discussed in this chapter was concerned about the problem of what ought to constitute the studies of students. Each developed a different solution to the problem. In the decade of the 1960s considerable controversy reemerged about what ought to be the criteria for structuring and sequencing subject matter in the elementary and secondary schools. This is a problem in the study of teaching that will probably always be debated. What we need to be aware of is that none of the writers discussed in the present chapter had any quarrel with the academic disciplines of their time; their quarrel was with the methods used to teach the disciplines. They called for more humane ways of perceiving and treating the learner, not for an abandonment or retreat from the quest for learning.

Summary

This chapter has been concerned with a brief discussion of a few of the great contributors to our thought about the practice of education. It is not intended as a comprehensive discussion of this subject. That task would require the writing of a comprehensive history of Western educational thought, and this volume is not intended as a history of education. Moreover, no claim is being made that other educational thinkers were not equally deserving of treatment in such a chapter. There are many great contributors to our thought about the nature, aims, and methods of education in the more than 340 years since Comenius published *The Great Didactic*. Spatial limitations required great selectivity. The ideas of each of the writers discussed in this chapter had great impact on the development of American elementary and secondary education. Their views on the aims and methods of educating are generally recognized as having had great influence in preparing the way for the scientific and logical conduct of inquiry into the problems of learning and schooling characteristic of present-day educational research in America.

QUESTIONS

1. Can you remember any of your former teachers using any methods of teaching that seemed to resemble the Herbartian "five formal steps of instruction"?
2. What similarities or differences can you identify in the points of view of the authors discussed in this chapter?
3. Why do you suppose Herbart's psychology and theory of teaching were so popular in America? Why did his followers have such a long-term, if indirect, influence on the development of instructional methods in America?
4. Which of the authors discussed in this chapter conducted experimental schools to try out their ideas?
5. How have our ideas about the nature of childhood been influenced by the views of the authors discussed in this chapter?

PROJECTS

1. Do an in-depth review of the literature on the conception of teaching advocated by one of the authors whose views were dealt with in this chapter.
2. Do a written project contrasting the major differences between any two of the authors dealt with in this chapter regarding the role of the teacher and the freedom of the student.
3. Develop a report on what your views are regarding why change in educational methods and institutions is often so slow.
4. Develop a report on the origins of lesson plans and unit plans in American teacher education. Find out what you can about this topic and give your own interpretation of the data you find.

chapter
9

The frontier heritage

There are several conceptual frames of reference from which the development of the American republic and its formal educational institutions can be examined. Urbanization and industrialization would provide a framework for a one-chapter historical narrative concerning American education as fruitful as that provided by our frontier heritage. The retention of the frontier heritage frame of reference in the present edition of this volume should not be taken to imply that the "frontier thesis" of Frederick Jackson Turner, creative and useful as it may be, is being put forward as the only way to view American educational development. In Chapter 10, where a brief discussion of major elements of the concept of cultural pluralism in American educational development is found, an effort is made to point up the importance of the factors of urbanization and intergroup relations as equally useful categories for discussing education in America. The image of the frontier is carried through the discussion in the present chapter not to imply the superiority of the Turner thesis, but to point up the significance of America's having been a frontier society, which had lasting effects on its cultural development. Therefore the balance of the present chapter in this edition has been left basically intact.

America has been settled by successive waves of immigrants from all parts of the world, both in our history and in our prehistory. Moreover, the present authors are aware that there are many urban, technological, and other "frontiers'" in American history that are critically significant in understanding American social development. Some contemporary social trends affecting our understanding of American educational development in the present are taken up in Chapter 10 and in various sections of the chapters in the following two units of this volume.

The present educational system in the United States had its origin in the streams of thought that grew out of the great social movements of history and the theories expounded by European leaders. Both were adapted to frontier conditions and altered by pioneer thinking. Understanding the nature of those earlier European influences is crucial to any evaluation of education in the United States. It is equally impossible to make a sound assessment without first recognizing and appreciating the significance of features that were molded by the frontier movement. The broad outlines of the movement are known to most students, but its direct influence on modern American education is not always fully understood. It is important to focus attention on the effects of the movement, on the character of what is perhaps America's largest social undertaking, its educational program.

The migration to America was only one of the numerous migrations of Europeans to many new, sparsely populated lands. Behind this European "invasion" lay one simple assumption, the assumption that the lands lying immediately ahead were free for the taking. This assumption was applied to the whole vast expanse of the American continent. It was the backbone of a philosophy of the people and resulted in one of the most dramatic population movements in all history. Its effects on educational policy in the United States are inestimable.

As the frontier continually moved westward from the first settlements on the Atlantic coast, it was marked not only by the development of new areas but also by a return to primitive conditions for the settlers. American social development was continually beginning again on the frontier. American life achieved a fluidity that was marked by a steady movement away from the influence of Europe, a steady growth in independence, a reliance on American strenuous endeavor, a remolding of the older ways of life.

The movement lasted nearly 250 years. Free land is not inexhaustible in a rapidly expanding population, and all exoduses end somewhere and at some time. Historians generally record 1890 as the year when almost all free lands in the United States had been settled. Thus the movement ended. However, the values established in the frontier period continue to be cherished, continue to influence the thinking and determine the action of modern Americans, who are part of the postfrontier period. The philosophy of the frontier was adaptable to rapidly changing conditions. That kind of adaptation is still in process. Educational institutions, and especially American educational philosophy, today reflect clearly the continuing influence of the philosophy of the frontier.

The Philosophy of the Frontier

Love of Freedom

The frontier brought about changed relationships between individuals and their neighbors. In crowded Europe the density of the population in 1500 was about 27 persons per square mile, or something like 24 acres of land, good and bad, for each person. On the frontier in America there was plenty of room and all the land one might wish to occupy. This meant release for the individual. The way of living began to reflect a hitherto unknown independence built on the challenge of opportunities, the privilege of choice. Individuals had freedom. Their biggest responsibility was to learn how to make the most intelligent use of the freedom they had more or less by accident become heir to. We do not pretend that the individual always used this newly discovered independence wisely. Ideas of democratic government, sometimes extravagant exploitation of natural resources, unconventional forms of behavior, rude manners, raw language, and the like, attest to the fact that the individual did not always make the best use of freedom. The point is that the new frontier conditions granted individuals a degree of freedom that they had never known before, and their knowledge that they had this freedom changed both their ideals and their fundamental social beliefs. In time, the ideal of freedom of the individual became strong, and, as the meaning was made clearer, it became a cherished guide to action.

The pioneer's esteem for freedom resulted in a reliance on individual intelligence. Pioneers did not want someone to tell them what to do. They believed that the application of their own intelligence, whether trained or not, was the best method of arriving at conclusions.

They did not have to appeal to the judgment of someone higher up in seeking a solution to problems. Their intelligence was sharpened by constant application to numerous everyday practical problems, some of which involved their very survival.

Freedom to arrive at their own conclusions and to use their own solutions led the frontier people to place a high value on the opportunity to develop their intelligence, to use it in solving the problems of life and in advancing their own material welfare. Freedom was a gift that, to them, became a right. Only through the development of intelligence could they learn to use freedom wisely.

Freedom of intelligence became a kind of religion. As the philosopher and essayist Ralph Waldo Emerson (1803–1882) said in his essay on self-reliance,

> Who would be a man, must be a non-conformist. He who would gather immortal palms must not be hindered by the name of goodness, but must explore if it be goodness. Nothing is at last sacred but the integrity of your own mind. Absolve you to yourself, and you shall have the suffrage of the world.

What kind of school would such freeedom-loving people build? What happened to the freedom philosophy as the frontier moved westward and civilization advanced? As schools become systematized in a developing civilization, must a degree of freedom be correspondingly relinquished? How much freedom must the average citizen surrender, and what methods should be used to achieve the surrender as the educational system develops and as smaller educational units are integrated into larger units? The frontier American cherished freedom, and established a halo of inviolability about it. How are those highly cherished, lasting, and theoretically desirable attitudes to be acknowledged as a new type of education develops under changed and still rapidly changing social conditions?

Regard for the Individual

The picture of the pioneer as a lonely, isolated individual is largely a myth. Pioneers had families and were members of a group. The pioneer was just as interested in having standing with other members of the group as would have been the case in a European setting. The difference was that on the frontier, standing depended on different factors—not so much on ancestors, education, or even money as on success in adjusting to the environment and in triumphing over current

His supreme generalization [Frederick Jackson] Turner presented in an address delivered in Chicago in 1893, entitled "The Frontier in American History." Within a few years his generalization became the most influential single interpretation of American history. Hundreds of disciples, inspired by Turner, diffused it in every section of the continent; and in time Turner was called to Harvard, under the presidency of Charles W. Eliot.

What had Turner said at Chicago? He had declared that the frontier and free land accounted for the characteristics that differentiated the evolution of society in the United States from the evolution of society in the Old World: "The existence of an area of free land, its continuous recession, and the advance of American settlement westward, explain American development." The statement, in its unqualified simplicity, was categorical and sweeping. Apparently Turner believed that if it had not been for the advancing frontier, for the free land on the frontier, if the English colonists had been hemmed in on the Atlantic seaboard, American development would have followed European patterns. If this was his belief, then American civilization, without the advancing frontier, would have duplicated the European process of civilization, at least in its main stream. . . .

This, however, had not been the main course of American history: "American development has exhibited not merely advance along a single line, but a return to primitive conditions on a continually advancing frontier line, and a new development for that area. American social development has been continually beginning over again on the frontier. This perennial rebirth, this fluidity of American life, this expansion westward with its new opportunities, its continuous touch with the simplicity of primitive society, furnish the forces dominating American character. . . . The frontier is the line of most rapid and effective Americanization. . . . The advance of the frontier has meant a steady movement away from the influence of Europe, a steady growth of independence on American lines. And to study this advance, the men who grew up under these conditions, and the political, economic, and social results of it, is to study the really American part of our history."*

* Charles A. Beard and Mary R. Beard, *The American Spirit*. New York: Macmillan, 1942, vol. IV, pp. 360–361.

vicissitudes, and on effectiveness in helping the group to do likewise. The pioneers were not satisfied with a new culture that would barely meet their biogenic needs. They also strove for the satisfaction of bio-social needs, including that for prestige. They were highly sensitive, social creatures with a natural concern for what others thought of them.

Pioneers expected the respect of other individuals; they also expected to accord respect to other individuals. This was a natural corollary to their love for freedom. Freedom of the individual must include freedom to attain prestige and standing, which, in turn, depend on respect for individual personality. What did the pioneer's respect for the individual imply? It implied first a recognition that each individual is unique. It implied also an appreciation that each must be allowed to develop a pattern of living in a way that gives full recognition to the need for individuality and individual expression.

Rousseau would have felt at home in this kind of philosophical surrounding. The social soil that nourished the individual afforded limitless opportunity for self-development. It was thought that there was something incommensurable about every person and that every person should have the opportunity to develop his or her natural endowments.

The whole idea of forcing the individual to conform to a norm, of reducing everything to an average, of emphasizing the mediocre as a reasonable standard for all was discarded as an untenable social theory. It was argued, instead, that all individuals should be encouraged to develop to the limit of their capacities. People were, by nature, constituted differently. One person should be as highly respected as another. Since each was different from every other, the talents possessed by each should be developed differently from those of all the others.

On the frontier there were always more jobs to be done than there was help available. All individuals, regardless of natural design, had the opportunity to be of worth. The pioneer family developed a philosophy toward the individual that recognized that worth. Everyone should and did respect the inherent worth of the individual.

Belief in Equality

Égalité is the French word for "equality." Under the influence of Thomas Paine and Thomas Jefferson, egalitarianism became a highly favored philosophy in the new land. Paine was a clever journalist, usually remembered as the author of an essay written during the French Revolution called "The Rights of Man." Jefferson, too, could write with compelling force. He was the author of the Declaration of Independence.

The attitude of frontier people was expressed in the Declaration of Independence and reiterated in the Bill of Rights. In essence, the American spirit was pledged to an extension of equality. Equality, it was held, was essential to the maintenance of the general welfare of the people and to raising the level of well-being of every American citizen.

Regard for the individual—with its implied appreciation of individual differences and recognition of individual needs for social standing—was woven into a philosophy broadly based on the principle of equality. On the frontier all people were important; each person had a significant job to do, and the worth of each was taken for granted. As the frontier moved westward, the pioneer expressed a belief in equality by insisting on universal suffrage. Property restrictions on voting were removed. Women got their first chance to vote on the frontier. The common person, whether educated or not, was elected to the highest offices.

As the nation developed, educators were constantly faced with the question, What does egalitarianism mean when incorporated into educational practice? What does it mean in terms of educational opportunity and in terms of teaching in the classroom? In the lands from which pioneers had come, it was held that people were unequal and that they should be educated as unequals. It called for thought and courageous action to build new schools and to follow new practices consistent with a philosophical position almost the reverse of that assumed by most leaders in other lands.

Faith in Oneself

The pioneer's love for freedom, respect for the personality of others, recognition of individual worth, and devotion to egalitarianism had certain correlative values. One of these was a deep and abiding faith in each person's ability to meet all problems. The pioneer possessed an almost unlimited and unbounded optimism. This is an attitude in sharp contrast to the pessimism that prevailed around 1700 among the individuals of Europe and that is reflected in the literature of such writers as Dryden, Swift, and Montaigne. Faith in oneself and one's future was a pronounced characteristic of the pioneer.

Faith in the Common Person

Life on the frontier also deepened the pioneer's faith in the common or average person. Once the door of opportunity was opened, common people proceeded to build a new nation. So great was their success that the European critics of the new American civilization, the European aristocratic leaders who had expressed misgivings about the ability of common people to build a great civilization, were confounded. To the pioneer, who believed that the worth and welfare of every citizen was important, the achievements of the common people forcefully verified his confidence. The pioneer simply assumed that the common people could achieve a stable government; develop and diffuse the material necessities of a civilized life; create literature, art, and music; develop education, recreation, and health—in short, do whatever was important for making life worthwhile. He had a boundless faith in the possibilities of himself and every normal person if adequately encouraged and wisely influenced. This faith in the intelligence of the common individual has often been expressed by liberal philosophers who have advanced the principle that the individual can, if he or she strives to do so, make an almost limitless advance toward perfectibility. This is true because human beings possess individually and collectively an almost infinite capacity for making new discoveries and for adapting knowledge to improving the quality of living. Like the pioneers, liberal philosophers today believe that human beings possess the intelligence to achieve in an almost unlimited degree. They need most to learn how to use that intelligence wisely. It is an important responsibility of education to develop that intelligence, not in a select few, but in all.

Belief in the Value of Work

Out of the experiences of the frontier a high regard for the disciplinary value of work developed in America. To the pioneer the value of actual work in educating the boy or girl was equal or superior to the training received in formal education. Somewhat like the Athenians, the boy and girl on the frontier were educated most by living and working with others. The future of a boy or girl who would not work was in jeopardy. It was work that brought a measure of unity into life and was considered the source of all enduring satisfactions. Not to *earn* one's living was like being a traitor to one's country. It followed, then, that a proper education of the young called for opportunities for the young to work, which they were given. Forcing or allowing the young to be idle was tantamount to leading them into paths of wickedness. From this came the now fully accepted principle of education that an individual develops more rapidly and more wholesomely when he is faced with and assumes responsibility. The pioneer believed that education should be essentially practical, that it should have a direct relation to building character. The idea of education for ornament, for superficial polish, was rejected as appropriate only to a leisure class.

Faith in the Common School

As schools became a necessity on the frontier, the ideas about education that the settlers brought with them were modified and incorporated into new practices. It cannot be said that the early frontierpeople believed strongly in formal education, but it is clear that some of the leaders did. Many expressed a conviction that the common school was the hope of our country.

Settlers in the earliest New England frontier communities unknowingly established a lasting pattern for educational organization in the United States. The unit of educational organization, the local school, was controlled and supported by the community. The one-room school that eventually led to one of America's most lasting, sentimentalized pictures—the "Little Red Schoolhouse"—was established in almost every community. It displayed inevitable and flagrant weaknesses, but it symbolized, nevertheless, the pioneer's acceptance of a plan to give children the benefits of a formal education. It was a manifestation of the belief held by most of the frontier leaders that a school was necessary to raise the level of American civilization.

This small school, meager in outlook and thwarted by the inadequacy of available teachers, was nevertheless the kind of educational institution that fitted admirably with the conditions and spirit of the time. It was a *little* school, close to the people it served. It was controlled locally by those who had complete confidence in their own vision and their own skill in management. It was supported locally. It truly belonged to the people it served. The influence of the traditions built up around this little school, the idea of neighborhood schools, local control of the school, and local support took a firm hold on the hearts and minds of all early Americans.

In studying the manner in which education is now conducted in the United States and in evaluating the paths being advocated for its future progress, it is important always to be conscious of the persistent philosophies of life and of education that were a natural and unquestioned part of the beliefs and attitudes of the frontier. The pioneer's faith in the common person, regard for the worth of the individual, belief in equality and freedom, and confidence in the common school are a significant heritage directly related to the qualities that make our present schools unique and culturally characteristic.

Education on the Frontier

It is well known that the American frontier movement was one part of a series of events—the conquest of a new continent, the planting of colonies, the conflicts between the incoming Europeans and the American red man, the fighting among Europeans for control of the new continent, the fight of new settlers for their independence, and the establishment of a new nation. From the very first arrival of settlers, civilization moved steadily westward. As the nation expanded, sectionalism—the identification of the people of one section of the country with that section rather than with the nation as a whole—nurtured competition for control of the west. New lands were exploited.

What sort of educational plans did the frontiersmen make as they adjusted to the conditions of westward expansion? By examining briefly some details of the educational experiences of the Puritans and the Massachusetts colony we can see, in some measure, how the frontier philosophy, in its early form, was put into action.

Puritan Education

In discussing Puritan education, we deal with the Puritanism of the American frontier, not, for example, the English Puritanism of John Ruskin, who defended puritanical ethics thus: "Observe, then, this Puritanism in the worship of beauty . . . is always honourable and amiable and the exact reverse of the false Puritanism which consists in the dread or disdain of beauty."

Within a few years after 1628, when the Puritans obtained a charter to establish a colony on the land between the Merrimack and Charles rivers, a large group of immigrants had settled in the colony of Massachusetts Bay. Many of the settlers were middle-class businessmen and country gentlemen who belonged to a religious group known as Puritans. Although these people were dissatisfied with the Church of England and wanted to "purify" it of the elements to which they objected, they were actually sufficiently conditioned to life in a church that for decades had been identified with the state, so that a shadow of ecclesiastical despotism was cast over the government they set up in the New World.

The Puritans believed that the principal reason education was necessary was to enable one to read the Bible. Of the many effects

Seven-year-old Abe walked four miles a day going to the Knob Creek School to learn to read and write. Zacharia Piney and Caleb Hazel were the teachers who brought him along from ABC to where he could write the name "A-b-r-a-h-a-m L-i-n-c-o-l-n" and count numbers beginning with one, two, three, and so on. He heard twice two is four. The school house was built of logs, with a dirt floor, no window, one door. The scholars learned their lessons by saying them to themselves out loud till it was time to recite; alphabets, multiplication tables, and the letters of spelled words were all in the air at once. It was a "blab school"; so they called it.

. . .

A few days of this year in which the cabin was building, Nancy told Abe to wash his face and hands extra clean; she combed his hair, held his face between her two hands, smacked him a kiss on the mouth, and sent him to school— nine miles and back—Abe and Sally hand in hand hiking eighteen miles a day. Tom Lincoln used to say Abe was going to have "a real eddication," explaining, "You are a-goin' to larn readin,' writin,' and cipherin.' "

He learned to spell words he didn't know the meaning of, spelling the words before he used them in sentences. In a list of "words of eight syllables accented upon the sixth," was the word "incomprehensibility." He learned that first, and then such sentences as "Is he to go in?" and "Ann can spin flax."

Some neighbors said, "It's a pore make-out of a school," and Tom complained it was a waste of time to send the children nine miles just to sit with a lot of other children and read out loud all day in a "blab" school. But Nancy, as she cleaned Abe's ears in corners where he forgot to clean them, and as she combed out the tangles in his coarse, sandy black hair, used to say, "Abe, you go to school now, and larn all you kin." And he kissed her and said, "Yes, Mammy," and started with his sister on the nine-mile walk through timberland where bear, deer, coon, and wildcats ran wild.*

* Carl Sandburg, *Abraham Lincoln: The Prairie Years.* New York: Harcourt Brace Jovanovich, 1926, pp. 19–20, 38–39.

the earlier attitudes of the Puritan leaders had on educational practice, perhaps the most enduring was on classroom methods of teaching.

From our present perspective we conclude that Puritanism led to a way of life narrow and petty in its formalism. Hard work, approaching slavishness, became a moral virtue. The arts were discouraged as needless and useless frills. Nurtured in such a soil, education sank to a low level. Traditional education was condemned as being associated with an aristocratic, idle, lazy type of citizenship. The Puritans felt that education as it had been conducted up to that time resulted in the creation of a class more ready to exploit than to serve, that it had acted as an alley of escape from the rigors of work, and that it did not adequately educate the pupil to meet conscientiously the requirements of a responsible and participant citizenship that the times demanded. It would be better for pupils to receive most of their education in the home under the guidance of watchful parents than

---

As visits and pleasure were interspersed with hard work for Robert, he developed rapidly in physique and in character, and by the time he was thirteen he had learned all that could be conveniently taught him at home and at Eastern View [a private elementary school]. Accordingly, by 1820, possibly before that year, Robert entered the Alexandria Academy. This had been established about 1785, and had been privileged to list Washington as one of its trustees. Occupying a one-story brick house on the east side of Washington Street, between Duke and Wolfe, the school was made free to all Alexandria boys after January, 1821. Here Robert met at their desks the boys with whom he had played in the fields, and here he came under the tutelage of William B. Leary, an Irishman for whom young Lee acquired enduring respect.

For approximately three years Robert studied the rudiments of a classical education under Mr. Leary. He read Homer and Longinus in Greek. From Tacitus and Cicero he became so well grounded in Latin that he never quite forgot the language, though he did not study it after he was seventeen. Later in life, he expressed deep regret that he had not pursued his classical course further. In mathematics he shone, for his mind was already of the type that delighted in the precise reasoning of algebra and geometry.*

* Douglas Southall Freeman, *R. E. Lee*. New York: Scribner, 1934, pp. 36–37.

to receive it in schools that divorced them from the values so highly respected in the home.

The Puritans put into practice what they thought were educational theories clearly dictated by the Scriptures. They modeled their laws to conform with these. Their educational philosophies harmonized completely with their religious convictions. In an atmosphere in which education was viewed so narrowly, superstition and ignorance thrived and opposition to learning in the schools flourished. They limited formal education to the study of reading, writing, and arithmetic at an elementary level. The principal textbook was a religious text for lay people known as *The New England Primer*. Teaching methods were primitive and grossly inefficient. Equipment was limited and neglected. At least two-thirds of the pupils' time was wasted or worse than wasted. At this distance the picture is, at best, dreary and discouraging. But the Puritan strain survived, and although some of the lasting effects on later philosophies have been harmful, some have been sound and helpful.

The emphasis of the Puritans on the principle that every future citizen should be a person who could read and write and cipher was antecedent to the acceptance in the United States of the principle that education should be compulsory. By 1918 each of the then 48 states had enacted a compulsory attendance law. Along with the increase in compulsory attendance went a gradual increase in the length of the school term. The school year averaged only 130 days in 1870, but by 1950 it had reached its present average—about 180 days.

The insistence of the Puritans on shaping elementary education so that it would contribute to building character gave an ethical em-

At that time [1830] there were no free schools in Ohio, but Georgetown, like many other communities, had a subscription school—so called because the parents of the scholars subscribed various sums for the support of the teacher. In this school a Professor John D. White, for three months in a year, scattered knowledge to his pupils as one scatters crumbs to sparrows. The crumbs were poor in quality and few in number, but this meant nothing to Ulysses, whose intellectual hunger was easily satisfied. The simple curriculum consisted of reading, writing, arithmetic, and nothing else.*

* W. E. Woodward, *Meet General Grant.* New York: Liveright, 1955, p. 16.

phasis to classroom teaching that still permeates both the theory and the practice of teaching in the elementary schools. Behavior is one of the uppermost concerns of every present-day elementary classroom teacher.

The emphasis the Puritans gave to reading, and especially to the reading of the Bible, and their insistence that the reader be given freedom to interpret what he read according to his personal values paved the way for the belief that a similar freedom should be granted in the whole world of thought. Freedom to think and freedom to act in terms of one's own thinking led to an emphasis in education on granting freedom and on teaching pupils to use this privilege wisely. Building habits of self-direction and achieving self-control became the abiding aims of the elementary schools. Such values are still cherished. In current professional literature we read that every citizen should be an enlightened citizen, that education in the schools should stress the building of good character, and that those of stronger character are those who have learned the lessons of self-direction and self-control and have learned to act in the light of a progressively more insightful intelligence that has been trained to think and to act. These effects of the Puritan doctrine have been deemed good, and they have been lasting.

Some effects of the Puritan influence that were also potent and lasting are now considered to be negative and unfortunate when viewed from the perspective of modern educational theory. The Puritans had a deep-seated belief in the efficacy of coercion and punishment to promote learning. It was assumed that children could never learn anything of their own volition. Their own interests were considered worthless. Teachers were to force the child to learn, using severe and vindictive methods of punishment as the chief instrument of motivation. As history so vividly shows, this philosophy was not only the philosophy of the teachers in the schools, but that of the whole of the Puritan society. Punishment, whether administered in school or out, was an ethical social instrument admirably suited to building the kind of society the Puritans desired. Believing that coercion is the most effective method of promoting learning is not surprisingly backward in a society that as late as the seventeenth century put 32 persons to death, some by torture, because they were accused of practicing witchcraft.

The nature of subject matter, its arrangement, the equipment of the classroom—all reflected the same severe, authoritarian atmosphere. All subject matter was laid out in advance, and all pupils

were to master precisely the same material. The teacher's desk was
in front. Pupils faced the teacher, never one another. The whole process of education was harsh, sometimes inhumane. Pupils generally
developed a dislike for the teachers—a dislike often kept through
adulthood. Everything done conformed to narrow interpretations
placed on the meaning of the Scriptures, with the approval of the
most learned men of the times. On August 9, 1681, Cotton Mather
wrote in his diary:

> This day I took my second degree, proceeding Master of Arts.
> My Father was president, so that from his hand I received my de-
> gree. Tis when I am Gott almost half a year beyond eighteen, in
> my age. And all the circumstances of my commencement were
> ordered by a very sensibly inclined Providence of God. My Thesis
> was *Puncta Hebraica sunt Originis Divinae.* ["Hebrew vowel points
> are of divine origin."]

Not only were the attitudes toward education deep-seated, but because
Puritan Massachusetts was a colony of great influence its attitudes
and practices prevailed rather generally throughout the rest of the
New England colonies. The Puritans left enduring traditions, some
of which can still be identified in many parts of the nation. This is,
perhaps, because wave after wave of the descendants of the Puritans
moved westward with the frontier until it reached the Pacific.

Education in Massachusetts

Some features of the educational experiences of the Massachusetts
colony are particularly significant because it was Massachusetts that,
early in American history, initiated certain educational legal principles
that have endured.

Massachusetts Bay towns sent deputies to represent them in the
General Court, as the legislature was called. This General Court,
which met in Boston, in 1642 enacted what is probably the first school
law to be passed in what afterward became the United States. Officers
chosen in the local town were empowered to find out whether parents
and schoolmasters were teaching the children "to read and understand
the principles of religion and the capital laws of the country" and
to levy a fine on those who failed to report on these matters when
required. As it worked out, a new legal principle toward education
was established by the law—namely, that *the education of children
is a proper subject for legal control.* Thus a first step was taken toward
building a legal system of education in the United States. In a law

passed in 1647, the General Court strengthened this principle. The student will profit from reading this law (page 244), as it contains a clear expression of both the Puritan theory and an early frontier attitude toward education.

The principle established by the two Massachusetts laws was generally accepted throughout the colonies. The Massachusetts plan of leaving control and support of the schools to the citizens was inefficient when local interest in maintaining good schools declined. The frontier practice of having small school districts had, however, become established. As we shall see later, largely because of deep-seated tradition no problem in education has, through the years, been more difficult to cope with than the problem of organizing state school districts logically. As pointed out in Unit III, it is only in recent years that progress has been made in solving this thorny problem.

Gradually, the small, local school districts in Massachusetts became centers of selfish political activity. Election of school committeemen, location of school sites, and payment of teachers' salaries became intense local political issues. Poor districts remained poor. The richer districts fought any action that would assign them a part in alleviating the weaknesses of the poorer districts. Poor districts, settled by poor people, were expected to have poor schools. Since poor districts greatly outnumbered wealthy districts, the typical school of the day was a poor one. It was only after poor schools in Massachusetts became so numerous as to constitute a disgrace that a reform movement set in.

In 1826 the state of Massachusetts passed a law that required every town to choose a school committee that would have general charge of *all* the schools within the town. The authority of this school committee extended to the selection of the textbooks, examination and certification of teachers, and other matters that hitherto had been left to the jurisdiction of the local school committee, which had authority over only one school in a town. The first significant step in regeneration of the schools had taken place. Control of and supervision over all the schools in a town had become centralized under a single authority. Thus was begun the policy of organizing school units into a school system. The reform movement had begun too late to change greatly the educational practices that by then had become fixed and had spread as the frontier moved westward to other colonies and to other states. The evil had mounted, and it would take a long time to eradicate its effects.

It is well to note, at this point, that efforts to regenerate education have many times been significantly influenced by farsighted laymen as distinguished from professional educators. The law of 1826 was a result of a vigorous, personally waged campaign conducted by James G. Carter (1795–1849), a skilled parliamentarian who had become deeply concerned over the flagrant evils that he, and many others, recognized were sucking the remaining lifeblood from the degenerate public school system. Once Carter got the reform movement started, regeneration of the schools continued. Instances of lay leadership to improve public education in the United States have been common in most of the states and throughout the history of American education. Lay leadership was, and still is, one of the sources of strength of American public education.

In 1837 the Massachusetts legislature created the first state board of education. The board had eight members appointed by the governor. Its function was to gather information about education in the state and to make recommendations to the legislature. The board employed a secretary to study the needs of the schools, point out these needs to the public, diffuse other information about the schools, and help the board formulate its recommendations to the state legislature. The first secretary was a lawyer, Horace Mann (1796–1859), whose achievements have captured the admiration of all succeeding generations interested in education.

In the law of 1837, Massachusetts had contributed another principle to the building of an educational system in the United States: *School administration is a branch of public administration.* The state is the unit of school administration and organization. It is the supreme authority. It can determine the conditions under which local schools operate. The implications of this principle, now accepted throughout the nation, are very wide and are not fully realized even today. (Some of the implications are discussed more fully in a later chapter.) Once Massachusetts accepted the principle and created a state authority over its schools, regeneration proceeded rapidly, and it has continued to the present time.

The Massachusetts story is but one example of how the social processes that built our national system of education during the frontier period and made a public school district a corporate entity in social organization tended to operate. As would be expected, however, since each state is a unit of administration, in each state the story would be different in many respects from all the others. For instance, New York furnishes an excellent example of how education in America came to be secularized; Texas, an example of how free lands have influenced education; and California, an example of how nonmineral underground resources such as oil have contributed to the building of a great system.

Education in the South

Despite hardships and failures at its onset, Jamestown, Virginia, the first permanent English settlement in America, grew steadily. Within 13 years its population numbered 4000, and by 1700 as many as 100,000 people lived in Virginia. In 1693 William and Mary College, the second college founded in America, was established at Williamsburg, a short distance from Jamestown. Many citizens of Virginia were men of culture, wealth, and refinement. From their ranks came some of America's greatest earlier political statesmen.

In Virginia and subsequently in other southern states, the development of education followed a distinctive pattern. This pattern was considerably different from that of the middle colonies, such as Pennsylvania, or of the northern range of colonies, such as New York and Massachusetts. Perhaps the views of the earlier Virginia settlers were somewhat like those that Governor Berkeley reflected in his reply to the authorities in 1671. He thanked God that there were no free schools and no printing presses in the Province of Virginia, and expressed the hope that there would be none for 100 years. "Learning," he said, "has brought disobedience, and heresy, and sects into the world, and printing has divulged them, and libels against the best government. God keep us from both." It was in 1779 that Thomas Jefferson showed that he had an extremely different view when he suggested his educational plan "for a more general diffusion of knowledge" among the people of Virginia.

The southern colonies, it seems, were not markedly influenced by the educational viewpoints of either Berkeley or Jefferson. Instead they developed plans for education along lines dictated by economic and social conditions. Children in the southern colonies did not attend school as we think of school today. Large plantations, located far apart and supported by a system of slave labor, led to a distinctive pattern of living and a special kind of educational organization. The more affluent plantation owners employed private tutors to teach their children. Sometimes planters cooperated to build a small schoolhouse in which the children from several plantation families received instruction. Plantation owners, in general, believed that schools should not be provided at public expense for all children but only for the children of indigent or near-indigent families. The Church also separated those who could afford to pay for their education from those who could not by providing education for the poor and underprivileged. Those who were able to pay for the education of their children were expected to do so or suffer a decline in social prestige. In the southern colonies public education was definitely to meet the needs of the poor. In other sections of the country this came to be known as the charity conception of education. Such a conception virtually placed a stigma on public education. Actually the demands of work kept education away from a major part of the population. Negro slaves and poor whites were so occupied that only a few of them could take advantage of what school experiences were provided for them. The effects of this flagrant neglect are still felt throughout America.

As the American frontier moved westward, people in the newer sections were not strongly influenced by southern traditions and practices in education. Instead they tended to be influenced by the policies that had been developed in such states as New York and Massachusetts.

The Educational Heritage

Doctrine of Free Schools

It is important that we neither exaggerate nor underestimate the amalgamation of peoples in colonial days. At the time of the Revolution probably three-fourths to nine-tenths of the white colonists were still of British blood; but the infusion of Dutch, German, French, and other continental groups was significant. A basic unity of tongue and basic institutions coexisted with a remarkable diversity in national origins.

To assess all the contributions of the frontier to American education would not be feasible because it would require study of how the frontier affected the entire scope of American life, including not only its institutions but also the philosophy that guided the nation in establishing those institutions. It is practicable, however, to focus on public policy toward economic support of schools extending from the kindergarten through the university. This seems especially appropriate and fruitful because economic support of an institution is one of the major factors in shaping the character of the institution. Economic support not only marks certain boundaries and to an extent limits what can be accomplished, but is also a reliable reflection of the philosophy of the rank and file of the citizens. One may learn a great deal about people and nations by observing what they spend their money for.

The frontier philosophy toward human beings made the doctrine of free education inevitable and easy to accept. Jefferson, at this time the foremost political philosopher, forcefully expressed the doctrine of free education as early as 1779 in his "Bill for the More General Diffusion of Knowledge" as follows:

> . . . And whereas it is generally true that the people will be happiest whose laws are best and are best administered, and that laws will be wisely formed and honestly administered, in proportion as those who form and administer them are wise and honest; whence it becomes expedient for promoting the publick happiness, that those persons whom nature has endowed with genius and virtue should be rendered by liberal education worthy to receive and able to guard the sacred deposit of the rights and liberties of their fellow-citizens, and that they should be called to that charge without regard to wealth, birth, or other accidental condition or circumstance; but the indigence of the greater number disabling them from so educating, at their own expence, those of their children whom nature hath fitly formed and disposed to become useful instruments for the publick, it is better that such should be sought for and educated at the common expense of all, than that the happiness of all should be confined to the weak or wicked.[1]

Jefferson's words constitute a liberal statesman's understanding of democracy as it was interpreted and applied to education. The sentiments he expressed were subsequently voiced by political leaders in almost every section of the nation.

Free schools, however, must be paid for, and it is the contribution of the frontier to a policy of economic support that we are primarily concerned with at this point. How were free schools paid for?

Free Lands for a Free Education

Democracy seemed to demand free education. Theoretically, free education seemed ideal. Those who were unable to pay for education themselves, of course, favored it. Many of the richer people, however, objected to paying for the education of the children of other families. To them free education at public expense was a startling if not radical step toward national or state socialism.

The pioneers resolved the problem of school support by granting subsidies of land to finance education. The income from the land would largely, if not entirely, remove the burden of support for education from the backs of the American taxpayer. Since all 13 of the colonies prior to the American Revolution had granted land at one time or another for the support of schools, the citizens of the new

---

[1] As quoted in Paul Leicester Ford, *The Writings of Thomas Jefferson.* New York: Putnam, 1893, vol. II, pp. 220–221.

nation were accustomed to the subsidy idea. When the Revolution ended, all the lands owned by the Crown—and the extent of them was astounding—became the property of the states. Income from these lands relieved taxpayers of some of their responsibility for financing free public schools. How land subsidy for the support of public education operated in just one section of the nation, in what has been called the Northwest Territory, illustrates the principle of federal support for schools that has since become a permanent policy. This also illustrates the policy, still in operation, of recognizing that funds given to a school in the form of an endowment cannot subsequently be taken away. An institution might be financed indefinitely from the income of a grant.

When the colonies finally won their independence in 1781, the western boundary of the United States was the Mississippi River. The great expanse of land known as the Northwest Territory—land that has since been made into the states of Ohio, Michigan, Indiana, Illinois, and Wisconsin, and a part of Minnesota—became the property of the federal government. The federal government, forced to plan for the administration of this vast territory, expressed its policy in the well-known Land Ordinance of 1785 and the Northwest Ordinance of 1787. The Northwest Ordinance was to the frontier settlers of the territory what, later, the Constitution was to the states. It was the framework of their government. The statement of policy concerning school support was forthright and unequivocal. A precedent was established.

The Land Ordinance of 1785 provided that after the land was surveyed, 1 section (1 square mile) of every township (36 square miles) was given to the people to help support the schools. During the last days of the Congress of the Confederation, the Northwest Ordinance of 1787 was passed. This ordinance contained, in Article 3, the sentence that is accepted as the charter of public education in the United States: "Religion, morality, and knowledge, being necessary to good government and the happiness of mankind, schools and the means of education shall forever be encouraged."[2] In a second ordinance passed later in the same year, provision was made for the sale of the lands. This repeated the 1785 provisions reserving lands for public education. Any income received from the school lands, whether by sale or from rent, was earmarked for support of the schools. Thus even before the Constitution was adopted, a policy of federal

---

[2] As quoted in Henry Steele Commager, *Documents of American History*. Englewood Cliffs, N.J.: Prentice-Hall, 1934, vol. I, p. 131.

support of schools was established. The federal government has never since withdrawn from the practice of participating in subsidizing schools.

As states were formed in the new territory, the lands of the Northwest Territory became the property of the individual states under agreements with the federal government. Since the lands then belonged to the central territorial government, or to the state, the schools, too, were viewed as belonging to the established central government. The subsequent story of education in the United States is largely a picture of how states have operated the schools under their authority. It is now an accepted principle of American education that the state, not the local government, is the unit of school administration. This principle, however, does not rule out certain of the interests of the federal government. The entire problem of the organization of schools is discussed in detail in Unit III.

Higher Education

Frontier thinking about school support for free public education did not end with the elementary and secondary schools. The federal land-grant policy also provided for the building of colleges. In 1862 President Lincoln signed a bill known as the Morrill Act, which made generous gifts of federal lands to states for the purpose of establishing what have since become known as land-grant colleges. The Act provided that each state was to receive from the public domain 30,000 acres of land for each member it had in Congress. The proceeds from the lands were to be used in establishing agricultural and mechanical arts colleges. Free frontier land was a wedge sufficient to influence state legislatures to establish colleges that have since blossomed into some of the best and largest of America's universities. Subsequent acts have further fortified the principle that federal support should also be extended to institutions of college level.

Summary

The frontier movement was a vast social movement that nurtured some of America's lasting educational traditions. Traditions brought from Europe were changed or abandoned as frontiers people accommodated to a new civilization, a new way of life. Free schools, first supported through land grants and later through taxation, are important among the elements of our modern heritage from the frontier period.

As we proceed, it will become increasingly evident that the frontier has had a striking effect on present education. Contemporary problems of education still revolve largely around how best to modify traditions so that they are appropriate to modern social conditions. We must understand our educational heritage and make no attempt to divorce ourselves from the past. We must recognize that the past lives in the present and that the wisest plan is to recognize and strive to build on the past.

QUESTIONS

1. In what ways were the effects of the American frontier movement on both America and Europe of a reciprocal nature?
2. How did the fact that the frontier movement in America was continuous affect the development of education?
3. What social ideals currently esteemed by the American people are associated with frontier development? In your opinion, how should these ideals be modified in the light of modern conditions?
4. Which had the greater influence on the character of education developed by the Puritans, religion or social conditions?
5. Why did the legal principles adopted in Massachusetts have such wide influence throughout the United States?
6. What were some of the lasting effects on education in the United States that can be traced to the fact that the frontier moved rapidly?
7. What are some of the difficulties that confront modern educators in their attempts to formulate a postfrontier educational philosophy?

PROJECTS

1. Consult some standard work, such as an encyclopedia, for information on the meaning of Puritanism. Note the ways in which later generations have tended to interpret the Puritan and what he advocated. Point out inaccuracies in popular interpretations.
2. Trace the main events in the history of education in some typical state, such as New York. Note the nature of the issues that arose and how they were settled.
3. Cite several examples to show that the use of free lands operated to shape the course of American education.
4. Trace the historical steps in the origin of the Northwest Territory. Show why it became a great influence on subsequent education.
5. Trace the principal historical events in the westward advance of the frontier subsequent to the establishment of the Northwest Territory. Indicate the possible effects of each of the events on the development of education throughout the United States.

chapter

10

Some contemporary social concerns in American education

There has been widespread debate in recent years about whether the historical functions of the American public schools should be subjected to critical reevaluation and whether the underlying values of American educational institutions require revision. The policies of public education in the United States have frequently been topics of grave concern in American history. The present chapter outlines some of the major social concerns regarding educational development in America. In the previous chapter the discussion of the historical origins of educational development followed fairly closely the manner in which the story of American education has been summarized in the past. In the present chapter we synthesize as one major concern to present-day Americans another point of view that has arisen in recent years to challenge the traditional view of American educational development. There have been several important books published since 1968 that have taken this more critical "revisionist" point of view about American educational development. The present authors do not choose to take sides in this controversy, since this volume is a textbook for introductory studies in education and should not be too partisan. However, we do wish to synthesize the basic position of the new revisionist position in the interests of fairness and a balanced commentary. We describe the revisionist view of American educational history in the following section of the present chapter. Other major concerns regarding the social functions of American education center around the debate about excessive bureaucracy in the American educational system and the problems of guaranteeing equality of educational opportunity. There is also a discussion of cultural pluralism and the social concerns to be considered when taking into account the cultural diversity of the American population. Finally, there is a brief synthesis of some of the social concerns involved in the effort to seek clarification of American educational values. Although this chapter represents a broad synthesis of views on these matters, the matters discussed here are integral parts of American social and intellectual history. Each of these concerns has affected the others in some way.

Revisionist Interpretations of the Role of the School in American Society

The revisionist points of view regarding the development of American education that have emerged in recent years have held that public schools in the United States in the mid-nineteenth century and nineteenth- and twentieth-century "progressive" educators failed to achieve equal opportunity for all. The rationale for the establishment of tax-supported schools centered on the idea of guaranteeing equal opportunity to all citizens. (The reasons given for developing the public schools in America were outlined in the preceding chapter.) The revisionist scholars argue that although the rhetoric of the early and later school reformers was highly humane, the functions (actual effects) of the forms of schooling they established were conservative and directed toward preserving the status quo. The revisionist position of recent years also maintains that the public school reformers in the mid-nineteenth century, such as Horace Mann and Henry Barnard, developed the basic bureaucratic forms that operated to centralize educational power in American cities in the hands of small groups of educational reformers and professional educators.

The dream of nineteenth- and twentieth-century school reformers was to establish an educational system that would assure each citizen's maximum development. Revisionist scholars argue that the public schools, as they were established and organized, actually benefited the children of affluent families more than others and thus perpetuated social class lines.

Michael B. Katz's 1968 study[1] of the efforts to establish publicly financed schools in Massachusetts in the mid-nineteenth century initiated a reappraisal of the beginnings of public education in America. Since 1968 some most perceptive revisionist interpretations of the development of public education and compulsory school attendance laws in America have appeared. The revisionist authors generally hold that the leaders of the public school movement, or the "common school" movement as it was called in the mid-nineteenth century, tended, however unintentionally, to serve large corporate wealth and the status quo.

Katz's study of early school reform in Massachusetts motivated other scholars to reevaluate the effects of public education in America since the mid-nineteenth century. Two of these other revisionist studies were *Roots of Crisis: American Education in the Twentieth Century,*[2] by Clarence J. Karier, Paul Violas, and Joel Spring, and *The Great School Legend,*[3] by Colin Greer. The essays by Karier, Violas, and Spring emphasize the conservative motivations underlying attempts to reform public education in the United States in the twentieth century. They argue, as noted in the preceding paragraph, that the basic thrust of such progressive reformers as John Dewey in the field of education in the twentieth century actually served the interests of conservative groups in industry and government, although their rhetoric often tended to be quite liberal.

Colin Greer's study of the "great school legend" in America also points out that the romantic rhetoric of school reform groups often did not correlate with social reality in major American cities, where millions of recent immigrants to the United States lived in the late nineteenth and twentieth centuries. The traditional view was that the public school would become the "great equalizer," opening opportunity to all citizens. Greer maintains that the children of the immigrants

---

[1] Michael B. Katz, *The Irony of Early School Reform.* Cambridge, Mass.: Harvard University Press, 1968.

[2] Clarence J. Karier, Paul Violas, and Joel Spring, *Roots of Crisis: American Education in the Twentieth Century.* Chicago: Rand McNally, 1973.

[3] Colin Greer, *The Great School Legend.* New York: Basic Books, 1972.

survived and prospered in spite of the public schools, not because of them; he cites statistical data from several urban school systems to support his point.

There are other equally forceful statements of the revisionist position on the social effects of public education in America by these and other authors published in the 1960s and the 1970s, and they deserve careful attention. We have stated here only the most basic elements of the revisionist position. Exceptions may be taken with their arguments by opponents of their position, but future historical studies of American education or any serious studies of contemporary American education will have to take their views into account, for they are having a strong impact on contemporary discussions of American education.

We will close this brief introduction to the revisionist point of view about past and present American education with a brief reference to some points made by Katz in *Class, Bureaucracy, and Schools*[4] in which he makes some forceful arguments that are generally shared by other revisionist authors. In this study Katz maintains that the critical period in the bureaucratic development of American education was between 1800 and 1885. By 1885 the basic administrative structure of American cities, in which power was centralized in a small board of education, had become the standard way of governing large school systems in America. He argues that the basic organizational structure of American education has not changed since that time,[5] and he advocates greater decentralization of educational power as one condition for any true educational reform in America. He says, "Bureaucracy had produced educational bureaucrats by the third quarter of the nineteenth century."[6] Later he asserts, "Urban educational bureaucracies developed with local idiosyncrasies that make each unique in some ways, but they were all responses to the same kinds of pressure."[7] Katz then engages in an in-depth analysis of the development of the Boston school system's organizational structure and argues that contemporary educational bureaucracies reflect the general pattern of organizational structure established by 1885.

Katz and other revisionist scholars have argued that the progressive educational reformers of the late nineteenth and the twentieth

---

[4] Michael B. Katz, *Class, Bureaucracy, and Schools.* New York: Praeger, 1971.
[5] Ibid., pp. xix–xx.
[6] Ibid., p. 57.
[7] Ibid., p. 59.

centuries did not produce any great democratization of schooling, nor did they transform the public schools into a great equalizing factor in American life, in spite of their idealistic rhetoric to that effect. Katz says, "Progressivism did not fail to work a fundamental transformation in American schools; it did not even try."[8] Katz and the other revisionist authors have argued that the highly centralized, hierarchically structured, and highly rigid forms of interpersonal relations characteristic of older forms of bureaucratic organizational structure cannot be sufficiently responsive to the interests and requirements of culturally pluralistic populations in large cities. They have also argued that the highly centralized forms of urban school organization have encouraged existing social class structures in urban settings and removed the power to influence urban schools from the common people. They insist that more decentralized patterns of school control and governance must be established in contemporary America. Again Katz asserts, "Bureaucracy provides a segmented educational structure that legitimizes and perpetuates the separation of children along class lines and ensures easier access to higher-status jobs for children of the affluent."[9] He and other revisionist authors thus insist that many progressive school reforms actually benefited those people already possessed of status and affluence. The intent of such progressive reformers as John Dewey was humane and democratic. However, when translated into formal organizational settings administered by people who modeled their administrative behavior after corporate managerial models, the views of the reformers produced results that were not those desired.

It is hoped that the preceding account of the contemporary revisionist view of educational development in America will be seen as an attempt to develop a summary of this position that is representative and fair. Not everyone agrees with all aspects of the revisionist attack on bureaucratic structures; some argue that it is not contemporary bureaucratic structure that is to blame for present-day educational problems but the uses to which it is put. Thus it is appropriate to consider next the meaning of bureaucracy and the nature of bureaucratic structure before we discuss cultural pluralism in America as it affects American education and the development of equality of educational opportunity.

[8] Ibid., p. 125.
[9] Ibid., p. 122.

Bureaucracy and the Structure of Schooling

In the everyday language of the average citizen and in the rhetoric of most American newspapers and popular magazines the term "bureaucracy" is used to suggest "red tape," inefficiency, and overly complicated administrative behavior of various sorts. Yet we must be concerned with the precise meaning of ideas when we are speaking of issues or circumstances that affect entire institutions, such as schools and school systems. Sociologists and other social scientists are aware that the everyday newspaper and popular magazine uses of the term "bureaucracy" do not convey its real meaning. The idea of bureaucracy is a social concern to many American citizens, but it would be well for us all to remember that it is the behavior of people, not of abstract organizational forms, that determines whether an institution, such as a school, satisfies the needs of its clientele. We need to take a brief but precise look at the nature of bureaucracy as a form of social organization before we judge whether it is defensible or indefensible as a mechanism for organizing the formal educational experiences of human beings in humane ways.

The revisionist historians of education have made a major issue out of their belief that bureaucratic structures cannot meet the educational requirements of culturally diverse and densely populated school systems. On the other hand, many educators and other citizens argue that without some forms of formally organized and hierarchically structured social organizational forms, a complex society such as ours would be unable to deliver adequate social services to its population. The revisionist historians of education and others argue that there must be more immediate neighborhood control over the public schools in urban neighborhoods, without which schools cannot be fully responsive to the desires of urban parents and students. We need to take a closer look at what bureaucracy entails; then each of us needs to make his or her own individual decision about how he or she feels about this matter. We can debate whether a centralized or decentralized form of organizational structure is the best for the delivery of a particular social service such as education, but this does not mean that because we do not think one of these forms is appropriate for the functions to be performed by a particular institution that the other one is inhumane. Forms of organization cannot themselves be inhumane; only people can be inhumane.

As noted earlier, the word "bureaucracy" has some very precise meanings to such students of human social structure as sociologists. (It is derived from a French word denoting a type of furniture in which important papers were stored.) Bureaucracy as a form of social organization was studied in depth by the famous sociologist Max Weber as well as by many other social scientists and philosophers since his time. When we speak of bureaucracy we are referring to a special kind of highly structured organization designed with vertical levels of authority and for achieving certain highly complex goals. At each level in a bureaucratic structure, whether one involving vertical lines of authority or one involving a series of circles in which the highest authority rests in the center of the circle and controls "levels" of authority viewed as concentric rings around the circle, there are positions or offices held by people. The people who create a bureaucracy give very explicit authorities and responsibilities to the various positions held by people at each level of the organization. Thus in any model of school administration, a school superintendent has authority over school principals and teachers and school principals have authority over teachers in their respective schools. In Unit III detailed attention is given to the organization of schools in America.

Every educational system represents, however centralized or decentralized its organizational structure may be, some form of bureaucratic structure; for "bureaucracy" is but a term designating a very specifically delineated series of levels of authority and responsibility for achieving highly complex purposes in the most effective manner possible. Any bureaucratic structure in a school system possesses the following characteristics:

1. There are levels of clearly defined roles in the organization, such as superintendent of schools, assistant superintendent(s), principals of schools, teachers, and other professional or support personnel.
2. The offices, or specifically designated roles, at each level of the organization are arranged in a hierarchical order, with the highest authority at the top and the lowest authority at the bottom.
3. There are rules, either formal or understood, for interaction both between peers and between superiors or subordinates.
4. Impersonal guidelines for interpersonal relationships within the organizational structure.
5. An informal organizational structure develops as members of the school system's professional staff interact within the organization.
6. An attempt is made to develop a rational system for achieving the organization's objectives.

7. There are always explicitly stated goals and functions that the members of the organization try to achieve or fulfill (manifest functions). (Formally organized bureaucratic structures also tend to have, or at least can have, implicit and either intended or unintended "latent" functions, as when the graduates of a highly prestigious high school are allocated status by employers for having graduated from that particular school.)

These, then, are some of the characteristics of organized school systems. The informal friendships among members of a staff in a school system tend to offset the impersonality of the formal organizational structure of the school system for those people who seem to benefit and to be successful in interaction with other people. Regarding criticisms of bureaucratic structure, Harold L. Hodgkinson has said:

> To blame bureaucratic organization for the previous exploitation of workers is as ridiculous as to give it credit for the enlightened approach which is now in effect. Patterns of social organization are after all created, maintained, and altered by human beings who must take the responsibility for them. Bureaucratic structure is per se little more than a "rational" system of organizing a number of people so that certain work can be done as effectively and efficiently as possible.[10]

This is not to say that bureaucracy is good or bad, for it is the behavior within a bureaucratic structure that determines the conduct of any organization's operations. There has been widespread concern regarding traditional and alternative ways of organizing school systems to achieve human needs most effectively, particularly in recent years.

Guaranteeing Equality of Educational Opportunity

The Fourteenth Amendment guarantees the equal protection of the laws to every American citizen, and this constitutional guarantee has been the basis for several major state and federal court decisions in the past few years regarding the rights of students. Equality is one of the most difficult concepts to deal with because people have different ideas about what criteria to use in defining it. For instance, equal-

---

[10] Harold L. Hodgkinson, *Education, Interaction, and Social Change.* Englewood Cliffs, N.J.: Prentice-Hall, 1967, p. 33.

ity can mean treating everyone the same or it can mean providing special opportunities that work toward counteracting disadvantages, which amounts to "special treatment" so that a disadvantaged person can compete on the same level with a person who has had more advantages. In 1954 the U.S. Supreme Court ruled in *Brown* v. *Board of Education of Topeka, Kansas,* that "separate but equal" education was inherently unequal. Providing someone with the same services granted to another may not be granting them equal treatment where one of these persons, in fact, requires additional help to have the same chance to achieve some objective. Equality of opportunity means an equal chance to develop one's potentialities.

Although the Constitution did not mention education and control of education thus passed to the respective states under the "elastic clause" to the Tenth Amendment, a fact noted in Chapter 13, the Fourteenth Amendment guarantee of equal protection of the laws provided the Supreme Court the means to intervene to safeguard the civil rights of students. It was not until the *Brown* case that this occurred in a case involving segregation of black students in the public schools. Since that time there have been many cases in state and federal courts involving such issues as whether students should be bused to achieve racial balance in the schools. Where housing patterns are segregated minority groups have often had to seek recourse in the state and federal courts if they wished to attend racially integrated schools. There are many economic and psychological issues involved in the matter of what constitutes equality of educational opportunity as well as social issues. In 1971 the Supreme Court ruled in the case of *Swann* v. *Charlotte-Mecklenburg Board of Education* that requiring racial integration of schools is a constitutional principle.

Equality of educational opportunity is also affected by the property tax base and income levels of different school districts. The relative affluence of a school district can affect opportunities for education because local property taxes and capital wealth are major factors in financing all local schools. The structure for financing local school systems in the United States is one of the topics dealt with in Unit III. The equal protection of the laws clause of the Fourteenth Amendment as applied to the financing of schools had not received the support of the United States Supreme Court as of early 1975.

In the case of *Rodriguez* v. *San Antonio Independent School District,* the Supreme Court, in 1973, refused to accept the equal protection of the laws argument for restructuring the financing of local and state school systems. There will be, in all likelihood, continuing efforts to extend the principle of equal protection of the laws in the field of guaranteeing equality of educational opportunity.[11] The work of Charles A. Tesconi and Emanuel Hurwitz, Jr., is referred to here as well as in the Suggested Readings for Unit II because it is an exceptionally useful review of data on this topic.

In addition to questions of legal equality, there is the matter of human attitudes and rights to be considered. Teachers have a moral duty, as do all citizens, to avoid prejudicial treatment of other people. A teacher's attitudes are easily communicated to his or her students. At the personal level of individual moral behavior we have the moral obligation to avoid "self-fulfilling prophecies" about other people, wherein one prejudges a person's behavior before one knows him or her as a person and then proceeds to think badly of the person. There are many dimensions to equal educational opportunity; when another person's equality of opportunity is diminished in any way there is a sense in which our own future equality of opportunity is diminished as well. This is a moral question as well as a legal one, for if we are not concerned for others we do not deserve concern ourselves.

Cultural Pluralism and American Society

In Chapter 7 we briefly noted the multicultural heritage that has been one of the products of the American experience. Many different national and religious traditions as well as all the world's races have contributed to the development of the United States as a nation. We described the difference between the fact of cultural diversity and a commitment to the desirability of a philosophy of cultural pluralism in Chapter 7, and it is particularly appropriate that we consider again the importance and richness of our multicultural heritage in these last few pages before we examine the American school as a social institution in Unit III. All the past and present social concerns of a people are produced in the context of their social interactions with one another. The rich and varied cultural assets that America possesses have contributed greatly to the development of its arts and sciences as well as to its political traditions. Cultural diversity was not always looked on as an asset by Americans in the past, but the tumultuous

---

[11] An excellent source that develops a most perceptive analysis of all facets of the question of equality of educational opportunity is Charles A. Tesconi, Jr., and Emanuel Hurwitz, Jr., *Education for Whom: The Question of Equal Educational Opportunity*. New York: Dodd, Mead, 1974.

social experiences of recent years have convinced most Americans of good will of the need to cherish and protect the constitutional rights of all ethnic, religious, and racial groups in the United States if the polarization of national emotions that plagued the nation in the late 1960s is to be avoided.

This discussion of the significance of cultural pluralism to American national life and education cannot be an in-depth exploration of the philosophy of cultural pluralism. However, one of the authors of the present volume has written on this topic elsewhere.[12] The first person to develop cultural pluralism as a philosophy of life was Horace Meyer Kallen, in two essays entitled "Democracy Versus the Melting Pot" published in *The Nation* on February 18 and February 25, 1915. Other authors who were to become famous, as did Kallen, for their writings on the need to preserve and cherish America's cultural heritages also contributed to the debate over this issue. John Dewey and Isaac Berkson also became prominent for their views on cultural identity and education, and in the last few years there has been renewed interest in exploring more humane ways of perceiving and understanding our cultural differences. As Milton Gordon noted in his 1964 study, "cultural pluralism was a fact in American society before it became a theory. . . ."[13] Gordon describes in detail the fascinating account of the emergence of cultural pluralist conceptions of intergroup relations as alternatives to various "melting pot" theories of assimilation into American life that encouraged citizens of non–Anglo-Saxon cultural or religious backgrounds to adopt Anglo-Saxon values.

Indeed, historians have well documented that the emergence of a large Roman Catholic parochial school system in the nineteenth and twentieth centuries was motivated by the cultural pressures Roman Catholic immigrants experienced when they first settled in America. Today the spirit of religious tolerance is much better established in the American consciousness than it was earlier in our national experience. It is the responsibility of every teacher to develop positive attitudes toward all people, particularly students and parents. We need to accept, not merely tolerate, the reality of cultural differences and the rights of people to cherish their cultural heritages.

Some teachers experience what cultural anthropologists refer to as culture shock when they are unaware that in teaching people who

[12] Frederick Marshall Schultz, *Social-Philosophical Foundations of Education.* Dubuque, Iowa: Kendall/Hunt, 1974, pp. 65–75.

[13] Milton M. Gordon, *Assimilation in American Life: The Role of Race, Religion and National Origins.* New York: Oxford University Press, 1964.

are culturally different from themselves they misunderstand student behavior. The phenomenon of culture shock[14] occurs where a teacher of one social class, ethnic, or racial group is unable to communicate effectively with students of another background. This is not an infrequent problem for beginning teachers working with students from cultural or social class backgrounds with which they have not had contact. Sensitivity to the feelings of others and a willingness to learn the values and behavioral standards of one's students so as to be able to understand and communicate effectively with them are usually all that is required for a teacher to learn to deal effectively with "culturally different" students. But the emphasis has to be placed on the phrase "willingness to learn" and with that characteristic teachers need to practice the art of communicating their concerns to students.

American Educational Values

Before we study in Unit III the school in American as a social institution we need to pause briefly to consider how our major educational thoughts are the products of cherished beliefs about what ought to be the values and goals of American education. Some of our values are rooted in the classical belief in the perfection of the potentialities of the individual human being. We have seen that the development of a new nation out of successive lines of frontier wilderness and out of the migrations of millions of people from all over the world to our cities and towns produced a certain faith in the power of education to improve the lives of people. Whether our schools have lived up to that faith is another question. The compelling faith of Americans in the concept that all human beings are entitled to at least a basic education was slow to grow into a universal national ideal, but we can perceive the origins of that ideal even in our earliest settlements.

Some Americans cling to classical academic values rooted in the Western educational heritage and others hold to more utilitarian and vocational beliefs about what forms of schooling or informal educational experiences are most desirable. There are also positions representing some compromise between these two opposing educational ideals. But most Americans have cherished beliefs about what education ought to do for them.

It has been said by many, and the present writers made this

[14] See Schultz, op. cit., pp. 17 and 91.

point in Unit I, that education is a value-laden enterprise. It is a process in which people develop beliefs about the "worth" of certain kinds of learning experiences and ways of learning. Education always involves value judgments about which knowledge is most worth teaching. For this reason education is a normative, or valuational, enterprise in which people, especially teachers and other educators, are involved in making decisions about how best to help other people learn. Virtually every activity of teaching involves making choices about why something should be done and how to do it.

America's educational values are as rich and diverse as her population. There is a strong national belief in the value of education, but beyond that Americans differ greatly about how to conduct educational and other social decision-making activities. This is healthy, for citizens of a democratic society must have the right to develop their own cherished values as well as to have government and other persons hold this right sacred. With such a right also goes the responsibility to tolerate the values of others.

Summary

In this chapter we have considered some of the broad social concerns about our national present and past that require the serious attention of any person who seriously desires to understand the American educational heritage. We considered some of the contemporary revisionist views about the development of American education, and we explored bureaucracy as a social phenomenon that influences the formal organization of American school systems. We noted the basic operational characteristics of bureaucratic organizational structures as they are usually applied in educational institutions. Some of the considerations involved in efforts to guarantee equality of educational opportunity in America were noted, and reference was made to the "equal protection of the laws" clause of the Fourteenth Amendment to the Constitution. The significance to teachers and other citizens of the factor of cultural pluralism was discussed, and a brief commentary was given on the origins of the idea in American thought and the importance of developing intercultural understanding and the ability to communicate with people of different cultural backgrounds. We closed the chapter by noting the sources of American educational values and the fact that education is a value-laden process. America's educational values are as rich and diverse as its population. The importance of understanding the need to tolerate differing values and to recognize the many value decisions that teachers have to make in teaching were also noted.

QUESTIONS

1. What questions do you have about educational development in America that were raised by the account of revisionist views of American education presented in this chapter?
2. How do you feel about the various characteristics of bureaucratic structures? Is bureaucracy necessarily good or bad? How do you react to the comments of Michael B. Katz and Harold L. Hodgkinson regarding bureaucracy? What questions do you have about the defining characteristics of bureaucracy in the light of the revisionist views on this matter?
3. What do you consider to be a good working definition of "equality of educational opportunity"? Is it always enough just to treat people "the same"? Are there situations in which other criteria must be applied to guarantee equality of opportunity?
4. What is your view of the significance of the cultural diversity in the United States? Can you think of any examples of culture shock in a classroom setting?
5. What do you think constitute the basic educational values of the United States? What are your most cherished educational values?

PROJECTS

1. Review some of the sociological literature on the concept of bureaucracy and evaluate this organizational concept as to whether you think it is a necessary or an unnecessary way of organizing school systems.
2. Review a book by one of the revisionist historians of education referred to in this chapter; then write as a part of your review your best reasons for your acceptance or rejection of the author's line of argument.
3. Write a research report on the literature you can find or that you have time to review on the educational needs or problems of any one minority group in America. Any such report could be very long, so limit yourself to five pages and only discuss your concerns about the most severe problems facing the group you choose to study. Concentrate on a wide range of reading, not on writing a long paper.
4. Write a brief essay or give an oral report on what you consider to be the most fundamental educational values in America.

unit

II

Suggested Readings

BLAU, JOSEPH L., ed., *Cornerstones of Religious Freedom in America,* Revised Edition. New York: Harper & Row, Publishers, 1964. This is one of the finest collections of major documents dealing with the development of religious freedom and the principle of religious liberty in America. The volume relates to the development of such American values as freedom of conscience, which were to influence the development of American educational ideals. Although the book does not relate to education directly, it is important for understanding the basic values that were to guide the founders of American school systems.

BUFFUM, WILLIAM B., "The UN at Twenty: An Instrument for International Cooperation," *Social Education,* 30 (No. 1): 13–18, January 27, 1966. The author, who was Deputy Assistant Secretary of State for International Affairs, reviews some of the accomplishments and problems of the United Nations. Teacher responsibility in helping to achieve world peace is pointed out.

BUTTS, R. FREEMAN, *A Cultural History of Western Education,* Second Edition. New York: McGraw-Hill Book Company, 1955. This is one of the finest histories of Western education. It provides an excellent perspective on the development of Western education and on how American education was influenced by European educational thought.

BUTTS, R. FREEMAN, "Search for Freedom: The Story of American Education," *NEA Journal,* pp. 33–48, March, 1960. This is a clear summary of major themes in the history of American education by one of the most prominent historians of education in America.

CRANE, THEODORE RAWSON, *The Dimensions of American Education.* Reading, Mass.: Addison-Wesley Publishing Co., Inc., 1974. Crane has compiled some basic documentary material on various dimensions of the development of American education, and he has written a commentary on the significance of these dimensions that makes this rather small volume a most useful text-anthology on this topic. This volume is clearly written and the author's insights are most perceptive.

EGGLESTON, EDWARD, *The Hoosier Schoolmaster: A Story of Backwoods Life in Indiana.* New York: Orange Judd, 1871. This novel provides an authentic description of a frontier school.

FROST, S. E., JR., and KENNETH P. BAILEY, *Historical and Philosophical Foundations of Western Education,* Second Edition. Columbus, Ohio: Charles E.

Merrill Publishing Co., 1973. This is a readable and comprehensive study of major men, ideas, and movements in the development of Western education.

GOOD, HARRY G., and JAMES D. TELLER, *A History of Western Education,* Third Edition. New York: The Macmillan Company, 1969. This is one of the most famous texts on the history of Western educational ideas and institutions; it ranks with Butts' work on this topic.

GOODLAD, JOHN I., "The Schools vs. Education," *Saturday Review,* pp. 59–61, April 19, 1969. The author attempts to answer the questions: Where are the schools today? What kinds of changes will be needed in the 1970s? What lies ahead for the rest of the century? His emphasis is on the elementary schools, especially the earlier grades. From the perspective of the mid- and late 1970s it might be interesting to react to this article.

GREEN, THOMAS F., *Education and Pluralism: Ideal and Reality.* Syracuse, N.Y.: Syracuse University School of Education, 1966. 35 pp. This short monograph on education and pluralism is one of the major essays regarding different patterns of social relationships in the United States and the relationships of educational institutions to American society. Green discusses three types of pluralist social relationships in the United States.

GROSS, CARL H., and CHARLES C. CHANDLER, eds., *The History of American Education: Through Readings.* Lexington, Mass.: D. C. Heath & Company, 1964. This is an excellent anthology of major documents and essays that have been significant in the history of American education. It is one of the best anthologies on this subject.

GUMBERT, EDGAR B., and JOEL H. SPRING, *The Superschool and the Superstate: American Education in the Twentieth Century: 1918–1970.* New York: John Wiley & Sons, Inc., 1974. This is a concise volume in which the authors provide a penetrating analysis of education in twentieth-century America.

KATZ, MICHAEL B., *Class, Bureaucracy, and Schools.* New York: Praeger Publishers, Inc., 1971. This is an in-depth criticism of bureaucratic structures in education and of the historical development of American public school systems from a revisionist historian's point of view. It is an incisive analysis and well written.

KATZ, MICHAEL B., ed., *School Reform: Past and Present.* Boston: Little, Brown and Company, 1971. This is an excellent anthology of essays from the nineteenth and twentieth centuries on school reform with very good evaluative comments.

LUCAS, CHRISTOPHER J., *Our Western Educational Heritage.* New York: The Macmillan Company, 1972. This is a readable history of Western education with some good original insights by the author. It is an excellent source and a fine study of its topic.

MEYER, ADOLPHE E., *An Educational History of the Western World,* Second Edition. New York: McGraw-Hill Book Company, 1972. This is an interesting account of the ideas, people, and movements that contributed to the Western educational tradition; Meyer's accounts of the lives of famous contributors to the development of Western educational thought are well done.

SILBERMAN, CHARLES E., *Crisis in the Classroom.* New York: Random House, Inc., 1970. Silberman's study of contemporary problems in American education is a useful source on contemporary efforts at educational reform in America, and his treatment of British informal elementary schools has proved particularly useful to many American teachers. His comparisons of British and American educational reform and his thoughts on the education of educators are well worth reading.

TESCONI, CHARLES A., JR., and EMANUEL HURWITZ, JR., *Education for Whom: The Question of Equal Educational Opportunity.* New York: Dodd, Mead & Company, 1974. This is truly an excellent text-anthology, containing in a brief volume the best thought on the topic of equality of educational opportunity.

TYACK, DAVID B., "Catholic Power, Black Power, and the Schools," *Educational Forum,* November, 1967. This is a perceptive brief article comparing and contrasting the struggle for equal rights of nineteenth-century Roman Catholic immigrants and present-day blacks.

WEBB, WALTER PRESCOTT, *The Great Frontier.* Boston: Houghton Mifflin Company, 1952. Chapters 1 and 12 and pages 84–85 contain, respectively, an analysis of the frontier factor in modern history, a description of education in its relation to the corporate age, and a discussion of how the frontier influenced education.

WEINBERG, MEYER, *Integrated Education.* Beverly Hills: Glencoe Press, 1968. This collection of some 50 articles, addresses, and documents selected from issues of the magazine *Integrated Education* surveys various aspects of this increasingly important contemporary problem in American education.

The schools in America

U p to this point we have
studied, first, the teacher in American education, noting some elements
that tend to increase satisfaction in individual work and others that tend
to diminish it. Second, we have studied certain ideas, customs, traditions,
and laws that have shared in making contemporary education in our
country what it is. Now, in Unit III we study directly, in three chapters,
the three closely interrelated, interdependent levels of government—state,
local, and federal—in their relationships with education. Each state has
the heaviest responsibility for education within its boundaries; therefore
we examine first what the states do with respect to control over and support of education, following this with examinations of local aspects of
educational organization and administration and then educational activities of the federal government.

Because authority over education is divided, there is some confusion
about who should have ultimate authority and what should be the relative roles of the three levels of government. The issue of relative roles has

never been even partially settled, and is, in fact, livelier now than ever before. Although these roles are constantly shifting, where the trends will ultimately lead seems to be anybody's guess.

In an earlier chapter it was pointed out that members of the teaching profession need to be sufficiently informed so that they may lead the public to a mature and intelligent view of what education in the United States should and could be, what it needs in order to build and maintain an excellent system of schools. Average classroom teachers are often so absorbed in daily teaching duties that they tend to overlook their personal responsibility to help build a strong education profession that can render broad educational leadership. Nevertheless, it is those who are responsible for the everyday duties of directing the vast educational undertaking who are in the best position to influence educational trends. The profession must be able to count on informed members who are actively concerned, and this concern must be based on sound understanding.

chapter

11

State public school systems

The Constitution of the United States separates the powers of the federal and state governments. The Tenth Amendment to the Constitution (1791) reads: "The powers not delegated to the United States by the Constitution, nor prohibited by it to the States, are reserved to the States, respectively, or to the people." The power of education is not delegated by the Constitution to the Congress, nor is it prohibited by the Constitution to the states. It therefore remains legally the right of the state legislatures to organize and administer education within the respective states.

Each state legislature has developed its own plan for administering education, and consequently state systems vary. It is obviously beyond the scope of this book to describe each state system. Instead, what states have done in general about education, paths followed, common structural elements, common problems, and some proposed plans for the future are explored. We begin by considering the legal structure that guides or controls actions of the state legislatures.

Legal Structure

As each state provided for education in its own constitution and from time to time passed laws relating to education within the state, it developed a legal structure. This legal structure includes the constitution, which is the fundamental or basic law of a state, subsequent legislation, and the decisions and precedents established by judicial review.

State Constitutions

Each state has a written constitution that follows, in general, the pattern set by the federal government. It provides for the popular election of a legislature and an executive—a governor—and for a system of state courts. Theoretically, the governor is free from the dominance of legislators because he is elected directly by the people. He is the titular head of his political party in the state. What the executive head favors with regard to public and private education, therefore, will be influential in determining how education will fare under his leadership. Thus education in a state depends somewhat on the party in power. The welfare of education, especially in the long run, is determined by the kinds of citizens who, by popular vote, are elected to the state legislatures.

All the state constitutions contain provisions for public education. Some of our current attitudes and prevailing traditions can be traced to statements about education found in some of the original state constitutions. Section 44 of the Pennsylvania constitution, adopted in 1776, said:

> A school or schools shall be established in every county by the legislature, for the convenient instruction of youth, with such salaries to the masters, paid by the public, as may enable them to instruct youth at low prices; and all useful learning shall be duly encouraged and promoted in one or more universities.

The constitutions of North Carolina of 1776 and 1835 contained an almost identical provision. The emphasis on "low prices" to the public occurs in the constitutions of several other states. The Vermont constitution of 1787, for instance, provided:

> Section XL. A school or schools shall be established in every town, by the legislature, for the convenient instruction of youth, with such

salaries to the masters, paid by each town; making proper use of school lands in each town, thereby enabling them to instruct youth at low prices.

A different pattern is found in the constitutions of states admitted to the Union later. Section 2 of the Indiana constitution, adopted in 1816, read:

> It shall be the duty of the general assembly, as soon as circumstances will permit, to provide by law for a general system of education, ascending in regular gradation from township schools to a State university, wherein tuition shall be gratis, and equally open to all.

Although it is evident that the states borrowed from one another in their constitutional provisions for public education, the systems of education that evolved later are the product of various interpretations and implementations by successive state legislatures. Considering, for instance, that the present constitution of Illinois was adopted in 1870 and geared to conditions very different from those of today, it is fortunate that the actual educational policies of the state have been determined by its succession of state legislators.

State Legislatures

Each legislature in each state passes school laws. Typically, citizens differ about how to solve specific problems of education—the transportation of pupils, for example. The state legislators may have public hearings, conduct research, weigh various suggestions, and then pass a law defining a uniform policy for the entire state. Throughout the state pupils will be transported for school purposes in a way that conforms to this law.

The laws in each state, determining such important matters as how public education shall be organized and administered, what the structure of authority shall be, how schools shall be financed, make it clear that actually the state legislature is the supreme policy maker for education in the state. Each new legislature, often characterized by considerable change in membership, passes new laws related to education or modifies old laws.

Generally speaking, these state laws are of two kinds: mandatory and permissive. Mandatory laws are to be followed uniformly throughout the state and concern such matters as districting, pupil transportation, and school taxation. Permissive laws give local school-governing bodies the right, within state-established limits, to use judgment, make interpretations, and determine implementations in terms of a particular situation. Matters related to salary provisions, security provisions for personnel, school building requirements, location of building sites, are the types of subjects covered in permissive laws. In all cases, how-

---

The attitude toward education characteristic of the times is reflected in a law passed in 1647 in Massachusetts that has often been called the "Old Deluder Satan Act." It is quoted with the original spelling.

It being one chiefe project of the ould deluder, Satan, to keepe men from the knowledge of the Scriptures, as in former times by keeping them in an unknowne tongue, so in these latter times by perswading from the use of tongues, that so at least the true sence & meaning of the originall might be clouded by false glosses of saint seeming deceivers, that learning may not be buried in the grave of our fathers in the church and commonwealth, the Lord assisting our endeavors,—

It is therfore ordered, that every towneship in this jurisdiction, after the Lord hath increased their number to 50 householders, shall then forthwith appoint one within their towne to teach all such children as shall resort to him to write & reade, whose wages shall be paid either by the parents or masters of such children, or by the inhabitants in generall, by way of supply, as the major part of those that order the prudentials the towne shall appoint; provided, those that send their children be not oppressed by paying much more than they can have them taught for in other townes; & it is further ordered, that where any towne shall increase to the number of 100 families or householders, they shall set up a grammer schoole, the master thereof being able to instruct youth so farr as they shall be fitted for the university, provided, that if any towne neglect the performance hereof above one yeare, that every such towne shall pay 5 pounds to the next schoole till they shall performe this order.

Two centuries later, Horace Mann paid eloquent tribute to the law in his tenth annual report (1846) as secretary of the Massachusetts State Board of Education. He said, in part: "It is impossible for us adequately to conceive the boldness of the measure which aimed at universal education through the establishment of free schools. . . . [This] was one of those grand mental and moral experiments whose effects could not be developed and made manifest in a single generation."

ever, local authorities are required to comply with both the spirit and the formal requirements of a law, whether mandatory or permissive.

State School Codes

In time, all the school laws of a state are brought together and published, making them easily accessible. The systematic collection of all the laws in force, together with judicial opinions and court decisions, makes up the state school code. Usually this published volume is sizable, technical, and detailed. For example, there will be an accumulation of many laws regarding such matters as compulsory school attendance, maximum liabilities of school districts, standards for teacher certification, charters for private schools, consolidation of school districts, the building and maintenance of school buildings, taxation for the maintenance of the schools, and policies toward pupil transportation—to name but a few.

Broadly speaking, the relations of American private and public schools to American society and to the pupils in the schools are defined in the state school codes. Nowhere else is there so complete and dependable a source of information about schools. The state school code is a valuable book of reference but, since much of it is expressed in legal terms, it is usually consulted only when special problems arise that call for legal answers—for instance, "What is the teacher's obligation to children taken on a field trip?" By going through the state school code, however, a classroom teacher can discover the nature and extent of school law in the state and may profit especially by noting those laws that apply to activities of classroom teachers. Direct acquaintance with school codes will impress a teacher with the importance of always acting within the limits prescribed by the law.

The Research Division of the NEA annually reports and interprets certain selected state laws that have been reviewed by the courts in cases involving teachers or schools—in suits for negligence, for instance. These court decisions, together with the analyses made by the judges, give information of professional interest. The cases selected by the NEA concern specific situations that have arisen, but they are representative of situations that might arise in connection with other schools, classrooms, or teachers.[1]

[1] See NEA Research Report 1967–R6, *The Teacher's Day in Court, Review of 1966,* and NEA Research Report 1967–R7, *The Pupil's Day in Court, Review of 1966.*

Judicial Review

The policy of an individual state toward public education is, then, expressed in the constitution and in the specific laws passed by legislatures. The state constitution is the fundamental law. State legislatures are subject to restrictions placed on them by the constitutions. The final authority to decide whether a state law is constitutional or unconstitutional belongs to the state court of highest appeal, usually called the supreme court. The state supreme courts may also invalidate an action of a state board or department of education.

As we shall see in a later chapter, the U.S. Supreme Court sometimes gets into the picture. A conflict over the way in which some state legislature or some state supreme court has decided a matter may, under certain circumstances, be carried to the U.S. Supreme Court, where the justices render what is expected to be, at least for some years to come, a final decision. However, state supreme courts have reversed themselves at times—and so has the Supreme Court itself.

State Controls

Basic Administrative Units[2]

As pointed out, ultimate responsibility for public education is vested in the legislatures of the individual states. The controls over public education, therefore, vary from state to state. There are, however, common policies of control among the states, and one of these, familiar throughout the history of American education, is the policy of establishing basic administrative units for purposes of state control. The state exerts its legal authority through these units (as explored further in the next chapter). Since the framework of administrative units, or the structure of exercising state authority, is about the same in all the states, it is essential to understand the nature of these basic administrative units as a step toward understanding public education in America.

When the earliest schools were established, a political boundary line was set around each school, designating the area from which its

---

[2] This discussion is limited to public elementary and secondary school districts; community colleges and state universities are briefly described in Chapter 15.

children were to come; the citizens who would support and control
the school would be those who lived within the area. This geographical
area, or territorial political division, was called a school district. Essentially, this is what a school district still is. Over the years, of course,
the states have seen fit to modify the character of school districts—to
enlarge the area, include more schools, redefine the prerogatives, add
to or take away some of the powers of control. This redefining of
a district, as explained later, has been continuous throughout our history, and is even now proceeding at an accelerated rate.

The National Commission on School District Reorganization de-
fines a school district thus:

> A basic unit of local school administration is an area in which
> a single board or officer has the immediate responsibility for the
> direct administration of all the schools located therein. Its distin-
> guishing feature is that it is a quasi-corporation with a board or
> chief school officer that has the responsibility for, and either com-
> plete or partial autonomy in, the administration of all public schools
> within its boundaries.

A clear understanding of this definition of the basic administrative unit requires some analysis. What is meant by referring to a state
school district as a quasi-corporation? It operates like a corporation
but it does not have articles of incorporation because it is an instru-
mentality of the state. It is operated under the laws of the state and
is created to facilitate the administration of public education by the
state government, to execute the state's policy. As the definition points
out, the state's authority is executed through a board, or chief school
officer, who, like any other important state school officer, is responsible
to the state government.

Full agreement among the states as to the relationship between
a public school district and other political divisions is lacking. It should
be emphasized, however, that what the relationship is makes a great
deal of difference in the way public school systems are organized and
administered. The basic administrative units in 29 states are established by the respective state legislatures as *independent* of all other
governmental units; in four states the school district has a dependent
relationship with the political division in which it is located; in 17
states the relationship is a mixture, some being more dependent
whereas others are more independent. Educational specialists in
public school administration almost unanimously advocate the separa-

tion of public school districts from municipal corporations. They believe that the boundaries of school districts, the basic state administrative units, can be more logically defined if political boundary lines are disregarded, that the financing of education in the independent district is more favorably considered by a community when costs are not compared with those of other government departments, and that it is much easier to reorganize school districts that are independent of other political ties. Some political scientists, however, for commendable reasons, believe otherwise. The fact that only four of our 50 states have established dependent districts seems to indicate that independent districts, at least in public opinion, seem best.

Before the present district system of elementary and/or secondary education began to prevail, the pattern set by the Massachusetts law of 1647 was followed. As the frontier moved westward, the northernmost states as far west as Kansas and the Dakotas established similar public school districts, typically one-teacher, one-room, eight-grade elementary schools. These contrasted with the school districts in small towns and in cities, which were allowed to establish complete systems, including secondary schools. Often the eighth-grade graduates of the rural schools were permitted to transfer to a nearby town or city school, their tuition being paid by the rural school district.

As the nation's population increased, the states were kept busy changing district boundaries to meet changing needs—about which more later. In the school year 1973–1974, however, there still remained 16,492 operating basic administrative units in this country. Six states—Nebraska, Illinois, Texas, South Dakota, California, and Minnesota had almost 40 percent of these units (Nebraska alone had 1224; Kansas, her sister state, only 310).

By and large, school districts in the states on the mainland vary greatly in size, school population, and financial support—that is, in quality of educational opportunities. One large city, for example, enrolls over 600,000 pupils, and has 25,000 teachers and 10,000 nonprofessional employees. In contrast, in 1973 there were still 322 nonoperating districts, districts that did not operate any school facility but functioned only to transfer their pupils to schools in operating districts.

All the states, in varying degrees, place responsibility for conducting the affairs of a school district on the citizens who live within the district. The way in which the states pass these responsibilities on to local citizens and how they are handled will be explained in the next chapter, which is devoted entirely to the subject of local school districts.

Reorganization of State Basic Administrative Units

Originally, except for the cities and towns, a district was just large enough to support a single one-room, one-teacher neighborhood school. Eventually, larger districts were organized and a number of eight-grade elementary schools were supported in one district. In Indiana a whole township under a political trustee became the basic unit of school administration. Other states followed other patterns, but very early in American history the movement to enlarge public school districts got under way and has continued at an accelerating pace ever since. Thirty–six years ago there were more than 100,000 basic administrative units operating elementary and/or secondary schools. By 1974, as stated earlier, this had been reduced to fewer than 17,000 operating districts; and, as we have also noted, almost 40 percent of these were in six states, where reorganization started later and has proceeded more slowly than in some other sections of the country.

What criteria should be applied to determine whether an area is qualified to be or to continue as a basic state administrative unit to do the job of education? Most educational specialists would agree on the following:

1. A minimum enrollment of 1500 pupils.
2. A somewhat homogeneous population.
3. Sufficient taxing wealth to support:
   a. Elementary schools and a high school.
   b. Such special services as health, guidance, and programs for the handicapped.
   c. Capable administrators and supervisors.

Organizing a school district so that it meets desirable standards of size and potential for support often means moving control over the schools farther and farther from the local citizens, placing it in the hands of fewer citizens, sacrificing some of the considerable advantages that accrue from fostering strong local interest in the schools. This has often led to conflict when efforts are being made to reorganize. The answer by the states seems to be to strike a reasonable balance between the size and efficiency of the district and the preservation of local interest and participation. The trend toward consolidation of assets and resources of corporations is a typical current social development. The move by the states to centralize control over public education by enlarging the basic administrative units is consistent with this trend. Although this similarity does not prove that every effort to enlarge a school district is wise, it does indicate that the trend is not likely to be reversed.

The Contemporary Picture

The public school districts that have the greatest influence on education in America, that enroll by far the largest proportion of the pupils, can be classified into three groups: large-city school districts, suburban school districts, and reorganized districts in agricultural centers. Public education is different in each of these.

The following discussion deals with these three kinds of districts, omitting the much smaller districts, which, although rapidly declining in number and importance, still operate small schools in a number of states.

Large-City School Districts

In present-day America, the school districts of large cities are to the educational world what the cities themselves are to the world. Usually, large-city school districts are laid out within the boundaries of the city, although, theoretically at least, they are independent quasi-corporations of the state. The responsibilities of citizens who are appointed or elected to serve on a school board for the public school system in a large city are tremendous. The New York City School District enrolls well over 1 million pupils and administers a budget of over a billion dollars. It takes a citizen of considerable ability and unusual civic dedication to share in the direction of such a system.

Currently, journalists are directing many harsh criticisms at America's large cities for their failure to provide adequate education for all pupils. Many criticisms are directed at the leadership of the schools, some at the teaching profession. It is often overlooked that although educational leadership has at times been deficient, some of the problems faced in the schools today are the outgrowth of broad *social* problems. The city schools did not create the ghetto or disadvantaged pupils. They are not responsible for the extreme heterogeneity of the population. The schools can, with adequate financial and civic support, provide many new and increased services and improve their adaptation to the needs of all pupils. The schools cannot, however, revolutionize the current social climate. Among the biggest problems of the large cities are those related to the socioeconomic structure of their inner cities. Improvement in education in the inner cities is a challenge that the schools must meet.

It is not our purpose here to discuss or even list all the critical problems of education in large American cities today. The reader will find these problems pictured, discussed, analyzed in many current professional and popular journals and books. Some thought-provoking articles, presenting various points of view on controversial issues, are listed among the readings at the end of this unit. Some aspects of urban school problems are treated in our study of the activities of the federal government in Chapter 13.

Suburban School Districts

We have pointed out that many affluent people have been moving in great numbers from the large cities and settling in the suburbs, thus not only creating new communities, but at the same time contributing to the social, economic, and educational impoverishment of the large cities.

The states have followed a variety of patterns in setting up new school districts in the new locations of rapidly growing populations. In some instances the new districts followed the pattern of the large cities, creating a single unified district with schools from kindergarten through high school and defining the school district boundaries as identical with those of the city-suburb. In other cases the boundaries crossed over political boundary lines, thus allowing the school district to be more independent of the influence of a single municipal corporation. Others created small districts for the elementary schools but created enlarged districts for the sole operation of high school education. Generally speaking, the salary scale for teachers in the dual districts was lower in the elementary school district than in the high school district, reflecting, perhaps, the earlier practice of requiring a longer period of training for a high school teacher than for an elementary school teacher.

It is generally held that the best education in America is in the suburban schools. There is much truth in this—suburban districts have

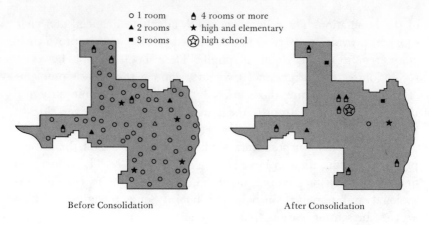

Before Consolidation   After Consolidation

Figure 11-1 How the formation of Unit District No. 10, Pittsfield and Pike County, Illinois, reduced the number and types of school units. (Data from Pittsfield Community Unit School District No. 10.)

many advantages: greater wealth, state taxing systems that favor these wealthier districts, newer and more modern school plants, more favorable teacher salaries and working conditions, more extensive citizen involvement, and local pride at a high level. It does not mean, however, that all suburban school districts fare alike in the educational benefits derived from being apart from, but contiguous to, large cities. Some suburbs have grown so large that they have taken on the characteristics of the city, the difference being that they have not yet developed an inner city, with its ghettos and substandard living conditions. An extreme range in quality of education can be found, however, among different types and sizes of suburban school districts.

Districts in Agricultural Centers

Although the problems of education in large-city school districts have increased, state programs for establishing school districts in agricultural centers have been achieved more smoothly and successfully. In part because of improvements in roads and other pupil-transportation facilities, it has been possible to enlarge the agricultural school district to a point where it can support schools that match the best programs offered in the cities. One can sense the change in education offered in agricultural centers merely by driving through the countryside. The elaborate school plants, beautifully landscaped, surrounded with ample space for parking and playing and, in many instances, located in a setting completely different from the crowded conditions of densely populated communities, are very impressive. From the standpoint of modern facilities, and citizenship involvement, these schools are the greatest improvement in modern education in America. As reorganization in districting continues, the old "country school" or "small-town school" is rapidly fading from the contemporary scene. (See Figure 11-1.)

If one may judge from these present trends throughout the nation, reorganization of the state's basic administrative units in agricultural centers will have three results:

1. A minimum enrollment figure or standard will be met in all except the more sparsely settled regions such as are found in the plains and mountain states of the west.
2. Districts that maintain only elementary schools will be consolidated or augmented so that they will be large enough to maintain a complete system up through the twelfth grade, including nursery schools, kindergartens, junior high schools, and all the special services required by such a system.
3. Districts that operate only a 4-year high school or a system of 4-year high schools will gradually—and not without opposition—be combined with districts that operate elementary schools, thus creating conditions required for a unified system of schools with no salary differentials among elementary, junior high, and senior high school teachers.

The State Educational Authority

The state, with its units for educational controls, its school districts, has mandatory and permissive laws that *regulate* education. The state also has laws that *insure* the execution of the state's responsibilities for both public and private education. Such laws set up a structure of authority to administer the educational affairs of the state; this is ordinarily a state officer or, in some cases, several offices, with specific and definite functions, with authority and responsibilities carefully spelled out. Characteristically, the states differ in the way the state educational office is organized and in the specific responsibilities assigned to it. There are, however, common elements in the national picture. Generally, the state's supreme authority over education begins with a state board of education, an office that greatly influences the character of education within a given state.

State Boards of Education

In 48 of our 50 states, a state board of education has authority over elementary and secondary school districts. (Illinois and Wisconsin are the two exceptions, although there are strong influences in both states that foreshadow change.) The state boards of education—sometimes called by other names such as the Board of Regents in New York State—uniformly constitute the highest educational authority in each of the states, although there is considerable variation in details related to powers, membership, methods of selection, and the like. Since some state policies are considered significantly better than others, a brief survey of current state practices may help in assessing proposed reforms. (See Figure 11-2.)

I. FUNCTIONS

Among the functions of the state boards of education, perhaps the most important are to appoint or have elected the chief state school officer, to designate the term of his appointment, to define his duties, and to state his salary. (Where there is no state board, as in Illinois and Wisconsin, this function is, of course, taken care of through state laws.) In broad outline the responsibilities of a state board of education are somewhat analogous to those of local boards of education, as described in Chapter 12. In general, the state board assumes responsibility for carrying out those aspects of education that must be administered at the state level and also for formulating educational policies related to the implementation, control, and supervision of statewide education.

In most states these functions are divided among several boards, each with control over some segment of the state's education program. In only 13 states, for example, are the state boards vested with general control over all elementary and secondary education. In many cases a separate board (or several boards) is responsible for universities, for junior colleges, for vocational education, for the education of the deaf and the blind, and so on. Boards originally set up to meet definite and timely needs have become deeply rooted, resistant to change. A more or less confused, diffused, and inefficient pattern of state boards of education, with overlapping functions and some of the resulting evils, persists.

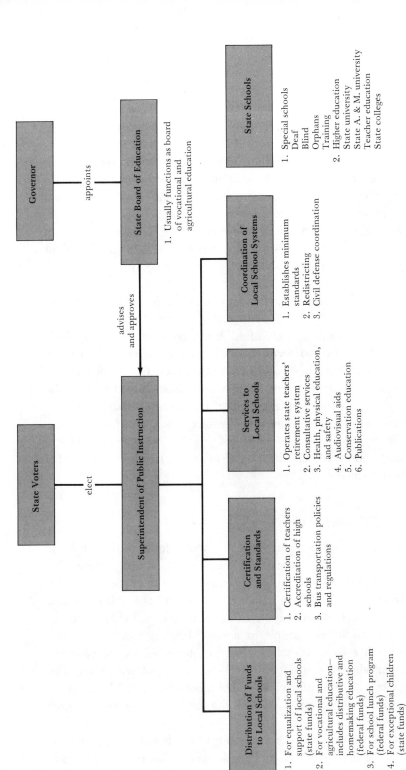

Figure 11-2 A typical state educational organization. The general trend is toward increased state participation in and control over local educational functions. This chart shows one of the more common ways of organizing state authority. The student may find it valuable and interesting to draw a similar diagram for his or her own state and compare it with this one.

State Voters — elect → **Superintendent of Public Instruction**

Governor — appoints → **State Board of Education**

State Board of Education
1. Usually functions as board of vocational and agricultural education

advises and approves → **Superintendent of Public Instruction**

State Schools
1. Special schools
   Deaf
   Blind
   Orphans
   Training
2. Higher education
   State university
   State A. & M. university
   Teacher education
   State colleges

Distribution of Funds to Local Schools
1. For equalization and support of local schools (state funds)
2. For vocational and agricultural education—includes distributive and homemaking education (federal funds)
3. For school lunch program (federal funds)
4. For exceptional children (state funds)

Certification and Standards
1. Certification of teachers
2. Accreditation of high schools
3. Bus transportation policies and regulations

Services to Local Schools
1. Operates state teachers' retirement system
2. Consultative services
3. Health, physical education, and safety
4. Audiovisual aids
5. Conservation education
6. Publications

Coordination of Local School Systems
1. Establishes minimum standards
2. Redistricting
3. Civil defense coordination

2. MEMBERSHIP

The state board of education is an important factor in the welfare of education within a state. Who serves on the board is vital in determining how effectively the board fulfills its functions. The states follow different policies in selecting the members. At present the board is elected by popular vote in only nine states; board members are appointed by the governor in 30 states; various methods of election and appointment are used in the remainder of the states.

The number of members on the state board varies, ranging from 21 in Texas to three in Mississippi. Nineteen states have from eight to 11 members. Ten states have seven members, and seven states have fewer than seven.

Numerous appointed commissions have made recommendations regarding the most acceptable membership of state boards. The commissions, almost without exception, have recommended popularly elected boards of five to seven lay citizens who serve without pay. No qualifications have been agreed on other than that each member should be a prominent citizen who has an unselfish interest in the administration of education in the state. It is assumed that some kind of preliminary screening process will protect the office from citizens who are incompetent or have selfish designs. Obviously, expert opinion about what constitutes the ideal state board of education has so far had little influence.

Chief State School Officers

It is generally agreed by specialists in school administration that the state board should select the state's chief school officer, whose title is usually superintendent of public instruction or commissioner of education. In actuality, however, the chief state school officer is appointed by the state board of education in only 24 states. In 21 states he or she is elected by the people as a candidate on a political ticket. In the other five states the chief officer is appointed by the governor of the state, who, of course, is also elected on a political ticket. The trend, however, is toward a chief school officer appointed by the state board of education—since 1947 the number so appointed has risen from 11 to 24.

In states where a nonpartisan state board is authorized to select the chief state school officer and to determine his or her functions, salary, tenure, and the like, the state can attract leaders of outstanding competence. But more than half the states still cling to partisan politics in connection with education. Politicians offer "good" arguments; they invent attractive slogans that influence people to oppose change: "Keep education close to the people"; "Make the chief state school officer independent of the board of education"; "Election by popular vote frees the chief state school officer from obligations to other officials, including the governor"; "If he proves incompetent, he can be recalled." Gradually, however, such political appeals are losing effectiveness as citizens become increasingly aware of the need for expert, not political, statewide school leadership.

State Department of Education

In all the states the chief educational officer uses the services of a professional staff. With his or her staff, the chief officer constitutes the state department of education. It discharges manifold responsibilities in connection with such matters as certificating teachers, distributing state aid to local school districts, assuming leadership in reorganizing school districts, enforcing various school codes, reporting the status of educational affairs to the public, and distributing large sums of money allocated to the state by the federal government for vocational education or other educational purposes. Responsibilities of a state department of education are indeed extensive. No school or school district in a state escapes its influences.

As is true of other aspects of education in America, there is wide variation among state departments of education in their relative importance in the overall educational organization. Assuming that importance in, and power over, education are relative to the size of the department, the influence and the extent of responsibilities are much greater in some state departments than in others. All departments, however, are rapidly expanding in power, in size, and in influence.

Judged in terms of time spent administering certain activities in the state, the most important areas are vocational rehabilitation, vocational education, instructional services, handicapped children, veterans' education, adult education, finance, teacher certification, research, statistical services, and school lunch programs. Obviously the state department in any state is important and influential.

Planning to improve the organization and services of the state department is in progress in all the states. All 50 states, and also Washington, D.C., the Virgin Islands, and Puerto Rico, have submitted to the U.S. Office of Education plans and requests for federal funds to help make such improvements. Federal funds are available for this purpose under Title V of the Elementary and Secondary Education Act of 1965 (discussed in Chapter 13).

State Involvement in Public Education

All the states face certain basic questions concerning the degree of involvement that the state should assume in education and the areas of education where the state should expand its control. Old and new issues that confront state governments include: What is a reasonable balance between the district's control of its education and the state's control? What minimum standards should the state require each district to meet? What financial policy will insure adequate and equitable financial support to each of the school districts? From what sources should the state derive its financial support? What policies regarding distribution of funds to each of the districts are educationally most sound? What minimum, foundation program should be required of all public elementary and secondary schools? These are all urgent issues that challenge the most expert educational statesmanship. Each issue really merits extended analysis, but for our purposes we necessarily choose only a few of the issues for brief discussion. These are, nevertheless, illustrative of the issues in general.

Centralization

One of the most difficult problems as well as one of the longest duration concerns state power over local school districts. As has been said, when the Tenth Amendment was adopted, because there was no reference to education in the Constitution, the responsibility for education went automatically to the states. Each state became a unit for the organization and administration of education within its boundaries. Under this policy the federal government had divested itself of control over a most important and costly social responsibility. The problem of how the state power over education should be exercised became, and to an extent continues to be, a problem for each state and, inasmuch as each state differs from the others, the problem was, and remains, in some measure unique with each state.

In the beginning the states had largely a laissez-faire policy. To start with, the Commonwealth of Massachusetts adopted what seemed to be the simplest solution by establishing very small school districts. Massachusetts' early system became the pattern for educational organization throughout the land. The citizens of the small administrative units truly exercised direct power over their schools. With time and changing social conditions, however, this simple solution became more and more impracticable and unacceptable. The various state legislatures had to face the problem of change, and the only direction that change could take was the removal of certain powers from the local school districts. Of course, when powers are taken from one group and given to another, there is a degree of conflict. From the beginning to the present, one of the most difficult educational problems of the states has had two aspects: What powers can and should be removed from local districts? What procedures should be used to accomplish the change? At the center of the difficulty the enduring issue is: What degree of centralization of power should the state attempt to promote? Or, to put it a different way: To what degree and in what ways should the state proceed to decrease local control over public education?

A state can move control over education farther from the people in two principal ways. It can pass more mandatory laws naming specific functions to be administered at the state level (e.g., taxation, pupil transportation, and the certification of teachers). Also, it can reorganize the public elementary and secondary school districts to make them much larger and more consistently able to maintain a full and complete system of elementary and secondary education. Many mandatory laws take much of the control of a function, although not necessarily complete control, out of local hands; they thus always reduce the extent of local control. Enlargement of public school districts, as previously discussed, would keep control over education in the hands of local people, but in the hands of fewer people.

Minimum Standards

The state departments of education establish minimum standards that local schools must meet or else suffer such penalties as may be stated in the law—cuts in state financial aid, for instance. As an example, a school may be required to employ only teachers who possess minimum qualifications for state certification. Schools may be required to have pupils in attendance a minimum number of days each year. Some states require that certain subjects, like U.S. history or health education, be taught. Some states have established a minimum salary for beginning teachers. If a teacher under contract should perform services for a local school board and receive less compensation than the minimum prescribed by law, that teacher is entitled to recover the deficiency.

When the state establishes minimum standards, in theory it guarantees the individual pupil a basic standard of education regardless of where the pupil lives within the state or which school he or she attends. All the states do not, of course, provide equal minimum standards.

Foundation Program

Despite the establishment of certain minimum standards, studies show that marked inequalities in educational opportunity characterize the schools in all the states. The discrepancy in educational opportunities between the poorest schools and the best schools in a state is, in some cases, so great as to constitute a social threat. The discrepancies in some states are greater than in others, but they are wide in all states. It might logically appear that poor schools are in communities of substandard wealth and that the discrepancy can be explained by lack of money. When we consider, however, that the entire state is an educational unit, it seems clear that it is not the substandard wealth of a community that is responsible. It is the policy of the state toward raising and distributing revenue for public school purposes that creates and perpetuates the discrepancies. The state organizes school districts. If a school district has low taxing ability and insufficient income to support the schools, the state has the responsibility for equalizing the educational opportunities. This can be done, if the state desires, by first establishing a foundation program for every district and then adopting a policy of school support that will ensure each district's ability to maintain the foundation program.

How can a state do this? The state must begin by defining its foundation program—the minimum program of education to be available to each child in the state. Every state now prescribes some kind of foundation program for its schools, often a bare minimum, but many of these programs have been developed haphazardly. In many states they have grown out of a long list of separate legislative actions. A legislature may decree, for instance, that every school in the state shall be open for a minimum of 180 days, that U.S. history shall be taught in all the secondary schools, and that all eighth-grade pupils shall be required to pass examinations testing knowledge of the federal and state constitutions as a condition for admission to the ninth grade. But can one call legal prescriptions such as these a program? Sometimes such foundation programs, if they deserve that name, do very little to reduce educational inequalities in a state. They may be legislated mainly to satisfy the passing fancy of legislators or to placate the persistent pressures of some highly vocal organized group.

A foundation program that will reduce educational discrepancies and equalize opportunities must be expertly planned and must be broadly acceptable to the school public. The state can act in either of two general directions. It can pass legislation defining in detail the standards each school district must meet. These standards might prescribe a school session of 180 days, a specified minimum salary for beginning teachers, and buildings and equipment that must meet definite quantitative and qualitative standards. The maximum size of a class might be established and the maximum teaching load stipulated. Many details of the state program are thus settled. They are defined by state fiat.

A simpler way, and one that is more in line with American local school tradition, is to set a minimum expenditure per pupil as the standard for all school districts. This leaves the planning of the details to the local district with a minimum of state intervention. The standard of expenditure may be changed from time to time as the occasion requires and as the state feels is warranted.

Once the state requires that each public school district shall maintain a foundation program for all the children in the school district, it must collect and distribute school revenues so that the financial burden for this foundation program is no heavier in the districts of low taxing ability than in the districts with higher taxing ability. The cost factor must be equalized. (In fact, in 1968 the Detroit school system sued the state of Michigan in a demand for an *unequal* distribution of state school funds, with more money going to big cities, so that larger amounts could be spent there in building good schools in economically disadvantaged areas.)

Financial Policy

What policy should the states follow in attempting to achieve a minimum program and at the same time to equalize the cost? It will require, initially, that each district in the state make an effort to support the foundation program equal to the effort of every other district. The local tax rate for the foundation program in a poor district will be exactly the same as the local tax rate in a wealthier district. Obviously the returns from taxes will be much greater in the wealthier than in the poorer districts. The wealthier districts will be able to support the minimum program with considerable ease. They probably will pay for the entire foundation program and will go as far beyond the program as they wish and further tax themselves accordingly. No limit is set on how much they spend on their schools or how good they make them.

The poorer districts, when taxed uniformly with the rest of the state, may find that they have collected insufficient funds to meet the cost of the foundation program. Funds from the state, called state aid, make up the difference. The poorer districts will receive larger sums from the state than districts with more taxable wealth. All districts make an equal effort to pay, but some must receive more state aid than others. This is not consistent with general state practice, which is to base state funds solely on average daily attendance.

State aid equalizes the cost of education for the foundation program but leaves the control of schools in local hands. The state remains the unit for providing school revenue. The words "state aid" are appropriate, since they imply that the state will assist local school districts but will not dominate them.

The state has the major responsibility for a financial policy that will eradicate many of the inequalities in educational opportunity within the state. By first defining the foundation program that all public schools must provide, it lets the people of the state know the minimum education they can expect from any school. This minimum standard will be tailored to the state's overall potential. Next, by establishing a foundation of financial support, the state will ensure that local public elementary and secondary school districts can maintain at least the accepted minimum program. Where a public school district is unable, through its own taxing powers with its own resources only, to support the foundation educational program, the state will provide the additional financial support needed. Wealthier districts may still, if they wish, provide education beyond the foundation minimum. The variable among the states will be the minimum or foundation program. This is a generally accepted plan, in broad outline. Working out the details of such a policy involves technicalities that require educational experts to formulate the foundation program and experts in state school finance to evolve the pattern for financial support.

In 1973–1974 state aid to local schools averaged around 43 percent of available local funds, with a range from 88.8 percent in Hawaii to 7.4 percent in New Hampshire. Perhaps, as a beginning, all the states should move up to or above the 50-percent point in providing state revenue. This might make a satisfactory start toward the ideal of satisfactory educational opportunity for *all* children.

Sources of State School Revenue

Where does a state get the money for its education program, including state aid? It is not possible to give a detailed analysis of all the sources of public school revenue in each of our 50 states. In any case, the picture is rapidly changing. A general trend is discernible, however: an increasing proportion of the financing of education in public elementary and secondary school districts is being assumed by the state governments. Nevertheless, the states, in varying degrees, still place a heavy responsibility for financing public schools on local governments. In the school year 1973–1974, for example, nationwide, about 49.5 percent of revenue receipts for public elementary and secondary schools came from local sources, with a range from 89.6 percent in New Hampshire to 3 percent in Hawaii.

The principal source of these local revenues is the property tax, both personal and real estate, a tax presumably conditioned on ownership of property and measured by its value. (The personal property tax is a tax on automobiles, furniture, jewelry, and the like.) Although specialists are generally agreed that the personal property tax is outmoded, it is still collected in some states, Illinois, for example. Making the real estate tax the principal source of school revenue also is seriously questioned, partly because the tax tends to be inflexible and also because accurate and fair valuations of real estate are difficult to achieve. The property tax has become increasingly inadequate as real estate has become less of an income-producing item in the economy. Many groups who have studied tax problems over the years advocate diversifying sources of public school revenue, but the property tax remains the principal local base for support of schools in public school districts.

School costs are a large part of the budgets of local governments. Although the property tax burden increases during an inflationary period American citizens have generally continued to approve raising the property tax ceiling and issuing bonds for school improvements. In times of inflation, the problem of adjusting to increased school costs is especially difficult because few items in the budget can be reduced. Often the only alternatives are to make needed faculty replacements from younger, inexperienced teachers who are lower on the salary scale, to increase class size, or to eliminate or reduce the services of such personnel as psychologists, fine arts teachers, or supervisory help.

Where does the state go for its revenue to distribute to the local school districts? State plans vary. Revenue from almost any state tax source may be used for school purposes if the state legislature desires. There is more and more dependence on general sales taxes. Sometimes excise taxes are levied on special products, such as alcohol or tobacco. The objection to the general sales tax is that it imposes a greater burden on the lower-income group, which spends a larger proportion of its income on necessary items for daily living and thereby pays proportionately more of the tax. Theoretically the income tax is considered most equitable. State constitutions and public opinion, however, sometimes make it difficult for a state to impose a state income tax. Up to now, reforms have developed slowly, probably because such reforms may call for constitutional changes, which are difficult to get passed.

The whole problem of state revenue, and especially of providing funds for public education, is a difficult one, the foremost problem in all the states. That education should be equalized throughout a state, and throughout any of the state's school districts, seems an essential, democratic principle. How to define the foundation program and how to raise the money to maintain it are, however, issues that arouse heated debate.

Policies of State Aid

All the states have programs of state aid, but the amount of state aid and the policy of distribution to the local public school district differ vastly. Some states have moved further toward equalizing the cost of education than have others. In all probability, the state that has a lower level of state aid has had to reduce its minimum education program in order to avoid putting an impossible tax burden on some of the poorer local school districts.

It is not difficult to reason logically that the state aid fund in any particular state should be larger, that improved foundation programs should be required, or that the brunt of the burden for local and state school support should not be concentrated on property taxes. Methods for making such changes, however, are not so readily apparent. Should the local school districts be further modified? Should the kind of taxes levied be changed? Should the methods of assessing, levying, collecting, and distributing tax money be improved, and if so, how? Should the authority and functions of the divisions of the state school system be clarified, simplified, and made generally more effective? Where should we look for intelligent and dynamic leadership for necessary reorganization of a state school system? These are, as yet, unanswered questions.

The state is the educational unit. What may be done locally depends on what the state constitution permits and what the state legislators feel inclined to do. The variations among the states regarding all details of state public school systems are imposing. Some states have advanced in their reorganization efforts, usually by gradual and continuous means. Some states have set up a permanent group, such as a commission on the reorganization of public school districts, to work on the problem.

Summary

Each of our 50 states is the unit responsible for the administration of education within its boundaries. The states vary greatly in their policies toward education, some states placing a much higher priority on education than others. State educational policies vary in leadership, public school districting, financial aid to districts, how revenue is raised and distributed, the manner in which local citizens are involved, the transportation of pupils, and many other aspects of state and community interrelationships.

Each state has a constitution (some are considered antiquated) and this, together with laws passed by the legislature and decisions by courts, forms an extensive legal structure that determines policies for conducting education within the state. When laws concerning education have become part of this legal structure—known as the school code—they tend to be solidified and difficult to change.

Not all state educational problems are financial, although financial policy is perhaps the most important element in determining the quality of education within a state. Also of great importance is a state's policy toward districting. Of the three basic types of public elementary and secondary school districts—large-city, suburban, and agricultural center—the agricultural area districts seem to have evolved a better climate for education than either of the other two. Even in agricultural districts, however, when older ones are reorganized, the relocation of individual schools, the problem of transportation, and the difficulties of obtaining adequate specialized services have been and remain pressing administrative problems. In other words, the many perplexing questions presented by districting are far from being answered. Each kind of district has crucial problems that, in fact, may not be solved by the present generation.

QUESTIONS

1. What in your opinion is the responsibility of a state when it establishes a public school district that does not have the resources to provide the foundation program prescribed by the state?
2. What is meant by equalizing educational opportunity within a state?
3. What logical steps may a state take to equalize educational opportunities within its borders?
4. Is it possible for a state to equalize educational opportunity without violating the principle of local control over education?
5. Why was the power to certify teachers taken over by the state?
6. What provisions for public education are made in the constitution of your home state?
7. When should a state school law be mandatory? When should it be permissive?
8. When do you consider it right and appropriate for a state teachers' association to attempt to influence legislatures?
9. In your opinion, how should a state board of education be organized?
10. What should be the functions of a state board of education?
11. How should the state commissioner of education, or state superintendent of public instruction, be selected?
12. What powers and duties should be vested in the state department of education?

PROJECTS

1. From a study of the state school code for your home state, list the major problems to which the legislature has given attention.

2. Describe the organization of the state board of education in your state and list suggested reforms.
3. Describe the organization of the state educational authority in your home state. Indicate the strengths and weaknesses.
4. Describe and evaluate the foundation program as prescribed in your state.

chapter

12

Local aspects of public school organization and administration

Students considering choosing public school teaching as a career may at this point say, "I'll give it a try!" They realize they must graduate from college and, in the process, qualify for a state teaching certificate and perhaps meet the requirements set by the AACTE. They must think about the grade level at which to begin teaching and consider the specific state or states with which to become identified. The public school is part of a state school district system, and what the school and the system are like will have much to do with initial success and feelings of well-being. When new teachers first meet their class of some 20 or 30 pupils, they may give little consideration to the school system as such. With time and experience, however, and with the growth that is sure to come, professional horizons will expand and views will broaden; ideally, teachers will continue this kind of enlargement throughout their careers.

In this chapter we study certain matters of great importance to all teachers but of special significance to those making plans to enter the profession.

What Is a Local School District?

As we have noted, local school districts are the units through which the state governs its public elementary and secondary schools. In other words, the state system for organization and administration of a public school corporation functions through those units known as school districts. As a part of the statewide system, the local school district is one thing; as primarily a local organization, it has a different set of characteristics, functions, and problems. It is the unit that encompasses a local area for the operation of schools for local boys and girls. It is the avenue through which local citizens act in establishing district-wide educational policies related to such important matters as financing, personnel, and curriculum. Local policies, of course, are always consistent with statewide policies set forth in the state school code.

Originally, school districts were small, and the state legislatures permitted them to be almost autonomous. Gradually, through the years, the states assumed more control over local school districts. In time, local districts were reorganized and consolidated into larger corporations, and thereby a measure of control was taken away from local people. Despite reorganizations, citizens of local areas still tend to think of local public schools as local possessions and of the operation of the schools as essentially a local responsibility. Some efforts at state reorganization have therefore encountered strong local resistance. Citizens, in general, wish to keep boundary lines constant so as to preserve what they believe is their rightful authority. Although, partly because of state district reorganizations, the meaning of the word "local" has undergone, and continues to undergo, change, what is done and what can be done in a school are matters of vital concern to people in the school district. Nevertheless, the way the local school operates has to change as the policies of the state and federal governments change. In other words, school districts have to be dynamic; despite conservative citizen effort to the contrary, they cannot be static.

The Structure of Authority

The Board of Education

I. POWERS

For efficient, democratic, local operation of public elementary and secondary schools, a group of lay citizens called a board of education, school board, school trustees, school committee, township board of education, county board of education, or something similar, has been given definite powers. Nearly every public school district in America is governed by such a board. In the school year 1968–1969, the number of citizens serving on boards of this kind was estimated at 110,380. This great reduction from 423,974 in 1933 has been caused in part by the great reduction in the number of local districts, but it also reflects the decrease in citizen service to school boards; the latter factor is more apparent when the growth in the nation's population since 1933 is considered.

A board of education is the legal agent specified by the legislature to be responsible for the conduct of education in the local district. By court decision such a board has been held to be a state agency, not an adjunct of local government—a fact often not recognized. (See Figure 12-1.)

From the viewpoint of the state, the board's primary responsibility is to put into effect state and community plans of education. The general power in the statute, which states that the function of a school board is "to do anything not inconsistent with this act," provides a broad basis for action. School boards authorize many activities on the assumption that it is proper to do so unless specifically prohibited by statute, and since many of these activities go unquestioned, they gradually become a part of routine practice. Such broad powers permit flexibility in action and provide opportunity for experimentation in new areas.

2. SELECTION OF MEMBERS

The membership of boards of education is decided in a variety of ways. Popular election is the most common, approximately 85 percent of school board members being selected in this manner. The others are appointed, usually by the mayor, city council, city manager, judge, or some other city, county, or state agency. The proportion of board members elected is considerably higher in the smaller school districts than in the larger. In large-city school districts, where the boundaries of the school district are coterminous with those of the city, the board is usually appointed by the mayor. By and large, American citizens have selected school board members in a manner consistent with the nonpartisan policy toward public education.

Whatever the method of selection, some kind of careful screening process often precedes the selection. Representatives of civic groups may meet in a district caucus to prepare the slate of nominees to

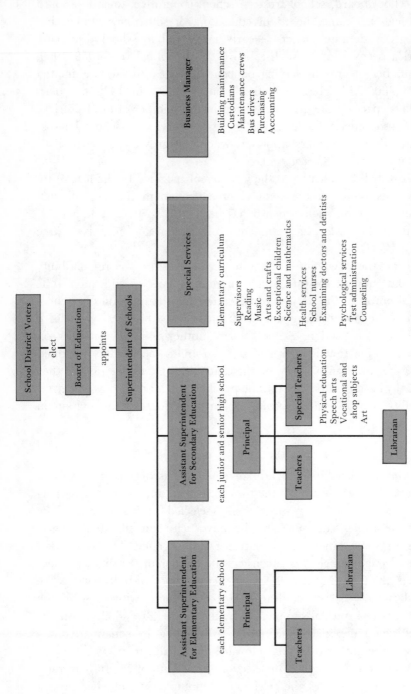

Figure 12-1 A typical local school system organization. The size and location of a system produce variations, but in all systems there are similarities in functions and in the way the functions are allocated and performed. Thus the pattern shown here is fairly common. The student may find it valuable and interesting to draw a similar diagram for a local system with which he or she is familiar and compare it with this one.

be presented to the voters at the special school board election. The nomination of some outstanding citizen by the caucus is almost tantamount to election. In other instances school board nominations are made by petition, primary election, mass meetings, or school district meetings or by an individual announcing that he is a candidate. Perhaps the most able candidates are those who are invited to run after careful screening by a sizable group of qualified citizens. Without some such process, public apathy toward voting for school board members could result in election of weak, perhaps narrow or selfish, citizens.

3. TERM OF OFFICE

Since it takes time for new board members to become informed of the needs of the local school district, it is desirable that they serve a reasonably long time—ordinarily a minimum of 3 to 5 years—and that, if warranted, they be allowed to serve a second term. For desirable continuity in board services, expiration of board member terms are generally staggered.

4. SIZE

The number of members of boards of education is related to efficiency in board action. A school board that is too small or too large has certain weaknesses. The number of members should be adequate to allow representation of the different points of view in the community. The one-member trustee, still found in some smaller communities, cannot fulfill this obligation. The question reduces to the following: What is the largest number that will assure a balanced judgment on school issues yet will be small enough to work effectively as a single group? According to a National School Boards Association survey made in 1965 of 42 cities with populations of 300,000 and over, 17 had boards of seven members; 12 had boards of five members; Milwaukee, Philadelphia, and Pittsburgh each had 15 members; Omaha and St. Louis had 12; Chicago had 11. Most experts in public school administration favor boards with seven members. It is felt that five is too small, because potentially a small political clique could gain control, and 9 is too large to serve as a single group. There is a tendency for groups of nine or more to act through committees. Therefore seven seems to be about the right number for a cohesive, representative unit. Because community traditions tend to be strong and the interests of the community and the schools tend to become intertwined, any established practice, whether in the best interests of the schools and community or not, becomes exceedingly difficult to change.

5. COMPENSATION

Membership on a school board has traditionally been considered as unselfish service to state, community, and children, and the chief reward has been the satisfaction of doing good work and receiving the respect of the community. In a few cities, however, the policy is to pay board members.

6. QUALIFICATIONS OF BOARD MEMBERS

Usually the law specifies only that the candidate for board membership be a qualified voter and a resident in the school district. Obviously, meeting only these minimum legal qualifications provides no guarantee that an individual can be an effective school board member or that the board will be broadly representative of popular interest in the public schools. Other factors that should be weighed in the selection of members include:

1. Whether the individual enjoys communitywide respect and is able to discuss educational problems intelligently and convincingly. Board members must cooperate with the community as well as with each other.
2. Whether the individual will be able to understand and direct the financial—business—affairs of the school system.
3. Whether the individual is willing and able to devote sufficient time and energy to the office.
4. Whether the individual is likely to minister to the educational needs of all the children in the district. The school board should be representative of and serve all the people. It cannot fulfill its responsibilities if it is faction-ridden, comprised of individuals each concerned only with promoting the interests of one socioeconomic, racial, or religious group.
5. Whether the individual has children or grandchildren attending school or is active in youth work. An individual with such a background is more likely to be interested in and understanding of educational problems than, for instance, a middle-aged bachelor whose concern for children has not survived his own childhood.

Generally the education of board members exceeds that of the total population—about 50 percent are college graduates. Typically the majority of the members are chosen from among the occupational groups called "successful men and women of business and professional affairs." Laboring groups and women are underrepresented. Women especially, it would seem, should be better represented, because as a group they have strong interests in and considerable insight into the education of their children, especially at the elementary level. Many women are qualified and have the time and energy required of a school board member.

7. FUNCTIONS

The functions of boards of education are implied in the broad powers, both specific and discretionary, granted them by the state legislatures. Ideally the school board acts as a kind of equalizer between the interests of the professional staff and the interests of the public. As state officers members also act as a counterinfluence to excessive state-centered authority over the public schools in their district.

More specifically, school boards hold meetings open to the public and to the professional staff, issue mimeographed or printed statements of their policies, employ a professional administrative staff (superintendent, business manager, and so on) to whom they delegate executive functions, map out or approve an overall educational program, fix salaries, draw up budgets, levy taxes, keep account of monies spent, decide the length of the school year, enforce compulsory attendance laws, determine where and when new buildings shall be erected, make rules and regulations for the management of the schools, purchase materials, provide pupil transportation, and so on. The list of functions is indeed formidable.

In recent years board practices in formulating policies have changed considerably. Boards now spend far more time in holding meetings to hear expressions of public opinion before making final decisions. Probably because of the growth in membership and influence of the teachers' national organizations, the National Education Association and the American Federation of Teachers, today's school board willingly enters into professional negotiations with teachers through well-defined procedures before making final decisions on such matters as salaries, sick leaves, and fringe benefits. In earlier times teachers were expected to—and usually did—accept submissively whatever the school board decided to give them. At that time school boards took the position that their authority was established by law and could not therefore be delegated to others. That is no longer held to be true. Boards have learned that through a series of orderly procedures many of their decisions can be shared. Among activities school boards have adamantly stood against are mandated mediation, sanctions, strikes, boycotts, and the like. Nevertheless, these techniques are being used increasingly by classroom teachers when they feel that a state or a district is not treating them fairly.

General Superintendent of Schools

The school board consists of laymen who do not profess expertness in school management. It is their responsibility to see that the work of the school is properly performed by professional personnel. They must employ a well-qualified professional educator to superintend the work of the schools. He or she is the chief executive, and as superintendent of the school district, occupies a central position in the overall structure of authority. The boards of education delegate many of their legal powers to the superintendent, but his or her policies are subject to board approval.

Since the superintendent's powers are broad, his or her duties are many and varied. As administrative head of the district, he or she is professional adviser to the board of education as well as supervisor, employer, and organizer of the professional personnel and supervisor and employer of the nonteaching personnel (e.g., engineers and janitors). He or she is the expert in relations between the schools and the community and formulator of the policies that rule the selection, placement, and transportation of pupils. In other words, the superintendent of schools is charged with the final responsibility for the efficient management and effective organization and administration of all the public schools in the school district. The position is important, calling for a high level of administrative ability and professional leadership. Because of its importance in school administration considerable study is devoted to defining the superintendent's work and to providing specialized training programs in graduate schools.

In a smoothly running school organization only the chief executive is legally responsible to the board. In all but the smallest systems, however, the superintendent has administrative and supervisory assistants to whom responsibility and authority are delegated.

There is a growing tendency to recognize the need for including the teachers and, in some cases, the public in defining school policy. In earlier years the superintendent was considered to be more sympathetic to the board than to the teachers. Today he or she is considered both the agent of the board and the representative of the teachers. The superintendent tends to include teachers when formulating plans and policies and encourages them to participate in making decisions. The superintendent's authority has thus been reduced, his or her opportunities for leadership enhanced.

In simple terms, then, the public school district is a state corporation, the board of education is the governing body, the superintendent of schools is the chief administrative officer.

County Superintendent of Schools

The professional staff of the school district in agricultural centers is sometimes headed by a county superintendent of schools. From the title "superintendent," one might assume that this position is analogous to that of city superintendent of schools. Such, however, is not generally the case. In states where the school district in the agricultural centers is organized on the town or township basis, the county superintendent's functions are mainly clerical. Only a few executive responsibilities are delegated to him. For example, in Illinois the county school superintendent, who is elected on a partisan political ticket, visits the rural schools periodically. State monies are channeled through his or her office. As the legal representative of the state, the county superintendent sanctions those who teach in county schools and interprets school law when the need arises. As a rule, steps in the reorganization of school districts are cleared through his or her office. In the 12 states in which the school districts coincide with the county boundaries, however, the position is somewhat, but not wholly, like that of the superintendent in a city district.

County and district school boards look on the county school superintendent as their professional adviser and leader. Whether appointed to be the chief executive officer for county boards of education, or elected on a political ticket and possessing only remote executive authority over individual school units within the county district, or selected by the elected trustees of the townships in the county, the county superintendent is an important person in the direction and improvement of public education in the agricultural areas of the United States.

The trend toward the reorganization of school districts and the reduction or abolishment of one-teacher schools tends to change the functions of the county superintendent of schools. Perhaps the future of the office cannot be predicted at this writing. In some cases, where, say, the county is made the organizational and administrative unit, the powers and functions of the office might be expanded. In other instances the opposite effect might even lead to making the office relatively obsolete. Different policies of reorganization in different states will almost certainly affect the official state and local relationships of the county superintendent of schools.

Abiding Traditions

The great variety of types of organization and administration results from (1) the unplanned development of education from semiprivate, short-term, low-cost schooling for the few to the huge public enterprise it is today and (2) the persistent emphasis on local initiative in educational planning. Despite this variety, however, traditions have persisted that cause schools throughout the nation to remain very much alike.

Self-government

An insistence on locally administered school systems is a manifestation of the deep-rooted American belief in the doctrine of popular sovereignty. The people elect school boards, vote bond issues, employ and live close to educational personnel, and in many other ways participate in school management. The degree of local control, however, is influenced by the policies of state and federal governments, and these shift with the times.

Local Interest

Throughout the nation citizens express pride in their local systems of free public schools. One way the professional staff fosters this interest is by encouraging wide, representative citizen involvement in public education. Furthermore, every proposal to shift responsibility and power from the local system to, for example, a statewide system is always examined closely to determine whether it may weaken the system by diminishing local control and stifling the local public's interest in schools that they have come to regard as "theirs."

Dispersion of Power over Education

Most Americans realize that power over education equals power over the nation's future. They know also that if this power were concentrated in a few "wrong" hands, education might be used to change the next generation's whole social outlook. Traditionally, we have rejected such concentration of power over education and, instead, have distributed control among many agencies and among many people. Of all traditions in American education, this perhaps is the one most likely to persist.

In 1974 there were 16,492 operating elementary and high school districts in the United States, and all of these were controlled by the local citizens. Some of these districts had boards with as many as 11 members—Chicago, for example. Some districts had only one school trustee, as in some township school districts in Indiana. The number of Americans who serve the schools on a voluntary basis is large indeed. Generally these people are capable and well-intentioned. Only rarely has control fallen into incompetent, corrupt, or selfish hands.

Teachers prefer to work in schools that are under the general control of local boards, principally because they are accustomed to this form of control and feel it can more readily reflect desirable local interests. Teachers cannot visualize what would be involved in adjusting to and influencing a highly centralized state educational system. Through their professional organizations teachers are encouraged to contribute to the formulation of school policies. Local school boards—which because they are local are accessible—are becoming more and more aware of the value of direct communication with teachers, of the value of consulting with teachers before defining policies. Teachers' relations with a nonlocal governing body would probably be too impersonal to permit such a direct relationship.

The public, of course, does not want the professional staff to conduct schools only as they, the staff, desire. On the other hand, the public does not want to dominate the schools. What it seeks is partnership. Partnership recognizes that the interests of staff and public are mutual. The public and the staff are closely related in the same venture, and its success depends on how each accepts and cares for the interests of the other.

Neighborliness

Neighborliness is a cherished characteristic of the typical American community. The school is highly suitable for the promotion of neighborliness because it is the one community institution that can cut across lines of class, religion, race, or political affiliation. With the current practice of busing children within a city district to schools that are not geographically "neighborhood" schools for purposes of achieving racial integration, and with the reorganization of many schools in agricultural centers, the dedication to the neighborhood school has had to change. Although in many communities the present-day school is no longer a traditional neighborhood school in the sense that it is the main center of recreation and social life, spirit of neighborliness is still cultivated by such events as PTA activities, parent's night at school, athletic events, parades, concerts, exhibits, and so forth. To the extent that the school is used to strengthen the tradition of neighborliness, it too is strengthened.

Free Choice

Parents are free to decide whether their children will attend public or nonpublic schools. This is in accord with one of our democracy's central tenets: the individual has the right to believe in whatever he chooses. The individual's beliefs direct his choice among political parties, churches, clubs—and the school that his children will attend.

Summary

We find great variation among school systems in the public school districts, even within the same state. Differences among the states and differences among districts in the same state are due in part to the fact that many state legislatures grant considerable authority to district boards of education. In some cases, for example, the laws are permissive, granting the boards wide latitude in interpretation. This means that America really has an educational system based on the principle of state-local cooperation. At present no complete or specific division of power has been developed, and experiments continue. There is a definite trend toward enlarging districts, especially in agricultural areas, and various patterns of enlarged districts are being tried. Whatever the answer to the question of local-state relationships, it is generally agreed that the self-governing school community should not be sacrificed. Problems related to the local school district should be solved without weakening the local interest of the community in its schools. Citizens, as they function through boards of education, are vested with authority over the schools. Fundamental changes in education are dependent on aggressive and intelligently informed citizenry.

Under widespread control, no single agency, it is believed, can ever gain control of the public schools, nor can any one propaganda agency influence education throughout all the nation's public schools.

From the start it was believed that it would be better to leave education in the hands of those who were most closely touched by it than in the hands of those far removed from the community. A local school system is more likely to respond quickly and sympathetically to a community's needs. Whatever the weaknesses of localism may be, it appears that the local school district, in some form, is likely to dominate the American educational scene for years to come.

QUESTIONS

1. What are the principal advantages of the American policy of operating the schools largely through home rule? What are some disadvantages?
2. What have been the principal advantages and disadvantages to education of the district type of organization as it has functioned in the past?
3. What is a local board of education? What are its principal functions?
4. In what ways has local school management become more difficult in recent years? What may school boards do to compensate for the increase in their responsibilities?
5. How is the superintendent of a local district appointed? What, ideally, are his or her principal functions?
6. How is a county superintendent of schools selected? What are his or her principal functions?
7. In your opinion, should the functions of the county superintendent parallel those of the city superintendent of schools?
8. What are the principal differences between a local municipal government and a local school district government?

PROJECTS

1. Survey the pattern of school districting that prevails in your state. Point out where and how improvement has been brought about.
2. Draw up a list of standards for local school boards on such matters as selection, term of office, size, representation, qualifications, and compensation.
3. List the powers and duties of a local school board. Indicate how a community may guard against misuse of powers.
4. State the pros and cons of keeping school government separate from municipal government.
5. a. Explain why inequalities in educational opportunities have been allowed to develop in large-city school districts.
   b. Explain what should be done to erase them.

chapter

13

Federal activity in education

In the overall picture of education in America the relative roles of the three levels of government—federal, state, and local—do not remain fixed for any length of time. Changes in educational policy at the federal level produce changes at both the state and local levels. Likewise, a new state law may modify the relationships between the local and state levels. It seems, then, that the interrelationships that exist at any one time among the three levels of government will continue to be characterized by constant change.

The most significant change in the past quarter century in American education has been, perhaps, the steady growth in the concern, influence, and participation of the federal government in many aspects of both public and private education at all levels—for children, youth, and adults of all ages. As will become clear as we proceed, it is most difficult to come even close to making an accurate estimate of the extent to which the federal government contributes to education because its contribution takes so many forms. This is strikingly illustrated by the growth in the amount of money the federal government spends on public education. In 1957–1958 the amount of public school revenue derived from the federal government was 4 percent of the total; 11 years later, however (1968–1969), it had increased to more than 8 percent. (The percentage remained fairly constant up to 1965–1966; then greatly expanded federal programs caused it to double.)

However, by the 1973–1974 school year the National Education Association estimated that the percentage of federal government support for elementary and secondary schools in the United States had dropped from the more than 8 percent level of federal support in 1968–1969 to approximately 7.5 percent. This drop in the level of federal support to elementary and secondary public schools reflected the decreasing federal emphasis on support for public schools resulting from continuing reductions in population growth, the increased costs of federal government services resulting from worsening inflationary conditions, and changes in recent federal priorities in the field of education. This has been a matter of grave concern to professional educators and boards of education at the local and state levels. The beginning of 1975 saw the United States confronted with a continuing dangerous rate of inflation in retail and wholesale prices as well as in the costs for such basic commodities as petroleum and steel. These economic changes created serious problems for all governmental agencies that have to provide vital social services. Since the costs of public education are financial responsibilities that fall primarily on local and state governments, any reduction in the level of federal revenues for public or nonpublic education is a serious problem. In the mid-1970s American educators were searching for new ways to motivate congressional and presidential interest in support for public education.

Congress passed several laws in the mid-1960s and early 1970s supporting programs such as school lunches and other aids to education. But the amount of federal support fluctuates, depending on the policy priorities of the federal government and the state of the American economy. The federal government does support many specialized programs to aid states on the basis of the relative ability of each state to pay for public education from its tax revenues. Thus not all states receive the same levels of support. Each fiscal year the federal government's aid to the public schools of the states is determined by the financial needs of the respective states. In the 1973–1974 school year it was estimated by the National Education Association that the state that received the highest percentage of support from the federal government for public elementary and secondary schools was Mississippi (about 24.5 percent federal support) and the state that received the lowest percentage was New Hampshire (3 percent level of support). Across all the 50 states the average level of support from the federal government for public elementary and secondary schools was 7.5 percent, as noted earlier. The difference between the 1968–1969 and the 1973–1974 percentages of federal government support for public elementary and secondary schools, a loss of less than 1 percent may seem slight; however, one must realize two things: (1) even 1 percent represents a loss of several millions of dollars of federal government support to the school systems in the United States that need such support the most, and (2) because of the very high rates of inflation each year in the period 1968–1974, the costs to local public school systems have increased at the same rate as those of private taxpayers and the federal government.[1] Furthermore, public school systems have encountered major problems in raising more tax revenues for public schools in the past several years as taxpayers have felt the pressures of higher prices and higher taxes on their property. The role of the federal government in the future development of public educational services in the United Sates will be a matter of major national concern for many years to come.

Because a classroom teacher's welfare is inevitably affected by changes in the federal government's activities, especially if the shifts in policy are sharp, no teacher will wish to remain a mere spectator to changes outside the classroom. As a member of the profession, the teacher will wish to evaluate educational changes, support those that seem desirable, skillfully implement those that are judged worthy from an educational point of view, and influence the direction of future changes. Government acts can produce good results only when the education profession provides the wise leadership needed to fulfill the provisions of the acts.

Since the influence of the federal government on education began even before the adoption of the Constitution, and since the long story of federal activities in the area of education has so many facets, we can select only a few of the more outstanding, more illustrative steps the federal government has taken. Let us consider first how the federal government justifies its considerable influence over education in America and note the ways it has, up to this time, limited its participation.

[1] See *Rankings of the States, 1974.* Washington, D.C.: National Education Association, Research Division, 1974.

Constitutional Provisions for Education

Why did members of the Constitutional Convention omit any mention of education from the Constitution? For one thing they were faced at that time with several other and more serious problems that had to be solved to preserve national unity. In the face of such emergencies it is not surprising that they should put less pressing matters in the background. We must remember also that at the time little thought had been given to public education. The ideas and the theories developed by Pestalozzi, Herbart, and Froebel had not yet been born. Education in early America was largely of interest only to those who could afford to pay for it.

In the preamble of the Constitution, however, the obligation to advance the cause of education is implied in the statement that it is the purpose of the Constitution to provide for the common defense and general welfare. The section of the Constitution that empowers Congress to levy and collect taxes likewise states that taxes shall provide for the common defense and general welfare of the United States. Although the founding fathers did not specifically mention education, they made statements that unquestionably obligate the federal government to advance public education.

On the other hand, the Constitution, by implication, also makes it clear that power over education is to be delegated to the states. Since power over education was not specifically delegated to the United States nor prohibited to the states, it was, according to the Tenth Amendment, definitely to be left to the individual states. That has consistently been the construction placed upon the wording of the Tenth Amendment.

There is general agreement that the federal government in America has complete control over certain segments of education, segments that are wholly outside the jurisdiction of any other unit of government. These are the following:

1. The education of residents of special federal areas, such as government reservations and federal districts lying outside the legal jurisdiction of a state and other regional governments.
2. The education of the American Indians and other indigenous peoples within the national jurisdiction.
3. The education of the peoples of the territories and outlying possessions.
4. The training of persons in the service of the national government.

5. Scientific research and the collection and diffusion of information regarding education.
6. The intellectual and educational cooperation of the United States with other nations.[2]

The federal government thus assumes complete authority over a considerable part of education in America. In addition to these six areas of complete federal authority, the federal government increasingly participates in education in the states and in local districts and even gives educational aid to certain individuals. A review of the historical development of such federal activity will lead to a better understanding of current federal activity in education.

Federal Grants to Education

Unconditional Land Grants

In 1785 and in 1787 the Continental Congress passed two ordinances that provided for surveying the Northwest Territory and planning the administration of the territory. The first of these ordinances established the policy of reserving the sixteenth section in each township (1 square mile out of 36) for the benefit of public schools. The precedent for this action was the reserving of land for school purposes by several of the former colonies.

The federal government did not put the land-grant policy into operation until 1803, when Ohio was admitted as a state. Vermont, Kentucky, and Tennessee, which were admitted to the Union as new states within a few years after the adoption of the Constitution, did not receive any land for common school purposes.

The provisions of the Ohio Act were extended in 1803 to the national domain south of Tennessee and in 1821 to the Louisiana territory. Only three states admitted since 1803 have never received some kind of federal land grant for public schools: Maine, where the federal government had no title to any territory because Maine had been part of Massachusetts; Texas, which was a sovereign state when annexed; and West Virginia, which seceded from Virginia during the Civil War. Since 1850, when California was admitted, two sections of each township have been given for schools in all new states except Utah, Arizona, and New Mexico, which were allowed four sections because of the low value of the lands.

It is evident that the early federal legislators did appreciate the

[2] National Advisory Committee on Education, *Federal Relations to Education.* Washington, D.C.: National Capital Press, 1931, pp. 9–10.

importance of public education and were interested in helping the states establish public schools. However, fostering education was secondary to other desired achievements. Their first interest was in selling and settling western lands. They believed that making school land available would promote the sale of real estate.

The land grants to education, considered an acceptable and essential federal aid policy, were to be out-and-out grants to the states, with no strings attached. After the state received the land, the federal government did not interfere with its use or management. This is an example of an early and prevailing attitude of the federal government—the principle of federal support without federal control.

In the states admitted early to the union, the general policy was to sell the land and to place the proceeds in a *permanent* fund. The interest from the fund was to be used for public school purposes. Often public land was the one source of support for education, and the lands could be kept or sold at the discretion of the state. Some states handled these permanent sources of income much more wisely than others. A few states virtually squandered their inheritance, allowing

The policy of setting aside a portion of the public lands for school purposes, rather than selling all the land or homesteading it, was first established in the Land Ordinance of 1785, enacted by the Congress under the Articles of Confederation on May 20, 1785.

An Ordinance for Ascertaining the Mode of Disposing of Lands in the Western Territory

Be it ordained by the United States, in Congress assembled, That the territory ceded by individual States to the United States, which has been purchased of the Indian inhabitants, shall be disposed of in the following manner:

A surveyor from each state shall be appointed by Congress. . . . The Surveyors . . . shall proceed to divide the said territory into townships of six miles square, by lines running due north and south, and others crossing these at right angles, as near as may be. . . . The plats of the townships, respectively, shall be marked by subdivisions into lots of one mile square, or 640 acres, in the same direction as the external lines, and numbered from 1 to 36. . . .

. . . There shall be reserved the lot No. 61, of every township, for the maintenance of public schools within the said township; also one-third part of all gold, silver, lead and copper mines, to be sold, or otherwise disposed of as Congress shall hereafter direct. . . .

dishonest individuals and greedy corporate interests to exploit federal land grants. However, in 1940 one-third of the land granted was still owned by the states. It is especially to the credit of the newer states that they have administered their share of public land for school purposes wisely. The value of their federal land grants is constantly increasing. The provisions of the early ordinances, which followed the policy of aid-in-general, stimulated sentiment for public education. In the older states the federal grants were especially helpful at a time when the idea of taxing citizens for the support of public schools was not generally accepted.

The policy of depending on permanent school funds, in its application, has had great influence on both public and nonpublic education. At present almost every university, whether public or nonpublic, has its own tax-free foundation built from contributions from many agencies—private individuals, industrial and commercial organizations, and the like. Also many tax-free foundations with exceedingly large financial resources make liberal grants to education, both public and nonpublic, and thereby exercise far-reaching influence on the course of education in America. Where the principle of permanent funds, called endowments by some universities, has been tested in the courts, the Supreme Court of the United States has consistently sustained the validity of a corporate charter given by a state to a school, denying that the state subsequently has the right to amend it, thereby assuring preservation of educational capital and the continuity of educational foundations.

From the history of federal aid to education, it seems that the question of future policy will not be concerned with categorical versus general aid to the states. We may expect a continuation of both policies—specific aid where needed and also general aid to the states to enhance their resources for designated state programs. Recent indications are, however, that categorical aid will receive first priority from the Congress.

Federal Grants for a Specific Purpose

I. THE MORRILL ACTS

The policy of no restrictions on management or uses made of the income from land grants was not followed in some of the later federal programs, notably in the Morrill Act of 1862. In part this was because the earlier grants had been squandered in some states and. in part because the earlier universities had remained almost entirely academic.

A proposal to establish a national agricultural college, analogous to West Point in the military field, had been defeated. The Morrill Act passed subsequently was intended to encourage the establishment in each state

The principles of federal aid to higher education and of the legitimacy of permanent school funds, sometimes referred to as endowments, are recognized in the Morrill Act of 1862, The wording merits careful reading.

An Act Donating Public Lands to the Several States and Territories Which May Provide Colleges for the Benefit of Agriculture and Mechanic Arts

Be it enacted by the Senate and the House of Representatives of the United States of America, in Congress assembled,
That there be granted to the several States, for the purposes hereinafter mentioned, an amount of public land, to be apportioned to each State a quantity equal to thirty thousand acres for each senator and representative in Congress to which the States are respectively entitled by the apportionment under the census of eighteen hundred and sixty: Provided, That no mineral lands shall be selected or purchased under the provisions of this act. . . .

Section 4. And be it further enacted, · That all moneys derived from the sale of the lands aforesaid by the States to which the lands are apportioned, and from the sale of land scrip hereinbefore provided for, shall be invested in stocks of the United States, or of the States, or some other safe stocks, yielding not less than five per centum upon the par value of said stocks; and that the moneys so invested shall constitute a perpetual fund, the capital of which shall remain forever undiminished (except so far as may be provided in section fifth of this act), and the interest of which shall be inviolably appropriated, by each State which may take and claim the benefit of this act, to the endowment, support, and maintenance of at least one college where the leading object shall be, without excluding other scientific and classical studies, and including military tactics, to teach such branches of learning as are related to agriculture and the mechanic arts, in such manner as the legislatures of the States may respectively prescribe, in order to promote the liberal and practical education of the industrial classes in the several pursuits and professions in life.

of at least one college where the leading object shall be, without excluding other scientific and classical studies, and including military tactics, to teach such branches of learning as are related to agriculture and the mechanic arts, in such manner as the legislatures of the States may respectively prescribe, in order to promote the liberal and practical education of the industrial classes in the several pursuits and professions in life.

This act, signed by President Lincoln, granted to each state

an amount of public land . . . equal to thirty thousand acres for each senator and representative in Congress to which the States are respectively entitled by the apportionment under the census of eighteen hundred and sixty: Provided, That no mineral lands shall be selected or purchased under the provisions of this act.

The act further established a measure of control by stipulating that each state claiming the benefits of the act should make an annual report "regarding the progress of each college, recording any improvements and experiments made, with their costs and results. . . ."

This act and another Morrill Act in 1890 led to the establishment of 69 land-grant colleges, some of which are now among America's largest and most influential state universities. At least one such college was established in each state. In some states (e.g., Illinois, Wisconsin, and Minnesota) the colleges were combined with the state universities. In others the federally aided colleges were established as separate colleges (e.g., Iowa State University, Michigan State University, and Purdue University).

Federal policy enunciated in the Morrill Acts was to give land grants to *higher* institutions, to state the principal objectives of the education for which the grants were to be used, and to require an accounting of the money spent. "Unconditional" grants did not constitute the only policy followed.

2. SMITH-HUGHES ACT

A number of congressional acts have authorized federal grants-in-aid to vocational education. The grants, in all cases, have been large and the effects upon public education have been far-reaching. The Smith-Hughes Act of 1917 was one of the first, and also one of the most influential, of a series of acts that gave aid to vocational education offered in the public high schools. It is a fairly typical example of how the federal government engages in educational activity.

> The term "land grant" is significant, implying that land was the foundation on which the present structure of agricultural and mechanical and also military colleges has been erected. It would be more accurate, however, to call them "land bait" colleges, because the grants were relatively small moneywise. They were large enough, however, to induce the states to set up a system of colleges which are supported partly by state taxation and partly by federal funds. . . .
>
> The purpose is to show how a relatively small gift of frontier land was used to establish a system of education that is nationwide, closely integrated, and now supported almost entirely by taxation, both state and federal. And it was created and raised by a little wedge of frontier land.*
>
> * Walter Prescott Webb, *The Great Frontier.* Boston: Houghton, Mifflin, 1952, pp. 402, 404.

Under the Smith-Hughes Act the federal government subsidizes high school vocational education in agriculture, home economics, and industrial education. The act also provides for the preparation of teachers of those subjects. Money is apportioned to the state on the basis of total population, and in order to receive it "the state or local community, or both, shall spend an equal amount" for this work. Each state and local community is required also to meet certain other standards. Congress has never failed to make the appropriation for these purposes—but it could, of course, refuse at any time.

Certainly many favorable effects have accrued from the Smith-Hughes Act and from similar legislation. High schools have become more conscious of the great need for expansion in the vocational field. New instructional materials and methods have been developed. Shops and laboratories in the high schools have been well built and adequately equipped. Education and salaries of the high school teachers of vocational subjects have been greatly improved. Improved salaries have attracted more highly qualified personnel.

The categorical-aid policy followed by the federal government in the Smith-Hughes Act and similar other acts called for the state to match federal funds to improve a single aspect of the educational program, perhaps at a given level. This was a departure from the earlier policy of giving general aid. Some educational leaders questioned the wisdom of the change. It was argued that federal aid to a given high school to help support a vocational education program, for instance, gave certain advantages to some staff members in such matters as salary, training, and number of months employed during the year, and was damaging to personnel relations. Also expressed was fear of the power of the federal bureaucracy over state and local programs, vocational or otherwise. Federal control was considered by some as a threat to the principle that the state is the unit of school administration and to the general practice of having the states control the powers given to the local school districts. With time, however, categorical aid from the federal government has proved a powerful and more or less welcomed stimulant which, once imbibed, continues to be sought despite objections in some quarters that its acceptance is a bad habit.

As the public and the teaching profession became accustomed to a degree of federal control of education, it became easier to accept an increase in federal power. For instance, the Morrill Acts extended a measure of control at the college level, the Smith-Hughes Act of 1917 extended it to the high schools, and as noted later in this chapter, the Elementary and Secondary Education Act of 1965 for the first time included the elementary schools.

Clearly, the federal government has not followed a single policy toward support of education. Politicians in particular seem to favor the aid-for-specific-purpose policy. Each act, however, has been independent of all the others. Many of the federal grants-in-aid have been crash programs, responses to sudden, pressing necessity. Each act, therefore, must be viewed as a separate episode in the history of the federal government's participation in American education.

Recent Federal Money Grants

I. MEASURES PASSED DURING THE DEPRESSION

During the depression of the 1930s, grants to education were mostly outright, with no requirement of matching funds. Laws set forth conditions under which funds had to be used but did not exert control over the programs.

The National Youth Administration was organized during the depression to provide aid for needy high school, college, and university students so that they might continue their education. The funds were administered and the work was assigned by the individual school in which the services were used. The federal grants-in-aid went directly to the high school or college students through institutional channels.

The Civilian Conservation Corps also was an emergency depression measure. Its purpose was "relief of unemployment through performance of useful public work." Camps were organized for young men, and an education program was made an integral part of the plan. The camps were under the administrative control of the army. So was the education program.

The school lunch program was an emergency relief program also started during the depression. With the passage of the National School Lunch Act of 1946, however, it became a regular part of federal participation in education. This act was designed "to safeguard the health and well-being of the nation's children and to encourage the domestic consumption of nutritious agricultural commodities and other foods." Under this act the federal government gives the local schools, through the states, both direct grants of surplus commodities for use in school lunchrooms and money to facilitate the distribution and use of these food products. This enables local public schools to provide federally subsidized low-cost lunches to their pupils. Although this is a direct form of federal aid to education, it was, in the beginning, designed primarily to help the farmers rather than the school children. Its value has been such as to assure its continuance as an accepted federal policy. In 1972, 48.8 percent of the public and private school enrollments were participating in the federally subsidized school lunch program. The range by states was from 24.9 percent in New Jersey to 84.8 percent in Georgia.

Many other federal programs of education were initiated during the depression, including the establishment of nursery schools, classes in avocational and leisure-time activities, special programs, and lectures. Funds for school buildings were also provided under the Works Progress Administration. It should be noted that federal aid to education has never been administered through a single agency such as the U.S. Department of Health, Education, and Welfare. Currently, several agencies are dispensing funds for various kinds of aid to education.

2. MEASURES PASSED BEFORE AND DURING WORLD WAR II

In the period immediately before World War II and during the war, disruptions growing out of such emergencies as the demand for many people with certain highly specialized training, the relocation of masses of people, and the large-scale employment of mothers led the federal government to conduct some emergency education programs and to make grants for the administration of others. For example, the Lanham Act, passed in 1941, provided general appropriations for training war plant workers under the direction of the U.S.

Office of Education, for constructing school plants in areas that were overburdened because of federal activity, and for maintaining child care for the children of employed parents.

3. GI BILL OF RIGHTS

In terms of influence and cost, one of the great federal participations in education is contained in laws collectively and popularly known as the GI Bill of Rights. The program began with the Vocational Rehabilitation Act and the Servicemen's Readjustment Act signed by President Franklin D. Roosevelt in 1944. Since then other laws have been added. In the peak year, 1948, nearly $3 billion was spent in subsidizing programs of education for veterans. Incidentally, only very rarely was any charge raised of "government interference" in the educational programs of high schools and colleges that were involved in this GI schooling. The GI Bill of Rights guarantees to veterans payment of tuition as well as payment for board and room for a specified number of months, based on length of military service rendered. The GI Bill has enabled millions of young men and women to attend high schools, colleges, universities, specialized schools, and adult education classes throughout the land. Several hundred also have studied abroad under the GI Bill. In addition to increasing the numbers enrolled in our schools, the GI Bill tended to change the character of our school population. It became commonplace for married men and men with families to be full-time students. Temporary housing for young families mushroomed on college campuses. The GIs were older and more serious. Their presence raised the age level of those in school and gave an impetus to adult education.

4. FEDERAL AID TO HIGHER EDUCATION

Millions of dollars are now flowing annually from agencies of the federal government into educational agencies and institutions of higher learning. The National Defense Education Act, signed into law on September 2, 1958, strengthened American education at all levels. Within 5 years the federal government had expended $800 million to assist educational institutions of higher education, both public and nonpublic, and to aid state agencies with programs believed important to the nation's security. This included, for example, $330 million assigned to a student loan program, 70 percent of which was lent to students of superior ability who intended to teach in the elementary and secondary schools. Another $65 million was spent on the education of school counselors. Over the 5-year period, 1958–1963,

$181 million was paid to the states and territories to strengthen instruction in science, mathematics, and modern languages in the public elementary and high schools. The number of language laboratories in public high schools rose from 46 in 1958 to approximately 6000 in 1963. However, in the early 1970s there developed a national trend among colleges and universities to cease requiring the study of foreign language in undergraduate studies, and this trend then damaged the large foreign language programs that had been developed in high schools, as many high school students decided that they did not need to take a foreign language in their high school years. By 1975 many of these federally funded language laboratories built in the 1960s were not being utilized as fully as had been anticipated when they were built. Many people who cherish the cultural benefits of the mastery of a foreign language have lamented this development, but this is one of the regressive educational developments that occurred in the late 1960s and early 1970s.

Equally large amounts were spent in improving other services. Periodically the U.S. Department of Health, Education, and Welfare issues a report on the National Defense Education Act, a report that describes in detail the many purposes for which federal funds are allocated. The annual report gives a vivid picture of the extensive scale of this federal excursion into a strengthening of American education, with the continuing support of the Congress.

5. ELEMENTARY AND SECONDARY EDUCATION ACT OF 1965

In response to a rather belated awakening by the federal government to manifest, and extreme, inequalities in educational opportunity among school districts and among states, the Congress of 1965 passed a number of significant laws. The most far-reaching of these was the Elementary and Secondary Education Act of 1965, officially designated Public Law 89-10 and unofficially referred to as the federal government's billion-dollar educational venture. The law was designed to reduce certain long-time cumulative deficiencies in both state and local education—the neglected education of young children in underprivileged areas of large cities, for example. A brief description of each of the law's five original titles gives an understanding of the extent and intent of the act as a whole:

Title I. Title I gives financial assistance to state school districts for the education of children from families whose income is less than $2000 a year. Five-sixths of the entire federal appropriation goes for the implementation of this title of the law. In an area where there is a concentration of such families, an area clearly identified by administrators of public or nonpublic school systems, all children are eligible to receive the benefits of the improved education made possible by federal funds.

Title II. Title II allocates some $100 million to the states to provide state public school districts and nonpublic schools with certain specified resources, such as school libraries, textbooks, and a variety of other instructional materials.

Title III. The purpose of Title III is to bring educational innovations into the school system. Application must be made to and approved by the U.S. Commissioner of Education. A wide variety of programs can be aided under this title. Basically, the hope is that the special and somewhat original local programs will make wide use of the community's resources, utilizing as never before its cultural advantages and talented leaders.

Title IV. Title IV provides $100 million over a period of 5 years for constructing and equipping national and regional research facilities. A rather broad interpretation is placed on the word "research." For example, funds are provided for building and operating national and regional laboratories, utilizing many existing resources such as universities, public schools, state departments of education, industrial research organizations, and the like.

Title V. Title V gives grants to the states for the specific purpose of strengthening the state departments of education.

The five titles cover a wide area; taken together, they represent an energetic federal attack on the weakest points of education as it has functioned in the past.

In addition to these original five titles or chapters of the Elementary and Secondary Education Act of 1965 [Public Law (PL) 89-10], there were other federal Public Laws passed as amendments to and extensions of the provisions of this act. Presented here are the Public Laws of 1966, 1967, and 1970, which either strengthened or extended the provisions of the original ESEA Act of 1965. The descriptions clearly indicate the range of educational concerns now being dealt with in response to pressing national educational needs since 1965.

Elementary and Secondary Education Amendments of 1966 (PL89-750)—in addition to modifying existing programs, authorized grants to assist States in the initiation, expansion, and improvement of programs and projects for the education of handicapped children at the preschool, elementary, and secondary school levels.

Elementary and Secondary Education Amendments of 1967 (PL90-247)—in addition to modifying existing programs, authorized support of regional centers for education of handicapped children, model centers and services for deaf-blind children, recruitment of personnel and dissemination of information on education of the handicapped; technical assistance in education to rural areas; support of dropout prevention projects; and support for bilingual education programs. Also, in order to give adequate notice of available Federal financial assistance, (this act) authorized advance funding for any program for which the Commissioner of Education has responsibility for Administration by authorizing appropriations to be included in the Appropriations act for the fiscal year preceding the fiscal year for which they are available for obligation.

Elementary and Secondary Education Assistance (1970) Programs, Extension (PL91-230)—authorized comprehensive planning and evaluation grants to State and local education agencies (State departments of education and local school districts); (this act also) provided for the establishment of a National Commission on School Finance.[3]

These amendments and extensions of the original Elementary and Secondary Education Act of 1965 point up the great concern felt in the United States in the decade from 1965 to 1975 regarding many social problems, including too many students dropping out of school, the now widely recognized need for bilingual education programs for Americans of Spanish descent and American Indians, the needs of both urban and rural poverty areas, and the need for continuing assistance in other areas of educational research and development.

Further, other federal laws were passed in the 1970s to deal specifically with such major issues as drug education and centers for the rehabilitation of young people with special problems, bilingual education, continuing provision of school lunch and breakfast programs where needed, reorganization of administration in the education of American Indians, and other areas of concern. Major federal laws providing aid to programs in drug abuse prevention and treatment (PL92-255) and environmental education (PL91-516) were also passed. Federal Public Laws constituting amendments to or appropriations for selected federal educational programs are passed in each

[3] See W. Vance Grant and C. George Lind, *Digest of Educational Statistics: 1974*. Washington, D.C.: National Center for Education Statistics, pp. 121–123.

2-year period of the U.S. Congress. Many professional and lay citizen organizations make strong efforts to gain congressional support for federal aid to educational programs. There have been federal laws to assist institutions of higher learning as well. In 1975 in the midst of the worst economic recession since the depression of the 1930s there was growing pressure on the federal government either to increase direct aid to state and local educational systems or to return more federal "revenue-sharing" funds to the states for use in meeting their educational needs. This pressure reflected the strains placed on state and local school systems by 10 years of severe inflationary pressures in the American economy. Amendments to the Elementary and Secondary Education Act and other federal laws were passed to prevent racially segregated school systems from receiving federal aid. This was mandated by the Civil Rights Act of 1964.

6. HEAD START PROGRAMS

The Economic Opportunity Act, signed into law in 1964, was one of the key measures in the federal government's "war on poverty." One program under this act is Project Head Start, which was begun during the summer of 1965 and is continuing as a summer and also as a year-round activity. Head Start was designed

> to improve the health and physical ability of poor children, to develop their self-confidence and ability to relate to others, to increase their verbal and conceptual skills, to involve parents in activities with their children, and to provide appropriate social services for the family in order that the child of poverty may begin his school career on more nearly equal terms with his more fortunate classmates.[4]

In some cases Head Start programs are operated by public school systems and in others by private schools and by nonprofit private agencies, such as settlement houses. About two-thirds of the summer programs and about one-third of the year-round programs are operated by the schools.

The government establishes criteria for selection of children but allows some leeway by asking that 85 percent of the children meet the requirements. Government requirements include family income of less than $3000. The age range of children included is 3 to 6.

---

[4] Office of Economic Opportunity, *Catalog of Federal Assistance Programs,* Washington, D.C., June 1, 1967, p. 554. (Head Start was moved to the U.S. Department of Health, Education, and Welfare in 1969.)

Chapter 15, "Units of School Organization," contains a discussion of Head Start as a part of the total school organization.

Public Reaction to Federal Grants to Education

It must be remembered that the major share of the nation's total educational program is still borne by the 50 states and the thousands of local communities that operate the schools of our country, even though the practice of making federal grants for the support of education is well established, widespread, and diversified. Even among those elements of the population who were, in the past, most vocal in their opposition to federal aid to education, the resistance has now subsided. The questions now before the American public are the following: How much federal aid should education be given? How should it be administered? What agencies are best qualified to administer it? To whom should grants be made? With what other governmental units should the costs be shared?

Other Educational Activity at the Federal Level

Education for National Defense

The U.S. Military Academy at West Point, New York; the U.S. Naval Academy at Annapolis, Maryland; the U.S. Merchant Marine Academy at Kings Point, New York; and the U.S. Air Force Academy at Colorado Springs, Colorado, are all supported and operated entirely by the federal government. These are a few examples of federal education conducted for reasons of defense. The total program for such education is extensive.

Education Under Special Federal Jurisdictions

Inasmuch as the District of Columbia is not part of any state, the operation of its education program is left to the federal government. Congress makes all the laws that govern the District of Columbia, including those that apply to the schools, makes all the appropriations, and provides the means for raising revenues, which are collected by a combination of direct taxes and direct appropriations from the federal treasury.

The citizens have the right to vote only in national elections for the President of the United States, and therefore those who are placed in control of the schools are not responsible to the community to the same degree as in public schools that are part of a state system. The school board appoints a superintendent of schools, who performs the functions usually assigned to such an officer.

Where the federal government has complete control, it shows its skill and reveals its attitudes toward public education. Generalizing from the Washington, D.C., school system, we may say that federally controlled systems operate about as efficiently and in much the same manner as do public schools in the rest of the country. None of the federally operated schools have ever been thought of as providing models or patterns to follow. For example, the school system in the nation's capital is noted for a predominance of the typical "inner-city" school, for schools characterized by a large proportion of disadvantaged children.

The federal government also assists in promotion of education in the federal reservations, territories, outlying possessions, and U.S. trusteeship territories. It aids other countries through the U.S. Point Four Program, the Foreign Operations Administration, the U.N. Technical Assistance Program, and the Peace Corps. The widely varying educational problems involved testify to the extensive range of federal activity in education.

Individual Schools

All the executive departments of the federal government engage in some kind of educational activity. Some of them operate schools to train government personnel and to help improve personnel once they are in the employ of the federal government. The Department of State, for example, gives instruction to all newly appointed diplomatic and consular officers. The Treasury Department maintains a training school for the Coast Guard service, one for stenographers, a correspondence school for the employees in the Bureau of Internal Revenue, and a number of others the department considers essential to the proper performance of its functions. The Department of Justice's school to train its personnel and the schools maintained by the Social Security Board are other examples of the numerous individual schools set up and administered by various departments of the federal government. Their educational activities are of great magnitude, affecting in some form well over a million civilians.

The U.S. Office of Education

The chief educational agency of the federal government is the U.S. Office of Education. It is the only federal agency devoted solely to improving the education of about 60 million students in American schools and colleges and to making educational opportunities more equally available to all.

The legal foundation for the U.S. Office of Education was laid in 1867:

> *Be it enacted by the Senate and the House of Representatives of the United States of America, in Congress assembled,* That there shall be established at the city of Washington, a department of education, for the purpose of collecting such statistics and facts as shall show the condition and progress of education in the several States and Territories, and of diffusing such information respecting the organization and management of schools and school systems, and methods of teaching, as shall aid the people of the United States in the establishment and maintenance of efficient school systems, and otherwise promote the cause of education throughout the country.

39th Congress, 2nd Session:
Approved by President Andrew Johnson, March 2, 1867.

In spite of the use of the word "department," the agency was not intended to have Cabinet status; a little over a year later its name was changed to Office of Education, and it was placed in the Department of the Interior. In 1870 the office was renamed the Bureau of Education, and that title was retained until 1929, when the title of Office of Education was restored. In 1939 the Office of Education was transferred from the Department of the Interior to the newly created Federal Security Agency. In 1953 the Office of Education became a part of the newly created Department of Health, Education, and Welfare, with a secretary in the president's Cabinet. In its present setting it naturally receives greater recognition than in earlier years.

Since 1918 bills for the establishment of a separate federal department of education and a secretary of education in the president's Cabinet have been proposed again and again. Those who favor these proposals believe that, at present, public education does not have sufficient prestige in the federal government and that a separate department could more effectively articulate the achievements and outstanding problems of public education. Opponents point out that placing a secretary of education in the Cabinet would move education into the arena of politics on a national scale and perhaps increase the danger of federal control over state and local education.

The Office of Education is one of seven operating agencies of the Department of Health, Education, and Welfare. Its early function—and a continuing one—was to collect and distribute statistical and other information on education in the United States. Today, however, its overriding responsibility is to administer financial aid to education, to channel federal funds allocated by Congress—several billion dollars annually in recent years—into programs developed by state educational agencies, local school districts, and colleges to upgrade the quality and broaden the scope of instruction. These programs cover the educational spectrum from kindergarten to postgraduate study, from vocational training in high school to adult education throughout life. Nearly all of some 19,000 public school systems and 2300 colleges in the United States participate. Students in parochial and private schools at the elementary and secondary levels also benefit from some programs.

The change in emphasis dates from 1958, when Congress responded to the first successful launching of a Soviet satellite and the immediate concern in the United States about the quality of our educational programs in science and related fields. The National Defense Education Act of 1958 was the first step by the federal government to assist school administrators in their increasingly difficult task of trying to provide quality education largely with local tax dollars and, in the case of colleges, with state or private revenues.

Even more far-reaching were the congressional decisions of 1965. The Elementary and Secondary Education Act authorized a multibillion-dollar program of federal aid to elementary schools and junior and senior high schools. By far the largest part of these funds was marked for special programs to help raise the quality of education for children from low-income families. The Higher Education Act set up seven new programs to strengthen colleges and universities and provide loans and grants to financially needy college students.

Other programs recently established or expanded by Congress and administered by the Office of Education include aid to vocational education, to the education of mentally and physically handicapped children, and to colleges and universities for construction or rehabilitation of classrooms, dormitories, and other facilities.

The U.S. Commissioner of Education

At the head of the U.S. Office of Education is the commissioner of education, who is appointed with the consent of the Senate by the president, on the recommendation of the secretary of health, education, and welfare. The commissioner serves an indefinite term. Sometimes a change in presidents is followed by the appointment of a new commissioner.

The commissioner's duties are listed in the act that established the Office of Education. In addition, his duties have been expanded over the years to include special tasks assigned by the president and imposed by congressional enactments, as well as voluntary cooperation with numerous educational agencies.

Judicial Controls

Although public education is a matter over which each state is sovereign, there are certain limitations on state action. State educational policy is in a most vital way subject to control by the Supreme Court of the United States.

Any state legislation, including educational legislation, is subject to review by the Supreme Court. If the Supreme Court decides that the law violates a provision of the U.S. Constitution, the law is declared unconstitutional and invalid. The authority to invalidate legislation affecting education is derived chiefly from the following provision of the Fourteenth Amendment:

> No state shall make or enforce any law which shall abridge the privileges or immunities of citizens of the United States; nor shall any state deprive any person of life, liberty, or property without due process of law nor deny to any person within its jurisdiction the equal protection of the laws.

The Supreme Court is the final judge as to whether a person has been deprived of liberty or property. Since the terms "liberty" and "property" are extremely comprehensive, all manner of social and economic legislation, including educational legislation, may be invalidated. Obviously, state educational policy is in a large measure subject to control by the judges of the highest of our federal courts.

Supreme Court decisions have influenced the states in such problems as the relationship between schools and religion, uniformity of treatment of different races in the schools, and contractual relations with teachers. None of these matters have to do with federal power over education, but rather with federal responsibility for protecting individual rights.

When the Supreme Court hands down a decision that affects the policies of public education, the decision itself constitutes an interesting public statement of educational policy. The decision is always accompanied by the reasoning behind it, and these analyses, broadly circulated by the press, radio, and television, serve to educate the American public effectively about fundamental issues in public education. In this way the Supreme Court has served as an educator to all the people of the United States.

The *McCollum* decision (1949) is one example of a Supreme Court decision concerned with the relationships of schools and religion. It grew out of the protest of Mrs. Vashti McCollum, a professed atheist, that her 7-year-old son, who attended a public school in Champaign, Illinois, was being subjected to ridicule and scorn because he remained in the classroom when the other children left to take part in religious exercises and training currently provided by the churches of the city on time released by the schools for this purpose. The school authorities, and then a series of lower courts, ruled against her plea that released-time practices be outlawed. The case finally went to the Supreme Court, which ruled against the released-time practices followed in this particular school system.

Another decision on religious education in the public schools was made in 1952 in the *Zorach* case in New York City. This decision declared the practice of released time constitutional. The opinions in the two cases were not contradictory. In Champaign those who were not excused to take religious instruction remained in school, whereas in New York all pupils were released from school, presumably to receive religious instruction. The reasoning of the Court in rendering such judgments can be understood by a layman only after careful study of the complete decision. The important point is that from the standpoint of the administration of public schools, the decisions of the Supreme Court are the final answers to controversies of a specific nature. Public schools may not be used to promote religious instruction, as was thought to be the case in Champaign. But where the public schools do no more than accommodate their schedules to a program of outside religious instruction, as was the case in New York, such action is deemed constitutional. Thus religious instruction on released time is legal under certain conditions. Sometimes the distinctions between legal and illegal practices are so fine that only an experienced judge or lawyer can make them.

Another conflict that has received the attention of the U.S. Supreme Court is that over uniformity of treatment of different races. In past years the prevailing pattern of education in the states of the South was separate schools for black children. Both white and black schools were under the same board of education and the same superintendent of schools, were financed by a common tax structure. In many communities, however, inferior buildings, old equipment, and poorly paid teachers were provided for black children. In the cities of the North the policy of segregation was not as complete nor as openly advocated, but in many cases the education provided for black children in the North was not much better than that provided in the South and was equally segregated. This pattern of separate schools was made more permanent when the United States Supreme Court, in 1896, handed down a decision in the famous *Plessy* v. *Ferguson* case. The theory underlying this decision, that separate but equal facilities did not violate the Constitution, gave the highest governmental sanction to the pattern of organizational segregation but not to any practice that denied black people equal educational opportunities with white people. Any school district could segregate the races if it maintained schools that were equal. The separate-but-equal doctrine became the legal basis of segregated schools in the North as in the South.

Many cases involving segregation of the races have entered the courts since then. On May 17, 1954, the Supreme Court handed down the famous decision that declared an end to the segregation of school children on a racial basis:

> We conclude that in the field of public education the doctrine of "separate but equal" has no place. Separate educational facilities are inherently unequal. Therefore, we hold that the plaintiffs and others similarly situated for whom the actions have been brought are, by reason of segregation complained of, deprived of the equal protection of the laws guaranteed by the Fourteenth Amendment.

When Chief Justice Warren announced this decision, he said that the Court realized that the decree presented problems "of considerable complexity." In attempting to solve the very complex problems, educational and government authorities have encountered obstacles rooted in bitter hate and deep-seated prejudice in both the North and the South. School integration is difficult to achieve, in part because it is only one facet of the much wider problem of cultural integration, including such areas as housing and employment. Deep emotions have led to incredibly violent reactions, to assassinations, arson, looting, even to the murder of children in a church.

Many cities, especially those in the North, where segregation of the races has been related to or has grown out of segregated housing, are using buses to achieve racial balance among the schools of their jurisdiction. Opposition of whites to sending their children by bus out of a neighborhood school and into a school with mixed racial population, or sending black children into a formerly all-white school, has often led to some form of violence.

Federal programs like Project Head Start are operating with the hope that they may help the underprivileged child, of whatever ethnic or racial background, to be prepared to take an equal place with his schoolmates in an integrated school.

Some leaders among black Americans now advocate separate but *really* equal, or even superior, schools, schools in which the black will be the policy maker, where the power of black persons will be equal to the power of white men in their schools.

Despite all the problems, many as yet unsolved, the movement toward school integration presses forward. Perhaps the ideal cannot really be achieved until racial discrimination has been removed from all our institutions—business, church, courts, housing, and, most important, from the attitudes and feelings of the members of each race toward the other.

On June 25, 1962, the Supreme Court rendered an opinion on the question of religion in the public schools. The Board of Education of Union Free School District No. 9, of New Hyde Park, New York, had directed the district's principal to have the following prayer said aloud by the teachers and pupils at the beginning of each school day: "Almighty God, we acknowledge our dependence upon Thee, and we beg Thy blessings upon us, our parents, our teachers, and our country." This daily ritual was backed by action of the state Board of Regents, thus making it a statement of authority by the state of New York. The parents of 10 pupils brought action against the regulation, contending that it violated both the New York State Constitution and the Constitution of the United States. The state courts of New York ruled the regulation to be constitutional. The Supreme Court of the United States held it to be unconstitutional.

That the Supreme Court has a vital influence over education in the United States cannot be denied. It makes the final decisions in many important cases as to what the laws pertaining to education mean. Since most Americans believe that law and not men shall rule, that known rules of procedure and not the whims of politicians or powerful pressure groups shall control in all exercise of governmental power, the judges of the Supreme Court are the final authorities who make the decisions that settle many concrete educational issues.

The Future

Equalization of Education

There is strong sentiment among educators toward having the federal government expand its efforts to equalize educational opportunities throughout the nation through some program of federal grants to the states. There are, admittedly, great variations among the states in the quality of public education and in their ability to support education. It is argued that the federal government has a responsibility to reduce such variations.

The quality of education is not determined solely by the amount of money spent. It is, nevertheless, one very important factor, and perhaps the best single gauge to the quality of education. Those states that maintain inferior school systems usually can raise little money, have little valuable school property, pay unreasonably low salaries to the teaching personnel, employ less-qualified teachers, and assign large classes and excessive teaching loads to the teachers. According to estimates assembled by the NEA, New York spent $1809 for each pupil in ADA (average daily attendance) in 1973–1974. During the same year Alabama spent $716. (The expenditure in the United States as a whole was approximately $1121.) By no combination of compensating factors could Alabama have offered its children educational opportunities equal to those of New York.

In 1973–1974, 19 states paid average annual salaries to public school classroom teachers of $10,500 and above, and the NEA estimated that the average public school classroom teacher's salary was $10,673. It was estimated that 45.9 percent of all public school teachers were paid at least $10,500; rating the states on a scale from the state with the highest percentage of teachers in public schools earning at least $10,500 to the state with the lowest percentage of teachers earning that much, 99.4 percent of Alaska's teachers earned that amount of money and only 0.7 percent of South Carolina's teachers did.

States also vary in birth rates and in the percentage of school-age children, aged 5 to 17, among the total resident population. In 1973 school-aged children comprised 24.5 percent of the total population of the nation. New York, a wealthy state, with 23.4 percent of its total resident population of school age, ranked forty-sixth (with Kansas) among the states. Other affluent states, such as Rhode Island, New Jersey, Pennsylvania, Massachusetts, California, and Illinois, also ranked below the national average. On the other hand, some less wealthy states, such as North Dakota, South Dakota, Louisiana, South Carolina, and Mississippi, ranked above the national average: a larger percentage of school-aged children was included in their total population.

Some states with limited resources available for public education must meet the greatest educational demand. Were such states as South Dakota, Mississippi, and Louisiana to adopt model tax systems and to assign the maximum amount they could afford to supporting public education, they would still be far short of the support needed for even an average state school system. Many of the less wealthy states are making efforts relatively greater than some of the wealthier states, but they are still unable to raise sufficient revenue to support the kind of schools their children need.

Because our population has a high rate of mobility and because the rate seems to be increasing, the social evils resulting from substandard education in one section of the country are not confined to that area but spread to all sections of the country. The public school problems of New York and Chicago are accentuated because of the substandard education received by many who move into New York and Chicago from other sections of the country. It is not just for humanitarian reasons that the people of Oregon are asked to approve expenditures from the federal budget to help education in Mississippi. It is more than mere neighborliness. The quality of education in any section of the United States affects the welfare of the entire country.

Equalizing education on a national basis, it is argued further, is justified also on purely economic grounds. If it is true that the amount of education received by an individual increases his productivity and his other contributions to society as well as his desire and ability to consume more and better goods, then elevating the educational level in all sections of the country is economically advantageous.

If the federal government increases its efforts to equalize education through a policy of making larger grants-in-aid to economically poorer states, or to those cities with a concentration of large numbers of disadvantaged children, will that lead local authorities to relax in their own efforts to pay for schools? Will it be a case of "easy come, easy go," of careless wasting of federal money? This is one danger. Such laxity, however, would probably be corrected and perhaps prevented by an objective formula and a definite audit procedure.

Tax Policy

For the federal government to tax wealth where it exists and to distribute funds where they are needed is in harmony with accepted principles of taxation. The federal government has tapped the most productive source of revenue—the individual income tax. Because of the huge federal debt federal taxes will probably be high for many years.

Local government agencies depend on the property tax for at least one-half of their total revenue. In most communities the expenditure for schools is the biggest item in the local budget. When property owners feel the pressure of adverse business conditions, they tend to demand relief first in property taxes. A reduction in school expenditures is a ready source of relief. The worst aspects of a demand for decreased school costs, it is believed, could be alleviated by having the states assume a greater share of the local school costs and, in turn, having the federal government assist the states through a policy of equalization of the cost burden. Such a plan would, however, meet with considerable opposition, especially from those reluctant to minimize local community responsibility for local public education.

A Statement of Basic Policy

If any one conclusion stands out in our review of federal participation in education, it is that there has been little consistency in procedures or purpose and little uniformity in policy. Grants-in-aid have sometimes been made without strings attached. In other instances the states have been asked to match federal funds granted. Grants have been made for higher education and for special fields on the secondary level. Grants have been made to ease emergencies in agriculture and other fields. Grants have been made to individuals. There seems to have been no pattern, no consistent trend, no emergent policy. It has been suggested that in order to aid in formulating future plans for the federal government in relation to education, a broad and basic statement of national policy be enunciated. This, it is believed, would serve as a guide to educators and legislators, contribute to stability, and lend direction and assurance to those involved in various aspects of the federal government's education program.

What are some of the matters on which clarification of position is needed? It would seem reasonable to expect that government aims should be stated. The statement of basic policy might say in broad terms what educational opportunities the federal government wishes to make available to all children in the nation. The policy statement should also set forth general procedures and types of activities to be used in implementing the general aims. A basic statement of policy would be adaptable to changing social conditions and to national emergencies. Such a statement of policy would provide a stable foundation and a guide for lawmakers and encourage consistency in future federal participation in education.

The difficulties of formulating a statement of basic policy are numerous and sizable. In a democracy the frequent changes in Congress tend to result in inconsistencies and in activities that do not fit into a stable and long-term plan. Then there is the question of who would draw up so important a statement of national policy.

Perhaps Congress, which has the final say, might itself issue a statement of policy on federal participation in education. To date, however, there has been little unanimity among members of the Congress in this matter. Since World War I there has not been a session of Congress that has not had at least one bill introduced providing money grants to the states for state school support.

As we have stated, there has been considerable support for the proposal that a Cabinet office be created to be devoted solely to education. The suggestion that a board of education at the national level be organized has received the support of the NEA and other influential groups. Perhaps the present organization, which includes a commissioner of education and an Office of Education under the Department of Health, Education, and Welfare, is potentially equipped to draw up a statement of federal policy. If this agency were endowed with adequate authority and were assigned administrative responsibility, it could, perhaps, give effective guidance.

Another possibility is the appointment of a special group with specific responsibility for formulating a general policy and for making recommendations. Beginning with President Herbert Hoover, who appointed a group that made a report in 1931, every president has called together a special committee of experts to study the nation's education and present recommendations for federal action. The weakness of such commissions has been their lack of influence on the legislators. It is the lawmaking body of the federal government that decides on the future of education in our country. Any special group—a national board of education, a Cabinet department, a strengthened Office of Education, or any other kind of organizational structure for this purpose—can only be as effective as the Congress permits it to be.

This brings us to the responsibility of individual citizens—and particularly members of the teaching profession. The federal program of education is not something remote, something complicated and removed from teachers and parents. Teachers owe it to themselves and to their profession to be acquainted with government activities in education on the local, state, and federal levels. It is important that teachers understand current political issues regarding such matters as federal support of education, taxation for education, and equalization of educational opportunities and that they be willing and able to discuss and interpret these issues for local citizens. It is this grass roots approach to the Congress through local voters that is the responsibility of individual citizens.

Summary

It is generally agreed that the federal government should continue but improve its program of equalizing educational opportunity throughout the nation. A broad statement of acceptable policy produced by a competent authority is a sound preliminary step. Such a statement will give direction and information to the Congress, and from Congress will come decisions about the future of the federal government in education.

QUESTIONS

1. What are some of the educational problems of the federal government that result from having three levels of government?
2. What legal principles have been developed by the federal government to guide it in its administration of education? How do you explain the lack of uniformity in these principles?
3. How is educational authority organized at the federal level? In what directions do you think improvements could be made?
4. What part does the U.S. Supreme Court play in shaping the policies toward education in the United States?
5. Do you consider the principal recommendations of the Hoover Commission on federal aid to education to be sound? Why? How do you

account for the small influence this report has had upon subsequent policy at the federal level?

6. How is the question of federal financing of education in the United States affected by population trends?

7. How do you account for the extraordinary amount of attention that Congress has given to encouraging vocational education in the schools?

PROJECTS

1. Appraise the effect of the Morrill Acts on higher education in America.
2. Appraise the effects on American education of the Smith-Hughes Act and other similar acts.
3. Analyze the arguments of the judges of the U.S. Supreme Court in some of their more notable decisions bearing upon education. Note particularly the social principles they used to justify their decisions.
4. Show why property taxes have, under present conditions, ceased to be a satisfactory base for public school support.
5. Show how certain problems like illiteracy are essentially national problems. Draw an analogy with education.
6. List and briefly explain what you feel is required to correct the deficiencies in elementary and secondary education, in addition to the massive federal aid given in the Act of 1965.

chapter

14

The
nonpublic
schools

Many schools in the United States may be termed "nonpublic," a classification covering a wide variety of institutions operating at all levels of education. Generally speaking, nonpublic schools are supported by private funds and their control is vested in private individuals or nonpublic organizations. In a few instances, such as a laboratory school in a state university, control and support may be both public and nonpublic. To achieve simplicity and clarity we will focus our discussion on schools that are mainly privately controlled and supported. Although the state has legal authority over nonpublic schools, in practice it normally exercises only a minimum of control, confining the use of authority to such matters as the competence of the teachers and the school's ability to satisfy certain minimum program requirements.

Enrollment figures are not available for all nonpublic schools. Little reliable data about specialized private vocational schools on the secondary level, for instance, are available. The ratio of nonpublic to public school pupils varies from state to state. Approximately 70 percent of the nonpublic school pupils are enrolled in schools in 10 states. The eight states that have the largest percentage of pupils attending nonpublic schools are Rhode Island, Wisconsin, Pennsylvania, New Hampshire, New York, Illinois, Massachusetts, and New Jersey. In these eight states the overall ratio of nonpublic school attendance to public school attendance is about 1 to 5. In the country as a whole the percentages range from 26.1 in Rhode Island to 1.7 in North Carolina.

In 1972–1973 the enrollment in Catholic parochial elementary and high schools was a little under 3.8 million (a major decline from about 4.94 million 4 years earlier). Of all American elementary and secondary school pupils, some 8 percent attend Catholic schools. About 90 percent of the total elementary and secondary school enrollment of the parochial schools of America is in the Catholic schools. Of the remaining 10 percent, 4 percent are in Lutheran parochial schools, 4 percent in nonsectarian schools, and 2 percent in schools under the auspices of other religious sects. Since little is known of the large number of pupils enrolled in such nonpublic schools as the vocational, commercial, military, and technical trade schools that give high school and post–high school training, the picture of nonpublic schools in terms of statistics is not complete.

The ratio of attendance at nonpublic colleges to public colleges has been approximately 40 to 60. It has been changing, and the Office of Education estimates that by 1975 the ratio will be 30 to 70, assuming that the present trend continues. The ratio of resident attendance at nonpublic and public colleges and universities varies with the individual state. Close to 97 percent of college students in the District of Columbia attend nonpublic colleges, whereas none attend nonpublic colleges in Nevada or Wyoming. Other states that rank high in attendance at nonpublic colleges are Massachusetts, Pennsylvania, New Jersey, and Rhode Island.

Many of the institutions of higher learning in the United States enroll nonresident students. Some of them give courses for college credit by correspondence. Some give short courses, individual lessons, and other adult education programs without college credit. Hence many more students are enrolled than the numbers indicate.

Basic Rights of Nonpublic Schools

The basic rights of nonpublic schools to operate in the United States are derived from two sources. First, the prevailing social philosophy of the people is pluralistic. It is an accepted American tradition that a citizen may have many loyalties—to family, church, club, and lodge—and still be loyal to the state. Second, the right of the nonpublic schools to function was officially recognized by the United States in the Fourteenth Amendment to the Constitution. As discussed in the previous chapter, the U.S. Supreme Court is the final arbiter when individuals or groups feel that some law is unconstitutional because it infringes on personal liberty as guaranteed by this amendment.

The Supreme Court has decided that the right to attend a nonpublic school is a personal liberty guaranteed by the Constitution. Its first decision on a violation of the spirit of the amendment was rendered in 1925. Oregon had legislated that all children must attend public schools. The Court ruled that the law was a violation of the Constitution because it interfered unreasonably with the liberty of parents to direct the education of their children. It was further held by the Supreme Court that a law requiring attendance at a public school would destroy the value of the property owned by the nonpublic schools. The wording of the decision is worth noting. It is a pointed statement of America's belief in the pluralistic philosophy.

> The fundamental theory of liberty upon which all governments in the Union repose excludes any general power of the State to standardize its children by forcing them to accept instruction from public teachers only. The child is not the mere creature of the State; those who nurture him and direct his destiny have the right, coupled with the high duty, to recognize and to prepare him for additional obligations.

The policy of the United States with respect to the basic rights of nonpublic schools seems clear. Parents are protected in their right to send their children to nonpublic schools. Freedom to choose is considered a fundamental right, one that is highly respected. The nonpublic schools are, in turn, protected in the ownership of their property and in their power to control that property.

Regulation of Nonpublic Schools

The nonpublic schools operate under the laws of the individual states just as the public schools do. The U.S. Supreme Court has consistently recognized the states' power to regulate schools. In the previously mentioned Oregon decision, the Supreme Court spoke as follows:

No question is raised concerning the power of the State reasonably to regulate all schools, to inspect, supervise and examine them, their teachers and pupils; to require that all children of proper age attend some school, that teachers shall be of good moral character and patriotic disposition, that certain studies plainly essential to good citizenship must be taught, and that nothing be taught which is manifestly inimical to the public welfare.

In line with its rightful prerogatives, each state, as we have pointed out in a previous chapter, has passed laws governing the education conducted within its boundaries. These laws, as they affect the nonpublic schools, are of two kinds. There are general laws that apply to the activities of all individuals and organizations conducting businesses or charitable undertakings within the state. Unless specific exceptions are made, these laws apply to the nonpublic schools. Under these laws an agency to which the state has delegated the responsibility must enforce regulations concerned with building codes, health laws, fire prevention, workmen's compensation, welfare of children in boarding schools, motor vehicle codes, codes regulating cafeterias and other boarding places, and any other provisions designed to protect public welfare. In other words, nonpublic schools, whether incorporated or not, are subject to all the general regulations that have been prescribed by the state for corporations.

A second kind of state law applies specifically to nonpublic schools, although it may be general enough to apply also to some other organizations within the state. This type of law regulates details of the articles of incorporation of the nonpublic schools that constitute a contract between each nonpublic school and the state. The Constitution of the United States prohibits the passage of any state law that violates the agreements made in the contract. The privileges accorded the nonpublic school under articles of incorporation usually extend to such matters as holding property, the right to sue and be sued, the right to make contracts, and such other agreements as may be deemed necessary to achieve the objects for which the institution was established. The articles of agreement always presuppose the principle of self-government under state regulation and thereby have proved to be the most popular and effective way a state has of regulating nonpublic schools. Incorporation also fully establishes the legal right of nonpublic schools to do what is deemed necessary to operate educational institutions under private auspices.

Besides basic legal regulations for nonpublic schools, state legislatures make interpretations that establish some limitations and privileges.

The interpretations vary quite as much with respect to the conduct of nonpublic education as they do for public education. They are found in the provisions made for education in the state constitutions, in the statutes passed by the state legislatures concerning nonpublic schools, and in relevant court decisions. This makes the state school code almost as important to the nonpublic school as it is to the public school.

Despite the variations among the states, two principles underlie state policy. The first is that, in general, a public tax may not be levied for the support of nonpublic schools. The second is that nonschool revenue may not be used for direct aid to nonpublic schools.

Even these principles, however, are subject to a variety of interpretations. Many of the differences arise in connection with the interpretation of the child benefit theory. This theory holds that benefits or services provided at public expense from revenue not collected for educational purposes should be given a child regardless of where he happens to attend school. Differences usually arise in a situation that involves indirect public aid to education—that is, the aid given to provide some service immediately for the individual pupil, not directly to the school. All children are entitled to the same free governmental services. In theory there should be no discrimination against children because they attend nonpublic schools. The question arises whether the aid provided actually goes to the pupil or to the school. Among the services about which there has been this kind of disagreement are free textbooks, free transportation, health services, and other welfare services usually described as auxiliary educational services. If an auxiliary educational service is provided for all public school pupils, is it unjust discrimination to deny comparable services to all pupils in nonpublic schools? Some state legislatures say it is. For example, the Michigan, New York, and Ohio legislatures have provided noninstructional services, textbooks, and transportation for pupils in church schools.

Other services that have been centers of argument are commonly called quasi-instructional services. Examples of this kind of service are recreation; child accounting (the keeping of instructional and executive records of the child throughout his or her school life); psychological, psychiatric, and sociological diagnostic services; and placement and follow-up of high school graduates. Should a social service considered vital to the welfare of every child of school age in a community be denied a child because he happens to attend a nonpublic school?

Decisions on such issues are related to the interpretation each individual state legislature makes of the child benefit theory when it is applied to a specific educational problem. What the interpretation may be cannot be predicted. In general, it is agreed that the state or the federal government may not directly make state or federal financial grants to nonpublic schools. It is expected, however, that certain social services rendered by the state to individuals will not be denied to an individual pupil, even though he attends a nonpublic school. The child benefit theory holds that the services of the state are to follow the child wherever he or she may be.

Classification of Nonpublic Schools

The great variety of nonpublic schools in the United States makes it difficult to arrive at a simple classification. The best we can do is to divide nonpublic schools into two main groups and state some of the features by which each group is identified. The parochial schools, one large group of elementary and secondary schools, are, as the name implies, operated by ecclesiastical organizations. A large majority of them are operated by the Roman Catholic church; the Catholic schools now enroll approximately 90 percent of all the pupils officially reported to be attending the parochial schools in the United States. Because of the number and importance of these schools, more information about them is given in a later section.

The second large group of nonpublic schools is private schools. The term "private school" in some educational publications is synonymous with nonpublic school. In popular usage, however, and in our discussion, the private school differs from the parochial school in that it is largely nonsectarian and is controlled by an individual or a self-perpetuating board of trustees. The two classifications of nonpublic schools might well be sectarian and nonsectarian. However, most educational publications use the words "parochial" and "private."

Parochial Schools

Parochial schools are those nonpublic schools that operate on the elementary and secondary level under the control and with the support of an ecclesiastical organization. The largest group of parochial schools is operated by the Roman Catholic church.

I. ROMAN CATHOLIC SCHOOLS

a. Origins. The Roman Catholic church has followed a policy of establishing elementary parochial schools in communities that have a Catholic population and organization sufficient to support such a school. Organizing schools as a regular and permanent feature of parish work began with the establishment of the first Catholic parish in Philadelphia in 1730. Philadelphia had a larger Catholic population than any other city in the country, and the system of parochial schools established there and throughout Pennsylvania became a model subsequently followed by Catholics throughout the country.

The schools were aided by the founding of teaching orders such as, for example, the Sisters of Charity, the Sisters of Loretta, and the Sisters of Saint Dominic. Members of these orders established religious communities where some kind of productive activity, perhaps farming, made the community more or less self-sufficient. With the support of the religious order and of the Roman Catholic church, the teachers were able to carry on their schools without aid from the state and to extend the Catholic educational system into new centers of Catholic life as fast as they became organized. Even before 1776, 70 Roman Catholic schools had been organized in the confines of what is now the United States. The Catholic church expanded rapidly after 1840, when there was a rapid increase in the immigration of Catholics from Germany and Ireland. This increase in Catholic population, together with the action of the Third Plenary Council of Baltimore in 1885 making it obligatory for every parish to maintain a school, resulted in a rapid multiplication of Catholic parochial schools. The action of the Third Plenary Council made it clear that the church leaders considered education a vital factor in the internal development of the Roman Catholic church in the United States.

b. Organization. The Roman Catholics followed the lines of their dioceses in their school organization. A diocese is the area and the population that fall under the pastoral care of a bishop. Each diocese has its school system with the bishop at its head. The bishops are bound by the legislation of the Third Plenary Council of Baltimore, which not only made schools obligatory but also prescribed a definite form of school organization for all the dioceses. Thus it is accurate to speak of Catholic schools as constituting a system, and it is this systematization of their schools that has provided a measure of unity and a source of strength.

Control over the schools in the diocese is in the hands of a board of education presided over by the bishop. The members of the board, except for a few lay people, are elected from the clergy. The executive officer of the school board is a priest, specially trained as an educator and school administrator. He serves as superintendent of schools in the diocese. The priest of the local parish generally serves also as head of the individual school supported by his parish. Beyond supervising financial and religious matters, he delegates the direction of the school to a superior of the sisters or brothers in charge. This superior is, in practice, the actual principal who administers the school.

c. Curriculum. The curriculum in the Catholic elementary and high schools is similar to the curriculum in the public schools in the same communities. The principal difference is in the emphasis on religious education. The curriculum is planned to give a well-rounded general education and at the same time to give a special place to religious instruction, an area that is usually not recognized in the public schools, which must remain secular and nonsectarian.

d. Kinds of Schools. The elementary schools are all diocesan schools and constitute the main part of the Catholic parochial school system. Some of the high schools are organized in the parish and are also members of the diocesan organization. Others are independent and are conducted by one of the religious orders of the church. The Catholic University of America at Washington, D.C., established in 1887 by Pope Leo XII and the American Catholic hierarchy, has as one of its purposes the preparation of teachers for the entire Catholic educational system.

e. Enrollments. The Roman Catholic school system in the United States has reached large proportions. Specifically, in 1972–1973 there were about 11,570 Catholic educational institutions: elementary schools, 8761; secondary schools, 1773; colleges and universities, 339; seminaries, 436; schools for atypical children, 260. They are organized in 147 different systems—one for each of the 147 archdioceses and dioceses in the country. About 40 percent of all these institutions, however, enrolling more than half of all the students, are in only 20 dioceses—Chicago, Boston, New York, and other metropolitan areas.

The total attendance at Catholic parochial elementary and high schools rose from about 405,000 in 1880 to almost 1.8 million in 1920 to 2.4 million in 1940 to a peak of about 5.6 million in 1964–1965. Around 8 percent of all American elementary and secondary school pupils are at Catholic parochial schools. There are difficulties ahead, however—a number of Catholic schools (most of them elementary schools) have been closed in recent years. Thus not only has the total enrollment not kept pace with the growth in the general school population, it has actually declined; in 1972–1973 the total Catholic elementary and secondary enrollment was down to 3.8 million. Rising operating costs, decreasing revenues, and a scarcity of teaching priests and nuns are all factors. Moreover, more closings are predicted.

f. Costs. The cost of attending Roman Catholic elementary and secondary schools, apart from services donated through the church, is borne by the parents. The annual costs of the elementary and secondary schools are well over a billion dollars.

g. Attitudes of Catholic Leaders Toward Public Education. Since those who send their children to Catholic schools must also pay taxes for the support of the public schools, the attitude of the Catholic leaders toward the public schools is of general interest. In the main, the parents of the children who attend the Catholic schools are appreciative of the privilege of freedom to make a choice between two kinds of schools and of being permitted to provide their children with religious education. The attitude both of the parents and of the clergy is positive, intelligent, and constructive. A short quotation expresses the sentiment that has long prevailed:

> Historically, we have had and, please God, we probably always will have a diversified system of education in this country. As American citizens, therefore, and especially as American educators, we must be interested in the improvement not only of our own unique kind of education, but of all kinds of American education—public, private, denominational—whatever it may be. . . . The public schools, as a complementary system to private education, are absolutely necessary for the thousands of Americans who are content with a purely secular educational pattern. Such schools deserve the interest and support of our Catholic population.[1]

2. PROTESTANT SCHOOLS

Some of the Protestant churches have, in recent years, conducted nursery schools for children who are younger than compulsory school and kindergarten age. These schools are operated by local churches

[1] Very Rev. P. C. Reinert, S.J., "American Catholic Educators Face New Responsibilities," *Proceedings and Addresses, Forty-ninth Annual Meeting.* Washington, D.C.: National Catholic Educational Association, 1952, p. 59.

more as a service to the members of the church than for religious reasons. Such schools diverge very little in their pattern of activities from those conducted under public auspices.

It is not easy to state the Protestant position toward elementary and secondary schools, because no official position has been taken. In general, and with notable exceptions mentioned later, it is the position of the Protestant groups that the parent should send his children to the public schools and that the child should receive his religious education in the home and in the church. Protestants, as a group, do not favor parochial education as an answer to the problem of religious education. Nevertheless, they "defend the right of all religious groups to carry on church-related education at any level, elementary, secondary, or higher, and the right of parents to send their children to these schools if they so desire."[2]

Although the majority of Protestants believe in sending their children to the public schools, they are favorable to church schools if member groups desire to have them. There are approximately 4000 Protestant day schools, which enrole approximately 385,000 elementary school pupils and 36,000 high school pupils. In the main, these are supported by the Christian Reformed church members, Missouri Synod Lutherans—which is the largest group, with an elementary school enrollment of 193,000 pupils and a high school enrollment of 14,000—Seventh-Day Adventists, Mennonites, Episcopalians, and Baptists.

There has been an increase in the. number of certain types of Protestant church-related private day schools in recent years, but it is very difficult to get accurate data on the extent of this growth and specific national enrollment figures. The growth in some types of Protestant day schools in recent years has not, however, been sufficient to offset the continuing decline in enrollments in Roman Catholic parochial schools. It was still the case in the mid-1970s that the Lutheran, Seventh-Day Adventists, Episcopal, Christian Reformed, and Quaker (or Friends) Protestant denominations were the most active in support of Protestant parochial schools. The Amish and other smaller Protestant denominations remain active in their support of nonpublic education. There is a National Association of Christian Schools (NACS) with member private Protestant parochial schools from 29 different denominations. Several smaller evangelical Protestant Christian groups are affiliated with this organization.

[2] D. Campbell Wyckoff, "The Protestant Day School," *School and Society,* LXXXII: 98, October 1, 1955.

Among Episcopal church groups in the United States there has been a continuing interest in provision for private Episcopal schools. The National Association of Episcopal Schools (NAES) is an organization of some 600 such Episcopal church schools of various types in the United States.

The National Association of Independent Schools (NAIS) includes about 780 nonpublic schools in its membership. However, there are some Roman Catholic and Protestant schools affiliated with this organization. The best single-volume source on both religious and secular independent schools in the United States to be published in the 1970s is Otto F. Krausharr's *American Non-Public Schools: Patterns of Diversity*,[3] which examines all facets of American nonpublic education.

3. JEWISH DAY SCHOOLS

Between 1940 and 1967 the Jewish day school (popularly known by its Hebrew name, *yeshivah*) grew to include 305 elementary and secondary day schools in the United States. More than 90 percent of these were established between 1940 and 1967. During this period, the pupil enrollment increased almost tenfold, from 7,313 to approximately 65,000 students.

Jewish day schools are distinct educational units founded and supported by parents and interested individuals and communally conducted by autonomous, self-governing lay boards, responsive to the needs of the parents and community. As Alvin I. Schiff, noted authority on Jewish education, has said, "The Jewish day school was not founded in opposition to public education, since Judaism does not challenge the state's right to control education."

The establishment of the Jewish day school is predicated, first, on a deeply felt need for intensive Hebraic-religious schooling. Second, the American Jewish community strongly believes in the value of a sound secular education and emphasizes the importance of effective training in the skills of good citizenship. The advocates of the Jewish day school feel that this institution is the best means of achieving this dual goal, which is, in essence, the blending of the Hebraic and American cultures.

In line with these goals, the Jewish day schools are organized into two divisions: the secular or general studies department and the religious or Hebrew studies department. In the elementary school the

[3] Otto F. Krausharr, *American Non-Public Schools: Patterns of Diversity*. Baltimore: Johns Hopkins, 1972, 387 pp.

pupils have two instructors, a Hebrew teacher and a general studies teacher; in the junior and senior high schools, where the programs are usually departmentalized, the students study under the guidance of two sets of instructors. Almost all schools are Bible-centered in the elementary grades. The concentration thereafter is divided between the study of Bible and Talmud and their major commentaries. The general studies programs are essentially the same as in the local public schools. The average Jewish day school has 225 pupils, although the range is from 50 to 1500. Some are all-boy and some are all-girl schools, but today 70 percent of the Jewish day schools either are coeducational or provide instruction for boys and girls under one roof.

> Exposed to both disciplines in a congenial environment the child learns to integrate the traditional with the modern, the secular with the religious, his Jewish heritage with American civilization. Through meritorious educational attainment, in an enriched program, he grows intellectually and culturally; via a program of intensive Jewish study he grows spiritually. In all, he learns to be a good American Jew. He learns that to be a good Jew is to be a good American. On this frame of reference, he builds a wholesome set of values. He loves Israel and wants to help it grow, as he loves America and strives to become a useful citizen in his native country. He is part of his Jewish people as he is part of American democratic experience.[4]

Private Schools

The private schools are the most independent of the nonpublic schools. They are subject to very little public control and are permitted to operate with a minimum of state supervision. They are numerous, and they maintain widely varying standards.

I. BELOW-COLLEGE LEVEL

a. Vocational Schools. Below-college vocational training, apart from the high schools, is almost exclusively the domain of the private school. Here vocational schools that are operated for profit prevail— technical institutes; business colleges; commercial or secretarial schools; art, interior decorating, drafting, design schools; charm, beauty culture, cosmetology, electrolysis schools; dramatic art, television, broadcasting, expression schools; trade, industrial, automechanics

---

[4] Alvin I. Schiff, *The Jewish Day School in America.* New York: Jewish Education Committee Press, 1966, p. 265.

The academy was introduced into America in recognition of the need for a form of secondary education broader than that given by the Latin grammar schools, with their highly restricted curriculum, which had dominated American secondary education for nearly 200 years. The academy became the principal institution in American secondary education, maintaining that position from the latter half of the eighteenth century until the beginning of the twentieth century, when the 4-year high school began its rapid growth. One way to get a picture of the purposes, programs, and achievements of the academy and of its place in American secondary education is to read the history of a successful one.* Phillips Exeter, for instance, one of the earliest academies, continues to be a distinguished institution. Incorporated in 1781, Exeter now has a campus of 775 acres—100 acres used for the school, 75 for playing fields, and 600 left in woodland. It has 125 school buildings and a faculty of 125 men. Enrolled in the regular session are 825 boys from all the states. In addition, there is a coeducational summer school attended by 250 boys and 225 girls.

Tax-supported high schools have grown rapidly in this century, but the number of able students who apply for admission to academies like Exeter has also increased. The quality of instruction offered by the academies has constantly improved. Also, their function has changed; in the late eighteenth century and for some time thereafter, the academies provided terminal education, as very few graduates went on to college; now, however, most academy graduates continue their education, many of them at private universities. For instance, for some time about one-third of the graduates of Exeter have entered three of the most prestigious private eastern universities—Harvard, Yale, and Princeton. (The 260 members of the Exeter class of 1968 went to more than 60 colleges and universities, but almost half entered five private institutions: Harvard, 50; Yale, 20; Stanford, 20; Princeton, 19; Dartmouth, 10.) The academies have, then, become college preparatory schools.

The academies in the United States are relatively inconspicuous in the total picture of secondary education; nevertheless, they perform significant and unique functions that give them great influence and prestige. They offer programs consistent with the ideals of high scholarship and they are dedicated to close, personal guidance of the individual pupil, with particular emphasis on character development.

* For a vivid account of the traditions, support, and functions of the academies, see Myron R. Williams, *The Story of Phillips Exeter.* Exeter, N.H.: The Phillips Exeter Academy, 1957.

schools; massage schools; baking, home economics, hotel management schools; jewelry and watch repairing schools. And there are many others that train specifically for some designated trade or commercial pursuit.

Information about such schools has not been collected thus far. Some notion of their magnitude, however, may be gained from estimates of enrollment made by the United Business Schools Association, with a membership of 500 institutions. One privately owned technical institute in Chicago, whose students are trained to enter the field of electronics, enrolls more than 20,000 post–high school students every year. Undoubtedly, since the enrollments in these schools number in the millions, their influence is tremendous. They answer the need for a kind of education—such as, for example, short-term, concentrated training—that receives little emphasis in the public schools.

b. Parent-Supported Schools. Another type of private elementary and secondary school is sometimes endowed and supported by wealthy parents. These schools are nonsectarian and serve approximately the same purposes as public schools of similar grade. The children are often selected so that they comprise a more or less homogeneous group in terms of economic or social background or special interests or problems. When the children are likely to attend college, attention is given to college preparation. Some of the secondary schools are endowed boarding schools. Some are known as country day schools, where typically some of the pupils are boarding pupils and others live at home. The purposes that justify the establishment and support of each of these private schools vary from school to school.

c. Academies. The academies, in part parent supported and in part endowment supported, are an important group of private secondary schools. Some of the academies have an illustrious history dating back to the early days of our country. Originally intended to provide a curriculum more flexible and enriched than was available elsewhere, the academies are now largely college preparatory. They are sometimes coeducational and are found in most parts of the United States. The military academies of high school grade emphasize military discipline.

The private academy emerged early in American history as a more popular form of secondary schooling than the old Latin grammar school. The private academies offered commercial and English curricula in addition to the older classical curricula for college entrance. The academy idea spread rapidly. By the outbreak of the American

Civil War in 1861, there were more than 6000 private secondary academies in the United States; it was the predominant form of secondary educational institution of the mid-nineteenth century in America. As noted, present-day academies are usually highly oriented toward strong, enriched college preparatory curricula.

Private academies continue, however, to play a major qualitative role in American education even though their numbers may not indicate this. There were in the early 1970s, according to Kraushaar,[5] 2369 "religiously unaffiliated" nonpublic schools of various types. Many of these are highly prestigious private academies. The early American secondary academies were developed in response to the demands by scholars and parents of financial means for high standards of academic and personal excellence that they believed could not be achieved in publicly supported secondary schools. The academies of today are usually boarding schools where students reside in dormitories on the schools' campuses, although day students may be admitted to some of these academies from their neighboring communities. When the academy movement was at its height in the mid-nineteenth century, many private academies were day schools, designed to serve the secondary education needs of students in particular communities. Andover (also referred to in educational history as Phillips Academy, Andover, after its founder Samuel Phillips, Jr.) was established in 1778 during the American Revolution. Phillips Exeter Academy was established in 1781 by John Phillips, who was an uncle of Samuel Phillips, the founder of Andover Academy. These two schools have remained outstanding examples of high academic and personal standards in nonpublic secondary education. The academy movement underwent major changes as it progressed; the academies were marked by a high spirit of academic innovation and individuality. A few of the present-day academies have large endowments to assist in their support, but most private academies do not have endowments sufficient to pay a large percentage of their annual costs. They thus rely on tuition payments and contributions from private individuals and foundations.

d. Industry-Supported Schools. Private business has, during the past 50 years, greatly expanded educational opportunities in industry. This has resulted in another kind of private school. Large industrial

---

[5] Kraushaar, op. cit., p. 368.

corporations have provided extensive industrial training for their employees and in some instances have provided other kinds of education for the families of their employees. Some industries engage also in cooperative education programs with various engineering colleges in order to meet the nation's demands for citizens well grounded both in the common essentials and in the occupational abilities necessary to insure economic and industrial efficiency. The number of people attending such schools is large, and it fluctuates greatly from time to time.

Since so many of these private schools operate quite independently and since so little information has been assembled on them,

Benjamin Franklin (1706–1790) is known to every American boy and girl as an American statesman, diplomat, author, scientist, and inventor. Few, perhaps, realize that he also influenced American education. In 1749 Franklin voiced progressive ideas about education in *Proposals for the Education of Youth in Pennsylvania*. Two years later he opened the Franklin Academy, which incorporated these ideas. His academy was far different from the other institutions of the time. Students applying for admission were offered a choice of three courses. They could enter one of what he called three schools—the English school, the mathematics school, or the Latin school. In typical Franklin manner he thus expressed his displeasure over the narrow classicism that characterized the Latin grammar schools of the time. Shortly after its establishment his academy was reincorporated as a degree-conferring institution. In 1779, 3 years after the signing of the Declaration of Independence, the University of Pennsylvania was established in its stead.

Franklin's intention was to displace the unsystematic practices of the private schoolmaster of the day with an institution organized and administered on a public basis. He attempted, also, to offer, so far as was possible at the time, a curriculum that was practical and useful. Even so great a man as Franklin, however, could not overcome the deep-seated prejudices favorable to educational emphasis on Latin. He saw English and other modern subjects gradually ousted from the curriculum of the school he had established in order to emphasize these very subjects.

Although Franklin's school was an initial failure, it was an expression of the progressive educational thought of the time. The Franklin Academy passed out of existence, but the ideas set in motion flowed on to exert a profound influence on succeeding generations.

few generalizations are possible except to say that they are numerous and their influence is great.

e. Laboratory Schools. Schools for children at the nursery, elementary, junior high, and senior high school levels are conducted on some college campuses. These are variously called demonstration schools, experimental schools, training schools, or laboratory schools. When they are associated with nonpublic institutions, they are private schools. Sometimes, however, they are part of a public teachers college or public university. Then they are public schools, which, however, differ from ordinary public schools in that they are not a part of any particular local school system. They are schools administered by the college or university for experimental and demonstrational purposes. Under Title III of the Elementary and Secondary Education Act of 1965, designed to establish or enrich exemplary elementary and secondary school programs, the federal government has given aid to demonstration or laboratory schools that are operated in public school systems.

Ideally, the laboratory school demonstrates the best modern educational theory in actual practice in the classroom. The philosophy of the school is carefully worked out; the curriculum is designed to meet the vital needs of its pupils; the teachers are skilled artists in teaching; the organization and the administrative machinery demonstrate arrangements that best serve the pupils and teachers and that foster wholesome human relations; and the building and equipment are thoughtfully planned.

Laboratory schools have contributed significantly to the improvement of education in both private and public schools. One main difficulty is that they sometimes operate on insufficient budgets. To supplement their budgets, they frequently charge tuition or fees, even though they may be part of a state university. This tends to result in an economically and sociologically favored enrollment of pupils, which makes the results of laboratory school research less applicable to a typical cross section of the general population. In addition to their contribution through experimentation and research, the laboratory schools have improved teaching in America's schools by providing opportunities for teachers in training to observe and to have actual daily experience in much better than average classrooms. However, because of increased costs in recent years and the feeling that laboratory schools provide a protected environment for undergraduate teacher education students, many universities have been forced to close or to consider closing their laboratory schools.

f. Private Segregated Schools. Title VI of the Civil Rights Act of 1964 explicitly forbids the granting of federal educational aid to any educational institution that has been organized as a nonpublic school to avoid racial integration. In the mid-1960s and early 1970s many small private schools were set up by white parents to avoid the racial integration required by federal laws and U.S. Supreme Court orders. All aid from Elementary and Secondary Education Act (ESEA) grants are affected by the Civil Rights Act of 1964. No school organized as a nonpublic school to perpetuate socially segregated schooling is entitled to receive federal educational aid. Kraushaar[6] has reported that in 1970–1971 some 450,000 to 500,000 students were attending private segregated schools. This sort of development is clearly a matter of considerable concern. The American commitment to the principle of equality of opportunity for all citizens should prevent federal aid from being given to any nonpublic school that has been organized to evade the federal law.

2. COLLEGE LEVEL

a. Colleges and Universities. No criterion has been established as a guide in the classification of higher-level institutions. The most dependable classification available shows that there are 132 universities in the United States, of which 70 are public and 62 are nonpublic. Since many public universities have numerous branches, the actual number of these far exceeds 70. Because of federal aid to nonpublic as well as public universities, the differentiation between the two types has diminished as far as support and control are concerned.

The nonpublic 4-year liberal arts college, usually just called a college, dominates the 4-year college scene. There are well over 500 such colleges in the United States, all of which are fully accredited. Very few such colleges are publicly controlled and supported. The dominance of the private liberal arts college is due in part to the fact that it was the earliest kind of organization for higher education in this country and also to the respect and faith that the American people place in these institutions.

The nonpublic institutions of higher learning have exerted and continue to exert great influence upon American social thought. Their programs penetrate almost every aspect of American life. Since it is estimated that currently over 2 million students attend these institutions, it seems that the American people will continue to accord non-

6 Ibid., p. 236.

public institutions of higher education a prominent position in the educational system of the United States.

b. Technological Institutes. There are between 60 and 65 private technological institutions of higher learning in the United States. Among them, to name a few, are such distinguished institutions as the Massachusetts Institute of Technology, the Carnegie Institute of Technology, the California Institute of Technology, the Case Institute of Technology, and the Illinois Institute of Technology. As their names imply, their contributions are mainly in the fields of science and applied science.

Contributions of Nonpublic Schools

The size and scope of the nonpublic school undertaking in the United States is in itself evidence of the high regard of the people of the United States for nonpublic education. The debt the nation owes to nonpublic education is indeed great. Although it is not easy to assess the total contributions made by the nonpublic schools to the contemporary educational scene, a few of the more obvious contributions can be identified.

First, the nonpublic schools have furthered the preservation and strengthening of the cherished American ideal of freedom of choice and of the pluralistic philosophy that nourishes that ideal. Although in some communities competition between the public and nonpublic elementary and secondary schools creates a degree of friction, in most communities a healthy and friendly rivalry exists—rivalry to excel in the quality of services rendered. Cooperation between public and nonpublic schools is common.

Second, the nonpublic schools have educated so large a proportion of the American school population that they have appreciably lowered the burden of public support. Since the nonpublic schools seek to achieve all the functions striven for in the public schools and, as is the case especially with the vocational schools, to answer certain needs not recognized in the public schools, the lessening of the costs to the public is accompanied by an actual increase in the breadth of education available.

Third, the nonpublic schools have made distinctive contributions to educational practice. Many of the forward-looking practices in the public schools were first developed in the nonpublic schools. The nonpublic schools have contributed particularly to experimentation at the elementary level. Nursery school and kindergarten education were first tested in nonpublic schools. Vocational education at the high school level was first introduced and developed in the nonpublic schools. A great deal of research in scientific and professional fields has emanated from the nonpublic universities.

These are only a few of the contributions made by nonpublic schools. Enough has been said, however, to show that public and nonpublic education in the United States have advanced together, with a minimum of conflict and a maximum of mutual appreciation. Both kinds of schools contribute to the preservation and advancement of our civilization.

Summary

The term "nonpublic schools" applies to many kinds of schools operating in America under various controls and methods of support and serving all ages and levels from nursery school through postgraduate education. The magnitude of the entire nonpublic school undertaking cannot be accurately or even approximately assessed. All one can safely say is that the enrollment is large.

Nonpublic schools are favorably accepted. The pluralistic philosophy of the American people and of their government encourages the establishment of many kinds of nonpublic schools. The states may, if they wish, issue regulations for such schools but, generally speaking, the regulations are not highly restrictive.

Appraisal of the nonpublic schools reveals that they have made a sizable contribution to education in America. By and large, these schools discharge all the functions performed by the public schools and maintain standards of professional excellence equal to those in the public schools.

Although the overall contributions of the nonpublic schools cannot be fully assessed, it is evident that they are serving specific educational needs and are valued as a vital feature of the complete system of education in America.

QUESTIONS

1. Why has it been the policy of the various states to exert so little control over nonpublic education?

2. What would be some uses that could be served by the states collecting complete information about all the nonpublic schools operating under their jurisdictions?
3. What are the principal justifications for the establishment of nonpublic schools and nonpublic school systems in the United States?
4. What evidences are there that nonpublic universities exert a great deal of influence on life in America?
5. Why are the 4-year colleges in the United States predominantly nonpublic schools?
6. How do articles of incorporation operate to protect a nonpublic school?
7. How do the articles of incorporation of nonpublic schools serve as a control over nonpublic schools?
8. In your opinion, what will the future development of nonpublic education in the United States be like?

PROJECTS

1. Secure information on one of the industrial education programs conducted by some large industry. Appraise the nature of the program.
2. Read the advertisements of nonpublic schools as found in some influential magazine. Itemize the claims of the various institutions.
3. Research the problems the Amish sect has had in Iowa, Pennsylvania, or some other state, in connection with their private schools. Give your own conclusions about a sound and just solution to the problem.

chapter

15

Units
of school
organization

There are several different types of schools in the United States, some of which the reader is already familiar with from his or her experiences as a student. In this chapter we describe the major features of the several types and patterns of school organization in America as they relate to the sequencing of the elementary and secondary school curricula. These patterns of schooling have evolved out of educational traditions and out of differing views of the nature of childhood and adolescence and differing theories of the best sorts of educational experiences to provide children and youth at various stages of cognitive (intellectual) and affective (emotional and valuational) development. Specific details of these general patterns of educational organization and development differ from place to place, but the patterns described in this chapter are representative of the forms of elementary and secondary schooling found in the United States.

Schools for the Early Years

The Nursery School

The nursery school is the latest unit of educational organization to bid for public recognition. Its growth in public acceptance is illustrated by the facts that in 1920 there were but three recognized nursery schools in the United States and that in 1972, enrollment of 3-, 4-, and 5-year-old children in pre-primary school programs had reached a total of 4,231,000. One impetus for extension of the nursery school has come from the federal government, most recently through the Economic Opportunity Act and the Elementary and Secondary Education Act, which provided funds for classes for preschool children, especially children from more concentrated population centers, where many homes are unable to provide for the needs of young children. New emphasis was thereby given to the role of early education. Although nursery education is now an accepted institution throughout the country and has been widely adopted both as a public and non-public school unit, it has not received legal status from state legislatures. It therefore operates as a nonstandardized unit under the sponsorship of a large number of different agencies.

Among the sources of early encouragement to the nursery school movement were public universities, such as the University of Iowa and the University of Minnesota, which operate nursery schools. In these schools, child development specialists made studies, the findings of which emphasized the importance of providing a suitable environment for the mental and physical development of children 2 to 5 years of age. The studies also demonstrated the importance of parent education, indicating that parents are the most important teachers of young children, because they are with the child for a greater part of the time than anyone else and share with the child a wide range of activities and experiences. It is mainly from parents that a child learns certain skills (such as talking) and develops attitudes, emotional control, maturity in his relations with others, and, hopefully, ideals that contribute to good living. Somewhere along the line a transition must be made from the narrower environment of the home to the wider social environment of the school. The shift from home to school is a major environmental change in the life of a child. It is often a time when the child feels his security threatened, a time when he must make major adjustments. The studies of the psychologists conducting nursery schools in the universities showed that skillfully directed nursery schools made the transition from home to school easier and safer for many 4-year-olds and for some 3-year-olds.

Early expansion of the nursery school movement was also encouraged by the Works Progress Administration (WPA), an agency of the federal government that, among other things, sponsored nursery schools for working mothers during the depression of the 1930s. The WPA operated some 1500 schools that enrolled well over 300,000 children. Being a branch of the federal government, it established a precedent by operating its schools in public buildings, including the public schools.

A third source of continuing encouragement comes from private, church, philanthropic, and other groups that have, with a considerable measure of success, operated nursery schools. During World War II, national defense was served by nursery schools that freed mothers of preschool children to work in industry or business. In the main these nursery schools have been well managed and have been fully accepted. In most cases the staff has been well qualified; often leadership has come from interested, dedicated experts who have volunteered their services.

Nursery school education serves two broad educational purposes—childhood education and adult, or parent, education. The location and equipment must be suited to the two purposes. An appreciation of the facilities required for such education can best be gained by a visit to a well-equipped nursery school. One will find that the selection of the room and equipment is dictated by what child development specialists have learned is appropriate for 3- and 4-year-olds. Psychologists who have studied the effects of nursery school education on children are agreed that a nursery school that is not adequately equipped and conducted by a competent staff can be harmful. In an adequate nursery school, playground and schoolroom are a single unit, separate from units provided for older children. Playground equipment is specially designed. A roofed area just outside the room is provided for special outdoor activities. The room windows face the playground. The room is large, well lighted, and properly ventilated.

Not all children need or profit from attendance at a nursery school. In deciding who shall attend, parents and teachers weigh many factors. Is the child an only child? Does he live in an apartment? Does the mother work? Does the mother feel that the child will do better if he is apart from her for some time each day? Does the mother feel that the child should have increased opportunity to expand his social adaptability? Attendance at nursery school is never required. It need not be regular.

The nursery school is here to stay. Social conditions such as increased employment of mothers, crowded housing, urbanization, poverty, and the like, appear to justify both a continuation and an expansion of the movement. Apart from social expediency, future expansion of nursery school education can be justified in terms of the immediate value to the children who attend and to their parents, who also participate in the program. Where nursery schools facilitate the transition from home to school, where they help parents understand and guide their children, where, all things considered, they help children make the adjustments required of them, the services and benefits justify the establishment and maintenance of nursery school units as a regular part of both the nonpublic and public school systems.

HEAD START PROGRAM

The statements made about nursery schools in general apply to the Head Start program also: it serves childhood and also parent education and it requires specially adapted facilities, highly trained teachers, medical attendants, and so forth. Although the Head Start program is not always a part of the public school organization, in many cases it is.

When the Office of Economic Opportunity initiated Head Start as a part of its war on poverty, the idea was to take youngsters from disadvantaged neighborhoods and give them preschool experiences so that they might more readily fit into the school picture and relate better to classmates from more advantaged homes when they started kindergarten or first grade. It was felt that what these children needed most was individual attention, to feel that someone cared about them.

The classes have usually included about 15 pupils with one highly trained teacher assisted by a number of teacher aides and volunteers. Doctors, nurses, psychologists, social workers, and nutritionists share also, especially in testing, guidance, home visits, and parent education. An effort is made to give the children a wide range of enriching experiences, including conversation, simple tasks they can do with satisfaction, group play activities, well-planned lunches often including food items new to the children, bus trips, and excursions. Enrollment is voluntary, and the 3- to 6-year-olds are selected from homes whose annual income does not exceed a certain figure (usually $3000).

That children entering kindergarten with experience in Head Start have had less trouble adjusting and seem happier is generally agreed. What happens, however, if the child finds that the pleasant surroundings and individual attention of the Head Start program are not part of the regular school? Perhaps in the regular school the teacher has to care for 30 or 40 children without all the aid, facilities, and equipment that were part of Head Start. Perhaps this teacher has preconceived notions about the limited potential of disadvantaged children. Will the early compensatory education be of limited, short-term benefit without positive experiences in the regular school? Hopefully, Head Start will call attention to the really crucial sectors in educational reconstruction—the primary and secondary inner-city schools—and will serve as the spark to bring about essential changes.

Even if we admit the important part preschool education can play, and even if the desirable features of Head Start could be continued throughout school, do we still perhaps overestimate the value of preschool education in American education? Can these experiences offset the effects of poverty, provide a substitute for the broad range of healthful, normative home and family experiences of small children? Just as it has never been demonstrated that preschooling is essential to the future educational success of typical middle-class youth, may we possibly find that it is not essential to school achievement for disadvantaged youth—once we provide really adequate buildings, teachers, and educational programs, as well as the genuine promise of future success in life?

The Kindergarten

In an earlier chapter the idea of kindergarten education for children of preschool age was traced to Froebel, who demonstrated the practicality of the idea by conducting an experimental school. He moved his experimental school to Blankenburg, Germany, and in 1840 gave it the name "kindergarten"—a garden of children. So rapidly did the idea take hold that in the 25 years following Froebel's death kindergartens were established in the leading cities of Germany, Holland, Belgium, Switzerland, Austria, Hungary, Canada, Japan, and the United States. The name "kindergarten" has become synonymous, in many parts of the world, with the kind of education program suited to preschool-age children.

St. Louis made kindergarten education a part of its public school system in 1873. A demonstration kindergarten was established at the Philadelphia Exposition in 1876. These two ventures are credited with demonstrating to the American people, many of whom had previously been skeptical, the merits of kindergarten education. Within 10 years, kindergartens had been established in all the major cities of the United States. All of these, with the exception of St. Louis, were under private control. As people became convinced of the value of the kindergarten, public schools enthusiastically adopted the unit.

Comenius had argued that at 6 the child was at the best age to enter school. We still accept 6 years as the logical age for entrance into the first grade. The kindergarten precedes first grade and, from the standpoint of organization, remains a more or less separate unit in the school system. The kindergarten is fully integrated with neither the nursery school unit, where one exists, nor the first grade. The separation is not considered undesirable. Psychologists believe that rapid maturation takes place between the ages of 4 and 5 and between the ages of 5 and 6, and that this must be taken into account in planning suitable programs. For example, in contrast to 4-year-olds, children at 5 are clear and complete in their answers to simple questions. They are more adept at building with larger blocks, more skillful in simple drawing, more critical of their inability to do something they would like to do, more likely to finish what they start, and more self-reliant in the performance of personal duties. They are ready for wider experiences than either the home or the nursery school can provide. Since the kindergarten must provide an environment quite different from other school units, the general practice of keeping it as a separately organized unit, even though in the same building, will probably be continued.

All large cities in the United States now have kindergartens, at which attendance is voluntary. Since there is considerable variation in the ages of children who attend the earlier grades—all children do not arrive at the age of 5 on the same day—it is not easy to interpret data on kindergarten attendance. It appears, however, that slightly over half the children of about 5 years attend kindergarten. This means that not all the communities in the United States that could support kindergarten education do so, and also that not all parents are inclined to send their children to kindergarten even when one is readily accessible. It seems that the acceptance and development of kindergarten education, like nursery school education, will depend on the wishes of the American public. Where kindergartens have been conducted according to the best known educational standards of practice, experts report that some of the most effective education in the nation has been accomplished.

The Elementary School

The common school, district school, or grade school in the early United States enrolled pupils from the first grade through the eighth. After that, if the pupil continued his schooling he transferred to a four-year high school. Since around 1910, there has been a strong tendency to reduce the unit of elementary education from eight to six grades. Even now, however, the eight-grade type of organization still·enrolls more pupils than does the six-grade type. In discussing the education program at the elementary level, regardless of type of organization, it is common practice to consider grades 1 through 6 as the logical unit.

The Curriculum

Elementary school pupils ordinarily follow a single curriculum, the chief aim of which is *general education*. In some schools the subject matter is classified under broad fields, such as language arts or social studies. In others the classification is more restricted; and reading, writing, spelling, penmanship, and grammar are classifications. This is discussed more fully in a later chapter. Since the elementary school must be adapted to the needs of children who vary widely in both abilities and interests, the curriculum is never considered as a set path, to be followed at all costs. The curriculum is more a suggestion to the teacher of what is desirable. The teacher in most American elementary schools is given freedom to modify and adapt as classroom conditions warrant. To the well-trained teacher this freedom to devise the most fruitful environment in terms of the needs of the pupils is what makes teaching in the elementary school most challenging.

The Teacher

The elementary teacher is a specialist in teaching at a particular grade level, for which he or she must have well-rounded training and experience. This is recognized both within the profession and in the community. It has strong implications for the preparation of elementary teachers. The elementary teacher must teach a very wide range of subject matter. He or she must therefore strive for broad, well-rounded preparation in college work, which is sometimes difficult within a rigid system of required majors and minors. Elementary teachers should try always to be aware of how important an influence they have on the formation of the future character of their pupils. They must understand how young children grow. They must be able to take the children's interests into account and make what they teach continuous with what the child has previously learned. They must be prepared to confer with and direct parents. Their relationships with parents place them in an excellent position to influence their thinking on educational problems.

The School Building

The modern elementary school building is typically designed along functional lines and is surrounded with attractively landscaped grounds and outdoor play facilities. It is one of the most attractive buildings in many American communities. By visiting such a building and noting the details that have been incorporated to serve the educational needs of pupils and teachers, one comes to appreciate what modern architectural school building science can contribute to the improvement of the elementary school.

Organization of the Classroom

The organization within the elementary school generally follows the self-contained classroom pattern, the service and resource unit pattern, or some modification of these. In either case the furniture in the classroom is completely movable so that discussion, laboratory activities, individual projects, and research by children can be conveniently cared for within the room. Many kinds of teaching-aid materials are available—not resting on shelves in neat arrangements but carefully catalogued and circulated throughout the school.

Although the self-contained classroom has a rather recently acquired name, it is the oldest form of educational organization in the United States. It is still considered by many educators to be the most desirable plan for elementary school organization. Under this arrangement, one teacher is responsible for the whole range of activities, and the equipment in the classroom is complete. Ideally, toilet and washroom facilities are included, as well as shop facilities, cupboards, work tables, art equipment, a piano, a record player, and perhaps a movie projector.

The service and resource unit pattern may shift some responsibility for teaching from the classroom instructor. To facilitate instruction, teachers have access to a library, a workshop, an auditorium, and other specialized facilities. A specialized staff of resource persons may also be available to help all classroom teachers. This may include a teacher-librarian, a psychologist, a teacher of dramatics, of music, of art, of crafts, of physical education, and a remedial teacher. The efforts of specialists are coordinated with those of the classroom teacher who, with the help of the principal, plans the activities so that there is no break in the unified development of the education program of a pupil. Coordination and scheduling of the use of the building and the personnel resources are the responsibility of the principal.

Whether the school is organized around the principle of the self-contained classroom, which is a more costly form of organization, or around the service and resource unit pattern, or some variation of either, personnel organization is kept simple. All the teachers are specialized, but in different ways. Ideally, there are only two ranks among the staff, that of the teachers and that of the principal.

There are still a few schools in the United States that include all eight grades, all under the direction of one teacher and all housed in a one-room building. In some cities grades 7 and 8 are included in the same building with the first six grades. In some instances subject matter is departmentalized and the instruction in each subject is handled by a specialized teacher as far as the fifth grade. Sometimes departmentalization is only partial, and children have one teacher for most of their schoolwork but have specialized teachers for music, physical education, or art.

Areas for Improvement

The elementary school is a fertile area for educational improvement. The success of any plan to build a continuous, organized, developmental program to serve all who attend schools through the twelfth grade is contingent upon the program built for children while they are in the elementary school. One indicated change in the elementary school is a better balance of men and women on the teaching staff. Elementary teachers now constitute about two-thirds of all the public elementary and secondary teachers in America, and approximately 85 percent of these elementary teachers are women. Perhaps the growth of young children should be directed and stimulated by mature, emotionally well-balanced men and women. A number of changes in such areas as social attitude, salaries, and organizational pattern will necessarily precede this kind of improvement.

Middle, Intermediate,
and Junior High Schools

The middle grades—grades 5, 6, 7, 8, and 9—united in the schools in various grade combinations, are the present-day answer to the problem of providing an organized school unit that will logically follow the one-curriculum lower-grade school and also facilitate transition into the more specialized programs of the secondary school. Most commonly, this in-between school unit embraces either grades 7, 8, and 9, or grades 6, 7, 8, and 9. This is not always the case, however. In fact, having no in-between school at all, but having the first eight grades together as one unit, is still typical in some agriculture areas and in some larger cities. Sometimes, legally established high school districts determine the grades included in the secondary school. In some parts of Illinois and California, for instance, the ninth grade is in a 4-year high school that operates in a district independent of the district caring for the elementary levels from kindergarten through grade 8. Opinions vary on the inclusion of sixth-graders.

Typically, the junior high school has attempted to care for the educational needs of 12-, 13-, and 14-year-old children, has directed teaching away from a single curriculum, from a uniform program for all pupils, toward an offering providing choice and opportunities for specialization. Ordinarily, opportunities for pupils to individualize their programs have been moderately introduced in the seventh grade and gradually increased through the eighth and ninth grades.

In the modern junior high school, pupils are usually provided a wide range of direct exploratory experiences. Although exploratory experience is not peculiar to the junior high school—basic science at the college level, for instance, may be exploratory—it is introduced in the junior high school as a special method of study through appropriate curriculums. Also, for the first time a pupil in an intermediate school ordinarily has the privilege of selecting an elective from among such areas as general shop, printing, crafts, ceramics, art, electricity, music, dramatics, or a foreign language. School marks are not usually given in the elective field, or, where they are assigned, they are not considered marks of relative achievement. Teachers are on the alert to discover special interests, aptitudes, and skills.

General science, mathematics, language arts, and social studies may be taught in the spirit of exploration and discovery. This consumes more time than conventional methods. Pupils are encouraged to observe, to read widely, to investigate independently, to write creatively, and to get a broad view of some field of learning before entering detailed study of it.

Extracurricular activities, under expert direction, in the athletic, social, musical, and dramatic fields are also provided. These are also especially designed to meet the needs of the preadolescent.

The work of pupils in junior high schools is customarily planned around homerooms. Homeroom teachers generally combine the function of counseling with their teaching. Large junior high schools usually make available the services of a trained psychologist also. The principal aim of the homeroom teacher, and of the other people on the professional staff as well, but perhaps to a lesser degree, is to help pupils solve problems peculiar to their respective ages. The teacher must understand the problems typically associated with the dawning of a social consciousness—physical development, recreation, home relationships, religion, school relationships, personal conflicts, and the like. At the junior high school level, partly because of these guidance needs, it is important that men teachers should be as well represented as women teachers.

A majority of pupils of preadolescent age now attend some kind of intermediate, middle, or junior high school that differs from the traditional eight-grade elementary school. Studies by psychologists recommend that even more attention be given to discovering better solutions to the ever-widening gap in individual differences that especially characterize pupils of the sixth-, seventh-, eighth-, and ninth-grade age groups. A potential weakness of the junior high school program is the tendency to veer too far and too rapidly from the older one-curriculum, elementary school program toward too much departmentalization. A pupil from a five- or six-grade, one-curriculum school, from a self-contained classroom with one teacher, going into a school where he may have as many as eight teachers, may find his problems of adjustment aggravated.

Psychologists, and particularly child development experts who have focused their studies and attention on preadolescent children, tell us that the physical, emotional, and intellectual characteristics of these youngsters leave little doubt that their needs and interests must be given special consideration. This is a crucial period in the life cycle, a period marked by the child's growth toward physical and mental independence, a period of widening gaps in individual differences. The age is considered the most difficult from the standpoint of discipline. Teaching at the junior high school level calls for special understanding and for specialized teaching skills. It promises commensurate teaching satisfaction.

The Senior High School

The senior high school, as we discuss it, embraces grades 10, 11, and 12, although some high schools include grade 9 as well. When the ninth grade is included as a part of the high school, the attitudes toward the pupil and toward appropriate education for him are approximately the same as when the ninth grade is located in a junior high school. The pupil is still the same age, and has the same psychological characteristics and the same educational needs.

Americans believe that an enlightened citizenry is necessary to the survival of our democracy. They believe that equal educational opportunity for all children and youth is a correlative requirement. At the beginning of the century, however, many communities prided themselves on the fact that very few pupils who entered the ninth grade ever finished the twelfth. Modern senior high school practices emerged from a social atmosphere where selection was a favored policy. At the beginning of the century, fewer than 8 percent of the 17-year-olds graduated from high school. The high schools actually were high schools. Only a few years ago the chances of graduating from high school were greater for those pupils who had intelligence quotients of 110 and above. A pupil's chances of obtaining an education were enhanced if he came from an economically favored home, if his parents were in the highest income brackets in the community. In other words, the high school program was planned with highly selected college-bound pupils in mind. Traditions that accompanied that kind of policy became very deeply established. Now, typically, at the completion of 12 years of school attendance each pupil receives a high school diploma. The diploma is the same for all, regardless of the quality of work or the subject matter studied. In most communities, completion of the twelfth grade is the terminal point of education for many pupils. The activities of commencement are a universal recognition of this achievement.

With the extension of universal education it has become necessary to cut the academic cloth to fit the needs, abilities, and interests of every educable youth who may wish to take advantage of a senior high school education. If education at the senior high school level is to serve all American youth, then it must be so planned and administered that all American youth can profit from it. High school teachers have moved energetically in the direction of attaining this ideal. Though their progress has been commendable, the conflict of new with old continues partially unsolved. One obstacle to progress has been the deep-seated tradition that high schools should select the fit from the unfit. Another obstacle to fitting the high school program to all American youth is related to disrupting social crises—the depression of the 1930s, World War II in the 1940s, the sharp upturn in population growth in the 1950s, the Vietnam War of the late 1960s. A faculty that favors making changes may be hampered by lack of funds and personnel. In timers of international conflict, industry and the government tend to exert pressure for a special kind of training in the high school. The rapidity of social change scarcely gives high school teachers a chance to keep up to date in their analyses of the adjustments currently needed.

The Curriculum

Typically, the modern 4-year high school is developed to serve the needs of students from 14 to 18. It offers in one administrative unit all the programs for the education of all the youth who attend high school in a given community or school district. There are, however, some exceptions in a few of the larger cities. In New York City, for example, there are a number of specialized high schools, such as those giving vocational education. Even though a high school may specialize in a particular kind of vocational training, it still remains comprehensive in that the pupils take a balanced program and can therefore continue on to college.

Building a satisfactory curriculum to serve all American youth has two main facets. There must be, on the one hand, a degree of specialized education and, on the other hand, an emphasis on general education.

No term has been coined to designate the program that achieves an adequate balance between integration and specialization, between general education and specialized education. The pupil, with the help of his counselors, can in most cases select studies that will prepare him for some field. This is referred to as fulfilling the preparatory function of the high school. The program of studies can be planned in terms of a future goal. Some high schools have been very ingenious in finding ways to meet the differentiated needs of young adults. Others have not been ingenious enough. They have stressed certain kinds of preparation, such as for college, but have not succeeded as well in meeting needs of pupils who have other goals.

Every high school curriculum should also foster cultural compatibility. It is not easy to say how a heterogeneous population of young adults should be educated so that they become sufficiently like-minded to guarantee the perpetuation and improvement of the present American society. That is, nevertheless, a responsibility of every American high school.

The high school's answer to what it believes are the activities that lead to a well-integrated personality can be judged by what all the pupils are required to study. All pupils are usually required to study English for 3 years and U.S. history, civics, mathematics, science, and health and physical education for at least 1 year each. To this minimum or foundation program, the pupil can add, through his own selection, other courses in general or specialized education to complete his requirements for graduation. In other words, approximately one-half of his program is general education and one-half is specialized education. The four subjects most important in achieving general education are, in order of the emphasis they receive, English, social studies, mathematics, and science.

The Core Program

One example of how high schools sometimes adjust to new demands has been the development of the core program, sometimes called core courses, corerooms, or core studies. The core program includes all the instruction thought to be needed by all pupils of a given grade level. For example, oral expression, written expression, and citizenship training would be integrated into a single course taught by the core teacher, who has received appropriate special training.

Traditional subject-matter classification is generally disregarded in planning core studies. The work may be planned, for example, around a study of the problems of the immediate community. A given project may reveal the important part individuals play in the community, principles that underlie the American way of life, and problems connected with developing responsible citizenship. The project may teach how to cultivate the art of oral expression and how to participate in planning and conducting certain social activities. The group—the core teacher *with* the pupils—determines the aims of the project and the resources and activities needed to achieve them as the study progresses. The period of working together is longer than a traditional class period. This allows sufficient time for use of laboratory techniques and for pupil-teacher planning. It permits use of the community, makes it possible to complete comprehensive projects, and allows participation in activities necessary for a realistic program of citizenship training.

Work accomplished in core studies varies considerably from school to school. But in all schools it is recognized that the core teacher must be with the pupils longer and that he must know them well. He must be assigned a moderate teaching and counseling load. The core teacher will teach a heterogeneous group, not pupils classified in terms of native ability or academic achievement. The teacher will be responsible for giving individual and group guidance to the pupils and will be free to plan the activities of the core program. Subject-matter examinations will largely be replaced by an evaluation that is planned by both the teacher and the pupil. This newer evaluation will focus upon citizenship, work habits, and ability to solve problems, to contribute to group thinking and planning, and to master subject matter. Although the coreroom is a unit in the high school plan of organization, it is also a unit of organization in which the teacher strives to fulfill certain functions with fairly definitely determined and generally accepted practices.

The core program is one recent attempt to improve the high school's effectiveness in achieving social integration. Other high school efforts at securing both specialized education and general education include the offering of extracurricular activities, counseling procedures, and special services such as psychological testing. The American high school is becoming a truly comprehensive school. It is being modified to serve well the needs of all the children and young adults of the nation between the ages of 14 and 18. The core program is an effort to make high schools that are comprehensive also socially unified, integrated schools.

The Nongraded School

For some time educators have been struggling with various plans to meet specific needs and to adjust to definite abilities of individual pupils. Such plans as the Winnetka Plan, the Platoon System, and the Pueblo Plan have been tried and for various reasons given up. A recent organizational plan is called the nongraded school. It differs from its predecessors in details, but it seeks to achieve the same service to individual pupils.

In traditional units of school organization, the pupils of any one grade are usually of about the same chronological age. The pupils in any one classroom, however, exhibit a wide range of differences in ability. Teachers have, of course, always made adjustments within the classroom to these variations. Special materials have been supplied for various levels of learning ability. In the nongraded school, however, an *organizational* plan is followed that creates a framework allowing for flexibility and continuity.

Nongraded schools are to be found more often at the elementary school level, although there are nongraded plans to be found in some disciplines in some secondary schools. As is true of all features of our American schools, the details of the nongraded plan vary from place to place.

The nongraded elementary school, for the most part, relies on levels of accomplishment in reading as the basis for advancement and assignment in a program of vertical progression through the six years of the elementary school organization. No grade designators are used. The nongraded sequence usually consists of a 3-year program (primary nongraded) or a 6-year program (elementary nongraded). Levels of sequential reading content are most often the first organizational basis for nongradedness. For instance, the children may all start together at level 1, and progress through to level 20, to a traditional sixth-grade reading book. At each level there are possibilities for lateral movement with enrichment materials and also for reinforcement materials if a child needs more work before moving on to the next level.

The pupil either moves on into the intermediate nongraded unit from the primary unit or has his program enriched. The amount of time it takes a child to complete a level varies. The slow learner may take four years to accomplish three. He does not have to repeat a whole year, as is the case in the graded school. Instead, he takes up in the fall where he left off at the beginning of summer. This is not retention, nor does it carry the stigma of retention. The decision about whether to enrich or advance the child who finishes 3 years in 2 is a basic one that involves many variables including age, size, intellect, and other social and psychological aspects concerning the child's life situation.

Nongradedness in the secondary school is linked with team teaching. It usually provides for as much as 45 percent of the student's time for independent study. Of the other 55 percent, 30 percent might be given to large-group instruction and 25 percent to small groups. This allows for flexibility in the time students spend on each course, depending on their rate of progress and the modifications the teachers make in it for individual students.

The Community College

In the United States the junior college or community college, as it is usually called now,—sometimes public and sometimes private—is a 2-year post–high school institution. Currently there is a dramatic increase in the number of public community colleges and in their services. The establishment of such a community college is typically initiated in the area to be served and may depend on approval in a referendum in the area. In some states the junior college (or "community college") is part of the state system of higher education; in others it is part of the local school district. At the beginning of the century there were fewer than 10 junior colleges in the United States; and only one—the junior college established at Joliet, Illinois, in 1902—was public. Now every state has public junior or community colleges. In the 1970s the community college movement has continued to expand.

Community colleges grew in number from 480 in 1947 to 929 in 1973. In 1947, 2-year institutions of higher (postsecondary) education in the United States enrolled 222,045 students; in the fall of 1973 such institutions had a total enrollment of 1,921,726. These figures include enrollment for both private and public 2-year postsecondary institutions incorporating many sorts of thirteenth- and fourteenth-grade-level curricula. Some of these curricula represented traditional academic programs in liberal arts studies preparatory to the third or fourth year of undergraduate studies. Many of the curricula of these institutions also included newer and highly specialized technical professional training programs leading to Associate Degrees in Arts or Science that would provide entrance opportunities in many new technological careers as well as older vocational careers. In the 1973–1974 academic year the number of 2-year institutions of higher learning had increased to 1003, of which 760 were publicly controlled and 243 privately controlled. Public control of a 2-year institution of higher learning can mean any one of three things: (1) that it is totally controlled by state government educational agencies; (2) that it is jointly controlled by both state and local educational taxes and agencies; or (3) that it is totally controlled by a local governmental unit and local taxes.

In the community college a large proportion of the program typically is devoted to courses that may be transferred to a 4-year college or university and that fit into a program leading to the bachelor's degree. However, especially in the public institutions, there is also emphasis on 2-year terminal curricula in the occupational, semitechnical, and technical fields such as business and secretarial, nursing, data processing, and electronics. The community college also serves as a center for the administration of programs for adult education through evening schools, adult forums, and the like.

All who graduate from high school are eligible to continue their education in a public community college. Tuition usually is charged. In addition to local tax funds, the support generally is shared to a relatively high degree by state funds and also by federal funds allocated to vocational and technical education and other areas of higher education. Federal funds are directly applicable to community colleges under the Higher Education Act of 1965 and its later amendments.

The community college has a position of unquestioned acceptance in America, and present trends suggest that it will have a prominent place in future plans for extending educational opportunities to the youth of America.

The State University

One of the most spectacular developments in American education is the state university, the apex of the public educational system. The state university—the answer to the American public's demand for higher education—has no counterpart in any other country. It is indigenous to the American cultural soil and suited to American tradition.

All the state universities have 4-year colleges, which award a bachelor's degree on graduation. Superimposed on the college is the graduate school, which (1) affords specialization beyond that given in the 4-year undergraduate college, (2) awards degrees, the master's degree for 1 year of study beyond the bachelor program and the doctor of philosophy degree for 3 or more years of study and research beyond the bachelor program, and (3) offers numerous degrees designating fields of specialization—doctor of education, doctor of laws, doctor of science. The faculties are made up of highly trained specialists who combine teaching, scholarly writing, and research.

Professional schools of law, medicine, dentistry, agriculture, library science, education, engineering, business, journalism, architecture, theology, and speech and a nonprofessional school of arts and sciences are all administered within the common university organization.

The public universities in some cases have become organizational giants. The comprehensiveness of their programs may be inferred from their size. For example, the University of California, with its seven campuses, enrolls well over 125,000 students. Its Berkeley campus alone has a teaching staff equal in number to a sizable university student body early in this century. So large have university enrollments become that some state legislatures—Illinois, for example—have established a system of independently administered state universities at strategic locations throughout the state. It is not at all uncommon for a state university to enroll more than 20,000 students. How large the state universities will be allowed to become is a matter of conjecture. One thing seems certain: their influence on American life and education will greatly increase.

The combination of college and university instruction under a single administration is the principal characteristic of the American state university and is considered one of its chief sources of strength. In some cases technical institutes within the university framework operate primarily for research purposes, for issuing learned publications under the direction of the teaching staff, for conducting programs contributing to the national defense, and for carrying on a variety of other undertakings deemed essential enough to call for recognition at the university level.

Many state universities have programs set up to serve special needs of the state. Extension divisions, organized in most state universities, provide credit and noncredit courses in various centers of the state for training in many fields. The state universities distribute visual materials and maintain lending libraries throughout the state, and offer short-course seminars, lectures, conferences, and other similar services.

Some state universities have branches in convenient centers in the state, making education more accessible and less costly.

State universities are supported mainly by direct taxation. They also, however, derive considerable revenue from federal funds, endowments, alumni foundations, private foundations, student fees, athletics, and the like. The annual expenditure for all state institutions is substantial. Their plans are extensive. Their educational influence is great. The state universities are large, colorful, liberally supported, constantly expanding institutions that form the top rung of the educational ladder.

Summary

The educational ladder of the public school system has been the pride of the American people. The ladder constitutes a continuous progression of instruction from the kindergarten through the most advanced training given by the universities. In the main the costs are borne by the public, and the opportunity of advancing to the higher levels is constantly being extended to more people.

The elementary school, the junior high school, and the senior high school are viewed as institutions for everyone. The desire of the American people to extend educational opportunities at the higher level is answered in part by the community college, the newest extension of free or low-cost popular education.

QUESTIONS

1. What factors should a parent consider before deciding whether to send his child to a nursery school?
2. How much should one expect a child's attendance at nursery school or kindergarten to contribute to his subsequent achievement in subject matter?
3. Why have the factors of continuity, gradation, and transition received such serious consideration in the establishment of school units of organization?
4. What kinds of specialized services would you expect to find in the better-organized elementary schools?
5. What are some of the instructional resources you expect to find in the better-organized elementary schools?
6. How is the transition idea reflected in the organization of the junior high school?
7. How has the movement to decentralize education affected the organization of the community college?
8. What are some of the problems the high school faces when it attempts to provide an education for all American youth?

PROJECTS

1. From a table of ages of the children in some particular grade of a school system, generalize on what some of the problems of teaching in that grade may be.

2. Describe the expanding role of the junior college and estimate the future of this public school unit.
3. Set forth what you consider the principal problems of teaching caused by individual differences among the pupils in the different units of school organization.
4. In view of the fact that the federal government provides aid to non-public higher institutions, state the pros and cons for its providing aid to nonpublic secondary schools; to nonpublic junior colleges; to nonpublic elementary schools.
5. Visit a local Head Start program. Evaluate the work in terms of specific observations.
6. Review some of the literature on middle schools and junior high schools and develop a short research paper on the specific rationales for each type of school and the major differences between them.
7. Investigate the rapid growth of 2-year community colleges in the past several years and report on the types of programs offered in them.

unit

III

Suggested Readings

ALEXANDER, WILLIAM M., "The New School in the Middle," *Phi Delta Kappan,* 50 (No. 6): 355–357, February, 1969. Explains why the middle school idea has grown so rapidly. "For the foreseeable future middle schools of grades 5–8 or 6–8 are destined to replace the traditional grades 7–9 junior high schools as the schools in the middle." Explains the rationale of the developing middle school idea.

ALFORD, ALBERT L., "The Elementary and Secondary Education Act of 1965," *Phi Delta Kappan,* 46 (No. 10): 483–488, June, 1965. Explains the provision of the acts and explains what local leadership must do to implement them.

American Education, pp. 12–22, 30–31, December, 1968–January, 1969. A series of short articles on the growth and development of junior colleges. Data on growth and enrollment are on pages 30–31.

American Education, "Federal Funds," 5 (No. 4): 22–25, April, 1969. A breakdown of the $3.5 billion distributed by the U.S. Office of Education to the states. Shows how the states used the money to improve education.

American Education, "Federal Money for Education: Programs Administered by the U.S. Office of Education," 5 (No. 2): 20–24, February, 1969. This lists 118 federal aid programs administered by the U.S. Office of Education. Of particular interest to the beginning student of education are the column "Authorization," which lists the specific act upon which a program rests, and the column "Purpose." It should be kept in mind that this vast endeavor is only one part of the federal activity in education. The list grows each year. In 1969, for instance, the Head Start program was added to the Office of Education list.

American Education, "National Defense Education Act—Years of Progress," 4 (No. 8): 2–15, September, 1968. Progress in American education after 10 years of administration of the National Defense Education Act of 1958 is reviewed.

BENSON, CHARLES S., "The Economics of Education in Urban Society," *Phi Delta Kappan,* 48: 316–319, March, 1967. This article is an excellent general account of the overall economic problems of city schools as the economics of schooling is compared with the economics of delivering other needed social services in cities.

COLE, ROBERT W., JR., "Ribbin', Jivin', and Playin' the Dozens," *Phi Delta Kappan,* 56 (No. 3): 171–175, November, 1974. This article is an interview with Herbert L. Foster in which he gives advice on teaching in the inner-city based on his 16 years as a public school teacher in inner-city schools and as a teacher educator. The title of this article was taken from the title of Foster's book on teaching in the inner-city schools of America, which was published in 1974.

CREMIN, LAWRENCE A., "The Revolution in American Secondary Education, 1893–1918," *Teachers College Record,* 56, pp. 295–308, 1955. This is a very good interpretation of the development of secondary education in America in the period from 1893 to 1918 when major changes occurred in the goals and curricula of American secondary schools that were to transform the American high school into the comprehensive high school of today.

DUKER, SAM, ed., *The Public Schools and Religion: The Legal Context.* New York: Harper & Row, Publishers, 1966. This is an excellent collection of selections from major court decisions affecting the relationships of American public schools with religious groups and religious education. The editor's commentary and selections from court decisions make this a valuable work. It provides a synoptic overview of the relationships of church and state in the field of education.

GOODLAD, JOHN I., "Directions of Curriculum Change," *NEA Journal,* December, 1966. Goodlad describes his conception of the directions to be considered if we are to develop what he describes as humanistic school curricula.

HAMILTON, CHARLES, "Race and Education: A Search for Legitimacy," *Harvard Educational Review,* 38 (No. 4): 669–684, Fall, 1968. This is a perceptive essay on the factor of race in American education. It is superbly written and very informative.

JACOBY, SUSAN L., "New Power in the Schools," *Saturday Review,* pp. 59–60, 70–72, January 8, 1969. This analyzes the position of black teachers in inner-city schools. "Black teachers and administrators are beginning to emerge as a power in the nation's city school systems at a time when the bitterness of black parents toward these schools is overflowing."

JENCKS, CHRISTOPHER, and MARY JO BANE, "The Schools and Equal Opportunity," *Saturday Review of Education,* 55 (No. 3): 37–42, September 16, 1972. A perceptive and widely read article on the authors' views about the often alleged relationship between schooling and equality of opportunity in society. They argue that many other factors are at least as important in accounting for success or failure in America as the factor of schooling. Jencks has published a book on *Inequality: A Reassessment of the Effect of Family and Schooling in America* with Mary Jo Bane and their research associates at Harvard University.

KOHLBERG, LAWRENCE, and PHILLIP WHITTEN, "Understanding the Hidden Curriculum," *Learning,* December, 1972. This is an article on value assumptions and approaches to valuing that operate in schooling, and it is a summary of Kohlberg's views about levels of valuing.

LA NOUE, GEORGE R., "The Establishment Clause: Requiem or Rebirth?" *Phi Delta Kappan,* 50 (No. 2): 85–89, October, 1968. This analysis of the U.S. Supreme Court's 1968 decisions on church-state relationships from the viewpoint of federal policy in financing education clearly highlights the issues involved in using public revenue for private and parochial schools.

For example, is the Pennsylvania law requiring the state to set aside horse-racing revenue to support instruction in mathematics, foreign languages, physical sciences, and physical education in nonpublic schools a wise law? Sound? Constitutional? A policy likely to be followed in other states? A lawyer analyzes the issue.

LEKACHMAN, ROBERT, "Schools, Money, and Politics," *The New Leader,* 55, pp. 7–14, September 18, 1972. This essay deals with Lekachman's views on the problems of financing school systems. He relates this concern to recent court cases challenging traditional ways of funding schools. This essay relates to finance and control of schools and the question of equality of educational opportunity.

LEVINE, DANIEL U., "Integration in Metropolitan Schools: Issues and Prospects," *Phi Delta Kappan,* 54, (No. 10): 651–657, June, 1973. This is a fine commentary on problems and prospects in efforts to achieve racial balance or integration in urban school systems. Levine is well known in the area of urban education, and this essay is most informative.

MARCONNIT, GEORGE D., "State Legislatures and the School Curriculum," *Phi Delta Kappan,* 49 (No. 5): 269–272, January, 1968. This is an excellent survey of the requirements imposed on classroom instruction by state statutes or state constitutions. The number of limitations varies from 1 in Alaska to 31 in Indiana, 36 in Iowa, 37 in California, and so on. Hawaii is listed as having no state limitations.

NATIONAL EDUCATION ASSOCIATION, Research Division, *Estimates of School Statistics.* An annual report of public school statistics, including pupils, professional staff, revenues, and expenditures for the 50 states, the District of Columbia, and the nation as a whole.

NATIONAL EDUCATION ASSOCIATION, Research Division, *Nursery School Education, 1966–67,* pp. 1–9. The introduction to this research report gives an overview of the nursery school movement in America.

NATIONAL EDUCATION ASSOCIATION, Research Division, *Rankings of the States.* An annual report that ranks the states in terms of teachers' salaries, relative wealth of the states, the financial effort made by each state to support schools, per pupil expenditure, and the like.

ORNSTEIN, ALLAN C., "Administrative/Community Organization of Metropolitan Schools," *Phi Delta Kappan,* 55 (No. 10): 668–674, June, 1973. An excellent critical review of three approaches to urban school-community relationships and administration of large urban school systems.

RICHARDSON, JAMES F., "The Historical Roots of Our Urban Crisis," *Current History,* 59 (No. 351), November, 1970. This essay represents a synthesis of the origins of contemporary American urban conditions. The author comments on the origins of public schools in urban centers.

REMSBERG, CHARLES, and BONNIE REMSBERG, "Chicago: Legacy of an Ice Age," *Saturday Review,* pp. 73–75, 91–92, May 20, 1967. Two free-lance writers analyze the dark sides of education in a large city, emphasize the job of the general superintendent, and by implication draw attention to the responsibilities of citizens who serve on boards of education.

SANDERS, STANLEY G., "Challenge of the Middle School," *The Educational Forum,* January, 1968. This fine article contrasts the "middle school" with the junior high school. The author describes the rationales for each type of school and provides some historical background.

SHAW, FREDERICK, "The Educational Park in New York: Archetype of the Future?" *Phi Delta Kappan,* 50 (No. 6), 329–331, February, 1969. Explains what the park system is ("a number of educational divisions grouped together in a common campus") and what the primary goals of such school organizations are.

SIZER, THEODORE, ed., *Religion and Public Education.* Boston: Houghton Mifflin Company, 1967. This is the best single-volume anthology of major issues relating to religion and public education in America to be published in recent years. The essays included represent all major religious and secular points of view. Several prominent scholars are included in this volume.

SHEED, WILFRED, "Don't Junk the Parochial Schools," *The Saturday Evening Post,* pp. 6, 10, June 13, 1964. A young journalist makes a plea that America continue to permit its pluralistic philosophy to govern the education of its children.

IV

Aims and methods in America

We began our study of education in America with the certain belief that the one most important figure in the profession of education is the classroom teacher, for aside from the quality of individual school administration, it is the teachers interacting with their students who play the key roles in the search for knowledge and human understanding. We know that families educate in a real and powerful sense, and we know that peer relationships influence how children and young adults view their world. Furthermore, we know that in a larger sense the entire community in which a child or adolescent lives can educate or miseducate as the learner interacts with his community environment. Nothing said in this book discounts these realities of human social life. When, however, we focus on the roles played in formal educational institutions we realize that the most important persons with whom students interact are the teachers whose job it is to aid and guide them in the search for knowledge and self-actualization.

In Unit IV we direct our concerns to the aims of education and the methods of educating that remain prevalent in American society. The different kinds of objectives teachers may have when they teach, as well as major relationships between the knowledge to be taught and the methods of teaching, are considered here. The use of the term "growth" to describe or imply the aim of education requires qualification here. When "growth" is used in educational writings in descriptions of pupil progress, the authors generally mean growth toward those sorts of learning outcomes that can be counted as "educative," outcomes that coincide with generally accepted definitions of "education" that are tied to beneficial learning experiences. It is understood that growth can be toward ends that meet the criteria of true education, or that it can be toward some undesirable end. Cancers grow but they are not viewed as desirable. When "growth" is used to describe positive educative achievement, therefore, we must plainly stipulate that the type of growth being suggested is qualitative growth toward personal self-discovery and toward development of one's cognitive and affective capacities, toward ends viewed as desirable by any rational person who might question them. Growth in a person's capacity to engage in autonomous, reasoned judgment in the search for the realization of their potentialities as persons, with respect for the autonomy of other persons, would certainly be such an educational aim.

Unit IV is thus undertaken with a commitment to examine, at an introductory level, a basic overview of matters to consider in understanding: the students, aims of education, methods of instruction, and their interrelationships. Our overview of American educational development ends with brief consideration of future studies and concerns that the reader will participate in if he or she decides to become an educator in America.

chapter

16

Understanding pupils

Clearly, the aims that are selected to guide in education must be related to the pupils, to unique and distinct individuals. Likewise, in determining what subject matter and teaching procedures are appropriate and promising, the decisions must be related to the pupils, to their capacities, interests, and needs. Understanding the pupils, then, is the prelude to the following chapters. This chapter describes some of the sources to which teachers turn for information about children and also for help in interpreting and comprehending what they learn about pupils—in refining their own insights.

Getting Information About Pupils

School Records

All schools collect and record more or less specific information about pupils. Generally, such information is included in a continuous, cumulative record that gives a picture of an individual as he or she progresses through the school grade by grade. Before the opening of the school year, a teacher often looks over these records before making tentative plans.

What kind of information is on the official record? Actually, this varies considerably from one school district to another, but, in general, the records include the following:

1. ATTENDANCE

Attendance gives the date of enrollment in the district and attendance by years in the school. Sometimes a record of tardiness is also included. This information may be important in understanding a child, because attendance is sometimes related to health, to delinquent behavior, to home problems, or to something else equally significant. The pattern of attendance over the years may be enlightening.

2. OUT-OF-SCHOOL BACKGROUND

The out-of-school record includes such items as where and when the child was born, where he lives, where his parents were born, the language spoken in the home, whether the parents are employed and what kind of employment they have, the number of brothers and sisters, older and younger, and with whom the child makes his home. The importance of this kind of information in understanding the child is obvious.

3. HEALTH

The health record includes results on hearing and vision tests as well as any other pertinent information about such matters as surgery. Some schools require dental reports, and these are also recorded. This part of the record should be scanned early because it is important for the teacher to know at once if a child is epileptic, for instance, or even if he should be seated near the front because of a hearing disorder or requires some other minor classroom adjustment.

4. ACADEMIC RECORD

The academic record may include report card grades over the years. Usually achievement test scores are also recorded. Where some kind of intelligence or academic potential test has been given, usually this score is also recorded as a help in interpreting the achievement test scores. This part of the record will also show whether the child has been retained or double-promoted at any time throughout his school career.

5. SPECIAL SERVICES

Many schools provide various kinds of remedial and guidance services such as remedial reading, speech correction, counseling. Usually the agency providing the service prepares a report of what activities have been completed, what progress has been made, and a recommendation for future assignment, and this is included in the cumulative folder.

6. TEACHER COMMENTS

By means of a checklist or brief comments, generally one teacher, annually, records impressions of the child's behavior and achievement in terms of personal adjustment, social adjustment, qualities of leadership, special aptitudes, creativity in various fields, and the like. Of course, the advantage of the insights and understandings of a pupil's previous teacher is inestimable. It is well to remember, however, that children do change and often go through "stages." An old record of problems should not be allowed to predispose a teacher unwisely.

A more extensive record is found in some schools, but in essence this is the information given to the teacher about each pupil. Without this kind of information supplied by the school, the teacher would be somewhat like a ship without a compass. A ship does not sink because it lacks a compass, nor does a teacher fail because of a lack of adequate initial information about pupils. Both, however, are safer with the guidance of dependable instruments. Of course, each instrument must be intelligently used.

Personal Observation

In learning to know a pupil, no approach is more rewarding than direct observation in a situation involving normal relationships with a peer group. Information from other sources becomes more meaningful as it is interpreted in the light of firsthand, everyday observation. With the pupil in the classroom the teacher observes evidence of maturity—personal, social, and academic. It may be significant to note, for instance, whether a pupil takes initiative in beginning an assignment, in going ahead on his or her own. How friendly, thoughtful, and helpful the pupil is in relations with fellow students and how alert in contributing to the class as a whole are the kinds of reactions that may be significant, especially as observed over a period of time. Evidence of a probable need for help in relation to emotional problems may be discovered initially through the teacher's observation in the classroom. Fears that seem to manifest themselves in such behavior as withdrawal or hostility or in excessive aggressiveness are usually identifiable in a classroom situation.

The teacher's direct observation of the pupil need not be limited to the classroom. In fact, quite important observations may be made of a pupil in the cafeteria, in the halls, at the lockers, in extracurricular activities. In situations of this kind the pupil is making decisions alone. That a pupil chooses to sit alone, to seek always to be with a particular group, or to attempt consistently to draw certain others around him may be significant. The pupil who has an untidy, crowded locker, the one who puts the lock on upside down to tease a locker mate, the one who regularly shouts to those across the hall, the one who races down the corridor without thought for the safety of others may be exhibiting behavior that is symptomatic, worthy of noticing.

Conferences with the Pupil

The most important of all the conferences a teacher holds are those with individual pupils. These conferences are related to any interests or problems the homeroom teacher or the pupil wishes to discuss. In conference the teacher learns of the general progress one child is making. The conference may reveal certain pupil needs, such as improvement in study habits or budgeting time. It may reveal information pertinent to changes in instructional materials, procedures, or some specific aim of current work. It is during these conferences that the teacher devotes attention to a single pupil, establishes rapport with the child. Most children and young people respond to evidence of a personal interest in their activities and concern about their progress. The teacher has an opportunity to discover how the pupil feels about his or her academic, personal, and social life at the school. Incidentally, the conference includes plans for a follow-up time, a time when the pupil will have an opportunity to report on any plan made during a conference, to continue it if it seems to be working well or to abandon it for some other plan if that seems desirable.

Conferences with the Pupil's Parents

In some schools at least one 20-minute conference with the parents of each child is required during each school year. In addition, parent conferences are arranged at other times when a need for them is indicated. In general, all schools encourage parents to visit the school or the teacher at any time that they feel it is desirable. In the conference the parent is encouraged to talk about the pupil—his or her interests, needs, and problems. The parent is also informed about the child's progress, his strengths and the areas in which he might be expected to improve. Where the child's major academic work has been in a team teaching situation, the regular conferences are sometimes group conferences including the parent, the pupil (for a part of the conference), and a teacher from each of the disciplines represented on the team. Getting to know the parents directly from conferences, and also from association in the PTA or at some gathering where teachers and parents get together, enhances the teacher's knowledge of the background of the pupils. In addition, what the parents tell about such matters as the pupil's out-of-school interests and activities, home relationships, or problems adds significantly to the teacher's understanding. If the pupil is present for a part of the parent conference, the relationship exhibited between parent and child may be enlightening.

Conferences with Professional Specialists

There are a number of professional specialists with whom the teacher confers to get help in understanding pupils. Professional services are typically rendered by a health department, usually represented in the school by a school nurse; a speech correctionist; a school social worker; and a remedial reading teacher. Sometimes psychologists are available. Also among the specialists with whom a teacher may confer are teachers who give special instruction to the orthopedically handicapped or the partially sighted or who give instruction at home or in the hospital. Although information related to the special services may be in the school records, a personal, direct conference with the specialists usually gives the teacher further help. The school social worker, for instance, typically has a series of conferences with a pupil who has an adjustment difficulty, confers with the pupil's parents, visits in the home, and confers with various community agencies dedicated to social service that have had association with the pupil. The social worker has much to add to what the teacher has been able to learn through direct conferences and observation.

Using Information About Pupils

The sources of information discussed here are not meant to be complete or exhaustive. They are typically the outstanding sources. Most teachers have other avenues to use in learning about their pupils—perhaps tests they administer to reveal aptitudes, social adjustment, or something else. From whatever source—direct observation, conferences, school records, or something else—all this information helps teachers understand their pupils. To make proper use of what they have learned about their pupils, teachers must know the meanings of certain terms ordinarily used in reports about pupils. Moreover, in order to comprehend the import of the entire collection of information from all sources, teachers also need to know some important generalizations that scientists in such fields as psychology, biology, and sociology have developed over the years.

Two Aspects of the Pupil

Learning, in school as elsewhere, is an individual process. Pupils' interaction with their physical and social environments, however, significantly influences what they learn and how well they learn it. For example, pupils may enlarge their vocabulary through personal, independent reading, but the actual meanings they attach to the words they acquire, their pronunciation of them, their manner of speaking, and their conversational skills are largely the result of interactions with those about them. The language of the child of the ghetto may be very different from the language of the child of the suburb. Think of pupils solving mathematics problems. They learn about mathematics as they work the problems. However, they probably interact with a teacher, fellow pupils, and, through the printed page, the writer of the textbook. What results from working a mathematics problem or reading a story is thus a complicated, personal, inner change, a change that embraces different kinds of learning. Simultaneously, while adding insights into mathematics or increasing vocabulary, pupils develop certain social attitudes—likes, dislikes, prejudices, for instance. Thus, to understand their pupils adequately, teachers must interpret them both as individuals and in terms of their social environment.

Meaning of Terms

When it comes to the meaning of terms used in material reported about pupils or information gained in conferences with professional specialists, the importance of having an accurate understanding of technical terms cannot be overemphasized. Definitions and explanations of such terms, however, are beyond the scope of this book. Ordinarily, technical terms are explored in other professional courses, or their meanings are discovered by teachers through their own research as the need to understand the terms arises.

It seems that every profession, as it develops, finds a need for words that carry more precise meanings than those conveyed by the everyday language of social communication. In addition to technical terms directly associated with education, the technical terms employed in relating information about pupils cover a wide range of areas. Each fact, quantity, or statement used to describe growth and development of pupils is concrete information about growth and development— mental age, vision acuity, or any one of numerous items. As we have noted, recorded information about pupils usually begins with the kin- dergarten and continues as long as the pupil is enrolled in school, perhaps through the twelfth grade. Of course teachers cannot appreci- ate the meaning and implication of the terms used in the entries unless they know the technical meanings.

One example of the kind of technical term whose meaning a teacher needs to understand is "mental age" (MA). A brief descrip- tion of the concepts implied by this term may show why mistakes are easy to make if technical terms are not accurately understood.

The term "mental age" is frequently used in schools where intelli- gence tests have been administered to pupils. It expresses the mental maturity of a child without regard to how long it took to reach it. Technically defined, it is the level of a child's mental ability expressed in averages based on the median test scores of a large group of children (called the standardization group) having the same chronological age. The procedure in determining the mental age of a pupil—always de- scribed in months—is to find the *chronological* age of the standardiza- tion group whose average score on a given test was the same as the pupil's. This is the mental age, regardless of chronological age. If a pupil whose chronological age is 74 months makes a score corre- sponding to the average score made by a standardization group whose chronological age is also 74 months, then the mental age is 74 months. If the same pupil makes a score corresponding to the average score of a standardization group whose chronological age is 80 months, then mental development is equal to that of the average child of 80 months. Since the pupil's chronological age is 74 months, he or she is judged to be abler than the average of the same chronological age.

Important Generalizations

Besides knowing the meaning of terms used in referring to items about pupils, it is essential for teachers to know some of the important gen- eralizations and conclusions regarding human growth and development that specialists have derived from researchers—especially from researchers in the life sciences such as psychology, sociology, pediatrics, psychiatry, biology, dietetics, education, and others—who have focused on some aspect of the growth and development of children and youth. Each valid generalization made by the qualified specialist serves as a background the teacher can use to make an intelligent interpretation of the specific information that the testers, dentists, nurses, caseworkers, and others provide about pupils.

We choose a few of the many important generalizations to illustrate their value to the teacher. The generalizations selected are related to concepts that are part of the broad concept of learning: habit, memory, forgetting, attention, and motive.

We are told that learning consists of the changes in behavior that follow behavior. When confronted by a situation a second time, one behaves differently from the way one did when meeting the situation the first time. To say this another way, learning is the modification in behavior that results from an earlier response to the same stimulus. A person responds differently to a stimulus situation when profiting from previous experience. A child, for example, will not be likely to touch a hot stove a second time. It is relatively easy to define learning and to provide simple examples, but some learning—such as, say, learning to be a great teacher, an outstanding novelist, a proficient surgeon, or a highly skilled mechanic—is very complex and occurs in many forms. The generalizations that follow are about concepts that help to clarify this broad meaning of learning.

I. HABIT

Current extensive study of habit as a kind of learning reflects the great importance professional psychologists attach to the subject. The generalizations derived from the many scientific investigations of habit are worthy of careful study by the classroom teacher. Those who take a professional sequence of courses in preparation for teaching are likely to find that their psychology studies give major attention to this aspect of learning. For our overview purposes, however, we merely introduce the subject by briefly exploring the answers to two questions: What is habit? What is its relation to learning?

A habit is a form of learned behavior that is engaged in without conscious thought. It is a pattern of behavior that has become stereotyped and hence is highly predictable. Habit is a kind of learning that is thorough. It is not a simple reaction, but a complex system of reactions. That the whole organism is involved in habit response is obvious as one watches a pupil walking, playing, talking, reading, or working a problem. By and large, one can roughly classify habits in three categories: motor habits, language habits, and emotional habits; all three are interrelated. In *deliberate* efforts at habit formation, the emotional factor must be emphasized, because consistent emotional reinforcement tends to make a habit an ingrained part of the organism.

Since many habits are readily acquired (some, in fact, result from a single response), it is important that, wherever possible, a pupil's first performance on a task be a correct one. There is always the chance that a pupil will repeat the first performance over and over again. Thus one cannot overemphasize the crucial importance of the teaching pupils receive in their early years and the habits they then establish. Accordingly, psychologists currently are intensifying their study of early intellectual development, and schools are emphasizing the need for identifying as precisely as possible a child's particular style of learning. These trends are reflected in the recent concentration on Head Start programs, nursery schools, and the like.

The skilled teacher notes a pupil's habits from information supplied and from his observation and then tries to influence the pupil to form good habits in the right sequence. The teacher shows the pupil that every step in the right direction tends to make learning easier, to increase self-mastery, to expand personal freedom, to help achieve his or her best. Efforts are directed toward getting pupils to channel their energies into directions that lead to the formation of desirable habits.

What should be done about the bad habits pupils—in fact, all of us—possess? The time-honored teaching device used to deter the development of bad habits and to encourage the building of good ones is punishment. Nevertheless, punishment in this connection does not always produce the results expected. For one thing, research has demonstrated that, to be effective, punishment must be so timed as to interrupt the course of the act and must be severe. Unfortunately, in school situations, punishment usually has to take place some time after the response that it is expected to disrupt. Furthermore, the degree of severity is very hard to judge. Punishment that is unnecessarily severe may lead to aversion, withdrawal, and other undesirable responses that may be worse than the bad habit the punishment is intended to correct. On the other hand, mild punishment may merely arouse interest and excitement among pupils, thereby actually reinforcing the bad habit.

In general, the principles that apply to the formation of good habits apply equally to the formation of bad habits. Neither good habits nor bad habits are formed in a day (with the exception of those formed under unusual environmental conditions that give strong emotional reinforcement). When incorrect responses are met with non-reinforcement, they are likely to decline. The emphasis should be on immediate reinforcement of correct responses and on no reinforcement of incorrect responses. In time, and with considerable patience, incorrect performance is likely to decline without reinforcement. *Correct* performance, however, is also likely to decline without reinforcement. In other words, the same principles apply to the formation of all kinds of habits—good, bad, or indifferent.

2. MEMORY

Memory is another area about which experts have given us helpful generalizations. Memory is the recall of past behavior or, more accurately, behavior that is reconstituted, or mentally revived, or adapted. Some cue in the present environment, perhaps a substitute cue within the body itself, partially revives or reconstitutes some form of behavior that the learner has executed in the past. The recollection is available as knowledge, the possession of which prompts the individual to behave—differently, if the recollection is adverse, or in the same way, if the recollection is pleasant.

Ability to reconstitute past behavior is strengthened by repetition. Pupils strengthen their ability to recall an event or an experience through narration, by telling their parents about something learned in school, by repeating what is to be learned themselves, or by just thinking it. Intention to remember is also a factor here, since pupils remember more vividly, verbalize more often, repeat more accurately, if aware that they are expected to narrate later what they learn.

Pupils are frequently required to memorize subject-matter materials such as spelling words, definitions, rules of grammar; basic formulas in mathematics, chemistry, physics; vocabulary in foreign languages; and the like. Repeated verbalization—going over the material orally, silently, and in writing—is indispensable reinforcement to efficient recall. Thorough, long-remembered learning is not a hurried process, nor does it proceed without conscious effort.

3. FORGETTING

Forgetting, the inability to recall, is a kind of learning in which new learning weakens older learning. This concept of forgetting leads to practices different from those resulting from the concept that pre-vailed in earlier times—that memory is a kind of storehouse of knowl-edge and that forgetting is caused by a lapse of time between learning and attempted recall.

The current explanation of forgetting is that when a pupil makes two or more different responses to the same stimulus—assuming that the same stimulus recurs—the last response has a physiological advan-tage over the first. New and different responses to older stimuli dimin-ish and eventually almost erase much of the earlier learning. What happens to what pupils learn in the early years of school depends, therefore, on what they learn in the later years. Children may learn to say "am not" in school. If later they are constantly with people who say "ain't," they tend to forget the earlier learned response be-cause when they make the new response, using "ain't," the former response is weakened—forgotten. Thus we may conclude, as Thorn-dike did at the beginning of this century, after many studies of forget-ting, that "there is no validity in the assumption that there is some magical curve of forgetting which every function at every stage will somewhat closely follow." How much one forgets depends on the new learning that takes place, the conditions under which it takes place, and how many new responses take precedence over old responses.

4. ATTENTION

There are also important generalizations about attention—called *stimulus selection* by psychologists. If the ·pupil's attention is given to a fly buzzing in the window instead of to the teacher's explanation of the meaning of a word, he or she learns about the fly and not about the word.

Teachers recognize the importance of stimuli in the classroom and are alert to those they may exploit to encourage pupils to give their attention.

Repetition or frequency of response under many, but not all, conditions, may favor attention and reinforce learning generally. The more often a given stimulus is responded to within a limited period of time and under favorable conditions, the more firmly learning is established. The effectiveness of this principle is illustrated in politics and advertising, where slogans, phrases, claims are repeated over and over again. In teaching (the reader may think here of learning to type or learning the multiplication table) the repetition of an appropri-ate response should occur under conditions that utilize other reinforce-ments, such as words of approval from the teacher, concrete evidence of progress made toward attainment of the goal-object, desire on the part of the pupil to improve, and the like. Without these, repetition becomes dull and can lead to a decline in attention and in performance. In classroom practice, therefore, teachers construe repetition to mean the repeating of an appropriate response under conditions that afford the pupil other reinforcements when needed.

Since elementary teachers are with younger pupils throughout the school day and since the attention span of their pupils is short, sustained attention is not easy to obtain. Teachers of young pupils must give much thought to the problem of developing teaching skills.

The concepts about which generalizations have been given are not mutually exclusive. Pupils can form the habit of making desirable stimulus selection, giving attention to what is expected of them, learning what is most worth attending to, and, conversely, learning not to attend to stimuli of little or no importance to them. Teachers, in addition to wisely selecting and managing the stimuli they use, try to get pupils to be conscious of their own responsibility in forming good habits of attention. In fact, teaching pupils how to study consists mostly of instructing them in how to develop good habits of attention.

It should be mentioned that undesirable behavior is often an effort to gain attention and that redirecting attention is frequently dependent on a desirable learning climate in the classroom.

5. MOTIVE

A motive is something that prompts a person to act in a certain way. The psychologist Woodworth defined "motive" as "a tendency toward a certain end-result or end-reaction, a tendency which is itself aroused by some stimulus, and which persists for a time because its end-reaction is not at once made." This seems to reduce the problem of teaching to the wise selection of a stimulus that arouses a strong tendency in the pupil, say, to read *Hamlet,* which persists until the reading of *Hamlet* is completed. How comforting! But a qualification is in order. A pupil never has *a* motive. He has *many* motives; some of them harmonize, some compete, some conflict. Picture the teacher confronted with 30 pupils, each of whom may have a tendency to act in many different ways because he or she has a multiplicity of motives. It is this kind of situation that challenges efficient teachers every day. Teachers know they can more intelligently interpret the behavior of pupils if they have some basic understanding of how motives operate to condition behavior.

Motives are closely related to, and possibly emerge from, the fundamental needs of the human organism, the more basic of which are air, food, water, sex, and perhaps exercise. Even these are not always of the same degree of urgency. At different times different ones take priority over others. It is believed that when the basic needs are met, higher needs emerge. A ravenously hungry growing boy will not be deeply interested in studying his mathematics just before lunch time. Nor will he be patient during a long wait in the lunch line. Food is the end result he seeks, and he does not like waiting to get it. The last period in the school day may seem dull to those pupils who feel a growing need for release of tension built up by an excessively long period of inaction. Improper management of the motive-to-exercise sometimes leads pupils and teachers alike to look with a feeling of dread on what they think of as the most difficult period in the day—the last one. Perhaps it has been preceded by too much physical inaction and the desire to exercise has intensified because the end reaction has been too long delayed.

Human needs seem usually to follow a kind of hierarchical sequence in which the learner seeks to satisfy the lower-ranking or more urgent needs first. Once the basic needs are satisfied, further needs, such as the needs for physical security, affection, self-esteem, feelings of independence, desire for adult and peer approval, pride in superior achievement, can receive attention. Somewhere in the upper reaches of this hierarchy come responses such as appreciation for the beautiful, desire to write creatively, intention to specialize in some field of interest to a point where one can utilize all his abilities.

The preceding generalizations are only illustrative. They relate to learning and help the teacher to understand information about pupils in terms of the learning situation. Knowing about motives, for example, may shed light on some adjustment problem reported. Generalizations about pupils as individuals, about their physical growth, their psychological development, and many other areas of growth are equally important tools for teachers seeking to improve their understanding of pupils. Fortunately there are reliable sources a teacher may consult for sound, guiding generalizations. Professional specialists, such as the school nurse or social worker, are helpful in stating generalizations in their areas. Well-indexed professional literature can be readily utilized. Many teacher organizations in specialized fields, such as the National Council of Teachers of English and the Association of Childhood Education, attempt to present through their publications significant research findings of special interest in their field, including the more recent investigations devoted to matters related to understanding pupils.

Neither of these two kinds of knowledge—an understanding of the specific information about a pupil and a comprehension of scientific generalizations that serve as a frame of reference—would be of any practical value without the other. Generalizations are derived from conclusions about many pupils; they are representative of none. They serve principally as a basis for studying one individual's performance in terms of what the scientists have said is generally true. With both kinds of information, the specific and the general, teachers have a part of what is needed to judge the educational needs of each of their pupils, to gauge the pupil's possibilities more accurately, to influence his or her pattern of behavior, and to guide and stimulate his or her growth and development with greater wisdom.

Heredity and Environment

Up to this point in our discussion of understanding pupils, it has sounded as if teachers' interpretations of what they know about their pupils—assuming the teachers are well trained—would be infallible, or at least highly dependable. That ideal might be a reality were it not for two factors that condition learning. Learning is conditioned by these two factors—*heredity* and *environment*—but they introduce an element of uncertainty, of possible error, into every action that we take because we are never sure in any given situation how much relative influence the two factors exert. This has never been established with certainty. Our interpretations and our plans for pupils, nevertheless, rest to a considerable extent on what we *believe* to be true about the relative importance of the two factors. In any discussion of what proportion of the wide differences in intelligence and achievement test scores, to take these as examples, should be attributed to genetic factors and what proportion to environmental influences, debate tends to become irrational and to be dominated by strong emotions and prejudices. These differences of opinion are not limited to matters involving 'allocation of relative importance to heredity and environment, but are, in fact, quite usual in many areas of human logic. The best that we can do in our brief overview is to indicate how the two factors somewhat complicate the picture when we attempt to understand pupils and make choices on how to stimulate them and direct their learning.

Heredity

Accepting, then, that personal interpretation is a necessary ingredient in understanding pupils, and that such interpretation rests, in part, upon judgment about heredity and environment, we will briefly explore both of these factors, turning our attention first to the natural forces that influence pupils—the inherited, genetic features. We approach this by an examination of what we call maturation.

From the biologists we learn that a close relation exists between natural forces that operate within children and their overall pattern of growth and development, that one cannot fully understand children without recognizing that some characteristics of their growth are biologically determined. A teacher's assessment of what pupils can achieve must give appropriate consideration to the hereditary factor, to the inner forces that influence the course of their growth and development.

The growth and development that result from purely hereditary forces are maturative; that is, in a friendly environment they produce maturation. The mechanisms of heredity are well understood, and the reader might profit by spending a few minutes reviewing the basic knowledge that biologists have supplied.[1]

The biological concept of maturation is that certain changes in the human organism are paced to a considerable extent by heredity. Succinctly stated, this means that certain kinds of learning will not take place, certain kinds of behavior will not emerge, until structural changes within the organism make such kinds of learning or behavior possible. What a pupil obtains, then, from instruction, from stimulation and direction, from favorable environmental influences, is determined by an inward, biological growth and development that are independent of environmental factors, that proceed at a rate *predetermined* by hereditary factors. What a pupil can learn at a given time is dependent in part on the growth and development of certain inner mechanisms, on his or her stage of biological maturation.

Because of biologically inherited characteristics related to maturation, pupils learn at different rates. In every sizable age group, learning rates range from slow to rapid, and as pupils advance from grade to grade the differentials in rates of learning result in progressively

[1] See, for example, Douglas H. Fryer, Edwin R. Henry, and Charles F. Sparks, *General Psychology*. New York: Barnes & Noble Books, 1954, pp. 131–134, 143–144. This is a condensed explanation of heredity and maturation in simple language.

widening divergencies in learning achieved. The persistent and perplexing problem of giving adequate recognition to individual differences caused both by heredity and by other factors, including previous learning experiences, receives and will continue to receive major consideration in America's schools.

With the exception of identical twins, no duplicates are to be found among the people of the world. Each newborn child inherits a natural design from his parents; his intrinsic growth will follow a unique pattern. No pupil escapes developing in accordance with the laws of heredity. Each is unique when he enters school; each will continue unique throughout life.

In one respect, however, all pupils are alike: *Each stage of growth follows the previous stage in a fairly well-defined sequence.* Although all normal pupils can, within reason, progress and achieve the same developmental tasks and, when older, can master certain subject matter and develop particular skills, they will not arrive at the same stage of development at the same age because of the unique pattern of individual growth. Knowing the present stage of development of a pupil, a teacher can, within limits, predict what the next *stage* will be. Inasmuch as natural growth patterns are not uniform, however, the teacher cannot predict very far in advance the specific *time* of full development in any area for a particular pupil. A child may be expected to creep or crawl before learning to walk, but the prediction of the ages at which a particular child will creep and then walk is subject to varying degrees of error. All normal pupils can, within limits, learn to perform similar tasks. Each, however, will learn in accordance with his or her own natural design.

Environment

Turning to the other of the factors whose relative effect on learning is so controversial, we examine some features of a pupil's physical and cultural environment and note the relationship these seem to have to some aspects of the child's growth and development. As pointed out earlier, the pupil is in constant interaction. Someone has said that through continuous social interaction a child is "able to traverse in a short lifetime what the race has needed slow, tortured ages to attain."

The cultural background of a child includes such material things as superhighways, ranch houses, and swimming pools (or dark, narrow streets, tenements, and poolrooms). It includes also such nonmaterial things as folk singing, birthday parties, church attendance, and loyalty to the Democratic or Republican party (or drunken brawls, crap games, and loyalty to the gang). Throughout human history a vast complex of social practices has evolved with so many variations that today certain cultural characteristics identify regions, others identify nations, and others are associated with class membership within a common community. These influence the social climate of even the smallest classroom.

1. REGIONAL AND NATIONAL DIFFERENCES

The cultural differences that characterize various geographical regions of our country may be trivial or fundamental, ranging from marked differences in pronunciation, in preferences for certain kinds of food or clothes, to differences in attitudes toward classes and minority groups and in ways of earning a living. In moving from one section of the country to another, a pupil becomes aware that he or she is different from those who have spent their lives in the new location. To avoid disagreeable tensions and to win approval of their peers, however, pupils usually adapt quickly and satisfactorily to the immediate cultural environment, even if in doing so they encounter family disapproval. Regional cultural differences tend to create more of a classroom problem in instances where a large migration results in a block of "minority" group members, such as the Cubans in Florida or the Mexicans in California.

2. CLASS DIFFERENCES

Cultural differences associated with regional or national differences do not usually, however, influence learning as much as differences that arise from membership in a particular class. Although many American citizens hesitate to admit that their society *has* classes, one can discern on a somewhat amorphous basis about six social classes: upper upper class; lower upper class; upper middle class; lower middle class; upper lower class; and lower lower class. Sociologists have identified the distinguishing characteristics of each class and have observed that class is important in determining, for example, an individual's associates, living quarters, churchgoing habits, reading materials, and quality of clothes worn; moreover, they have determined that class greatly influences a person's educational interests and aims. In their choice of life plans, friends, leisure activities, and educational goals, pupils show that they pattern themselves after members of their own social class. As one sociologist has said:

Evolving effective methods to help the educationally disadvantaged child is a problem that remains acute, in spite of the extensive and expensive programs that have been set up. These programs in general focus on compensatory services—remedial classes, counseling, cultural experiences, and so on. Many concerned people suspect, however, that a little-studied aspect of the problem— teacher attitudes and behavior—may deserve more attention than it has been given.

Robert Rosenthal, professor of social relations at Harvard, and Lenore Jacobson, principal of a San Francisco school and a former teacher, investigated the effect of teacher attitudes; they reported on their study in a thought-provoking book, *Pygmalion in the Classroom*. At a public elementary school in a lower-class community, they led the teachers to believe that the results of a test showed that certain pupils would "spurt" in achievement. Actually, the designated children were picked at random. Later testing showed that these children had improved in their school work to a significant degree, whereas those not designated as "spurters" had made far smaller gains. Some of the achievements of minority-group children who had been designated as "spurters" were particularly dramatic. (The authors describe their procedures, their careful scientific methods of analysis, their results, and their conclusions in detail in their book.)

Nothing was done directly for the disadvantaged children at the school—no crash programs, no tutoring, no museum trips. There was only the teachers' belief that certain children had competencies that would become apparent. Rosenthal and Jacobson speculate that the teachers who brought about intellectual competence simply by expecting it must have treated those children in a more pleasant, friendly, and encouraging way. In other words, they must have indirectly communicated their expectations to the children. Such behavior is known to improve intellectual performance, probably because it increases motivation. They speculate further that additional research might show exactly how teachers can effect dramatic improvement in their pupils' competence without changing their teaching methods. Then other teachers might be taught to do the same. They eloquently conclude:

> As teacher-training institutions begin to teach the possibility that teachers' expectations of their pupils' performance may serve as self-fulfilling prophecies, there may be a new expectancy created. The new expectancy may be that children can learn more than had been believed possible. . . . The

new expectancy, at the very least, will make it more difficult when they encounter the educationally disadvantaged for teachers to think, "Well, after all, what can you expect?" The man on the street may be permitted his opinions and prophecies of the unkempt children loitering in a dreary schoolyard. The teacher in the schoolroom may need to learn that those same prophecies within her may be fulfilled; she is no casual passer-by. Perhaps Pygmalion in the classroom is more her role.*

* Robert Rosenthal and Lenore Jacobson, *Pygmalion in the Classroom: Teacher Expectation and Pupils' Intellectual Development.* New York: Holt, Rinehart and Winston, 1968, pp. 181–182.

Everyone knows that students come to school with widely varying interests and aspirations, but the social categories to which these differences are generally linked are less well known. The most important of these background differences, leaving race and ethnicity aside, is the socioeducational level of the family—a combination of father's (and mother's) occupation, income, and education.[2]

Studies of the specific attitudes and forms of behavior of middle-class and lower-class children and of the effects of these on learning show that there is an increased divergence among the classes both in social attitudes and in specific forms of behavior as the children grow older. Class differences influence the motivation of pupils to learn in many ways.

America's schools are largely under middle-class leadership. Most classroom teachers reflect middle-class values, and their instruction favors middle- and upper-class children. Children who come from middle-class homes have the values, manners, habits, and attitudes that teachers share and stress at school. The vocabulary used by the teachers is the vocabulary with which upper- and middle-class children and youth are familiar. Even tests typically contain terms more readily recognized by children of the middle and upper classes than by children of the lower classes.

3. INFLUENCE ON THE CURRICULUM

Unless a definite effort is made to overcome it, the curriculum prepared by middle-class personnel contains a middle-class bias. In the lower grades especially, the curriculum has often included material

[2] Burton R. Clark, *Educating the Expert Society.* New York: Intext, 1962, pp. 58–59.

that gave little recognition to the cultural backgrounds of pupils from lower classes. Newer textbooks, however, particularly readers for the elementary schools, do show changes. The material is no longer so completely oriented to middle- and upper-class traditions, reflecting ethnic and class bias. Americans used to be consistently pictured as almost exclusively North European in origin and appearance, almost exclusively blonds, and always quite well-to-do. An attempt is made now to have the materials deal with ideas and experiences that include the lives of lower-class children. An effort is made to lead children of black, Puerto Rican, South European, and possibly Jewish origins not only to feel that they belong, but to be proud of their backgrounds.

Pressure from black groups has been successful in calling attention to deficiencies in the treatment of the black's part in American and world history, and in bringing about curriculum changes to include more emphasis on these matters in the regular courses or special, definite courses to include black history and contributions.

The pupil who comes from a middle- or upper-class home where reading is common, where books, paintings, music, and the like, are important parts of the home surroundings, has an educational advantage. Perhaps this weighting of the curriculum explains, at least in part, the positive correlation of high school marks and dropouts with class membership.

4. INFLUENCE ON SCHOOL ATTENDANCE

Poor school attendance and dropouts are definitely greater among lower-class and lower-lower-class children. This may be caused in part by the fact that pupils from the lower classes usually receive a greater proportion of the lower and failing grades. Studies of school records show that pupils who drop out of school early usually had a difficult time in school. Studies also show that, on the average, the less competent a pupil has shown himself to be in meeting school tasks, the more quickly he is released to face out-of-school problems. The youngsters who are least able to acquire socially useful habits, information, and points of view without formal instruction are those to whom the school has given the poorest preparation.

Summary

This chapter is the first of four that deal with aspects of the central problem of all formal education—stimulating and directing the growth and development of pupils. To fulfill his or her teaching responsibilities with reasonable skill, the teacher must understand each pupil, which requires being in command of two kinds of information considered fundamental. The teacher must have a reasonable grasp of generalizations the scientists have formulated that concern learning and human growth and development in general. In addition, he or she must know the technical meanings conveyed by specific items of information assembled about the pupils. These will aid in determining teaching methods, materials, guidance needs—the host of activities related to stimulating and directing the growth and development of *each* pupil.

QUESTIONS

1. What are some possible mistakes with and misuse of information from a pupil's cumulative record that a teacher may make?
2. What do you see as problems related to an upper-class person teaching in a school in a disadvantaged area of a large city?
3. Someone has referred somewhat sarcastically to the technical language educators use in intercommunication as "pedegese." In your opinion is this implied criticism justified? Why, or why not?
4. What are some of the problems related to the fact that differences in learning rates increase with chronological age?
5. Does an educational program such as Operation Head Start imply adherence to a point of view toward the relative importance of the influence of heredity and environment? Explain your answer.

PROJECTS

1. Make a list of what it is necesary for a school system to provide so that a classroom teacher has the resources to know his or her pupils well.
2. In terms of an imagined or an observed classroom activity, point out how the generalizations about attention have been exploited or overlooked.
3. Write an essay on the ethical standards that ought to govern teachers' use of the cumulative records of students.

chapter

17

Aims
in American
education

The methods by which we arrive at what we think ought to be our educational aims are as important as the aims themselves, for our educational aims are supposed to be based on reasoned evaluation of what we ought to do. As R. S. Peters has so well argued in his essay "Must an Educator Have an Aim?"[1] in the field of education this means that we need to be concerned as much with the manner in which we choose or develop our aims in life as with the substantive objectives we may have. Peters has argued well that we need to be as much concerned with the "principles of procedure," the reasoned methods by which we develop our educational aims, as with any other matter we may deal with as educators. Peters has argued in his essay that much of the discussion over broad, universal educational aims is often the result of differences over the principles that should govern our rational procedures for developing educational aims. Some of the

[1] See R. S. Peters, "Must an Educator Have an Aim?" *Authority, Responsibility and Education*. London: George Allen and Unwin, 1963.

principles that he asserts should govern our methods of arriving at educational aims are "respect for persons and facts, toleration, and deciding matters by discussion rather than by dictate."

Much of the discussion in this chapter centers on the sorts of broad educational aims that people develop so often in discourse about education and that overlook the importance of developing sound principles of procedure. We wish to emphasize the importance of the procedural dimensions of educational aim development in this introductory section of this chapter. If we are really to understand the nature of educational aims we must realize that all our aims are products of those basic ethical or valuational principles by which we develop our decisions about how to treat other people. In other words, our aims are deeply rooted in our most fundamental principles as to how we think we ought to behave toward other persons. The development of educational aims is fundamentally a moral enterprise, and the more we inquire into the principles of procedure by which we arrive at all our decisions as persons, the more precise we will be about the meaning of our actions. Peters would probably say that such broad goals as self-actualization or democratic citizenship cannot be precisely understood until we get clear on the procedures by which to attain them and on the moral principles that should govern those procedures. He closed his essay "Must an Educator Have an Aim?" with the following statement:

> My point is that arguments about the aims of education reflect these basic differences in principles of procedure. The Puritan and the Catholic both thought they were promoting God's kingdom, but they thought it had to be promoted in a different manner. And the different manner made it quite a different kingdom.[2]

When we refer to broad, universal aims of education we must remember that our moral work has just begun. We cannot understand such aims until we inquire into the reasoned methods by which we choose them. It is most important to know the criteria we use to choose our aims.

In Chapter 5, "The Teacher's Philosophy," it was pointed out that what teachers attempt in the classroom and the way they go about it reflect individual educational philosophy, and educational values. We focus now, in this chapter, specifically on educational *aims,* not this time from the viewpoint of their philosophical base, but in

[2] Ibid.

terms of all the other factors that have an influence on educational aims in the restricted setting of an individual classroom or in the expanded setting of a school district or even of the nation.

In comparing two individuals, both well informed, we may discover that one is expert, efficient, and esteemed and that the other is a bore and ineffective. They have had different aims for acquiring the knowledge that made them well informed. The efficient, interesting teacher accumulated knowledge for a purpose, so he or she had direction and this teacher's information is organized and useful. The boring, ineffective teacher lacked purpose and organization. This teacher's information is like scraps of metal in a junk yard. Such a teacher displays motion without direction.

In exploring how learning takes place in the preceding chapter, the importance of motivation was highlighted. A desire to learn is the magic that leads to learning. We have said that the teacher's job, in essence, is to stimulate and direct the growth of pupils. Successful stimulation leads to self-motivation, and self-motivation implies accepted aims or goals.

Some self-made, or at least self-directed, people who have achieved expert or leadership status despite the lack of a college degree and perhaps even of formal schooling, show that a definite aim can unify and direct learning to a point of dramatic achievement.

What Determines Educational Aims?

The Individual Teacher's Philosophy

The teacher's aims, then, are related to his or her values, to personal philosophy. The teacher will seek, within the limits discussed in Chapter 5 and later in this chapter, to achieve those ends that are personally worthy and practicable. Some of the teacher's aims will be broad and sweeping. He or she may seek, for instance, to promote attitudes of fair play. Such aims underlie all his or her teaching. In addition, the teacher will have immediate aims associated with what he or she seeks to achieve in a single activity. The teacher may also have a specific aim for a particular child. For example, a goal might be for one child to develop the habit of paying attention to instruction. The teacher might have a conference with this child during which the wording of this goal could be worked out by the child. Checking with the child on the advancement toward that goal might occur weekly. When the goal is satisfactorily achieved, another goal might be

John Dewey emphasized that aims and means are related, that ends are always pluralistic, and that all the consequences of an act, not just one, must be considered.

. . . Ends arise and function within action. They are not . . . things lying beyond activity at which the latter is directed. They are not . . . termini of action at all. They are terminals of deliberation, and so turning points in activity. . . .

In being ends of *deliberation* they are redirecting pivots in action. . . . A mariner does not sail towards the stars, but by noting the stars he is aided in conducting his present activity of sailing. . . . Activity will not cease when the port is attained, but merely the *present direction* of activity. The port is as truly the beginning of another mode of activity as it is the termination of the present one. . . . We know without thinking that our "ends" are perforce beginnings. . . . Common sense revolts against the maxim, . . . that the end justifies the means. There is no incorrectness in saying that the question of means employed is overlooked in such cases . . . that overlooking means is only a device for failing to note those ends, or consequences, which, if they were noted would be seen to be so evil that action would be estopped. Certainly nothing can justify or condemn means except ends, results. . . . Not the end—in the singular— justifies the means; for there is no such thing as the single all-important end. . . . It is not possible adequately to characterize the presumption, the falsity and the deliberate perversion of intelligence involved in refusal to note the plural effects that flow from any act, a refusal adopted in order that we may justify an act by picking out that one consequence which will enable us to do what we wish to do and for which we feel the need of justification.*

* John Dewey, *Human Nature and Conduct.* New York: Holt, Rinehart and Winston, 1922, pp. 223, 225, 226, 228, 229.

adopted. Such immediate and specific goals give direction to effort and provide a measure for judging progress.

Sometimes the work in a specific area of teaching is organized in a unit. Such a plan includes a statement of aims to be achieved in the unit. The aims, in this case, help the teacher select relevant material and unify teaching. In such a unit in English, for instance, the aims might be (1) to participate courteously in a group discussion,

(2) to build up understanding and consideration of others, and (3) to use concrete and vivid words in speaking and writing. The teacher is guided usually by *sets* of aims, not by a single aim. These aims, moreover, will be ineffectual if the pupils do not share, whenever possible, in their formulation, or do not feel that they are acceptable. The teacher's individual aims must always be flexible so that they can be readily modified in terms of the unexpected, in the light of changed conditions.

As America's schools are administered, however, the teacher is not always completely free to decide on his aims. Various influences and pressures affect his or her choice. Some of these are from external authorities—the school board, the local teaching group, state and federal governments, and accrediting agencies. There are also pressures from various groups, from the home, and from commerce and industry. The press may exert a strong and significant influence. Professional commissions set up to establish general educational aims, or supervision within a system, may also affect what the teacher attempts to do in the classroom. Sometimes, in fact, except for details related to an immediate situation, the choice of goals is made *for* the teacher, rather than *by* the teacher. When the influences do not operate in a consistent direction, a measure of confusion is introduced and then each teacher must decide, in his or her own way, to which influence to yield. Perhaps his or her teaching will be a compromise between personal aims and those of others.

External Authorities

I. PROFESSIONAL GROUPS

In order to promote unity and give consistency to the direction of teaching at a given grade level or in a particular subject, teachers, or their representatives, frequently get together and produce a general plan of work. The plan is typically preceded by a statement of aims that the group agrees should be striven for; the curriculum or other material worked out should promote these objectives. Often an instructional group looks for guidance to some national organization, such as the American Society for Childhood Education or the Modern Language Association.

As an example, representatives of the English teachers in three junior high schools drew up a proposed English curriculum in which they set forth the following objectives:

1. Instruction in the language arts should prepare pupils to use efficiently the skills of listening, speaking, reading, and writing requisite to effective learning.
2. The language arts are avenues to all learning; therefore, a good language arts program should (a) integrate the language arts courses, (b) integrate with other courses of the school, (c) enrich personal living.
3. All good teaching in the language arts results in the development of individual personalities in the direction of their highest potentialities.[3]

Although such aims are general in the sense that they must be interpreted by the individual classroom teacher, they are sufficiently specific to give direction to the teacher's immediate aims.

2. SCHOOL STAFFS

In many cases individual school staffs formulate statements of aims for their own school. Such goals have an influence on the aims adopted by individual teachers. The following is an example:

We aim to help each pupil—
1. to succeed in school.
2. to learn to get along in the school where he is and in the classes of which he is a part and with the people with whom he works.
3. to form the habit of doing what is known to be right.
4. to be of service to other pupils and to the needs of the school.
5. to expect to abide by the rules and regulations that are made for the good of all.
6. to recognize and use the abilities, talents, and creative thinking of individuals in all lines to make an interesting school.

Sometimes this kind of statement of school aims is worked out by pupils in collaboration with the faculty and perhaps with parents.

3. STATE AND FEDERAL GOVERNMENTS

The aims of the school and of the individual teacher are influenced significantly by the state and federal governments. The federal government, we have noted, has often influenced aims by means of such acts as the Smith-Hughes Act of 1917, which gives grants-in-aid to high schools that meet certain federal requirements. The grants

[3] These objectives were based on the teachers' interpretation of the philosophy expressed in National Council of Teachers of English, *Language Arts for Today's Children*. Englewood Cliffs, N.J.: Prentice-Hall, 1954, vol. 2.

are administered through the state departments of education, thus giving some power over the program to the states. The grants-in-aid given by the federal government under Titles I, II, III, IV, and V of the Elementary and Secondary Education Act of 1965 are made for many different purposes and distributed in various ways. However, as pointed out earlier, the federal government, through this act, has become an active participant in education to an unprecedented extent. The Office of Education, especially, now has a greater degree of authority than it had ever before been given. Through these two acts alone—Smith-Hughes and the Elementary and Secondary Education Act of 1965—the federal government influences the aims of the schools significantly. The Smith-Hughes Act determines to a considerable extent the aims of agricultural education, home economics, and industrial arts in the high schools. The Elementary and Secondary Education Act further extends federal influence, now for the first time, into the elementary school. These are but two of the many avenues through which our national government influences the aims of American education.

State legislatures and state educational authorities also influence the aims of the school. For example, state laws stipulate that schools teach, and pupils study, certain subjects. In some states it is required that American history be studied for a full year in high school. In some states pupils in the elementary school are required to participate in physical education for a stated number of periods each week. Sometimes, through the office of the chief state school authority, the states have prescribed the matter of study required of teachers who desire certification. The state foundation program is an influence on the aims of the school. Each governmental act is motivated by an aim, and the act in turn almost, if not entirely, legislates an aim for teaching.

4. INSTITUTIONS OF HIGHER LEARNING

Colleges and universities exert some influence on the aims and objectives of the high schools by their admission requirements. Sometimes high school pupils feel that the all-inclusive aim of their high school education is to prepare for college board examinations. Pressure on the high schools from institutions of higher learning may be cause for the high schools to attempt to influence what is taught in the junior high schools and even in the elementary schools.

It has been stated that high schools tend to credit the colleges with being more of an influence than they actually are. In defending the emphasis placed on the study of grammar in high school, it has been said, "Our children must be well prepared in grammar in order to do well on the college entrance examinations." A review of some of the college entrance examinations used, however, shows that little stress is actually placed on formal grammar. Some high schools are using college entrance examinations to justify something they include in their teaching for some other reason. This is not to imply, however, that the colleges do not influence the aims of the high school teachers considerably.

5. ACCREDITING AGENCIES

Accrediting agencies such as the North Central Association of Colleges and Secondary Schools determine to some extent what subjects a pupil in high school must pursue for graduation. In this sense they too have an influence on the school's aims and on the aims of the individual teacher.

Societal Pressures

Pressure groups are characteristic of modern America—there is no escape from them (this was discussed in Chapter 10). It is up to the teaching profession, then, to work out ways of dealing intelligently with those groups that have the greatest influence on the schools. There are many such agencies; here we will briefly examine four of them as examples—the home, industry, the press, and professional organizations.

I. THE HOME

If the home does not fulfill certain needs related to achieving maturity, then the school is expected to add the fulfillment of these needs to its aims of instruction. The home or the community may, for instance, expect the school to undertake activities related to sex education, social dancing, grooming, and the like. In some instances the objectives of the school are tied in with certain activities in the home. In an agricultural community, for example, the school may teach the conservation of food by correlating work in methods of freezing, canning, and otherwise preserving food with the materials and facilities the children have in their homes and the instruction they have received there.

2. INDUSTRY

Industry, both through many organizations and through individual enterprises, shows a strong interest in education in America. Sometimes attempts are made to bring pressure on a particular segment of education, as when the public utilities, through advertising and printed materials, have tried to persuade social studies teachers to emphasize the advantages of private ownership of public utilities and, by implication, to minimize the values of, say, the Tennessee Valley Authority.

In a more positive direction, some American industries are spending large sums on developing and manufacturing teaching materials, such as teaching machines and many kinds of classroom aids. The promise of ultimate profit is a factor in such expenditures, of course, but the executives who authorize these programs are also motivated by a genuine desire to advance modern education. Each year many large industrial corporations make sizable contributions to educational institutions, to university foundations, and for the establishment of scholarships for students in certain selected fields. Through their expertly directed public relations departments many large corporations—without any thought of influencing the direction they wish education to take—provide schools with a wide variety of skillfully prepared materials on many subjects of interest to teachers and pupils. The principal intent seems to be to build and maintain a favorable public image, an image that includes an abiding interest in encouraging education. There also is an obvious, and logical, factor of self-interest behind all these activities—better education for all results in more qualified workers for industry and in more consumers of corporations' products; in other words, when industry aids education, it anticipates long-range benefits.

3. THE PRESS

Journalists, television commentators, and news analysts exert pressure on the public and also directly on the schools to shape their programs to fulfill objectives that come into the public limelight, usually because of current crises. When Russia surpassed the United States in the development of space satellites, journalists led the hue and cry for education to be patterned more on the Russian plan. Our assumed inferiority to Russia was attributed to inadequate education. "Our children should work harder, be more serious." "Stress mathematics and science and foreign languages." "Select the gifted children early; see that they are adequately motivated to pursue the required subjects."

One trouble with journalists is that they quite naturally tend to be dramatic, to distort the true picture. They may overemphasize some of the aims of education because they are devoted to promoting a "cause." Often they are not completely informed about education but make an impression on the public by mounting emotional or irrational assaults on the waste of school funds in elaborate school buildings, on the school's failure to teach Johnnie to read, on the school's failure to keep America abreast of Russia in technical advances—matters that lend themselves to the journalist's art. Often, however, the effects of journalistic efforts—urging, for instance, that teaching be made more attractive as a means to improve teaching conditions—are socially very desirable. The restrictions of authoritative external bodies and the pressures of official statements, the press, and industry will be greater in fields of specific subject areas, especially in vocational fields. In the areas of the basic education that is given to all children—that is, the education of the elementary school and that portion of the high school program that is not differentiated—the teacher has more freedom in making the final decision as to aims and the subject matter that he or she believes is potentially most profitable in terms of those aims.

4. PROFESSIONAL ORGANIZATIONS

From time to time groups of outstanding educators have taken up the task of formulating statements of the aims or purposes for education in America. Such statements may contain many helpful suggestions for the teacher. They may indicate what the teacher should emphasize, what results may be expected, what kinds of materials are best to choose, what directions the pupils' energies may be turned toward, and the like.

Statements of Aims

One of the first difficulties encountered in attempts to state the aims of education in American schools is terminology. The words used have had various meanings. In various lists of aims prepared as guides to teaching, many different kinds of terms have been used. This has led to some confusion and misunderstanding. Because of the subtleties of learning it may be that some confusion is unavoidable.

Consider the basic word "aim." The meaning of this word seems clear when one uses it to describe a physical object at which one is shooting a gun, or when, in war, the object is to destroy a certain bridge. When the act, however, is a mental one, no one word can describe all the different kinds of objectives, and sometimes different words are used interchangeably to describe precisely the same objective. In most instances where mental processes are concerned, each of the various terms used carries a slightly different emphasis. Let us note how this is true in the following sentence: "The student whose *aims* are worthy, whose *aspirations* are high, whose *designs* are wise, and whose *purposes* are steadfast may reach the goal of his ambition and surely will win some *object* worthy of life's *endeavor*." Writers who attempt to describe the direction education should take by stating what it should seek to achieve have to clarify the meaning of such terms. The choice of a particular word, however, results in slightly different emphasis.

It is, perhaps, not surprising to find writers in education using such phrases as "purposive learning," "objectives of education," "object lesson," "purposeful effort," "ends in view," and others that reflect a philosophical viewpoint toward the relation of aims to teaching. It would be easier, of course, if all the writers used the same terminology. In all the lists the attempt has been to do the same thing—to make carefully formulated suggestions to guide teaching practices in schools, even though there have been different approaches that have led to different kinds of statements.

Quantity of Subject Matter

One common criticism of teaching aims is that American schoolteachers sacrifice a desirable concern with the total product of their teaching—understanding, interest, desirable attitudes—to a concern with covering a certain amount of prescribed subject matter. In literature, pupils are expected to read a specified *quantity* of material; in algebra, all ninth-grade pupils are expected to advance rapidly enough to arrive at quadratics by the end of the year. Teachers are criticized for adopting too completely the aim to "cover so much ground in so much time."

Summary

It is perhaps obvious that teaching aims cannot be static, rigid, or fixed. As one aim is achieved, the next aim is defined. Each accomplishment leads to a definition of the next aim. When one end is achieved, it becomes the means to the next. Ends that are worthy function to free learning activities, to direct them, but never to freeze them.

This generalization is true of aims that are set by the school, by government authorities, by nations. History tells the story of Greece, a nation at one time alive with new and noble ideas that engendered aims that led the whole nation to socially desirable action. At a later time the people of the same nation found themselves no longer motivated by appropriate and collective aims. The nation lost direction and floundered. For education to have direction it must be guided by aims, but the aims must be appropriate, must make an appeal strong enough to evoke strong individual and collective action. The failure to recognize that effective aims are not static explains in part why Greece flourished at one time in its history and declined at another.

Forward-looking and active institutions sometimes, with the passing years, become stagnant and lose their strength and popular appeal. The early leaders in the schools of the Christian church were inspiring teachers. Later, much of the teaching by churchmen became pedantic, catechistic, formal, and uninspirational. Such deterioration is caused, in part at least, either by adherence to aims that are outmoded and therefore inappropriate, by the adoption of new aims inappropriate for some reason, or by a change in social conditions that renders all the general purposes of the institution obsolete.

Aims influence education, constitute a challenge to action, only when the aims are acceptable because they can be and are adapted to current conditions. The dynamic nature of the complete educational picture calls for a constant reinterpretation and reappraisal of the aims sought. Changing social conditions bring new educational demands into focus. Changing conditions in the classroom bring new demands into focus also. Conditions are never static. Effective aims also cannot be static.

QUESTIONS

1. How does the age of the pupils affect the aims of instruction?
2. How are teachers to formulate aims that reflect the social viewpoints of the people when these viewpoints are sometimes in conflict?
3. How are the aims of education in American schools affected by the character of the community?
4. What functions are served by statements of aims carefully formulated by official bodies?

5. Under what conditions are educational aims apt to be static in nature? Dynamic?
6. How do you account for the great variety in the manner of stating aims? Would it be advantageous to have a single statement of the aims of education? How can one select from among the many statements?
7. When may a statement of educational aims be an aid to teaching? A hindrance?

PROJECTS

1. Explain how one's educational philosophy shapes the character of one's educational aims.
2. Give an example that illustrates the interrelationships of aim, subject matter, and method.
3. State the aims that guide you in your professional study. Justify your professional studies and activities in terms of the process you go through in establishing your aims. What methods do you use to determine what your aims ought to be?

chapter

18

Subject matter in America's schools

Subjects of study probably date back to the earliest schools. The Babylonians had schoolhouses in 2100 B.C.; other civilizations may have had them earlier than that. Archeologists have established that one of the skills taught in the early schools was writing. Words and phrases and, later, complete sentences and quotations were copied from old documents. Inasmuch as the documents were available for copying, writing—using symbols—must have predated even these very early schools. It also can be assumed that some had been taught to read these early documents and that there were some who could teach others to read. In all likelihood, when the earliest schools were set up over 4000 years ago, they aimed to perpetuate and extend the ability to read, to write, to interpret, to appreciate, and eventually to add to the store of manuscripts. No doubt these ancient manuscripts were the earliest forerunners of the subject matter in today's schools.

As time passed and it was recognized that certain social groups—especially at first the priests—needed knowledge in particular areas before beginning their work, pertinent information and skills were selected and organized for instructing potential members of these groups. It appears now that the advance from barbarism to civilization was marked by stages of development in the classifications of knowledge—classifications made partly to facilitate instruction of an oncoming generation.

The orderly organization of subject matter into classifications that were generally considered appropriate for young pupils was quite advanced by the time America began to be a settled country. When the first colonial schools were opened, there was available a great deal of material that those in charge felt was, with very little modification, ideally suited to their aims.

Evolution of Subject Matter in the United States

In Elementary Schools

Initially, American elementary schools borrowed their classifications from Europe. Our first educators and those who supported the schools were religious leaders and other church members. Children were viewed as the children of the church. Schools were established to teach children to read and write so that they might read the Bible, which, in turn, might lead them to be better church members.

Many different religious groups set up schools that varied somewhat because of differences in religious beliefs. By the time the Declaration of Independence was signed, however, the elementary schools were essentially alike in that they all emphasized the study of reading, writing, spelling, and arithmetic. In all these subjects they utilized scriptural quotations and moral platitudes.

After the passage of a half century there were discernible changes in the common subjects. Although reading, writing, spelling, and arithmetic remained the chief subjects, modifications took place within each, both in content and in organization. English grammar became a separate subject equal in importance to the others. Knitting and sewing were included for girls in some schools.

By 1876 the subject matter of the elementary schools had been greatly expanded. Conditions had changed and some of the new ideas of European educators had filtered into practice. Following a trend toward secularization in the schools, education became less concerned with religion. In teaching reading the teachers helped the children not only to develop proficiency in reading the Scriptures but also to develop skill in reading and appreciating literature other than the Bible. Declamation, oral language, geography, U.S. history and the Constitution, elementary science, music, drawing, and physical education were now among the subjects. Many textbooks were rewritten. In addition to textbooks, actual objects were used for instruction. Such direct experiences as field trips and laboratory experiments were added.

The expansion of subjects of study continued, and by the end of the century, manual training, nature study, and a new outgrowth of reading—a subject called "literature"—had made their appearance. In fact, by the beginning of the present century all the elements of the modern subjects had been introduced into the elementary schools. As our aims, our conditions, our knowledge, and our understanding change, the evolution continues, and our classifications, our emphases, and our textbooks continue to change.

In 4-Year High Schools

The evolution of subjects in the American 4-year high school constitutes a story almost as independent of the evolution of the subjects in the elementary schools as though the two had never belonged to the same family of institutions. The effects of this earlier disregard of articulation of eighth-grade and ninth-grade subject matter are still an acute problem in America's schools, especially where the elementary and the high schools are in different, independently organized school districts.

When the Declaration of Independence was signed, the subjects in the high school were almost exclusively Latin and Greek. The dominance of what was studied is implied by the name of the school, the Latin grammar school. The aim of the secondary school was largely vocational—to prepare individuals for further study for entrance into the ministry of the church. The transition from elementary school to high school was so abrupt that it amounted to an almost complete break.

Fifty years after the Declaration of Independence, high school subjects had undergone considerable change. By 1825 the Boston Public Latin School, considered in that day an extremely progressive school, had included in its program such well-defined subject matters as arithmetic, geometry, trigonometry, geography, declamation, reading, English grammar, English composition, debating, chronological

history, and the constitutions of the United States and of Massachusetts. Slowly but surely the subjects covered by the high schools continued to undergo modification.

The influence of the Latin grammar schools waned after 1800,
and the private academy became the dominant secondary school institution. The number of subjects expanded amazingly, reflecting the
rapid development of new subject matter, especially that related to
the specialized sciences. By 1837 the academies in New York State
were offering 73 different subjects, including architecture, astronomy,
chemistry, botany, conic sections, embroidery, civil engineering,
French, geology, analytic geometry, German, Hebrew, Italian, law,
logarithms, vocal music, instrumental music, mineralogy, political
economy, statistics, surveying, painting, Spanish, trigonometry, and
principles of teaching.

After 1890, the date that coincides with the end of the American
frontier movement, the private academy ceased to be the dominant
institution and its influence rapidly waned. The 4-year public high
school became the prevalent institution. As the high schools grew in
number and enrollment, new subjects were rapidly introduced into
the curriculum. The passage of the Smith-Hughes Act of 1917, which
gave federal grants-in-aid to high schools offering training in vocational education, spurred expansion of vocational education programs.
In some larger, comprehensive high schools the entire program of
some pupils was built around study in one of the areas of vocational
education. The new subjects included motor mechanics, machine shop,
radio, advanced electricity, agriculture, business law, stenography,
beauty culture, commercial cooking, and aeronautics. Music and art
subjects also multiplied. The older fields—such as English, science,
mathematics, and foreign languages—also were expanded. As many
as 19 different subjects were offered under the broad heading of
"homemaking." Not all of these, of course, were offered in a single
school. Driver training and mathematics and chemistry for nurses are
further examples of the trend both toward completeness in curriculums
to meet today's needs and toward selecting subject matter directly
related to an explicit aim.

No attempt has been made here to establish relative importance
among the many subjects offered. This is partly because no reliable
data showing the percentage of pupils enrolled in the various subjects
are available. Moreover, since there is no consistency in high school
policies in requiring the pupils to pursue certain subjects, generalization about their relative prominence would be unreliable.

Selection of Subject Matter

The brief review of the history of subject matter in the schools in the United States reveals significant and continuous changes over the years in scope, content, organization, and emphasis. Apart from actual classroom instruction, perhaps more teacher time and energy have been given to selecting subject matter appropriate to the learning needs of pupils than to any other one activity. Reconstruction of the curriculum is a continuous process and is so complex that only a brief treatment is possible in this chapter.

Subject matter is a tool designed to move children in the direction defined by a school's educational goals. The relative values of various areas of subject matter have always been judged in terms of their probable potential contribution to the desired ends. As aims have changed for various reasons, subject matter has likewise changed.

When educators began to state aims for education and were asked to justify subjects in terms of aims, the question of the relative values of different subjects also came under serious consideration. Even assuming that all the subjects had value, the extent of that value, the relative value of one subject as compared to all the others, had to be determined.

If, as the great English philosopher John Locke (1623–1704) believed, the mind at birth is like a blank piece of paper with nothing written upon it, a *tabula rasa,* with inherent powers that can be strengthened by "exercising" with subject matter, then it could be argued that certain kinds of subject matter better serve this need for exercise than others. From this, it follows that subject matter for all pupils should be uniform. Teaching each learner the same spelling or grammar or mathematics is all right because these subjects provide the best kind of mental exercise for all learners. "The faculties of our souls are improved and made useful to us just after the same manner as our bodies are . . . would you have a man reason well, you must use him to it betimes, exercise his mind in observing the connection of ideas and following them in train."[1] Actually, the "blank paper" theory was not accepted for very long, so it had little influence on the selection of subject matter.

Another belief that came to be known as faculty psychology had

[1] John Locke, as quoted in Paul Monroe, *A Brief Course in the History of Education.* New York: Macmillan, 1907, p. 265.

more of a following. It explains, in part, some of the perplexing lack of direct value in subject matter, especially in the high school. For instance, early spelling textbooks contained many words that would never be useful to most of the pupils, even in adult life. English grammar, emphasizing sentence structure, seemed to have little connection with developing powers of expression. Faculty psychologists believed that the mind was composed of a series of distinct and separate faculties—such as thinking, memorizing, feeling, willing—and that each of these could be trained through exercise just as a muscle could be strengthened through exercise. Moreover, it was assumed that training received in one area of subject matter was transferred to another. This meant, for instance, that the powers developed through memorizing poetry would be transferred to memorization of grammar or multiplication tables. The study of Euclidean geometry was considered particularly valuable because it developed prowess in logical reasoning that could be used in studying other subjects and in out-of-school activities. When we recall that Euclid's *Elements,* a very early textbook on geometry (300 B.C.), has served as a model for all the later textbooks on the subject, we get some notion of how long this approach to learning and subject matter survived in at least one area.

Knowledge about how children learn, about child development and growth, and about differences in capacities and interests today influence the selection of subject matter much more than in the past. Currently the trend is to select subject matter that is as flexible as possible, is *directly* related to the achievement of aims, and is appropriate to the age and needs of the learners. Knowledge and insight are required in deciding what subject matter will contribute most. Usually teachers have broad boundaries of subject matter determined for them by the school district, the school, or some other authority. Where textbooks are supplied or prescribed, the extent of teacher choice is further limited. In most systems, however, teachers participate in developing the curriculum, in determining the subject matter to be taught, and also usually any prescribed materials will allow the teacher some leeway to make adaptations. Today the American people are tending to become progressively more dependent on formal education to educate youth for citizenship obligations. The selection of subject matter, therefore, becomes increasingly important. In earlier times much of the education of the young was received outside the school. At that time, because of social conditions, advanced education was highly selective and based largely on the ability to pay. Higher education was almost monopolized by specially privileged people who used graduation from higher institutions as a stepping-stone to rising on the social scale. That tradition is gradually disappearing in the United States. Formal education is becoming a requirement for entrance to most adult activities. The trend is toward greater attention to what graduates of high schools and colleges have learned or have learned to do and less attention to how long the graduates have attended school or from what units they have been graduated. There is greater interest in the content of what children in the elementary and high schools study and in the degree to which efficient learning is promoted. The future promises even more emphasis on the practical values of the subjects provided in our schools.

Classification of Knowledge

One of the greatest advances human beings have made in their attempts to achieve a high level of civilization through education has been in the classifications they have made of accumulated knowledge. Their ability to organize and to systematize knowledge into such broad classifications as physics, geology, and mathematics and to make systematic classifications within these subjects has contributed to research, to the preservation of knowledge, and to learning. The future, it seems, will depend largely on the uses human beings make of their growing accumulations and classifications of knowledge. These uses hinge, in part, on the way young people are taught to apply and expand knowledge. And knowledge in this context does not mean merely information that is immediately and obviously useful. The future also depends on the way knowledge of the humanities is used.

For Preservation

Preservation of knowledge is essential to the continued existence of any civilization. Classification and organization of knowledge into logical, usable, understandable systems are essential for its preservation and transmission to succeeding generations. In botany, for example, material may be classified beginning with broad divisions and proceeding to successively smaller units such as class, order, family, genus, species, and, finally, variety. Geology or zoology or history will follow some other pattern, each appropriate to its own field. In each of the divisions, organization is a value in itself. The practical purpose served is determined by the one who uses it. The more logical the classification and the more logical the various divisions within the organization, the more suitable is the whole for preservation for the future.

For Research

Logically classified categories of subject matter serve as a ready reference for those who wish to extend the range of human knowledge. Diligent and systematic research demands a previously well-organized body of subject matter to serve as a springboard for new discoveries, which, in turn, may modify previous classifications.

For Learning and Transmission

The major classifications of knowledge have formed the bases of the subjects offered by the schools. Modifications in classifications have been evolved to make them more practical and more usable in teaching the young. By the end of the first grade, pupils are aware of fairly sharp distinctions between reading, writing, spelling, and mathematics. As they advance through the grades, they rapidly learn to distinguish numerous other subjects. Usually the distinctions are emphasized by the way the subject matter is prepared for use—in textbooks, workbooks, study guides, and the like.

It would be a mistake, of course, to conclude that all children learn in school is a result of exposure to what is ordinarily thought of as subject matter. What children learn before they begin school and what they learn in school apart from the materials in the subjects of study are thought by teachers to be quite as important as what they learn through association with organized subject matter.

There is one division of subject matter that is quite different from the rigid, logical classifications associated with the preservation of knowledge and the advancement of research. This is the classification of subject matter in terms of its relation to direct and indirect experiences of the child. Subject matter in books, for instance, would be classified as part of indirect experience. The subject matter is part of direct experience, however, if the child comes into direct contact with the original matter. For example, the child learns as he or she sees a house burn down, climbs a mountain, watches a plane take off, observes a mother bird feeding her young, sees a TV program. His or her growth is promoted by the opportunity to preside at an assembly, make a dress, dissect a frog, or write a poem. The subject matter may be unorganized, lacking in sequence, and unplanned. It is not, however, without purpose. Learning in this way is natural and, perhaps, most rapid and most efficient.

Learning that is related indirectly to the experiences of the child utilizes subject matter that is more or less systematically arranged so as to facilitate learning. The pupil learns through vicarious, not direct, experience. He or she reads, listens, observes, learning through participating in the experiences of others.

Both kinds of learning, both kinds of subject matter, have a place in the school. In the earlier grades particularly, direct learning, associated with personal experience, the method of direct discovery, is emphasized. In science or mathematics, for example, the pupils work with objects at first hand, experience them as concrete realities. As the child progresses through the grades, the subject matter tends to be related more to indirect experience. Gradually a conceptual order in subject matter is introduced as a substitute for the perceptual order that preceded it. The important point to remember is that the perceptual precedes the conceptual.

There is a natural limit to the amount of subject matter that can be learned through firsthand experience. The time element must be considered. It becomes necessary to expand the world of the pupil through learning subject matter that depends on language, pictures, mathematical symbols, stories, historical episodes, and maps. Sufficient direct learning experience makes the indirect learning more meaningful. A perceptual background is a sound base for a conceptual understanding. In mathematics, for instance, pupils may learn about symbols in such a way that they have no meaning apart from the mathematics lesson. In science, pupils may work with subject matter that has little relation to their everyday lives. On the other hand, the symbols used in mathematics can be so related to direct experience that they will be meaningful. If the materials of science provide an opportunity for direct experience in observation and manipulation, are related to, or are built on, direct experience in the everyday life of the child, then the child has a background for the understandings that are conceptual. He or she can read, understand, and learn about science by building on a background of percepts from direct learning. Thus the two kinds of subject matter are complementary. When properly balanced, the one reinforces the other.

Organization of Subject Matter
for Teaching Purposes

In discussing the organization of subject matter for teaching purposes, the two terms "curriculum" and "course of study" are used frequently and are therefore explained here. Keep in mind that such terms as "integration," "correlation," "core," and "interdisciplinary team approach" are used to refer to various plans for unifying subject matter for teaching purposes.

1. Curriculum. The term "curriculum" is now commonly used to include all the activities and experiences that have been planned for the pupil in school, or that are sponsored by the school, to advance his desirable growth. Originally "curriculum" referred only to activities that had been planned for the classroom. This left outside-of-the-classroom activities to be "extracurricular." The current trend is to consider the entire school experience of the pupil as a unit and to determine the emphasis on any particular kind of activity in terms of individual needs, interests, and abilities. As progress has been made in discovering and adapting to pupils' needs the curriculum, the total school offering, has been enriched by visual aids, plays, excursions, and various types of pupil activities in and out of the school. A specific plan of organization is implied when we talk about core curriculum, subject-matter curriculum, or integrated curriculum.

2. Course of Study. A course of study is usually worked out in a particular subject area to serve a variety of purposes. The area covered might be something like U.S. history, or it might cover a broader area such as social studies. Typically the course of study begins with a statement of aims that the teacher will be expected to implement in his instruction. Organization, time allotments, teaching materials, methods, and activities are suggested. In a sense the course of study sets a minimum common denominator for a grade level or a certain subject within a school system or a school. Besides these purposes, it serves as a tool for guidance workers who counsel high school pupils in their choice of subjects and helps a teacher by providing information about what a child studied last year and what he probably will study next year.

A course of study is usually developed by teachers and supervisors working together. Sometimes they have the help of a curriculum specialist in a particular area or given grade level, and sometimes they also have the help of scholars in the field. For instance, in developing the course of study in U.S. history, an outstanding scholar in the field of black history might work with the committee.

Unfortunately, the course of study becomes an educational hazard when it is overly specific instead of suggestive, when it is too mandatory to allow for adaptations in terms of all aspects of a learning situation. It is a help but never a substitute for the kind of teacher planning that is built on an understanding of the pupils involved.

Language Arts

The emphasis in this broad field is upon the word "language." The raising of language to the level of an art signifies the attempt to cultivate language so that it may be used as an expression of beauty, by appealing, and have more than commonplace significance. Language arts is concerned mainly with developing skills in expressing ideas and in receiving ideas from others, through both the written and the spoken word.

In earlier schools, subject matter focused on developing the mechanical skills of reading, speaking, spelling, and writing. Listening and appreciations were largely disregarded. The current trend is toward selecting subject matter that will contribute to much wider growth. It is assumed, for example, that development of the powers of communication is closely related to the development of a rich, attractive, well-adjusted personality. The trend is toward emphasizing the values as well as mechanics of communication in the wider aspects of social living.

As the broader concept of the language arts has been adopted, subject matter has been increasingly diversified. As yet, no clear agreement has been reached among language arts teachers as to the relative emphasis different aspects of the program should receive, nor has a logical sequence in specific areas been developed. Some teachers deviate very little from the older practices of teaching reading, writing, and spelling as separate mechanical skills. Others place the greatest emphasis upon well-rounded development. Most teachers feel that a realignment of the subject matter of the language arts field is inevitable.

Science

Subject matter in science is selected in terms of an integrated-general approach for the elementary school through the eighth grade and for ninth grade where science is adapted to certain students who are not preparing for college. The crucial problem in the selection of appropriate science subject matter is related to these early grades where the integrated-general course is expected to include a range of nonspecialized science material. The emphasis in these grades is on the selection of material relevant to basic concepts to be explored, concepts considered appropriate to an individual school population and its particular community. The curriculum and courses of study outline units are prepared by the school as well as for the school. This results in the subject matter of science in early grades strongly reflecting the locale of the school and obviously rules out a standard subject matter for a state, as was once a common practice, or a standard sequence even for one large school system. In terms of concepts to be learned, each school selects subject matter appropriate to its own pupils and to the environment of the school. It attempts to choose subject matter that *is* inherently interesting as contrasted to materials the teacher is asked to *make* interesting. This approach tends to build favorable attitudes toward science by utilizing what is close to the pupils, that exists in their surroundings: seasonal changes, animals, plants, airplanes, food, air, water—literally hundreds of items. This practice of selecting subject matter in science that is closely related to the lives of the pupils is generally advocated by leaders in science education. This obviously invalidates the idea of having a rigid science sequence in the elementary schools.

The science courses in the secondary school, selected by or for students preparing for college, are specialized courses such as biology in the ninth grade, followed by courses in physics, chemistry, the earth sciences, and, for some, college-level courses in physics and chemistry. With the great expansion in knowledge, subject matter in all the specialized sciences has been greatly modified during the past decade, although the topics studied in each of the specialized science fields are fairly well standardized.

Mathematics

Mathematics is what educators call a constant in the curriculum—that is, a subject to be studied by all pupils for a considerable length of time. Education in mathematics begins with the very young and continues, with varying degrees of emphasis, up through all the grades of the elementary school and in some grades of the high school. Mathematics is a *tool* subject, an essential instrument with which to think. Its value continues to increase as civilization advances. This is dramatically true in our current age of electronics. Knowledge of mathematics and skill in its application are essential to advanced study in most major subject fields: science, economics, geology, psychology, sociology, education, and so on.

Judged in terms of time devoted to mathematics in the schools, one would expect the graduates to have a high degree of competence and an ability to apply their knowledge where quantitative thinking is required. Actually, there has been a wide discrepancy between what is expected and what has been achieved. Hence mathematics educators in recent years have been investing great effort to discover and rectify the mistakes of the past. They tackle such questions as: Why do high school graduates show glaring mathematical deficiencies? Why do many pupils exhibit a strong antipathy toward mathematics—even fear of it? Why do many elementary school teachers dislike teaching mathematics? Why are many elementary school teachers inadequately prepared to teach mathematics effectively? The first approach to the problem was to examine critically the subject matter traditionally studied in mathematics courses, subject matter considerably standardized: arithmetic in the elementary schools, algebra in the ninth grade, plane geometry in the tenth grade, solid geometry and advanced algebra in the eleventh grade, trigonometry, in larger schools, in the twelfth grade. Most teachers adhered closely to adopted texts, so the writers of mathematics textbooks really determined the subject matter taught. Textbooks written in the early 1890s in algebra and geometry were still in common use in the 1920s and 1930s and are in use in some places even today. For example, the popular textbook by Wentworth and Smith, *Plane and Solid Geometry,* was copyrighted in 1888, 1899, 1910, 1911, 1913, and 1939.

By 1950 the entire teaching profession had become aware that the subject matter of the old mathematical sequence should be revised and a different approach made. A much-concerned federal government and numerous private foundations made large contributions for the support of projects to improve both mathematics and science in the schools. The federal government subsidized the reeducation of mathematics teachers. In addition, numerous colleges and universities, the U.S. Office of Education, manufacturing corporations, and other agencies joined in an all-out effort to improve the subject matter and the methods of teaching mathematics in the schools. Experiments, perhaps influenced by the training programs of the National Science Project financed by the National Science Foundation, are now being conducted in elementary and secondary schools throughout the nation to improve both the subject matter and the methods of teaching mathematics.

The so-called new mathematics is subject matter in development. Concepts that constitute the central theme of mathematics are introduced early. Unifying ideas such as sets (any well-defined grouping of distinguishable objects) receive emphasis with the very young. Pupils are introduced to sets of objects, pictorially perhaps, before being introduced to symbols. The basic idea is first learned through direct experience; symbols and terminology follow later. Structure is a concept that is introduced early. The subject matter of structure sets forth principles and properties traditionally associated with the classifications of later mathematics, not excepting college calculus. A child can visualize a line as an infinite number of points. He can grasp the idea of infinity. Space, time, and distance are realized intuitively. As he advances, the subject matter includes measurement, systems of enumeration, the meaning of operations, logical deduction, graphic representation, valid generalization, and, as the pupil develops, other unifying themes. Throughout his elementary and high school experiences with mathematics, subject matter is so selected and the pupil so directed that from the beginning mathematics is a series of unifying concepts and integral relationships. The future of this new mathematics seems most promising; it has been a challenging innovation in modern American education.

Social Studies

As long as social studies was confined to a study of only one aspect of social living, the classification into specialized fields such as geography or history was considered adequate. Teachers became increasingly aware, however, that within such a scheme of classification many important phases of social living were not even being touched. They reasoned that pertinent subject matter related to the whole of a current social process, not just a small segment of a process, should be included if pupils were to develop an intelligent appreciation of the broad area of human relations in modern society. In locating materials that would shed light on crucial and urgent present-day social problems, it was necessary to investigate all fields, not just the social sciences. The reorganized subject matter, focused on selected problems of social living, was called social studies.

The trend is for teachers, perhaps in terms of a curriculum or a district or school course of study, to formulate the course pattern, to direct the selection and organization of the subject matter, and to use any materials that promise to develop insight into human relations, to promote a better understanding of social processes, and to build competence in living and dealing with one's fellows.

Sometimes as a preliminary step to the achievement of these kinds of social aims, specific social concepts are assigned to be developed at a particular grade level. Such concepts might include, among others, colonialism in the seventh grade, for instance. Subject matter to assist in developing this concept will be social studies materials as defined earlier—not confined to history or to the United States or to any other limited area of time, place, location, or discipline. In fact, emphasis on the world, on international relations and international aspects of areas of study, is now replacing the older pattern of restricting study largely to the United States and western Europe.

Whether social studies is concept oriented or not, the subject matter is selected to develop competence in intergroup relations, skills in group action, concern for the welfare of others, tolerance for the viewpoints of others, respect for and ability to work with others who have different cultural backgrounds, and understanding of the elements that contribute to the increasing interdependence of human beings everywhere. In other words, the social studies emphasize skills, traits, attitudes, and understandings needed for the improvement of human relations everywhere.

The subject matter of social studies in the elementary and secondary schools has perhaps departed more radically from the older and more specialized patterns of organization than has that of any of the other fields. This is, it seems, partly because social problems are so numerous and varied that they, more obviously than other problems, can be approached only through the avenues of more than one kind of specialized subject matter.

Social studies in our schools, however, has never been organized uniformly according to any definite scheme or pattern or logical sequence. This is one criticism made by those who advocate the more traditional, specialized, schematic arrangement.

Fine Arts

The fine arts include painting, dance, music—any mode of expression thought to be significant and beautiful. The expression may be in the form of both appreciation and actual production or creation. Fine arts are emphasized throughout the elementary school, including the kindergarten, and also through most of the grades of the secondary school. They are recognized, also, as important in adult education.

The attention given to the fine arts at all levels of education in the United States is a recent phenomenon. In the past the tendency was to consider the fine arts as a "frill." Music in the nursery school and kindergarten, rhythms for younger children, handicrafts for all ages, including those who are handicapped or suffering from some nervous ailment, are now typical. Perhaps the relatively recent social changes—shorter work week, mandatory retirement, mechanical housekeeping aids—bringing about increased leisure have been responsible, in part, for the upsurge of interest in the fine arts.

The subject matter of the fine arts, drawn from many fields, is neither highly systematized nor standardized at any of the levels of education. In selecting and organizing the subject matter, the interests and the maturity levels of the pupils serve as the main criteria. Thus a ninth-grader with no background in art and a fourth-grader who studied art in second and third grades might be able to handle the same subject matter. The subject matter is determined largely by the needs of the individual pupil as they are revealed to the teacher, not, as is the case with mathematics, by a progressively increased level of difficulty arbitrarily allocated to grade levels.

Children, particularly those in the elementary school, use a great variety of forms of expression—drawing, painting, singing, listening to music, acting out stories, playing in a school orchestra, playing musical instruments they have made. The subject matter may include almost anything thought to be beautiful and aesthetic, anything that will provide an outlet for children to communicate in a creative or in a receptive, appreciative way.

Health

In all the official statements of aims of education in the United States, high priority is given to health. Sometimes the aim is divided into two aspects—physical health and mental health. This is one of the dualisms first introduced into educational philosophy in the Middle Ages. The use of the two terms indicates the emphasis desired in the education program and probably causes little harm, providing one remembers that the two terms merely designate the health aim from two different angles. Health is health of an organism. When there is a threat to good health, the whole of the organism is involved.

Study in the health area is varied. Children in the grade schools often make a special study of diets, record and rate their own diets, study the relative numbers of illnesses pupils have, and look for a relationship between illness and diet. The classroom and the school building with its lighting, sewage disposal, and the like, may also provide subject matter for health education. Sometimes the health services of the school are used as source material. School dental services have led science classes to study the fluoridation of water, the relation of diet to good teeth, and the relation of eating sweets or drinking sweetened liquids to the preservation of teeth.

Much of the subject matter of health studies involves direct experience from actual activities. Free play, particularly in the elementary school, may, for instance, make a significant contribution to self-control, fair play, and physical efficiency.

Health, as a major object of education, cannot be achieved by studying logical categories of subject matter. It is an aim that embraces the needs of every pupil at all levels of education. What is studied in health education even in a single grade cannot be standardized. Perhaps in this field more than in any other, expert planning is of paramount importance. The subject matter must be flexible—adaptable to the growth characteristics and primary interests of the individual pupils.

General Trends

The trend in organizing subject matter is toward larger units. Traditional organization is in terms of more or less isolated subjects. The teacher in the elementary school conducts a class in reading, a class in arithmetic, or a music class. In the high school one teacher has a class in geography, one a class in algebra, and another a class in chemistry.

To overcome the disadvantages of too great emphasis on the separateness of subject matter, to move from fragmentation toward greater unity, various plans have been followed. One such plan is called "correlation." Interested teachers working together discover relationships in their subject matter. The teacher of literature, for instance, may correlate Dickens' *Tale of Two Cities* with the history teacher's treatment of the French Revolution. Teachers and administrators tend to like this plan since no subject loses anything and traditional organization is not basically upset. Actually, the barriers between the subjects are not eliminated. Rather, they are adjusted to; teacher planning achieves some unification despite them.

Another approach to unifying small areas of subject matter is called "integration." This type of organization is more readily adapted to the lower grades of the elementary school than to the secondary school. The teacher selects, or directs the selection of, projects that will give the child experiences educationally desirable, promote learning specifically suited to academic level, and provide an opportunity for the teacher to give the kind of guidance that promises to lead to social and personal maturity. If, for instance, the project selected is the operation of a grocery store, in setting up the store and running the business the children would read, draw, add and subtract, and engage in many learning activities that ordinarily are taken up separately. They would also have such experiences as planning and working together, sharing, and cooperating.

Sometimes the fragmentary character of traditional subject-matter organization is lessened by combining areas and having an expanded unit. Typical large divisions are social studies, general science, language arts, health, physical education, general mathematics, and general arts. The subject-matter area known as "unified studies," embracing English and social studies, is an even broader kind of classification.

The core program as a part of the junior and senior high school organization was described in Chapter 15. The term "core studies" is used to describe another plan for unifying work in the elementary school. Under this plan a basic unit or problem on such subjects as housing, family, or civil liberties is the "core." Children who pursue the core give to this phase of their work all the time that is allocated to "general" education, that is, to education common to all students as differentiated from specialized education or vocational training. In working on the basic problem children use material from any subject. Emphasis is on pupil activity. A wide range of reading materials as well as the resources of the community are used.

Among the aims of the various forms of team teaching is that of unifying instruction by using the interdisciplinary resources of all the members of a team in developing a concept. Contributions from mathematics, science, social studies, and language arts may be utilized in a single unit of work.

Within the general plans called correlation, integration, unified studies, team teaching, and core studies, the variations are numerous. They all mark the trend toward organizing subject matter in larger units. They are of increasing interest to those who wish to improve the instructional programs.

Subject Matter in America's Schools

At Grade Levels

Subject matter has long been organized into levels paralleling the grades of our schools. In the Middle Ages, subject matter was limited to the knowledge systematically organized in books somewhat like encyclopedias for the purpose of being learned. Eventually the easier parts of accumulated, organized knowledge became the subject matter of the earlier grades. The more abstract, the more conceptual, and the more difficult to comprehend became the subject matter for the later grades. The most difficult to assimilate was to be taught by the graduate schools in the universities. Grade placement of subject matter was determined on an empirical basis. Eventually, for example, Euclidean geometry was placed regularly in the curriculum for sophomores in high school. Adaptations of Euclid's textbook are still used in some high school geometry classes at the sophomore level.

It was believed that subject matter, in time, found its own natural level and settled there. Its natural level was that stage of educational advancement at which it could be understood. Any other reasons why it should be studied at a predetermined level were never probed. From earliest time a systematic, arbitrary arrangement of subject matter was accepted as appropriate entirely apart from utilitarian or interest values. It is related that even about 300 B.C. a pupil, having learned the first proposition of demonstrational geometry, raised the question of what he would get by learning these things and was answered by Euclid, who called his slave and said, "Give him threepence, since he must needs make gain by what he learns."

In the ninth grade, algebra begins with the intuitively conceived axioms and proceeds to quadratics. Demonstrational geometry, which follows, is a tenth-grade subject and is given a full school year. Advanced algebra is learned in the first half of the eleventh grade, and solid geometry is learned in the second half of the eleventh grade. The subject matter of Latin is grammar in the ninth grade, Caesar's *Commentaries* in the tenth, Cicero's *Orations* in the eleventh, and Vergil's *Aeneid* in the twelfth.

Subject matter in American schools thus became crystallized. Materials in numerous fields have been systematically sifted, sorted, and organized, and their pedagogical uses have been prescribed according to grade-level sequence. Currently, however, traditional grade-level classifications are being modified. The determination of grade-level placement of subject matter is still made on an empirical basis, but improved understanding of pupils, of learning, and of subjects themselves has led to some drastic changes—to the teaching of geometry in the primary grades, for example. Because there has perhaps been most resistance to change in the grade-level placement of subjects in the secondary schools, pupils now in the elementary schools may need accommodations in grade-level placement when they reach the secondary schools.

Total Learning

A somewhat expanded notion encompasses as subject matter *all* that a pupil learns. This concept does not exclude the idea that subject matter is organized in grade levels or that it includes what is in the textbooks. Subject matter, however, is not limited to that which is in a book, but includes what goes on within the pupil, the reaction to what is studied. In this case the subject matter consists of the facts and ideas that are communicated to the pupil. Here the subject matter is only that which the pupil assimilates. In this sense no two pupils ever study the same subject matter, even though they use the same textbook and are taught by the same teacher.

Purposive Learning

Clearly, an individual's belief about what constitutes the subject matter of a school is directly related to what he or she thinks the aims of the school should be. If it is considered that learning should contribute to purposes shared by the teacher and the pupils, then subject matter may be defined broadly as the "facts observed, read, recalled, and talked about, and the ideas suggested, in course of a development of a situation having a purpose."[2] This definition emphasizes that a classroom constitutes a special place for deliberate education and that there is more to the mastery of subject matter than learning what is included in the textbook. Importance is placed on the management of a situation so that learning proceeds with a purpose. It is the purpose uppermost in the minds of the pupils and the teacher that dictates what and how subject matter shall be learned. In this concept the subject matter varies with the individual pupil, since individual reactions to what is read or talked about will vary. In addition, it is recognized that how the pupil organizes what he learns depends on various factors, only some of which are within the pupil himself.

The Teacher and Subject Matter

In our discussion of the qualifications, training, and experience necessary for teaching, it was pointed out that the successful teacher has acquired a breadth of knowledge far wider than that possessed by even the most advanced of his pupils. This knowledge is like a huge reservoir—it stands ready at all times to be drawn on as needed.

The teacher's knowledge of subject matter and of pupils is a necessary complement to textbooks. Frequently textbooks are divided into sections, and perhaps into subsections, for purposes of organiza-

[2] John Dewey, *Democracy and Education*. New York: Macmillan, 1916, p. 212.

tion, reference, clarity, and emphasis. The textbook is a tool, and the divisions, sometimes minute, may be a definite aid to instruction. If, however, the teacher does not have a wide range of knowledge, the textbook with its detailed subdivisions tends to give subject matter a quality of rigidity, to make it less adaptable to momentary situations and less appropriate to teaching with a purpose. The teacher's knowledge must extend beyond the limits of the subject matter established in the textbook, limits unavoidable in the preparation of specialized books. The boundaries of a textbook are never the boundaries of the most fruitful subject matter.

The chances are that the teacher will organize his or her knowledge in a way somewhat paralleling the specialist's organization of subject matter because the teacher has studied under and mastered that kind of arrangement. The physics teacher, for instance, tends to think of physics around words such as measurement, mechanics, heat, static electricity, electricity-in-motion, sound, light, and invisible radiations.

The pupil's orientation to subject matter is different from the teacher's. The pupil's organization, growing out of limited past experiences, is inchoate. The successful teacher is aware of the discrepancy and is alert to providing opportunities for a pupil to develop his or her own organization and application. In drawing on the reservoir of knowledge, the teacher will not be influenced by the organization characteristic of his or her own school experience, but will draw from any area, whether in textbooks or in the world of practical affairs, appropriate to achieving the end desired. For instance, the teacher's knowledge may influence the subject matter of the literature class to include something that might traditionally be classified as history, philosophy, economics, or something else. In our review of the current trends in the organization of subject matter, it will be noted that the importance of organizing subject matter in larger units is recognized.

Subject matter, it has been pointed out, may include direct experience and indirect or vicarious learning. In advancing educationally the tendency is to move from emphasis on the direct toward progressively greater emphasis on the indirect. A learning situation may include both direct and indirect features in varying degrees. In the biology laboratory pupils may have such direct experiences as learning about circulation by dissecting a rabbit. They will also use the textbook, library reference materials, and perhaps filmstrips and movies. Sufficient direct experience is necessary to make indirect learning effective. The indirect must be associated with the direct by meaningful symbols, vocabulary, and examples. The successful teacher is resourceful in making appropriate connections. For instance, in teaching mathematics it will be less difficult for a child from a farm to make a meaningful connection between the symbols of measurement applied to a bushel of oats or an acre of ground than it will be for a city pupil who buys oats in a cereal box and thinks of land divisions as city blocks and 50-foot lots.

Unfortunately, students often arrive at college, even at the graduate level, without having built firsthand experiences with quantitative subject matter sufficient for clear understanding of the meanings various words and symbols are expected to convey. For real appreciation, a meaningful connection between subject matter and human living is essential.

Summary

It is important to remember that selection and organization of subject matter are never isolated activities. They are closely related to the educational aims of the school and of the teacher, which, in turn, are influenced by the teachers' understanding of the pupils. In deciding what is worthy and desirable subject matter and what would be the best organization of that subject, just as in selecting methods of instruction, the criteria have a philosophical base.

At present, subject matter designed to promote specialized and vocational competences tends to be relatively adequate and satisfactory because the specialized areas have immediate and definite aims and the subject matter appropriate to advancing these aims is readily available. Further progress is required in selecting subject matter potentially more significant in advancing the aims of general education. There is a current tendency to give too much emphasis to specialized subject matter and too little emphasis to subject matter that contributes to the aims of general education, to a sound cultural background. Chemistry teachers, for instance, tend to stress the kind of subject matter that prepares chemists, not the kind that makes citizens intelligent about the physical world. Unfortunately, there is a continuing lack of agreement about what subject matter best contributes to the general education of all learners. The development of materials appropriate to general education in all subjects, selection of suitable subject matter, and planning adequate curriculums are among important areas for study and leadership.

Another path to progress is unmistakably indicated in the selection of subject matter that is more adaptable to the vast range in pupils' backgrounds, interests, and learning abilities. Balanced reading programs, textbooks suited to different levels of ability, and workbooks and other instructional aids that permit pupils to advance at individual rates are becoming increasingly effective. Including more direct experience, particularly in the high school, is another improvement in the selection of subject matter that may be profitably extended.

Present trends indicate that in the future, organization of subject matter will continue to be progressively more in terms of unity and less in terms of specialized, fragmentary fields. Specialists in the psychology of learning, in child development, in social psychology, and in social biology have effectively challenged the soundness of a theory in which education is viewed mainly as the acquisition of material as it is arranged in textbooks.

Regardless of the way subject matter is selected or organized, its value in the educational experiences of the pupil depends largely on the effectiveness of the teacher. Progress here lies in the direction of improved training and experience. In order to exploit fully the potentialities of the entire learning situation, the teacher must not only understand the learning process and be thoroughly acquainted with his pupils, but also must have both a broad, general background and an extensive reservoir of information and understanding.

QUESTIONS

1. What is your definition of subject matter?
2. What is the curriculum? the course of study? a subject of study?
3. How may one judge the relative values of the various subjects of study?
4. What should be the relationship between school textbooks and the subject matter used in a given classroom?
5. What are the characteristics of a suitable textbook?
6. How, in your opinion, is continuity in a subject such as the fine arts or social studies to be achieved?

PROJECTS

1. Consult some specialized publication on the subject matter of your chosen field. Set forth what seem to be the principal trends in the selection of subject matter.
2. Look over materials in the curriculum resource center or consult professional publications—yearbooks, periodicals, and so on. Make a list of changes that have occurred in a field other than the field of your major interest since you were a pupil in elementary school.

chapter

19

Methods of teaching in America's schools

Four kinds of understandings are essential to effective teaching: (1) basic knowledge about pupils; (2) knowledge of the part played by aims in giving direction to the educative process; (3) knowledge that is classified as appropriate subject matter; (4) understandings related to methods, procedures, and skills required to utilize effectively, in directing learning, the knowledge of subject matter and understandings about pupils. In a sense, these four kinds of understandings constitute a unified whole in that they are inextricably interrelated, each constituting one component of the educative process.

For a teacher in preparation or an experienced teacher to keep informed about educational developments, it is important that a reasonably balanced interest be maintained in all four aspects. Since each kind of understanding is of such breadth and magnitude as to sustain a lifetime of study, it is relatively easy, even tempting, for teachers to allow their interests to become one-sided. That a balanced interest in the four essential aspects—knowledge of pupils, of aims, of subject matter, and of methods—is a valuable goal for teachers in training and for teachers in service cannot be overemphasized.

Methods, a Deepening Concern

Problems relating to teaching methods have become a matter of rapidly expanding interest in recent years. This seems due, in part at least, to an intensified awareness on the part of teachers after they have gained teaching experience that all they knew about human growth and development and about subject matter to be learned could be translated effectively into learning only with wise use of skillful methods. Without the ability to select and utilize appropriate procedures, without the requisite skills to communicate effectively with pupils, a teacher is somewhat comparable to a family with a swimming pool that is only an ornament because no one in the family can swim.

The expanded interest in teaching methods is due in part also to the accelerated change in curriculum, to the expanded background of interests and experiences of pupils, and to the extensive variety of teaching aids now available. A teacher today looking back at the days before TV, plane travel, automated manufacturing, and Cold War international maneuvering, recognizes at once that many classroom methods geared to conditions of a decade ago are now out of date. Also, there is the realization that technology is contributing to increased effectiveness of teacher communication. In the wake of current rapid change, teaching methods are inexorably swept along.

That the teaching profession is responding to the current demand for improvement in methods of teaching is attested to in part by the great amount of time and money that industry feels can be wisely invested in developing and producing a wide range of teaching aids. Attention is given to improving teaching methods by numerous groups of educators—for instance, the National Council of Teachers of English and the National Council of Teachers of Mathematics. Information about teaching problems, experiments, recommendations, and innovations is widely disseminated by many such organizations through their national publications. Teachers will find among these much material to stimulate their interest in teaching methods and to guide them in determining the methods and procedures appropriate or adaptable to their teaching responsibilities.

Approaches to Study of Methods

One may approach a study of methods of teaching by focusing on so-called general methods. General methods include the basic principles, generalizations, and concepts that are, presumably, applicable to teaching in general. In his five formal steps to conducting the recitation, for example, Herbart assumes that teachers in general conduct recitations and that they can use the five formal steps as a guide regardless of the subject matter they are teaching. Likewise, Dewey, in his *How We Think,* assumes that all teachers are attempting to help pupils learn how to think. All teachers are assumed to ask questions, evaluate pupil achievement, engage in telling, and the like. A study of general methods would be expected to cover what teachers do in general to stimulate and direct the learning of pupils.

Another approach to the study of methods focuses on special methods. This approach relates to problems inherent in the teaching of a specialized subject-matter field or in the teaching of a particular age group, usually very young children. It assumes that there are methods that apply particularly to the teaching of English, mathematics, and the like, and that these can be better studied in special courses. The study of special methods is thought to have the added advantage of providing an opportunity for the logical combination of a study of teaching methods with a study of subject matter. Thus colleges now give such courses as intermediate mathematics, physics for teachers, and chemistry for teachers. Furthermore, in some universities the study of special methods and student teaching in the subject field are closely correlated.

No attempt will be made here to evaluate the two approaches to the study of methods. It seems that both have certain advantages. There is some advantage in the broader approach that gives consideration to such topics as the aims of education, how rewards and punishments operate to condition learning, how interests, motivation, and other affective factors can be utilized. On the other hand, concentration on a study of the problems peculiar to the primary or preschool level is likely also to result in certain advantages. Certainly it is profitable to explore under the guidance of a skilled college teacher problems related to any special field. Study of both general and special methods may be needed for a satisfactory command in any one field.

A Comprehensive Field

Methods of teaching cover a comprehensive field. This is due first to the fact that education is established for the very complex purpose of promoting human improvement. As pointed out in Chapter 16, this involves a twofold continuing problem—on the one hand, problems related to the biological character of each human being, which is the product of the interaction between the individual and the environment, and on the other hand, problems related to the environment, including the school with everything that makes it an important part of that environment.

The great breadth of the area of teaching methods is also due to the extended range of subject matter, each element of which presents its own novel teaching problems. Take, for example, the field of English. Some of the questions a teacher might need to answer are the following: What is the best method for the study of words? Children seem to learn slang terms easily, but have difficulty learning some more standard terms. Why? How should punctuation be taught? Will a single method such as phonemics suffice? Can a poem be taught to high school pupils by programed instruction? If so, how does one program a poem? One might similarly proceed to other elements of English—such as reading, writing, grammar, spelling, listening, viewing, and mass media—only to find that each presents peculiar problems of teaching, none of which is easy to solve. In seeking an answer, a teacher may recognize the need for knowing, in general, about available teaching aids, team teaching, programed learning, curriculum construction, program evaluation, and so on.

In the fields of language arts, social studies, science, and mathematics, a great deal of emphasis is at present given to the inductive method of teaching. This method allows students to *discover* knowledge, skills, understandings. The teacher's role is to provide students with structured situations, to pose questions that call on the student to make the discoveries. An example is the teaching of the concept of the noun. Instead of telling the students "a noun is the name of a person, place, or thing" the teacher may give the class a sentence with nonsense words used as nouns and then ask the pupils what the words have in common, will let them discover clues that indicate how the words used as nouns function in the sentence. Later other examples will be given without nonsense words, and by careful analysis, by asking well-planned questions, the teacher will help the student better understand the concept.

Those who favor the inductive method contend that a student learns and retains facts and rules best when putting forth effort to discover or build them individually. Modern psychology tends to favor the inductive method, the presentation of arranged learning situations so that the student may discover through individual activity the facts, principles, and structures of the subject. The student may thus attain understanding and intellectual growth by engaging in an activity through which he or she discovers structures of knowledge.

Since methods of teaching are such a comprehensive field of study, the survey that follows in this chapter and the next makes no attempt to deal with concrete analyses of the many problems of teaching method. Since our objective is to give a brief overview, the treatment is necessarily limited to overall trends in various subject-matter fields.

Teaching Subject Matter

Language Arts

The aim in teaching language arts is twofold—the development of the abilities to express ideas and feelings and to receive and interpret messages. Writing and speaking constitute the media of expression of ideas and feelings. Listening and reading constitute the media through which the ability to receive and interpret messages is developed.

I. WRITTEN EXPRESSION

After judging a pupil's present capacity to write clearly and effectively, the teacher next concentrates on finding ways to encourage growth in this skill. Growth is emphasized rather than expertness, which is held in mind as a remote goal. The pupil should always have a clear notion of the next step in the development of his abilities.

The material best suited for study, discussion, and rewriting is the sentences and paragraphs from a pupil's own written expression. Variations in word meanings receive attention, with a view to selecting words that express the precise meaning desired. Published paragraphs, which may be read by the pupils at home and which serve as examples of better forms of written expression, are also discussed in the classroom. The contributions made to expression by correct spelling, punctuation, and grammatical structure are made an integral part of the instructional procedure.

How does the assignment contribute to the growth of an individual's powers of expression? This is the paramount criterion for the selection of a method. For example, teachers help their pupils see that socially acceptable forms of written expression are important, not because they represent the ends of good written expression, but because they make a pupil a more effective social individual. An effort is made to help the pupil recognize that there is a place for the language, especially the oral language, that is a natural part of his everyday conversation, even though this may be different from the so-called formal language that is considered socially correct. The pupil is helped to understand that the informal language, or the dialect of a group or a neighborhood, is not *wrong,* is actually the most appropriate medium of communication under some circumstances, but that there is, however, a place where the socially correct language, the language characteristic of the educated people of the community, is needed. Younger children are taught to know words, to use them, and to write them in proper context. Knowing words helps them to think and adds to their development of capacity to deal with other persons and to provide solutions to individual personal problems. Pupils learn that their potential powers cannot be developed in a day, but will, with some effort by the pupils, develop gradually.

One of the problems in attempting to promote growth in the abilities of written expression is the pupils' lack of interest. To encourage them to develop their capacities, teachers use as many lifelike situations as possible. Pupils write useful letters, prepare scripts for an assembly program, devise school posters, or originate captions to announce special events in the school. Pupils may be asked to read a written digest of something they have read in order that the class may also know about it, to write an occasional verse just for fun, to write a formal composition in order to demonstrate how one should be written, or to take notes on a talk they will hear in order to transmit effectively and faithfully the ideas of the speaker to the class. The use of lifelike situations has been effective because it brings into play the pupils' interests and helps the pupils to see that they write in school for the same reasons that people write outside school. Resistance to writing is easier to overcome if the pupils are encouraged to write about things of concern to them and if writing can be done in ways of some immediate use.

The question of methods in teaching spelling, punctuation, grammar, and handwriting often arises. Teaching written expression includes all these subject matters. Spelling is combined with, and is a part of, written expression, but the central emphasis is upon word study—the meaning of words and the form in which they convey the meaning. Both the words studied and the spelling of the words are taken from the words the pupils use. Meaning and structure are considered together. A word wrongly spelled usually does not carry its true meaning. "It reigned yesterday" is an example. Teachers focus attention upon words. A number of words are examined, analyzed, and reviewed each week, but always by a method that leads to growth in the powers of expression. Both punctuation and grammar are given careful attention—but, again, as means to developing powers of written expression.

Many current changes in methods of teaching language arts are consistent with recommendations by scholars in the field of linguistics. The language arts teacher oriented to the linguistic approach, instead of presenting a collection of facts for rote learning, instead of teaching rules for spelling and punctuation and grammar, shows students how to examine and test the facts of language and expression for themselves. The teacher frequently uses nonsense sentences to illustrate grammatical structure and emphasizes position as a means of identifying parts of speech. There is some new terminology. For instance, "determiners" and "noun-markers" are what traditionally have been called "articles" and "adjectives." In teaching spelling and word comprehension the phonemic principle is stressed for a clear understanding of the difference between letters and sounds. The oral language factors of pitch and stress are utilized for help in understanding and using punctuation. Common, basic sentence patterns are examined and the pupils have experience with the infinite variations that can be made in terms of these patterns. It is contended that this kind of language arts teaching will pay off in a noticeable improvement in the students' handling of the language in writing and oral work, that understanding the system of the language plus purposeful practice will result in improvement of language use.

2. ORAL EXPRESSION

In helping pupils develop the powers of oral expression, teachers must realize the importance of full recognition of the child's native resources and his level of maturation. The native capacities are developed by putting natural organs—ears, vocal cords, larynx—to use. The way the child is taught to use the organs determines the nature of the development that takes place.

Teaching speech in school is important because speech is man's basic mode of expression. It is his most effective way not only to give expression to his wants but to preserve his techniques and knowledge and to pass them on to the next generation.

Unfortunately, methodical teaching of speech in the schools has been somewhat neglected. This may be in part a legacy from the past, when schools were places where children were forced to be quiet. Studies show that a 4-year-old speaks 10,000 words a day, a 5-year-old speaks 12,000 words a day, and the longest period for either age group without audible speech is 19 minutes. The average length of periods of inactivity—and these are infrequent—is 4 minutes. Children are naturally highly stimulated to talk, and if silence is not enforced, speech in the schoolroom is an almost continuous process. The methods for correcting, modifying, and directing the pupils' speech are continuously in use.

Considerable attention is given to the development of a speaking vocabulary. There are many differences between a speaking and an understanding vocabulary, and the problem of developing one differs from the problem of developing the other. Each entails different methods.

Training the voice has received much attention. Schools often provide specialists to direct the speech instruction of pupils with exaggerated defects. Methods that have proved very effective in speech correction are adaptable to teaching the normal pupil in the school. In normal classroom situations, a few simple rules are followed. Good speech calls for good listeners. The teacher sets an example with his own speech habits. A pupil is directed to speak plain and loudly enough to be heard. He speaks to the class, not just to the teacher. Good articulation is striven for. Careless speech, even in the most informal discussion, is discouraged. The pupil is made conscious that he is speaking his thoughts, that others are thinking with him, and that they are occupied with the thoughts he is trying to express, not with their own thoughts.

Most of the methods that teachers use are informal and are selected to help a certain pupil or to fit some special situation. As with written expression, as many true-to-life situations as possible are used, such as assemblies, announcements, presiding over the class, and discussion. Teachers find the tape recorder particularly helpful.

The linguists stress the importance of oral language, and recommend beginning with what students, as native speakers, already know, what they have learned from imitating those around them. The great variations in oral speech are not necessarily undesirable, something to be stamped out, and there are no permanent, absolute rules to follow in language arts, because language is constantly changing.

3. READING

Reading is language development that interprets what is seen on the printed page. Reading English is the reverse of writing and speaking English. Writing and speaking are processes in which meaning is translated into words, whereas reading is a process in which words are translated into meaning. Both are active processes, but they differ; hence the methods of teaching the two must differ.

The discovery of printing brought reading into prominence. Hopefully, printed symbols cause one to think. Ideas come to the students through their eyes rather than through the medium of sound. The response a pupil makes to a symbol depends on the ideas and emotions that are aroused in him by the sight of the symbols. No two pupils make the same response to a symbol because the symbol carries different meanings to different people.

How children are taught to read obviously influences the nature of their ability to comprehend and to interpret what they read. Reading is not taught as an absorptive process. It is treated as an active process in which readers express themselves through the interpretation of what they read. It is a process that stimulates their thinking, feeling, and acting.

Powers of expression, whether oral or written, expand as the ability to read develops. The development of this ability is a constant and continuous process. It begins when the small child first points to a picture in a book and continues throughout life. Growth patterns in ability to read, to comprehend what is read, and to interpret more meaningfully what is read vary in different individuals. Thus the student who reads with ease the most difficult technical treatise is one who has gradually sharpened his or her powers of distinction, enlarged the scope of knowledge of meanings, and developed a highly specialized vocabulary. What one person reads may be easy for him or her and difficult for someone else. Ability to read depends not only on how well a pupil has learned to read previously, but also on the lines along which growth has been directed. The pupil may read one kind of material expertly and read and comprehend another kind poorly.

In reading, the overall growth pattern of each pupil is unique. A method of teaching that takes into account the natural design of the learner gives promise of contributing the maximum to the development of the ability to read.

In view of the nature of reading development, the efforts made in earlier schools to classify reading into grade levels and to establish standards for each of the grades seem hopeless gestures. The range of reading abilities in each of the grades is inevitably very wide. Method, to be effective, must take into account the extensive differences among pupils of the same age in reading interests, abilities, and all-around reading competence.

Teachers in the lower grades of the American schools have developed and use highly successful methods of teaching reading, principally because they have accepted the guidance of child development specialists. The quality of teaching reading deteriorates somewhat in the higher grades; teachers too often use methods that largely disregard the findings of the psychologists. Consequently, high school and college students do not read as well as they should. Their progress in language facility has been slower than it should be, considering the amount of training these pupils have had. Since the methods of teaching have been partly responsible for this situation, language arts teachers at all levels have made the improvement of methods of teaching reading one of their goals.

Thus the reading process, as is the case with the learning process itself, should not be considered as isolated from other conditioning factors. The teacher should keep this in mind when deciding whether to have pupils read orally or silently and whether to use the word method, telling method, phonetics methods or one of the several phonetic systems, questioning method, discussion method, or some other system. The teacher may often have to make arbitrary decisions— simply because some decision has to be made. In the final analysis, as has been said, methods are inseparable from other factors. Indeed, one can think of the choice of a reading method as the end of a sequence: understanding pupils and knowing their needs and interests; evolving and following definite, specific, and worthy objectives for each of the lesson units; having a diversity of suitable materials available; and then choosing those methods that are best suited to directing the learning of the pupils effectively toward the desired ends, using, when needed, appropriate instructional aids (such as those described in the next chapter).

4. LISTENING

Attentive, sympathetic listeners are necessary to the cultivation of good oral expression. Listening is also a form of expression on the part of the one who listens. It is a somewhat neglected area of language arts. In teaching children to be good listeners the teacher is concerned with the impact the spoken word makes on the listener, the ideas it arouses, and the reactions to which it leads.

Pupils are taught that listening may have different purposes—for example, listening carefully to a question to answer it, to a record just to be entertained, to a persuasive advertisement on the radio to criticize the logic of the argument, or to the reading of a beautiful poem to appreciate it. Life presents many opportunities for listening, and the school has an obligation to encourage growth and development in the skills of listening quite as much as in the skills of reading. Just as, at times, spelling, punctuation, and sentence structure are made the focus of direct instruction, so also is listening. The subject matter is carefully chosen, the purpose is agreed on, and the procedures are defined just as carefully as they would be in any other language arts instruction.

5. TRENDS

Language arts teachers are aware of the individual differences among their pupils and know that the differences expand as growth in language arts progresses. Individual needs are given as close attention as are group needs. Much thought is devoted to choice of material and to deriving ways whereby subject matter may be effectively directed toward desired ends. Currently the inductive, linguistics approach is in vogue.

Language arts teachers carefully analyze the language development of preschool children, of children in the primary grades, and so on, up through the graduate school of the university. Observation of growth in large numbers of children does not obscure their vision of individual differences. It does help in setting up levels that can be used as standards or guides in planning instruction.

The language arts teachers, whose methods are based on current educational theories, tend to be nonconformists in the profession. They ignore some practices that were sacred to the older language arts teachers—such practices as adhering to established grade-placement of subject matter and demanding standard achievement for promotion.

These teachers insist that good language arts teaching can proceed only when the individual pupil is fully understood, when an attempt is made to discover his individual requirements. Only then can appropriate subject matter and methods be selected.

These language arts teachers are not, however, the educational rebels they are sometimes pictured. They are, in fact, realists. They are practicing psychologists. They are convinced by their studies of human growth and development that their methods of teaching are better, that these methods are essential to the proper promotion of human growth.

The language arts teachers seek to coordinate their classroom work with the social experiences of the school and with the experiences the pupil may have in other subjects, such as geography and social studies. Language is a social instrument, and a broadened range of social experience widens the range of the subject matter that can be used in teaching language arts. When correlating the language arts with other subjects, the language arts teachers may be accused of overlapping the other fields. If they do, it is with a distinct instructional aim in mind. When pupils read, they cannot just read "reading." Growth in reading implies a broadening of the range of experiences as well as growth in reading skills.

The language arts teachers have been especially resourceful in choosing functional subject matter. In reading, for example, schools have placed great emphasis on having suitable library materials readily accessible to teachers and pupils alike. Paperbacks, popular with pupils, enhance the breadth of reading materials available. The librarian, who is usually also a language arts teacher, serves mainly as a resource person to help teachers or pupils. Single textbooks for reading have almost disappeared from the better schools. The wide range of pupil needs, interests, and abilities demands a wide range of reading materials. Efforts are made to develop balanced reading programs. A wide range of sources is made available. The differences in cultural backgrounds, interests, and abilities of the pupils are taken fully into account. This change in methods has impregnated many language arts classrooms with new spirit, has ventilated them with a breath of fresh air.

All teachers in the school are, in a sense, language arts teachers. Pupils are taught to read in mathematics and science classes. There they learn the use of specialized words. Language arts teachers attempt to coordinate the language arts of all the classes. When school work has been compartmentalized into rigid divisions of subject matter, the work of the language arts teachers to coordinate language arts skills with other school subjects tends to be more difficult. Critical reading, vocabulary building, spelling, sentence structure, and collateral reading become submerged in many. of the classes in specialized subject matter because of the dominance of other aims. The trend at all levels, however, is to stress growth in the communicative arts through the conscious efforts of the teachers of all the subjects.

Planning a sequence in the language arts area remains an unsettled problem. There is agreement, however, that methods should place greater emphasis on written and spoken communication, less on isolated drill. Speaking opportunities should far outnumber writing opportunities. Overt attention should be given to developing the skills of listening. Both practical and imaginative writing should be taught. What a pupil reads should be in answer to that pupil's interests, needs, and abilities. The teaching of reading should emphasize reading with a purpose. Ordinarily the purpose of reading for information and enjoyment should outweigh, but not displace, reading to improve the mechanics of reading. Pupils should share their reading experiences with others as often as possible. To set forth in advance specifically what is to be covered in the language arts instruction or to define the methods of directing the instruction is not possible. Much is left to the intelligence of the well-trained language arts teacher.

Science

A precipitately heightened interest in science education among the American people has been reflected in the school program. Our discussion deals with the methods of teaching science only in the area of general education, where all pupils, regardless of interest or ability, are studying the same subject matter.

Much thought and effort have been devoted to the formulation of a developmental program of teaching science. The old problem of sequence is still unsolved, but instruction in science now begins in the first year of school and continues as general science up to the seventh grade. In the seventh, eighth, and ninth grades, science is usually still general science, but the instruction is given by a specialized teacher. The subject matter after that becomes more specialized. There are classes in physics, chemistry, and biology.

Teaching general science has two principal purposes: (1) to lead the student to an accurate understanding and appreciation of the physical world and (2) to cultivate the student's ability to use the scientific method.

One of the age-old stumbling blocks to teaching in this area is the complex form in which the sciences have been organized by the specialists. The connections of the highly systematized subject matter with the experiences of everyday life have often been hidden from both the pupils and the teacher. Teachers in the earlier grades now teach science without the use of textbooks. The inductive approach is generally followed. Much attention is given at first to obtaining concrete experiences and to connecting the subject matters studied with those experiences. Even in the first grade, the pupil begins to recognize the nature of a lever or the relationship between sunlight and life. The teacher begins with what the pupil has learned from his previous experience and develops from that experience the proper modes of scientific treatment. Time is sacrificed to understanding and to fostering a vital interest. The cue to method is that nothing is learned by the pupils unless they understand it fully.

The teacher in general education never assumes that he or she is obligated to produce a scientific specialist, but leaves that to the later years, when selection operates. The teacher does assume that everyone should learn something about the method scientists have used to perfect their knowledge as well as something about the results they have achieved. A pupil's understanding grows as he or she learns *how* to look and for *what* to look.

Facilities for teaching science, generously furnished by most schools, are as highly varied as the methods that they are expected to serve. Laboratories, library materials, visual aids, books suited to the age of the pupils—all contribute to and influence the teacher's methods. The selection of science teaching methods is ideally left to the discretion of an able teacher who has considerable knowledge of pupils' needs.

Mathematics

Methods in the teaching of mathematics in America's schools might have been included in the preceding discussion, except that American schools treat mathematics as a specialized subject apart from science. This specialization begins in the very early grades and continues through all the remaining grades. The subject matter of mathematics traditionally has been organized in relatively narrow areas, such as algebra and plane geometry. Changes that have resulted in the so-called new mathematics have brought about an organization into more comprehensive fields.

Perhaps in no field of teaching have the results been more subject to critical scrutiny. Criticisms have been heeded, and great changes have been made in methods of teaching mathematics in recent years. One of the common criticisms was that most pupils at the elementary and high school levels did not learn mathematics, and that what was learned about mathematics was largely forgotten as soon as the pupil left school and entered adult life. Another criticism was that in studying mathematics many pupils developed a fear of it, or an antagonistic attitude toward doing any kind of quantitative thinking. As already pointed out, quantitative thinking becomes increasingly important in this age of computers.

Teachers were the first to admit that the methods of teaching mathematics for the purpose of general education have not been as effective as desired, and efforts to improve these methods over the past years are continuing. Traditions, however, have a strong hold, changes have not been easy to make. If, as some contend, teachers of mathematics have placed too much emphasis on manipulation, such as applying formulas, and on getting the right answers, rather than on processes of thinking out answers, then a key to progress seems to be a change in the emphasis of teaching. Setting up equations in the ninth grade will become just as important as solving an equation that has been set up. Teachers complain that in systems where city-wide standardized tests are administered, the tests are scored right or wrong, sometimes with a machine, according to the correctness of the answer, regardless of whether pupils can think through the processes or not. This places pressure on teachers to emphasize rapidity and manipulation rather than thought processes. The emphasis is shifting to methods that train pupils to think quantitatively as well as to manipulate accurately and rapidly. The accuracy and speed are considered a follow-up to thinking rather than an antecedent.

The subdivisions of mathematics—algebra, geometry, and the like—have been taught in the general education programs as isolated, specialized subject matter, little related to one another or to the experience of the pupils. Current stress is therefore on the development of a unified mathematics field that emphasizes relationships and attempts to make all that is taught meaningful. It has become more important to have the children comprehend basic structures inductively than to have them advance through established steps, often going on to a new step without mastery of what went before. The emphasis is now being placed on developing an understanding of mathematical concepts through the pupils' own directed discovery, rather than on studying specialized arithmetic, algebra, or geometry. The trend is to strive to have the pupils fully understand those fundamental mathematical concepts that are part of their own living and those that are common to mathematics generally. There is also an increased concern with the children's growth patterns, with their background and readiness. Teaching conceptual thinking without regard to whether the concept should be labeled "algebra" or "calculus" is a path to progress in teaching mathematics. All children, with adequate instruction, can learn mathematics, and many will enjoy it. Meaning, relationships, and processes serve as a truer guide than emphasis on the so-called fundamentals so necessary to the manipulative tradition.

Social Studies

The social *science*s are the orderly, systematically arranged bodies of knowledge that deal with various aspects of social living. The social *studies* of the elementary and high school consist of portions of the subject matter of the specialized fields that have been selected and organized for instructional purposes in general education.

Although the content of the social studies is similar to that of the social sciences, the methods of teaching are different because the purpose is different. The subject matter in social studies is simpler, less compartmentalized, and less logically organized. The methods of teaching social studies strive to utilize broader generalized interests of the pupils rather than the specialized interests that may later develop.

One area of life in which the teachers of the social studies seek to promote growth is that of social relationships and understandings. Civil rights, human relations, intercultural and interracial relations, and the like, are very lively topics in present-day society. The methods used in teaching subject matter related to such topics as these demand considerable skill. Obviously, this area cannot be wholly separated from the language arts. Nor can the social studies assume the whole of the responsibility for achieving growth in social development. They can merely give more emphasis to the problem. The methods of the social studies teacher will be selected to help pupils develop greater maturity in the socialized aspects of their behavior.

The affective factors involved in social development present one of the most difficult problems of method. Teachers and pupils alike have social attitudes, feelings, prejudices, and biases that they bring to school with them. Recognizing deep-seated predispositions among pupils, social studies teachers promote social interaction in the classroom that leads pupils to consider the bases of their opinions, beliefs, and prejudices and to understand and respect differences.

As in science, mathematics, and language arts, the inductive method is used increasingly in social studies instruction. The students discover for themselves answers to such questions as what something is, how it got that way, why it got that way, why it is important, what its current effects are, what its future effects may be. In this inductive method, in structuring the pupils' activities, the teacher may use as a base or goal the development of understandings of a broad social concept, thinking of a concept as a group of meanings that cluster around or belong to a social term. Such a concept might be democracy, nationalism, or rebellion, for example. A range of suggested methods and activities may be given the teacher in a course of study or curriculum outline.

In building a comprehension of a broad social concept, pupils may be directed to seek understandings related to various subconcepts—perhaps mercantilism, for example, as a step in the process of discovering what colonialism is and has been. Sometimes the concepts to be developed in a social studies program are organized in a sequential manner, building consecutively from kindergarten through the junior high school. Sometimes the geographical areas or historical or current events to be utilized in helping the students acquire the conceptual understandings are also suggested in the curriculum or course of study.

Social studies teachers have developed considerable skill in dealing with controversial problems. The technique is one of getting the pupils to understand both sides of a question and to make their own decisions. This teaches pupils to deal intelligently with controversial aspects of life. The teacher is free to express his bias, but purely as a matter of opinion.

Social studies teachers at all levels of education have many opportunities to use lifelike stituations. They make contact with issues in home life; study firsthand the operations of the police, fire, judicial, and other departments of local government; study the safety department programs and school board and municipal elections; participate in school government and other school activities; and hold mock political conventions. Study of such situations is combined with the study of the more formal kinds of subject matter. The two kinds of activities are complementary. Study of the causes of poverty, for example, may lead to a trip to several sections of the city where poverty is most prevalent, to the clubs, community organizations, settlement houses, and the like, that work with the poor. Pupils are carefully prepared for the trip in advance through the study of pertinent books and pamphlets and by discussions. After the trip a scheduled follow-up lesson is devoted to reviewing what was learned on the trip, to making conclusions and generalizations, and perhaps to applying the generalizations to other situations or problems.

As mentioned earlier, the problem of developing a logical sequence in the subject matter of the social studies is similar to the problem encountered by the language arts teachers, and the same generalizations apply. There is a trend in the school to integrate the subject matter of the social studies and language arts for the purposes of general education. The core program of the junior and senior high schools, which was described in Chapter 15, is an attempt to do this. The integrated approach, shown by the increased number of schools in which the curriculum includes integrated studies, interdisciplinary team teaching, and core programs, seems likely to continue. The movement now reaches from the first years of the elementary school through college.

Fine Arts

The purpose of the fine arts is to develop the pupil's sensitivity to, and appreciation of, what creative artists seek to express. The teacher of fine arts seeks to provide an environment appropriate to this end and to cultivate the powers of expression.

We have noted that the logically organized subject matter of mathematics is used in directing pupils to develop their powers to think and express their thoughts quantitatively. In marked contrast, when directing growth in the area of the fine arts, loosely organized, and sometimes unorganized, subject matter is used.

The trend among teachers of the fine arts at all levels of education is to stress direct participation as a means to enlarging the scope of the esthetic experiences of the pupils. Painting, singing, acting, and playing instruments can add a great deal to the pupils' understanding and appreciation of what the arts are about. Listening and observing, too, have their place, but overly emphasized they can dull the pupils' interest in the fine arts. They can have a superficial or even a negative effect.

Although the emphasis in the fine arts is on creativeness and participation, the element of the technical is not omitted. As the children work to improve their acting in the play, or to sing in unison, or to perfect the rendition of instrumental music, they, of course, consider with the teacher the technical problems involved. As they study the technical aspect of the art, however, it is not just to learn more about the art. Always the purpose of technical study is to develop a higher level of expression.

Esthetic responsiveness and expression are closely bound up with emotions. The teacher therefore takes into full account the personal nature of responsiveness and expression and their emotional foundation. Respect for personality should be high on the scale of values of the teacher of fine arts, and his methods and the complete learning environment should reflect this at all times. Children will not sing or paint or act if they are ashamed or embarrassed or fearful. Teachers of the fine arts, themselves conscious of the values that lie in the arts, tend to demonstrate what teaching is like when teaching is viewed as an art. They follow their own, perhaps untraditional, methods in creating conditions most productive of the kind of pupil growth they seek to achieve.

When teachers of other subjects imply that fine arts is a somewhat inferior or unnecessary field of study, it is usually because they do not understand the purposes of the teachers of fine arts. Persistent traditions associated with other fields of teaching tend to set fine arts apart. For example, if a teacher of fine arts attempted to give pupils numerical or letter grades in music or art appreciation, not only would it be impossible to evaluate a child's appreciation of music or of art, but it would damage the climate for advancing such appreciation by introducing competitiveness, desire to please the teacher, anxiety, and other undesirable attitudes. The moment a teacher of fine arts attempts to emulate the evaluation techniques of, say, the mathematics teacher, his effectiveness in achieving growth in fine arts starts to wane. Creativeness, free expression, and appreciation of the beautiful flourish only in a sympathetic atmosphere.

Summary

At all levels of education there is an increasing concern for improvement in the methods of effectively directing subject matter to desired ends. As Skinner points out, "human behavior is far too complex to be left to casual experience. . . ." In line with the overview purpose of this book, the overall trends in both general teaching methods and methods in specific fields are explored. Trends in teaching language arts, science, mathematics, social studies, and fine arts are given extended treatment because they are studied by all pupils—that is, they are the subjects that together ordinarily constitute the bases for general education.

The great breadth in teaching methods is caused in part by the complexity of the human organism and in part by the range in materials included in each subject field. Wherever possible, however, the inductive method of teaching is favored. It is believed that pupils will attain better understandings if learning situations are arranged so that the facts, principles, structures of the subjects studied are discovered through their own activities. It is believed that, if there is a general method applicable to teaching in all subject-matter fields, the inductive method comes closest to meeting the requirements. Nevertheless when used in specific fields, its applicability has to be decided in terms of each new unit of subject matter. Perhaps teachers can err by placing too much emphasis on any one teaching method, either deductive or inductive. Both have their places.

QUESTIONS

1. Why is it not appropriate to separate method from subject matter for purposes of analysis?
2. What purpose is served by an acquaintance with several methods of teaching in a given field?
3. For what reasons are teachers more likely to be effective with their teaching methods if they know the subject matter well?
4. What is remedial instruction? When should it be used?
5. What is meant by the inductive method of teaching?

PROJECTS

1. Analyze a recent publication of a subject-matter professional organization such as the National Council of Teachers of Mathematics or the

National Council of Teachers of English. List the suggestions made on methods of teaching. State your conclusions as to what experienced teachers think is of greatest significance.

2. Set forth what preparation is necessary for teachers who are to engage in team teaching.

3. Explain what challenging problems are encountered in any attempt to individualize instruction completely.

chapter
20
Instructional aids

Related to subject matter and methods of teaching are instructional aids, aids that help the teacher achieve the aims of the lesson or the unit of study. There has been a great increase in the variety and refinement of instructional aids in recent years. Some predict that even the chalkboard, oldest of the instructional aids, may disappear from classrooms of the future, to be replaced by the perhaps more effective overhead projector.

Certainly instructional aids help to bring teaching more closely in line with factors that psychologists say encourage effective learning, help instruction to capitalize on factors of attention and reinforcements to learning, and also help make possible a fuller recognition of wide divergencies in learning rates. Instructional aids, teacher and pupils agree, tend to make both teaching and learning more interesting. Every year shows an increase in their popularity and in confidence in their effectiveness.

The kinds of teaching aids available are numerous. One college textbook devoted 500 pages to describing audiovisual aids. Several manufacturing companies list hundreds of such items as long-playing records, filmstrips, tape recordings, and models. One company alone lists, for example, 52 long-playing records that reproduce Shakespearean plays as recorded by the most famous Shakespearean actors. Another company specializes in making records for the elementary schools that reconstruct history through dramatizations of such themes as the Pony Express, the California gold rush, and the building of the first transcontinental railroad. Each year more than 6500 sound-motion pictures are produced and adapted by several manufacturing companies for use in every grade and in almost every subject. Perhaps variety and quantity of instructional aids stem from a heightened recognition of the part played in effective learning by the senses, from an increasing knowledge of how perceptions are formed and of how perception and thought are related. The accepted assumption—that mental images result from sensations—reinforces the belief that variety in the stimulation of the senses in the classroom greatly enriches learning, and hence contributes to more reliable and mature thinking.

When teachers decide on the use of instructional aids, they are guided by the same considerations of purpose that guide all other decisions related to the stimulation and direction of learning. Some aids are designed to serve but a single purpose; a slide rule is used for computation; a lifelike model of the human heart is used to explain the design and physiological functioning of the heart. An overhead projector, on the other hand, is an instructional aid adaptable to many purposes. The discussion of instructional aids in this chapter is intended to acquaint the student with some that teachers use, to give an overview. Because of their great variety, the purposes that guide teachers in the selection and use of aids are omitted.

Books and Periodicals

Well-prepared teachers use textbooks and workbooks as valuable aids to teaching. They do not make the mistake of thinking that within the pages of the textbook they will find complete subject matter. They will not use the textbook and workbook as substitutes for their own knowledge or resourcefulness, but instead as a supplement, a guide, and a source of suggestions. In addition, they do not restrict themselves to one textbook but select one or more books, perhaps books geared to different reading abilities, as basic texts and several others for the classroom reference shelf. The pupils use the basic textbook for study and the others as supplementary reading.

Paperbacks are taking an increasingly important place on the classroom list of reading materials. Their colorful covers appeal to young readers, especially if they can be displayed on the kind of wire revolving rack that the salesmen have found so useful in the corner drugstore. Paperbacks are relatively inexpensive and are an effective answer to the problem of prohibitive costs in making a wide range of reading materials available. As Daniel Fader has pointed out in a.report on his work with delinquent youth, the paperback appeals to young people who have had only unpleasant experiences with the hardcover textbook or library books displayed on a shelf with only the dull title on the spine showing.[1] It is sometimes good to have a book that fits well into a hip pocket to be taken out for reading at any time. The tremendous range of titles in paperback provides the teacher with ample opportunity to appeal to the interests of the pupils as well as to find books appropriate to their individual ability and to further the aims of the course.

Newspapers and magazines are also a valuable aid on the classroom shelf. In some cases they are used as a core and lessons are prepared around them. Often they are supplementary, used for class work or for individual and committee work. Some city newspapers have "education editions" that contain material especially adapted to the classroom.

Frequently classes use a periodical prepared for boys and girls in school, perhaps *Junior Scholastic* in the upper elementary and junior high grades. Such a magazine has interesting material on current affairs, history, geography, arithmetic, social living, and science, together with exercises in reading, grammar, and vocabulary building.

How are textbooks selected? In approximately half of the states the local school district has jurisdiction over textbook selection. Usually a committee made up of teachers, supervisors, and administrators selects one or more books in a field or level. Unfortunately, under this plan there is no uniformity, so that children who move from one district to another may be handicapped because they have become used to different books. In the remaining half of the states, statutes require uniform textbooks throughout the state. In some of these states the state department or an authorized committee selects several books or

[1] Daniel Fader and Elton B. McNeil, *Hooked on Books*. New York: Berkley, 1968.

series of books for each subject, leaving the final choice from among these to the local district.

To aid in selecting textbooks, committees frequently use a checklist containing such items as authorship, date of publication, content, vocabulary, organization, suggested pupil activities, recommended teaching aids, illustrative material, format, and durability. No matter how high a particular book may rate on all the checklist items, however, the most important deciding factor will be how well it will contribute to the needs of the pupils who will use it. (As we have noted, it is in connection with adopting textbooks that pressure groups frequently try to use their influence to determine what students will or will not read and study.)

The textbooks today are far superior to those used even 50 years ago. In early America the hornbook, a paddle-shaped contrivance that hung from the pupil's neck, usually contained the Lord's Prayer and the alphabet. *The New England Primer* is an example of the small, morally slanted, compact textbook also used in colonial days. McGuffey's *Eclectic Readers* emphasized the Bible and morals by means of interesting stories. Until relatively recently, geography textbooks described countries merely by listing their boundaries, principal cities, rivers, mountains, and products; and history textbooks focused on dates, battles, and strictly political events without much attention to their implications.

Authors of today's textbooks determine content through experiment based on knowledge of child psychology. They attempt, as nearly as the pages of the book will permit, to enter the classroom and assist in the instruction. As with other teaching activities, the authors set up their goals and then draw on their knowledge and experience as teachers to meet the goals. The better present-day textbook is proficiently written, attractive, usable, and long-wearing. The improvement in appearance, format, durability, and illustrations has come about through research and advancement in publishing generally. The modern textbook is an invitation to learning.

Library and Library Materials

The typical elementary and secondary school contains a central library, often one of the most inviting places in the building. In larger schools the school library is administered by a trained teacher-librarian; in small schools a classroom teacher doubles as school librarian. The resources housed in the library for both pupils and teachers vary with the policies of administration. In some the resource materials are limited to books and graphic materials, whereas in others they include teaching aids such as films and records.

In general, school libraries are administered by trained individuals who fulfill a coordinating function and serve teachers and pupils in many ways. Supplementary materials flow from library to classroom and back again. Pupils use the library for round-table discussions, group study, individual reading, research, and study, and as a place to learn to locate and use such resource materials as indexes, reference books, bibliographies, catalogs, encyclopedias. Pupils have the opportunity to browse among many books. They are guided and encouraged to choose books in harmony with their individual interests and abilities.

Administrators, teachers, and librarians cooperate to make the library a rich center for many kinds of resources and educational activities. Wisely coordinated, the library and the teacher-librarian are indispensable adjuncts to effective classroom teaching, vital in wisely planned programs.

Audiovisual Materials

The human organism constructs images that are a consequence of seeing and hearing. Since one's perceptions are closely related to one's ability to think, learning through a wise use of audiovisual materials in the classroom may be of paramount importance to effective teaching. From the images constructed by the pupils on being exposed to wisely selected audiovisual material, understandings of the true nature of external objects and of spatial, social, and temporal relationships are expanded. Furthermore, this type of learning tends to be vivid and lasting. Perceptions resulting from effective audiovisual experiences are integrated by the human organism through some process the nature of which as yet is unknown. It is by some such reasoning as this that the wide use of audiovisual materials in American education has been justified.

In recent years, and particularly in the elementary schools, serious attention has been given to encouraging good habits of listening. Besides being an effective learning experience in general, good listening is precedent to effective speech. Skill in communication is considered closely related to habits of listening. Many audiovisual aids are designed to utilize fully the advantages of good listening.[2] The Shakespearean records and the recorded dramatized historical incidents mentioned earlier, for instance, are excellent examples of a kind of device that promotes understanding and appreciation while also encouraging habits of good listening.

The following overview of audiovisual aids frequently used by classroom teachers gives an idea of the great variety and educational potential of these aids. Teachers, guided by the purposes they have in mind, of course, use discrimination in selection of particular devices.

It has been suggested that the minimum equipment for each classroom include dark shades, permanent screen, tape recorder, overhead projector, maps, and a globe. If audiovisual aids are not easily accessible, teachers just do not have the time to round them up.

Films and Filmstrips

Four types of projection machines are at present used effectively in the classroom. The opaque projector needs no special material for projection, but will reflect on a screen the image of any picture, printed page, or flat object of suitable size. It is used successfully in projecting pictures of which there is only one copy and in projecting pages of pupils' written work for discussion and criticism by a whole class. To make maps or drawings, students may project the map or picture on a tag board, follow the outline with a felt pen, and later add details or colors.

Because the overhead projector has the special advantage of being used at the front of the room by a teacher who is facing the class, it has proved useful at practically all grade levels and in all subject areas. This type projects materials prepared on transparencies by the teacher, the pupils, or commercially. The teacher can mark or write on the transparency while it is being projected, and this action will show on the screen behind him. Maps used in this way are very effective.

The 16-mm film projector is widely used, and a large number of excellent sound films are available for use in all areas of the curriculum. Some of the films provide background or introduction, some add to appreciation or understanding. Many films are prepared for use in helping young people solve problems of getting along in school

[2] See section on listening, p. 437.

and in life, touching on such matters as study habits, personality, friendships, part-time jobs, and dating. Usually when a film is used in the classroom, some preparation should be made in advance, although some of the films, those related to personal and social problems, for instance, require little preparation because the motivation and introduction are included in them. Better films lead to discussion, criticism, and evaluation of their contribution by the class immediately after they have been seen.

Many large commercial organizations, such as Bell Telephone, Ford Motor, or American Oil, produce excellent educational films, sometimes as an outgrowth of a television program, and supply these without charge to schools as a part of their public relations programs.

At present most schools have available sound-motion equipment. In larger schools usually a teacher or a teacher-librarian or one who specializes in the use of sound-motion pictures serves as coordinator. Coordination is necessary partly because films and projectors are so expensive that their maintenance and use must be systematically provided for and partly because it is wise to have someone in the school who knows what films are available and takes responsibility for scheduling previews, obtaining the films, and returning them. For all teachers to know how to use such equipment as the movie film projector is highly desirable. Selected students in each class are often trained to be the operators.

The filmstrip projector has largely replaced the simple slide projector, although the instruments commonly used for filmstrips can also be used for slides. The filmstrip contains 25 to 100 frames, or still pictures, which are projected on a screen in sequence by manual operation of the projector. Some filmstrips are accompanied by tapes or records containing commentary on each frame. A great many filmstrips, both single and in series, are available. They are especially helpful with material that the class needs to have time to discuss as the projection proceeds. Filmstrips are less expensive than regular movie films, so a library of filmstrips related to the curriculum will often be assembled in the school and be readily available at any time. A color slide is like one frame in the filmstrip. Such slides may be prepared by the teacher or purchased from commercial outlets. An entire biology class may, for instance, use a color slide to see in a greatly enlarged picture what each could see under an individual microscope, and the teacher can call attention to the parts that are especially significant. In the geography class a three-dimensional color slide may show a stereoscopic, lifelike view of an entire mountain scene and focus the attention of the students on such features as the terracing of farms on the mountainsides. (Also, both filmstrips and slides may be used individually by means of small portable viewers.)

Recordings

The use of records has become an important part of teaching in recent years. In the language arts classroom, records serve as aids to understanding and appreciation, as enrichment, as supplementary material. Listening to literature read by professionals has proved valuable. In the music classes, by means of records students hear great works performed by outstanding artists. Dramatic readings of important episodes in history, a presentation of the music of a particular period, are the kinds of recording that bring color and a feeling of realness to the pages of the social studies textbook. Records are frequently used in the classroom, but they are also used for independent study, extra credit, or small-group activities. Records, like filmstrips, are often a part of the school's library collection. Sometimes the producers of the records supply text or workbook materials that the students may follow along with the sound.

The resourceful teacher will also find many uses for the tape recorder. Oral presentations of students may be recorded and later played back for student and teacher criticism. A panel discussion recorded in one class may be played in other classes. An address by a guest speaker in one class may be recorded and played to other classes. The teacher may record material that he or she wishes to use in several classes. The tape recorder may be stopped at any time for oral discussion or comment.

Many teachers feel that listening skills can be greatly improved through the use of the tape recorder. Students are asked to listen to recorded materials with a specific purpose in mind—listening for the main ideas, listening for supporting details, listening for "loaded" words, and the like.

From outside the classroom the sources of materials for tape recordings are unlimited. The best in radio and television programs can be brought into the classroom by means of the tape recorder. Public addresses and other performances of talented people of the community may be recorded for classroom use.

At present most prepared tapes are related to social studies and language arts. There are, however, tape recordings that make the new mathematics meaningful even to young pupils, their parents, or teachers of other subjects who may wish to know what the subject is about. Some state universities maintain lending libraries of tape recordings to encourage the use of tape recorders in the classroom. They issue catalogs of available recordings that include valuable hints on how teachers can profitably use the recordings. The National Education Association has an extensive tape-recording library located in the Audio-Visual Division of the University of Colorado. The great encouragement received by classroom teachers from agencies such as the NEA and the state universities attests to the confidence these agencies have in the educational value of tape recorders.

Television

For some years now the classroom teaching uses and potential uses of television have been explored and discussed. The actual use of TV in schools indicates that though it can improve the effectiveness of classroom teaching in all subject-matter fields, the most valuable results so far have been achieved in social studies, mathematics, and science. Extensive experimentation is now being carried out to discover the most advantageous ways of using the new medium.

Teachers utilize television in a number of ways, but the most common procedure is to tell pupils, sometimes by means of a bulletin board, about programs they wish them to see. Since programs are announced a week in advance, any teacher has at hand a listing of a great many programs, some of which are likely to include the kind of material he wants the pupils to see. When commercial programs are of special interest to schools, the sponsors make available carefully prepared printed materials that can be placed on the bulletin board. Often, after a TV projection of an educational program the material will be available on film for teacher use on a movie projector in the school.

Educational television, both open circuit and closed circuit, is an aid to direct classroom instruction. Open-circuit television refers to programs that originate outside the school system. These offer front-row seats to televised lessons by well-known professionals. Closed-circuit television has become an important adjunct in schools that can afford to install it. Here master teachers within the school broadcast to large audiences of students by means of receiving screens in various classrooms. The professional lecturer and the master teacher form "teams" with the regular classroom instructors. Lessons received either by open-circuit or closed-circuit television may be preserved on video tape and scheduled for use in the classroom at any appropriate time.

Televised lessons are organized in some places—in Chicago, for instance—in a so-called cluster plan. The closed-circuit televised lessons are designed and taught by superior teachers in the Chicago public schools and are televised daily into the classrooms of approximately 30,000 children through the cluster plan, which links a studio school in a circuit with four or more adjacent schools by means of a coaxial cable. Televised teaching in five such clusters in Chicago located in areas of cultural disadvantage adapts the curriculum to the specific educational needs of the children in each cluster. In the cluster plan all television teachers are also classroom teachers. Since the cluster links neighboring schools together, the teachers have a real understanding of the educational needs of the children to whom the lessons are telecast.

Experimentation with television as a medium of classroom instruction continues throughout the country. At present the trend is for the schools to obtain from both commercial and educational television stations special tapes or recordings that can be transmitted on the school's own closed-circuit equipment in any desired way or at any time. The effectiveness of television instruction, however, has not yet been adequately assessed, either from the educational or the relative-cost standpoint. All that can be said with certainty is that it is an innovation that will receive increasing emphasis.

The Language Laboratory

The language laboratory now found in many high schools is an instructional aid to foreign-language teachers who stress building conversational skills. The equipment in the language laboratory enables pupils to listen to the spoken word, to repeat it in return, and then listen again to their own pronunciation, thus comparing their own speech with that of the native.

It is general procedure to have the lessons taped and for all the pupils to listen to the same materials through individually provided earphones. The teacher also can join in with explanations. Each pupil may imitate what he has heard and have his own voice recorded. He may then play his version back, judge his response, then repeat the procedure until he is satisfied. As the reader probably knows, tapes can easily be erased and used over again many times. The language laboratory permits each pupil to proceed on his own and to practice building conversational skills in accordance with his own needs.

Pictures and Charts

For centuries flat pictures have been the means of effectively conveying a message, expressing an idea, portraying an event, reproducing the historical likenesses of persons and scenes. Pictographs in ancient caves and the large circulation of modern pictorial magazines attest to the everlasting appeal of flat pictures. Quite naturally, classroom teachers utilize all the advantages of their universal appeal.

Usually teachers in subject-matter areas such as geography, social studies, history, literature, and science have a continuous but changing display of appropriate pictures in the classroom. Many such pictures are attractive, accurate in detail, and instructionally sound. The pupils know what Ann Hathaway's cottage or the Wright brothers' airplane looks like, and the same holds true of many historical figures and places and scenes in the world. The effective use of color in modern photography adds to the vividness of the pictures. In addition to real pictures, there is a vast array of pictures that are wholly imaginative. An ancient battle, the sorrows of a displaced people, illustrations of literary themes are often shown in artists' imaginative drawings.

Some publishers make available to teachers charts that are excellent teaching aids. Such charts show, for instance, historical time lines for world history, how to use the dictionary, or the evolution of the English language. Charts related to various aspects of science tend to be valuable instructional aids. Book jackets make a colorful and stimulating bulletin board. Unfortunately, many other types of free material have been discontinued either temporarily or permanently because of higher operating expenses and postal rates.

An effective bulletin board display should be planned with and by the students. In fact, the best bulletin board display exhibits the students' own work—their writing, drawing, charting, painting.

Maps and Globes

Maps and globes are a part of the everyday equipment of elementary and many high school classrooms. They are made in attractive, contrasting colors and are constructed so as to be readily accessible for classroom use and easy to read. They are accurately drawn to scale and can conveniently be used for such activities as locating places, measuring distances, computing areas, tracing great-circle air routes, ocean currents, and wind systems, or showing the number and position of heavenly bodies or the division of the country in the Civil War.

Often maps and globes are so constructed that they may be marked on with water-soluble felt pens and easily washed off. Manufacturers of school maps and globes recognize the principle of readiness through gradation of their product in detail and complexity. They make materials for younger children that show fewer details and acquaint the child with only basic map symbols. For older pupils all standard map symbols are used for details such as elevation, rivers, falls, cities, railways. Often small desk globes give the pupil a chance to handle the globe individually, to experiment, explore, and follow directions. Wall maps may be printed with few details and supplemented by transparent overlays that add the kind of details the teacher desires—population, resources, battlefields, or something else.

The art of map making for educational purposes has been highly developed by a number of manufacturers who combine their know-how in the manufacture of maps with the knowledge and skill of professional cartographers and educational specialists. Through cooperative efforts a great variety of maps is available to serve in such special subject-matter areas as history, economics, and literature, as well as almost any particular branch of geography from world climate to geological evolution.

Models

Models, among the oldest of instructional aids, are still considered by teachers to be among the most helpful. Models appeal to all ages; children have played with them from infancy in the form of toys; adults flock to view and manipulate them in museums of science and industry, where they are used on an elaborate scale to elucidate a wide range of subjects. The gyroscope and pendulum, for instance, are models that reveal the rotation of the earth.

Models are designed for use in elementary and secondary schools to aid in teaching in almost every subject-matter field and to serve a wide variety of purposes. True models are manufactured on an accurate scale and usually are three-dimensional representations of some principle, fact, or idea. An exact replica, for example, of an automobile or of any of its working parts is available to high school teachers of auto mechanics to make clear their or the text's explanations. A model may illustrate how the human heart functions or how the blood circulates in the body. With a skillfully designed model a pupil virtually "sees" the explanations.

Manufacturers often use true models (including full-sized mockups) to make clearer certain kinds of explanations. Sometimes they make models that utilize intentional exaggerations, as, for example, in size, color, or transparency. Thus in the Chicago Museum of Science and Industry a viewer can stand inside a modified model of the human heart and study each working part at leisure. Another kind of modified model, the best examples of which are in museums, is the diorama. It consists of a combination of figures, background pictures, actual specimens, and symbolic materials, which, with the ingenious use of direct and indirect lighting, make a scene appear almost real.

In larger cities classroom teachers may supplement their own use of models with field trips to museums where skilled lecturers instruct the pupils on a great variety of subjects.

Models available in the schools usually are readily accessible, easily assembled and disassembled, and therefore conveniently adaptable to any logical teaching plan.

Tachistoscope

The tachistoscope is a device for projecting words, phrases, sentences, number combinations, formulas, and the like, for short durations—as low as 0.01 second. The image is either reproduced on a small viewing screen or flashed as a lantern slide on a larger screen. Viewers are warned when the shutter is about to be tripped; they look at the screen and then reproduce what they have seen. As a rule, the device is used for remedial work, to speed up the reading of slow readers or to increase the rate and accuracy of computational skills.

Programed Learning

Programed learning is a different kind of instructional aid. Learning is achieved by using subject-matter materials that permit an individual pupil to study efficiently without the continuous help of a teacher and independent of membership in a study group. To enable a pupil to learn independently, the subject matter to be learned is broken up into a series of small, psychologically related segments that are logically arranged in steps. With the aid of a teaching device, such as those described in the following pages of this chapter, pupils proceed independently, at their own rate, through each of the steps.

Since in programed learning pupils learn at a rate commensurate with their ability, individual differences in learning rates are fully recognized, even though, theoretically, all pupils will eventually achieve at least a minimum standard of mastery. Programed learning is more satisfying to pupils than learning through traditional processes because the results are immediately known to them. Since the programed learning activity is an individual one, pupils who learn slowly do not feel the sting of competitive comparisons that make them feel inferior. Finally, programed learning utilizes the advantages of motivation. As one psychologist says:

> Human behavior is remarkably influenced by small results. Describing something with the right word is often reinforcing. Other simple reinforcers are to be found in the clarification of a puzzlement or simply in moving forward after completing one stage of activity.[3]

The proponents of programed learning in America's schools—a rapidly growing number—believe that it is an important step to correcting past omissions. Why, say the educational psychologists, do schools put forth such prodigious efforts to gain understanding of pupils, to discover their more urgent needs, and then give so little attention to their individual needs? Why should teachers learn about the psychological bases of education and then teach as though such bases did not really exist? If these omissions have been due to the lack of a practical method, then, it is contended, programed learning will contribute to eliminating that lack.

Two difficult problems in programed learning are related to, first, selecting the kinds of material that can best be taught by this method, and, second, arranging these materials into a series of steps that are reasonable and are psychologically related. Obviously, not all kinds of subject matter can be taught by the programed method. The selection must be carefully made. It is only by actual experiment with pupils that the soundness of the steps in a program can be evaluated. Many attempts are now being made to select suitable subject matter and to program it. Although the method is relatively new, the results have been most promising.

---

[3] B. F. Skinner, "Teaching Machines," *Scientific American,* 205 (No. 5): 97, November, 1961.

Once the difficult tasks of programing are completed—the materials are selected and the logical steps for learning devised—the question remains: How shall the materials be presented to the pupil?[4] Three means of automated instruction are the programed textbook, the teaching machine, and the electronic learning laboratory.

Programed Textbooks

The programed textbook is an incomplete textbook that pupils complete by filling in key sentences, words, or numbers in so-called frames. They check their own answers by comparing them with the correct answers given elsewhere in the book, usually on the succeeding page, where they also find their next frame. Many attempts are being made currently in universities and in lower schools to produce improved automated textbooks. This calls for extensive tryouts of the materials and careful study of the results to refine the materials and improve the sequence.

A number of programed textbooks have been published for use in the schools. The books cover a wide range of subjects. Each presents the basic skills and information to be learned and allows pupils to proceed at their own rate, evaluate their own progress, and correct their own weaknesses.

Teaching Machines

With teaching machines, instead of marking an answer in a frame in a book, pupils respond to the programed subject matter by making the response on a machine that indicates immediately whether they have chosen the correct answer. They cannot proceed to the next step until a correct response is registered to the current one. A right response is always a prerequisite to the next task. Like the programed textbook, the value of teaching machines depends on skill in selecting the subject matter and in arranging it in a logical series of steps. Like experiments with programed textbooks, experiments with teaching machines are being conducted in many schools, and there is considerable confidence that many kinds of learning can be achieved through their proper use. In fact, many manufacturing concerns have planned

[4] See, for example, the explanation of difficulties encountered by an astute book editor in "An Adventure in Programing Literature," *The English Journal,* 52 (No. 9): 659–673, December, 1963.

ambitious expansions and are building newer and better teaching machines.

Research has given us no detailed information about the interactions of students with teaching machines and with their content materials. As we have pointed out in connnection with any kind of programed learning, the practical value depends on the effectiveness of content materials. At present, only a few instructional programs have been adequately developed through a series of empirical trials and revisions. Most of the well-developed programs today are short sequences prepared for research purposes. Also, we do not have verified information about the effect of individualized instruction on children of varying abilities. For instance, a very bright child may be as far along in his or her studies as another child several years older; the student's scholastic peer group may thus be quite different from his or her social peer group. Is it possible that the sociological and psychological effects could be harmful to the students?

Electronic Learning Laboratories

The electronic learning laboratory is an exciting innovation in programed learning. The learning laboratory is a kind of wired classroom. Usually 30 or more students are seated in booths, each containing a tape recorder, earphones, a microphone, and master tapes. The students can play and respond to master-tape lessons in English—such areas as grammar, phonetics, vocabulary, remedial speech—and in foreign languages. From a master console, the teacher can direct the tape or hold a two-way conversation with one student or talk to all the students. In this technique the teacher is not replaced by machines; his or her capabilities are multiplied, and individual differences are handled adroitly.

Computers

It is easy to appreciate the potential of the computer in teaching high school mathematics students something about programing and computer operation and use, as well as in preparing them to use the device in more advanced mathematics work. The computer also has potentials in other areas of education, but many of these are highly technical and many others require more research before they will become generally applicable. Computers can definitely be helpful with more general school functions, such as counseling, relating census to budget, and distributing teacher loads.

The expense involved in installing computers has prevented their widespread use. For this reason and because the machines are constantly being changed and improved, even when they are used in the classroom or administrative office, they are often rented rather than purchased. In the final analysis, present trends indicate that the cost of computers will decrease as their practical educational functions increase; thus their use is likely to become general within the next few years.

Resource Center

As a facility particularly important for independent study as a part of team teaching, many schools are placing increasing importance on an area known variously as a resource center, an instructional materials center, a learning center, or something else. The center is usually located near the library and is, in a way, an extension of the library except that, in addition to the facilities of a regular library, the resource center also provides equipment for a kind of laboratory experience—individual work spaces and areas for individual and group activity.

The resource center contains books, magazines, pamphlets, pictures, maps, films, filmstrips, recordings, tapes, slides—all the learning aids and reference materials the school owns. Those items not located in the resource center are cataloged, and their school location is indicated.

The center is typically divided into three sections: a section provided with carrels for quiet reading, study, pursuing programed lessons; a section equipped for the use of various audiovisual materials and such aids as typewriters and office machines; a section for pupil-teacher or small-group discussion and conference. A specially trained personnel member is in charge of the resource center, and often he or she is assisted by paraprofessionals and other aides.

Pupils ordinarily go to the resource center to pursue independent study, sometimes for small-group study, in terms of their individual needs or special interests. As independent study is increasingly emphasized, the use of the resource center will likewise be increased. In time standard equipment will probably include carrels equipped with individual television screens; earphones and facilities for dialing for videotape presentations and demonstrations; a signal device for notifying teachers when assistance is needed; tapes of lectures, lessons, speeches.

Aids Requiring Organizational Modifications

Ability grouping, team teaching, and providing opportunity rooms are also ways of making instructional aids available to teachers. These differ from audiovisual aids and programed teaching in part because they require organizational modifications.

Ability Grouping

The prevailing pattern of grouping children in America's schools is by age-grade. Ordinarily, children enter the kindergarten at age 5, then advance together from grade to grade, graduating from the high school at about 18 years of age. Ability grouping refers to classifying and regrouping pupils of a given age-grade for teaching purposes. This is usually done more or less in terms of ability to learn, in terms of relative intelligence.

Ability grouping in the lower grades usually involves three, four, or five groups within one classroom. These groups may work at different rates on reading, spelling, and mathematics. The teacher works with one group while the others proceed with their individual activities. In the intermediate grades practices may vary from school to school and from subject to subject within the same school. For instance, classification and grouping may be used in mathematics and science but not in social studies or English.

For classification purposes within a grade level, intelligence scores are usually used for younger pupils. Achievement test scores, together with earlier measures of intelligence, are generally the bases for classifying older pupils, those above elementary school age.

No set pattern has been followed in the high schools in ability grouping. In some large high schools pupils who rank high on achievement tests are assigned to advanced placement. For them the subject matter studied is more advanced and the rate of progress is stepped up. College-level subject matter may be studied and college credit given for work in the last two years of high school. A second-level group may consist of the moderately gifted, who are assigned to courses, perhaps called "honor" courses, which are also advanced, both in subject matter studied and in rate of progress, but less so than the advanced-placement classes. The third level, which may comprise as many as two-thirds of the pupils of a given grade in high school, is more conventional in curriculum and methods of teaching. The lowest group is the smallest, and for this group the studies are largely limited to basic skills and vocational subjects.

It appears that, in general, the American people look with favor upon ability grouping in the schools when it is done to meet the educational needs of pupils at the extremes—those at very high ability levels and those at very low ability levels. The attitude toward the practice for pupils between these extremes is not clear. Some teachers say they find that ability grouping makes teaching easier and more challenging, and that it enables them to depart from teaching all the pupils the same kind of subject matter and judging them by the same standards. At the same time, teachers generally recognize that the practice has unmistakable disadvantages, which, up to the present, schools have been unable to eliminate. In larger high schools, teachers and administrators have generally believed that ability grouping encourages a higher degree of achievement; in these schools, therefore, the practice has largely been taken for granted. Currently, however, community groups are challenging ability grouping, and in some high schools the number of different graduated groups has been reduced.

Up to now research has not provided evidence that ability grouping is educationally more productive than heterogeneous grouping. Certain questions remain unanswered. What are the effects of the practice on the social attitudes of the pupils? of their parents? Will those labeled inferior have such a poor self-image that they will be defeated to start with? Will they come to dislike those considered superior, to hate school, to build up a personal protection against teachers? Will those labeled superior become smug? How do parents feel about having their children labeled slow learners, or fast learners? Might the lowest group consist mainly of children from disadvantaged homes who feel they are being degraded by the school? Are the criteria used in labeling the students infallible? Will teachers lessen their efforts to adapt subject matter and methods of teaching to the needs of individual pupils in an ability group? Is such a group really homogeneous? Will every group have some who, relatively, are slow learners? These are only a few of the many difficult questions related to ability grouping to which we do not at present have sound answers based on research. Questions of this kind need to be answered in any evaluation of ability grouping as an instructional aid. Perhaps the only valid conclusion we can draw from long experience with ability grouping is that it has been proved to have a number of worthwhile advantages but has not come even close to being the final answer to the problem of recognizing individual differences. The schools continue to experiment with and search for other answers.

Team Teaching

Team teaching is a currently popular instructional aid that, at least in some forms, calls for some basic organizational and structural modifications. Some features of team teaching are not entirely new; we have had some of them in some form for a long time. Now, however, under a team teaching organization, sharing of teacher resources in terms of talent and interest, cooperative planning, and flexible grouping are not a casual part of interteacher relations; they are definitely and specifically provided for and their continuity is guaranteed.

There are many different ideas of exactly what team teaching is and how it should operate. In the universities a general plan of team teaching has been followed for some time. There it has meant having a number of teachers, each with a different but related specialty, teach certain broad, basic, or overview courses as a team. In some cases a similar organization is followed in team teaching in the junior and senior high schools. Another plan is to have the teaching team comprised of a group of teachers in one field—say, high school English—organize for and share the responsibility for high school English instruction for a specific group of students. Still another plan is to have the team organized in terms of a grade level and include, say, all seventh-grade teachers of specified fields—perhaps mathematics, science, language arts, and social studies. There are numerous variations to all of these plans.

Experience seems to indicate that team teaching is a profitable way to use teacher resources. Teachers on a team have the opportunity to specialize when they plan units, develop materials, or conduct large-group instruction. This specialty will be decided in the light of interests and talents, and personal choice as worked out cooperatively by the teaching team. It is important to remember, however, that the team teacher is also informed about what is going on in all the areas included in the team and is prepared to share in small-group and special-help activities in all team areas. He or she is alert to and capitalizes on all opportunities for worthwhile interdisciplinary integration. It seems reasonable to conclude that added incentive and increased satisfactions are among the rewards of the successful team teacher.

From the pupil's point of view, there are also potential advantages. It is expected that the pupil will have increased intellectual stimulation as a result of contact with several teacher personalities instead of one. With learning experiences directed and stimulated through team teaching, the pupil has an enhanced opportunity to develop skills in self-direction, perhaps partly through large-group instruction, but also, however, through the considerable advantages of individual direction in small groups.

Flexibility in grouping and time allotments are among the essentials of team teaching. The team determines the time and grouping in terms of the particular learning experience. The pattern followed in a high school in Decatur, Illinois, is somewhat typical of a team devoted to English on the secondary school level: 20 percent of a week's time spent in large-group lectures (held two or three times a week); 50 percent of the time spent in small-group classes (held on days alternate to lecture days); and 30 percent of the time given to independent study (arranged according to the individual student's schedule). This kind of flexible schedule eliminates the need for a teacher to make a boring repetition of instruction. Time saved by large-group presentations is utilized for individual conferences with pupils, for team planning, and for preparation of quality lectures.

Of special importance to the success of team teaching are adequate help from teacher aides and paraprofessionals and the provision of enough time in the team teachers' schedules to allow for team planning.

Many new schools and remodeled buildings incorporate architectural features adapted to team teaching, especially movable partitions for classes of various sizes. The instructional aids we have described as audiovisual aids are an important part of team teaching. For large-group instruction a microphone, an overhead projector, and a large screen are standard equipment. Other items such as an opaque projector, a record player, and film and filmstrip projectors should be readily available. Programed instruction, including electronic devices, will probably become a regular part of the team teaching of the future.

Summary

Large sums of money are being spent on instructional aids to help teachers, make classroom teaching more rewarding, and encourage more effective and more significant learning. Instructional aids do not lighten the load of classroom teachers although they do help teachers to teach more effectively. Instructional aids emphasize the responsibilities of classroom teachers to adapt to methodological change. The traditional pattern of teaching was face-to-face verbal presentation and response. Today new media of communication require of the teacher additional specialization and extra preparation, which require extra time and energy. Instructional aids are not contrivances that lessen the work teachers do. Other ways must be found to accomplish this.

QUESTIONS

1. What are some of the factors that must be considered by a classroom teacher in making a selection of teaching aids?
2. In what ways do teaching aids add to the direct experiences of the pupils?
3. What are some of the teaching advantages of mock-ups?
4. What are the advantages of programed learning? What are the possible dangers?
5. Which do you consider to be the better teaching device—programed textbook or teaching machine? Explain why.
6. To what extent do you believe that teaching methods will be changed by the introduction of automated learning materials in the classroom?
7. a. What, in your opinion, are the disadvantages of the statewide adopted uniform textbook policy?
   b. What causes the statewide adopted textbook policy to linger on?

PROJECTS

1. After reading a textbook on audiovisual aids, write some of your conclusions about their uses in the classroom.
2. List the skills you feel you must develop while training to be a teacher in order to use teaching aids effectively.

3. Examine a programed learning textbook. Write your evaluation of the book and of this approach to teaching.
4. Write some principal conclusions to be drawn from your study of the analyses of the 20 specialists writing in the *Phi Delta Kappan* on programed instruction. (See readings at the end of this unit.)
5. Examine a teaching machine. Write what you conceive to be the advantages of teaching machines over other aids.
6. Some elementary schools are experimenting with nongraded rooms. Explain how this kind of grouping is achieved. Explain the advantages over ability grouping.
7. Write an evaluation of team teaching in terms of your own experience with team teaching or in terms of an interview with a teacher doing team teaching or a student in a team teaching situation.

chapter

21

A look to the future

The principal aim of this book has been to describe what the American people have done to provide adequate education for all citizens and particularly for those who attend the schools. Trends in development have been noted, and in some instances future trends have been indicated. Selection of aspects of education to be included was made in the light of two critiera: the material chosen should contribute to an *overview* and should serve as an *introduction* to American education, especially for the reader getting his first view of American education. For some readers this book may be a terminal point. For others— students who have decided to enter teaching or who, for various reasons, wish to explore professional education further—the following brief view of some more specialized fields in education may be helpful. We have in mind here the freshman or sophomore—the student who has a few years of undergraduate work to do before entering teaching.

As described in our discussion of how the teacher qualifies, college programs for teacher preparation are made up of three parts. One is the general education, the liberal education, the common cultural knowledge and understandings expected of all college graduates. Another is specialized education. This includes work specifically selected to contribute to a specialized field of teaching. If the subject for specialized study is one that is included in the general education of all students, the courses pursued are more advanced than those required of all students. The third is devoted to professional training. It is to this third part that we now turn our attention.

Professional Study

Professional education differs from other areas of study in three general ways. First, the subject matter is professional in nature. The aim is definitely vocational. It is assumed that the student has chosen teaching as his future vocation, as his chief means of earning a living. Second, the content of specialized methods courses in which the student learns to teach in his field of choice is not ordered on the principle of gradually advancing difficulty in the same degree as is content in such fields as mathematics, physics, a language, or history. For example, a course dealing with the teaching of the new mathematics may use some simple mathematical materials that were learned by teachers to be long ago but that they must now relearn with the new approach. They may also have to learn some mathematical concepts that are new to them. In the course in the teaching of physics in high school there is also a new physics: the whole field of physics, or any part of it, whether it is advanced or not, may be drawn on for illustrative material. The main objective is to develop skill in teaching the physics that is modern. The assumption is that students already have a good basic understanding of the subject they are going to teach, but that they will continue to learn more about it.

The third difference lies in the backgrounds of the professors of education in the college or university. In addition to their college work, which includes advanced training in professional education, they have had considerable practical school-teaching experience on the elementary and secondary levels. Their principal function is to help the teacher in preparing to become a *successful* teacher.

Aims of Professional Study

The all-inclusive aim of the professional program is to develop competent and interested teachers. Professional study is not always fully understood. Among students in professional education courses it is often possible to identify three quite different attitudes toward the work. There are, for instance, students who think the work in professional courses, with the possible exception of student teaching, is abstract, theoretical, and quite unnecessary as preparation for a teaching career. They think that native intelligence, common sense, will provide adequate support when they get into the teaching world. They think that they can guess about the things they have not studied and do not know about, that they can choose among alternatives after some trial and error in the classroom. In other words, they expect to get professional training through experience in the classroom—obviously at the expense of the pupils.

Then there are the students who expect the professional courses to do so much by way of preparation that all they, as beginning teachers, will need to do is to apply some rule-of-thumb method learned in college. They expect the experts who teach them to give specific solutions that can be applied to any difficult discipline case or to the selection of techniques in any particular learning situation. Of course such students are destined for disappointment when they discover there are no ready-made answers. They will then tend to deny the value of any and all professional study, and perhaps even lose interest in teaching.

A third attitude is characteristic of students who are not willing to begin teaching directed by caprice and depending on trial and error, and who are not willing to try to accumulate a collection of routine procedures to use in teaching. Courses in professional education are designed to meet the needs of such students, to help them improve their understanding of all aspects of teaching, to become intelligent about the problems of education, so that they can become effective teachers.

Such understandings may be expected to reduce the number and seriousness of the errors that beset inexperienced teachers. The background of professional study may be expected also to add to the satisfactions of teaching. It is a common observation that, on the whole, no people are more seriously devoted to their work than teachers. The teacher who tends to be most devoted, to get the most gratification from teaching, is the one who understands the students, the materials, the aims—and all the other aspects of the complete educational picture. Courses in professional education are designed to build the understandings and insights that will enable teachers from the beginning to be intelligent, fully informed members of the education profession, ready to play a role in whatever is required to discharge their obligations with professional skill.

Perhaps a part of the satisfaction in teaching comes from the kind of creativeness and independence that a teacher with a well-founded background in professional education enjoys. Teachers with confidence and knowledge will have the incentive to use their own initiative. The textbook and the course of study are their tools and aids; they know how to utilize them on their own terms. In earlier days even the daily topics of classroom work were selected for teachers, and pages to be covered each day were indicated by overseeing authorities. Now the well-trained teacher decides, within limits, what subject matter pupils will study, how much ground they will cover, how work will be coordinated with that of his or her colleagues, and what relationships with parents will be. In general, the teacher enjoys the privilege of deciding how to advance the achievement of the aims he or she selects.

Professional study is also expected to help teachers become prepared to use their influence effectively—not only as leaders in the classroom, but as active members of the professional group and also as enlightened citizens. This does not necessarily imply holding elective offices, making speeches, or writing articles. These may be included, but not all teachers exercise their influence in these ways. The influence may come through activities that are individual, on a rather personal plane, and dedicated to long-term progress in education. People in the United States have all kinds of ideas for the improvement of education—some wise, some foolish, some constructive, some selfish. American schools are not all they should be, as has been made obvious in many of the discussions in earlier chapters. They fall short of what the teaching profession and the American people would like them to be. Many old educational traditions are outmoded. Methods of taxation need revising. The organization of schools needs overhauling. The curriculum needs reconstructing. Methods of teaching require improvement. Some colleges and universities have flagrantly neglected their most important function, training education leaders. Well-educated members of the teaching profession, though they may not dominate the future trends in American education, certainly must furnish some of the significant insights to help the American public make decisions about problems related to education.

The aims of professional study in education for the undergraduate are usually implemented through four main types of courses: foundation courses; specialized courses, including such areas as history of education, philosophy of education, and human development; student teaching; and specialized courses designed for advanced study.

Foundation Courses

All the beginning courses in any phase of professional education are foundational in character. This means that they provide an introduction to a particular field. They open the door to more advanced study in the area. The undergraduate student will study what deliberate education in America is about, will have "foundation" courses in philosophy of education and in child growth and development, for instance. In each of these areas, work advanced beyond the semiprofessional level will be offered to the undergraduate who is specializing in a professional area and to the graduate student who is doing work on a higher level. They differ from the more highly specialized courses, devoted to such topics as taxation, school law, school buildings, educational statistics, advanced child development, school supervision, and school administration, that are designed for experienced teachers.

Colleges and universities vary in their requirements of study in foundation courses. The foundational fields—education in America, history of education, philosophy of education, educational sociology, psychology of human development, methods of teaching, and student teaching—will, however, at sometime and in some form be part of any program of professional preparation. In general, students will take at least the beginning course in these areas.

In some schools the courses named History of Education, Philosophy of Education, and Human Development or Educational Psychology, together with an Introduction to Education in America (such as the course for which this book is designed), are combined in a series of units each lasting for a semester and known as Foundations of Education. Usually such an integrated course is taught by a teaching team of specialists. It uses appropriate materials from such sources as social psychology, sociology, political science, and anthropology. The integrated course has proved a successful base for more specialized professional study.

Specialized Courses

In addition to so-called foundation courses in education—either basic, unified courses or more or less specialized beginning courses—undergraduate professional education offers beginning and advanced study in such fields as history of education, philosophy of education, and child development or educational psychology. Since this book itself illustrates the nature of the subject matter in the first course in professional education, Education in America, we need not further discuss the nature of that course.

I. HISTORY OF EDUCATION

In some teacher education programs a foundation course in the history of education is taught as a separate course. In others the historical aspects of some phase of education are included in the separate course devoted to that phase of education. If reading is studied, for instance, the student may begin with material related to the historical development of our present practices in teaching reading. Either kind of course, if taught by an able teacher, may achieve the desired understandings.

The general purpose in studying history of education is to make clear that the education of one generation is influenced by the education of the generation that preceded it. The student learns that it is profitable to study the thinking and practices of able educators throughout history and realizes that the key to what comes after is often found in what went before.

An eminent historian says:

On every hand the past controls us, for the most part unconsciously, and without protest on our part. We are in the main its willing adherents. The imagination of the most radically minded cannot transcend any great part of the ideas and customs transmitted to him. When once we grasp this truth we shall, according to our mood, humbly congratulate ourselves that, poor pygmies that we are, we are permitted to stand on the giant's shoulders and enjoy an outlook that would be quite hidden from us if we had to trust to our own short legs; or we may resentfully chafe at our bonds and, like Prometheus, vainly strive to wrest ourselves from the rock of the past in our eagerness to bring relief to the suffering of men. . . . Whether we are tempted to curse the past as a sort of chronic disease, or bless it as the giver of all good things, we are inevitably its offspring; it makes us its own long before we know enough to defend ourselves. It is almost all that we have, and to understand it is to understand ourselves, our possibilities of achievement, our frustrations and perplexities.[1]

Education is a fundamental influence in the development of all civilizations, and the continuity in the development of education is a fundamental historical fact. Citizens of today, for instance, hear

---

[1] James Harvey Robinson, *The Ordeal of Civilization*. New York: Harper & Row, 1926, pp. 3–4.

much about the educational programs of the national government, the programs of expediency, sometimes suddenly put into operation without any forward-looking planning. Yet this is not a new goverment attitude. The Morrill Act of 1862 was a crash program, as was the Smith-Hughes Act of 1917. Numerous other examples could be cited. The old traditions, like tenacious bulldogs, tend to hang on long after reason tells us to let go. The history of education indicates that the traditions of the past will only be changed after enlightenment is sufficiently widespread to make acceptable the fact that there are other and more efficacious ways of solving educational problems.

Study of the history of education can easily be dull unless attention is focused on the future of education as it is understood in the light of the past. The history of education points to what education in the United States may become, as well as to what it has been. Knowledge and interpretation of the history of education can throw light on difficult educational problems and bring encouragement to those who might, without this understanding, be completely discouraged. A study of the history of education can do a great deal to improve our understanding of present education and to accent the challenge ahead.

From a historical perspective we get a notion of the relationship between an educational event, situation, or problem and certain other social events, situations, or problems. Further, we see the relationship between the educational events, situations, or problems and the whole of the American educational scene. By studying the history of education or some aspect of it, we get a picture of the relative place of education in the present scheme of social life in the United States.

2. PHILOSOPHY OF EDUCATION

The philosophy of education is a comprehensive, critical evalution of the principles that underlie the practices in education in the United States. When organized into a system, these principles serve as a guide to intelligent practice. The study of educational philosophy helps each of us to formulate a consistent and comprehensive viewpoint toward education so that we may know why we do what we do and so that we may be able to give reasons for all that we do and be willing to examine our practices critically in order to assure ourselves that our practices are well founded. In other words, the philosophy of education is studied for the purpose of helping us clarify our own educational viewpoints.

The study not only will help the student formulate a comprehensive viewpoint toward education and educational practices but will also help him resolve within his own mind the conflicts that exist between the varied viewpoints Americans hold toward education. Some of the conflicts are rather troublesome to beginning students in education and, as they begin teaching, may be a source of worry. The conflicts exist not only among the citizens of a community but also among the members of the educational profession. Sometimes the sharpest critics of educational viewpoints and classroom practices are themselves teachers. At times the editors of popular, influential magazines and newspapers develop a philosophy of education for their publications and attempt to sway the American people to accept their views. These views are expressed with a positiveness and persistency that attract the attention of the public but that may disturb many classroom teachers whose fundamental views toward education are in direct conflict. Does a study of philosophy help resolve such conflicts?

After all, in the last two centuries the human race seems to have made little progress either in improving the quality of human relations or in working out universally accepted and generally effective ways of resolving conflicting social viewpoints. We must accept the fact that conflicts in viewpoints on almost every social issue exist. These a single individual cannot resolve. What the individual can do, however, is to resolve his or her own conflicting viewpoints. A philosophy of education can then be formulated that is both justifiable in the light of what the person knows and defensible in terms of its consequences.

There are three steps used by educational philosophers in arriving at judgments about what is the best educational theory and practice. The first is the establishment of a standard of values. Educational philosophers place a higher value on the path of action they follow than on the one they do not follow. They direct their actions in terms of widely accepted basic values such as democracy, morality, and so on. We constantly engage in selecting values to guide our action in everyday life. The process of establishing values and of evaluating education in terms of those values is no different in the school than outside, except perhaps that we formalize the process to a greater extent in the schools.

The second step involves a critical and methodical examination of the assumptions of each educational practice and an evaluation of these assumptions in terms of our chosen standards of value. What assumptions underlie using coercion? administering standardized tests to all pupils of a particular grade? giving marks to pupils? giving examinations? unionizing teachers? requiring demonstrational geometry in the tenth year of school? Every requirement in the school and every technique of administration or of teaching is based on some fundamental assumption related to values.

The third step used by the educational philosopher is to evaluate what is done in the schools in terms of its actual or possible effects. Before one decides what it is good to do in school, one considers what the consequences may be in terms of one's standard of value. The teacher who contemplates keeping a student after school to study algebra must think of all the consequences. Might this student be led thereby to dislike algebra, to dislike the teacher? All educational philosophers are interested in the effects of what is done in the schools on the character and personality of the pupils. They therefore consider the possible outcomes of what is done in the schools and judge the merit of what is done in terms of all the possible outcomes.

The practical and common problems of everyday classroom teaching are a rich source of subject matter for educational philosophy. What are the ordinary beliefs of the members of the teaching profession about what is good education? What philosophical generalizations about teaching do teachers draw from the knowledge of child growth and development? On what kind of educational philosophy do practices rest—such practices as marking pupils, classifying or refusing to classify children into ability groups, awarding honors, withholding honors, using the results of standardized tests, punishing children?

Educational philosophy examines all teacher activities critically, with the purpose of testing the validity of all that is done. This does not mean that teachers of educational philosophy find fault with everything that is done. Criticism is developed as a method of philosophy. It is pursued methodically. Familiar practices are investigated beyond what is ordinarily known about them. Inconsistencies in thinking are revealed, confusions dissolved, conflicts resolved, and order, clarity, and consistency introduced to educational studies. Philosophers in education go to many fields for information and ideas. They examine the information and ideas critically, and as they do this, they evolve both a method of criticism and criteria to use in criticism.

Some of the greatest philosophers have addressed themselves to educational philosophy. Some of the works of such men as Charles S. Peirce, William James, Josiah Royce, John Dewey, Bertrand Russell, A. N. Whitehead and others, including Plato, were directed to a discussion of education. It may well be that this linking of education and philosophy occurs because education is viewed as an organized, deliberate, conscious attempt to mold the viewpoints and the dispositions of the young. Truly professional philosophers can scarcely refrain from considering a matter that is of such social significance and ethical importance.

Educational philosophy can be as trivial or as deep as one wishes to make it. The foundation course, however, can only be the beginning of a study of a very extensive field. As a rule, the beginning courses deal with such philosophical topics as the aims of education, the nature of subject matter, appraisals of the methods used in teaching, and the various practices related to the organization and the administration of schools. Among the ideas that are critically examined may be such practices commonly associated with teaching school as those of grouping pupils, of promoting and failing pupils, of giving examinations, and so on.

Students who wish to develop the art of critical thinking, who favor constructive change, who wish to chart the paths to future progress, who believe that interests, attitudes, and emotions are factors to be considered in the education of people and feel that what has been discovered by the specialists in human development and in the other fields of the social sciences should affect the practices followed in educating the young will find their future study of educational philosophy a highly fascinating, practical, and significant experience. Above all, they will receive from such study help on one of the most important problems, one for which they must formulate a workable solution. That is the problem of their own reasoned, defensible point of view toward what the education of a growing, developing human being should be.

3. HUMAN DEVELOPMENT

Human development is a fascinating field and one of undeniable importance to those who wish to teach intelligently and to derive a great degree of personal satisfaction from their work.

The scope of the field of human development is wide. As a professional field of interest to teachers, however, the focus of the course, regardless of title, is on using education to promote growth in the quality of human behavior. Behavior and development of behavior patterns receive pronounced emphasis. A study leading to understanding of the learning acquired by the infant, the nature of childhood fears, the source of attitudes, the way children learn to talk or read or think or reason is helpful in planning classroom activities that promise maximum desirable growth among children.

The typical college textbook on human development devotes considerable attention to learning, growth, individual differences, personality development, emotions, attitudes, and the like. Perhaps the most fundamental idea underlying all the concepts is that of the total development of the pupil. Hence the textbooks include such topics as growth in ability to make generalizations, the effects of repetition on learning, how emotions promote or inhibit growth, what has been learned about memory, habit formation, the breaking of bad habits, the effects of approval, the effects of punishments and rewards on learning, how growth in skills is effected, how intention affects learning, how growth in habits of attention is encouraged, what the nature of thinking is, and so on. Each of these topics relates to factors that shape the character of total growth of the human individual. The subject matter of the course in human development may be almost as broad as life itself. All the topics included apply not only to the learners in the school, but to everyone who learns. It is, however, only when these findings are made directly applicable to the problems of learning in the school that we call the course Educational Psychology.

Student Teaching

In their last year of training, students customarily spend part of their time as student teachers. The course in student teaching is the most obviously practical of all the professional courses because it gives students an opportunity to do on a limited scale what they have looked forward to doing and have prepared to do. The nature of the course varies greatly from institution to institution. Usually student teachers are assigned to work with some teacher in a public school as an assistant or cooperative teacher. What students do, of course, depends on the teachers with whom they cooperate. Usually the senior teacher has been selected because he or she is a successful teacher and is interested in helping in the education of teachers.

Under the immediate supervision of the classroom teacher, student teachers gradually assume more and more responsibility and engage in a constantly expanding number of practical activities. As they teach, they continue to study with the object of personal and professional improvement. If the time is spent wisely, the students build skills and understandings and develop confidence that are of inestimable value when they enter a school as one of the regularly employed teachers.

Advanced Study

The student in education will find many avenues open for advanced professional study. University catalogs list specialized courses given in departments and schools of education that deal intensively with almost every problem the teacher is likely to encounter. Teachers of nursery school, kindergarten, and the primary grades may study one kind of course grouping; middle-grade teachers another; and high school teachers still another. Courses are designed specifically for each of these levels in the teaching of reading, mathematics, science, social studies, geography, creative dramatics, arts and crafts, music, speech, physical education, and other related subjects. All such courses, when taught by able teachers, afford many insights into the handling of rather narrowly classified but important problems connected with the promotion of child growth. In the light of their interests and choice of a field for specialization and with the aid of their advisers, students will decide what advanced courses to pursue.

In contemplating future fields of study, if students can select courses that are compatible with their vocational plans, not only will they enjoy them more but their profit will be much greater. By and large, the later courses in education, pursued for the purposes of professional preparation, include both subject matter and methods of directing the subject matter, combined in such a way as to promote human development to a maximum degree. Some may, however, emphasize one aspect much more than the other.

Most students find the more specialized courses in professional education a source of great interest, perhaps because these courses are then more closely related to the student's vocational objective and are usually taught by specialists who themselves are deeply immersed in their subject. If one is going to teach reading, for example, then a course in the teaching of reading, taught by an inspiring psychologist who has specialized in that aspect of child development, can indeed be most rewarding.

Perspectives for the Future

In analyzing American education—what educators and the people are doing to provide American youth with an adequate formal education—we have examined primarily the past and the present. As this book closes we think back over some current trends, some current problems, and raise questions about the future. Will current trends continue in their present directions? How will vexing problems of education be solved? It has been said that coming events cast their shadows before. Can we peer into the shadows and identify a few outlines that seem to indicate what is emerging?

Will Faith in Education Persist?

From our earliest frontier on the Atlantic coast, through various stages of western expansion to the Pacific coast, the American people have always manifested a faith in the power of education. The early provisions for free public education were based on a conviction that education is a bulwark and indeed an essential in the foundations of democracy. Immigrants from Europe have recognized that education was the important portal to an improved life with extensive opportunities. Despite crosscurrents in educational theory, conflicts in educational philosophy, numerous diversions such as wars and depressions, distractions, intrusions, and criticisms from dissatisfied elements in the body politic, education has gradually and unmistakably improved from generation to generation. Are the pride and confidence of the American people in their educational institutions sufficiently strong so that they can withstand present and future efforts to weaken or destroy them?

Will Current Trends in Education Continue?

Throughout the story of education in America we have observed trends, springing sometimes from ideas that go back to early movements and leaders in Europe, trends that have led to current practices. Sometimes, as we have noted, trends have continued for a time and have then been reversed. Sometimes they have moved in cycles, recurring after an interval. Looking at some trends that seem current, what can we say about their future? Will they be maintained in their present direction? reversed? abandoned?

I. ADJUSTMENTS TO TECHNOLOGY

We have noted many recent changes in education that have received their impetus from dramatic changes in social life in general, or that can be traced to rapid technological progress. These have included modifications in all aspects of the educational picture from building construction to curriculum and general aims.

Present predictions are that coming generations will have increasing time for their own personal use. Will the schools have to continue and expand their work in helping pupils build the kind of foundation that will equip them to utilize this free time in a satisfying manner? With shorter working days, shorter working weeks, longer vacations, and early retirement for the majority of employed people, will present trends of modification in the curriculum and other elements be adequate if continued? Should there be a more sensitive and insightful awareness of the school's responsibility in this area?

And how about preparation for actual careers or vocations? Are present trends appropriate for fulfilling the demands for a broad educational base, for training in skills needed today but training sufficiently flexibile and broadly based so that the pupil is equipped to adjust to rapidly changing demands of science, industry, and business? Are present practices adequate to supply pupils with a background that allows them to adjust to one of a number of employment opportunities if the specific one they have selected to prepare for has become obsolete even before they have completed their training?

Will the present trend in expansion of teaching aids that have been and continue to be produced in line with technological advances in other areas, be continued? accelerated? decelerated? Some of the aids have, apparently, proved themselves in the classroom. Many are still in a more or less experimental stage, although great achievement is promised for them. Will these benefits be realized? Will teaching machines, for instance, be the great help in meeting individual pupil needs that is predicted? Will their expense on a wide scale be so prohibitive as to counteract their value? Will they impersonalize instruction unduly? Will they reduce the number of teachers needed? What *is* their future?

2. MEETING INDIVIDUAL NEEDS AND ABILITIES

We have said that instructional aids are designed in part to assist the teacher in meeting individual needs and adjusting instruction to individual abilities. What about other current adjustments in schools to serve these purposes? Will the present trend toward increased numbers of nongraded classes and nongraded schools continue? How about team teaching? ability grouping? Have they proved themselves to be sound and practical? Should, or will, present trends continue? Are they still so new that they are really unproven, are still experimental, and the future cannot be predicted? Are there other trends in practices to meet individual needs and abilities that are more promising?

3. TRENDS CAUSED BY POPULATION SHIFTS
   AND EXPANSION

We have noted that the current trend in school district organization is toward fewer and larger districts in agricultural areas. Has this proved to be desirable? Will the consolidation of smaller districts, the removal of control of education from a small community or neighborhood prove sound? How far will the corporate trend lead in district organization? Should it continue?

The great range of differences in neighborhood areas in large-city districts has led to a number of trends intended to eliminate racial segregation and minimize variation in educational opportunities caused by cultural deprivation in such areas as the inner city. Will the present attempt to achieve equality and racial integration by busing be continued? expanded? What is the future of the so-called cluster school plan? Will people become accustomed to, and reconciled to, having their children educated outside their immediate neighborhood? Will the trend toward integration be reversed and the black children who live in highly concentrated black communities remain segregated in school as they are in life, but be supplied with schools that are better than the other schools in the city, so that they can be compensated for years of inferior education?

Will the size of large-city school districts reach a point where they can no longer be efficiently administered, where they are weighted down with bureaucracy? Of the population in general, 71 percent now dwell in urban centers—in New Jersey more than 88 percent. The New York City District School System alone is responsible for educating more than 1.1 million children and youth and employs more than 59,000 classroom teachers. Will the present trend toward expansion of districts be allowed to continue? Or will the states have to limit the size of large public school districts—force them to divide into a number of smaller administrative units (in much the same way as they have eliminated small districts by enforcing consolidations)?

unit

IV

Suggested Readings

ANDERSON, ROBERT H., *Teaching in a World of Change*. New York: Harcourt Brace Jovanovich, Inc., 1966, chaps. 5 and 6. Chapter 5 treats of team teaching. Chapter 6 discusses the people who work with teachers—paraprofessionals, parent volunteers, and other teacher aides.

BALLINGER, STANLEY E., "Of Testing and Its Tyranny," *Phi Delta Kappan,* 44 (No. 4): 176–182, January, 1963. A review of a book by a professor of mathematics called *The Tyranny of Testing.* The review gives substantial analysis of the testing movement, revealing its major strengths and weaknesses.

BAREN, DAVID, "Do You Dare . . . Negro Literature and the Disadvantaged Student," *Phi Delta Kappan,* 50 (No. 9): 520–524, May, 1969. The author "challenges teachers, and particularly teachers of English, to examine in their classes the most fundamental and sharply probing studies of the Negro in America—made by Negro authors." Includes a short bibliography.

BECKER, JAMES M., and LEE F. ANDERSON, "Riders on the Earth Together," *American Education,* 5 (No. 5): 2–4, May, 1969. Explains some of the implications for education when the earth is viewed from afar. "Scrapping the segmented view of the earth that is our legacy from schools and maps and pre-space-age thinking, let us consider the lunar view of this world as a basic unity and examine its implications for education."

BEGGS, DAVID W., III, and EDWARD G. BUFFIE, eds., *Nongraded Schools in Action.* Bloomington: Indiana University Press, 1967, part II. Thirteen different nongraded schools are described by those connected with them.

BENNETT, MARGARET, "Teaching Is Better With," *Saturday Review,* pp. 82–83, February 16, 1963. A classroom teacher who began teaching without courses in education concludes, "My attitude toward education courses can be summed up with a paraphrase of that old saying about money: 'I have taught with education courses and without education courses, and, believe me, *with* is better.'"

BERKMAN, DAVE, "You Can't Make Them Learn," *Atlantic Monthly,* 210 (No. 9): 62–67, September 1, 1962. Analysis of the problems confronted by teachers who teach in schools in economically depressed areas.

BERLIN, I. N., "Desegregation Creates Problems Too," *Saturday Review,* pp. 66–68, June 15, 1963. Explains the problems created by teaching children who have widely divergent sociological origins.

BETTELHEIM, BRUNO, "Stop Pampering Gifted Children," *The Saturday Evening Post,* pp. 8, 10, April 11, 1964. "Segregating the gifted, I am convinced, harms both the advanced student and the not-so-advanced." A psychologist's analysis of the effects of ability grouping.

BIDWELL, JAMES K., "A New Look at Old Committee Reports," *The Mathematics Teacher,* 61 (No. 4): 383–387, April, 1968. Traces suggestions on reform in mathematics subject matter beginning with a report made to a National Education Association meeting in 1892. "Thus we have seen that these reports in the nineties sometimes presented a point of view similar to what we consider good curriculum practice. . . ." The pronouncements of committees are not always carried out in action.

BLOUNT, NATHAN S., "Fructify the Folding Doors; Team Teaching Reexamined," *The English Journal,* 53 (No. 3): 177–179, 195, March, 1964. Views team teaching as "the most exciting prospect in English." Explains why.

BROWNELL, JOHN A., and HARRIS A. TAYLOR, "Theoretical Perspectives for Teaching Teams," *Phi Delta Kappan,* 43 (No. 4): pp. 150–157, January, 1962. A rather complete analysis of what is required for team teaching, written by two men involved in an extensive experimental program of team teaching.

BRUNE, IRVIN H., "Some K–6 Geometry," *The Arithmetic Teacher,* 14 (No. 6): 441–447, October, 1967. An interesting article for the general reader who may not understand how geometry can begin at the kindergarten level and continue to be taught through all the grades of the elementary school. Clearly sets forth the basic concepts on which mathematics is built.

BURNS, JOHN L., "Our Era of Opportunity," *Saturday Review,* pp. 38–39, January 14, 1967. Explains how the essential tools for improving the quality of education have become available through the development of a large number of teaching aids. "The first step toward improving quality would be to free the classroom teacher from much of his daily routine in order to give him time to help individual students." The author enumerates the devices he believes will accomplish this.

COULSON, JOHN E., "Automation, Electronic Computers, and Education," *Phi Delta Kappan,* 47 (No. 7): 340–344, March, 1966. This article is based on a presentation at a conference on cybernetics.

CRONBACH, LEO J., "What Research Says About Programed Instruction," *NEA Journal,* 51 (No. 9): 45–47, December, 1962. A clear explanation of what is involved in the current attempts to build well-designed programs of instruction, and some discussion of the difficulties encountered in arriving at a fair appraisal of the educational results.

DARLING, DAVID W., "Team Teaching," *NEA Journal,* 54 (No. 5): 24–25, May, 1965. A university consultant to an intern in team teaching in the University of Wisconsin Improvement Program explains his concept of team teaching in elementary school. "We believe that team teaching . . . offers a greater opportunity for achieving the objectives of elementary school education . . . than any other organizational plan that we know of."

DAWSON, KENNETH E., and MORRIS NORFLEET, "The Computer and the Student," *NEA Journal,* 57 (No. 2): 47–48, February, 1968. Explains how one computerized program works and its advantages. "The biggest advantage of the computerized program appears to be its ability to adapt to individual differences. . . . It automatically adjusts to the student's ability level and constantly leads him to more advanced problems as he progresses."

DU BRIDGE, LEE A., "Physics," *NEA Journal,* 52 (No. 9): 24–28, December, 1963. Shows in simple language the changes that are taking place in the field of physics and explains how the changes lead to many new developments.

ELDRED, DONALD M., and MAURIE HILLSON, "The Non-Graded School and Mental Health," *Elementary School Journal,* 63: 218–222, January, 1963. Discusses advantages of nongraded schools from the standpoint of mental health.

FISHER, MILDRED OGG, "Team Teaching in Houston," *The English Journal,* 51 (No. 9): 628–631, December, 1962. Describes the plan for modified team teaching that is working successfully in Houston.

GEDDES, DOROTHY, and SALLY I. LIPSEY, "Sets—Natural, Necessary, Knowable?" *The Arithmetic Teacher,* 15 (No. 5): 337–340, April, 1968. Explains why the idea of sets is fundamental to successful teaching of beginning mathematics. "The concept of set is an intuitive and natural one; every child has made use of it long before he enters school."

GIBB, E. GLENADINE, "Some Approaches to Mathematics Concepts in the Elementary School," *NEA Journal,* 48 (No. 8): 65–66, November, 1959. Analyzes the nature of the current discussions centering on the question of developing a better sequence of subject matter in mathematics.

GIBEL, INGE LEDERER, "How *Not* to Integrate Schools," *Harper's Magazine,* 227: 57–66, November, 1963. The writer, who is a mother in a large city, analyzes the effects of school policy, such as ability grouping, having mostly middle-class teachers, and the like, on the education of children.

GOSLIN, DAVID A., "The Social Impact of Standardized Testing," *NEA Journal,* 52 (No. 7): 20–22, October, 1963. A sociologist analyzes the effects of standardized testing both on the individual and on what is taught in the school.

GROBMAN, HAROLD, "Biology Is Changing Too," *Saturday Review,* pp. 67–69, 75, September 21, 1963. Describes the new instructional practices and materials in biology that are being introduced into the schools, beginning with first grade and extending through the basic courses in college. Stresses particularly the trends in vitalizing the instruction at the high school level.

HANDLIN, OSCAR, "Are the Colleges Killing Education?" *Atlantic Monthly,* 209: 41–45, May, 1962. A professor of history analyzes the stifling effects of the stress given to competition in college instruction.

HOUSTON, W. ROBERT, and ROBERT B. HAWSON, eds., *Competency-Based Teacher Education.* Chicago: Science Research Associates, Inc., 1972. This is a collection of recent essays on the various developments in the conception, development, and implementation of behaviorally grounded "competency-based" programs of teacher education.

HUDGINS, BRYCE B., *The Instructional Process.* Chicago: Rand McNally & Company, 1971. This is a text that looks in depth at some basic processes, concepts, and arguments relating to teaching and learning. Attention is given to the classroom as a social environment as well as to instructional innovations.

HUNTER, WILLIAM A., ed., *Multi-Cultural Education Through Competency-Based Teacher Education.* Washington, D.C.: American Association of Colleges for Teacher Education, 1974. This is a collection of several essays on competency-based, or behavioral, approaches to teaching American cultural groups and on the preparation of teachers for such teaching.

HYMAN, RONALD T., ed., *Contemporary Thought on Teaching.* Englewood Cliffs, N.J.: Prentice-Hall Inc., 1971. This is one of the finest collections of essays on different theories of teaching to be published in the last several years. It contains essays by many prominent scholars on the ways in which teaching proceeds, theories of teaching, and the evaluation of teaching.

ITZKOFF, SEYMOUR W., *Cultural Pluralism and American Education*. Scranton, Pa.: International Textbook Company, 1969. This is a most important study of cultural pluralism in America as it relates to contemporary and future problems of education. The author discusses past points of view on cultural pluralism and then presents his own position.

INGRAHAM, LEONARD W., "Teachers, Computers, and Games: Innovations in the Social Studies," *Social Education*, 31 (No. 1): 51–53, January, 1967. The author gives a clear explanation of how a computer in a school can serve social studies teachers, points out that every social studies teacher should know something about computers, and appends a helpful bibliography.

JOHNSON, DONOVAN A., "Enjoy the Mathematics You Teach," *The Arithmetic Teacher*, 15 (No. 4): 328–332, April, 1968. Explains how enjoyment in learning mathematics is the key to success in teaching mathematics. Explains how many recreational topics can and should be used to discover mathematical concepts and to build positive attitudes toward learning the subject.

KLIGER, SAMUEL, "The Workbook and the Programed Text," *The English Journal*, 52 (No. 9): 674–676, December, 1963. Are programed textbooks merely old workbooks in new format? Answers the question from the programer's point of view.

KORB, SISTER MARY VICTOR, "Positive and Negative Factors in Team Teaching," *The Mathematics Teacher*, 61 (No. 1): 50–53, January, 1968. Reports on team teaching in high school mathematics clearly explains how it was organized, and points out the benefits that accrue to teachers and pupils.

LANGE, PHIL C., "Selection and Use of Programmed Learning Materials," *NEA Journal*, 53 (No. 4): 28–29, April, 1964. Sets forth the assumptions about teaching procedure that underlie programed learning.

LARRICK, NANCY, "The All-White World of Children's Books," *Saturday Review*, 63–65, 84–85, September 11, 1965. This analysis of children's books shows that they do not portray the lives of all kinds of racial groups but are representative mainly of the white group. Describes what the Council for Interracial Books for Children is doing to give direction to future children's books.

LEAR, JOHN, "What the Moon Ranger Couldn't See," *Saturday Review*, pp. 35–40, September 5, 1964. Shows the rapidity of change in the world of subject matter to which school children are exposed.

LEAVITT, WILLIAM, "Individuals, Front and Center," *American Education*, 5 (No. 2): 4–6, February, 1969. Explains how children in Washington, D.C., were used to demonstrate how innovative techniques employed in various school systems throughout the nation operate to individualize learning.

MAC KENZIE, VERNON G., "Health in a Changing World," *School Science and Mathematics*, 68 (No. 5): 380–384, May, 1968. Explains the impact of rapid social change on the health of the American people. "The giant and often conflicting scientific, social, and political forces within our society . . . move inexorably forward." Decisions affecting public health are often made without reference to certain vital health concerns. A good problem to interest pupils in the study of science in school.

MANNING, JOHN, "Discipline in the Good Old Days," *Phi Delta Kappan*, 41 (No. 3): 94–99, December, 1959. A professor of humanities vividly and authentically describes how our ancestors handled the problems of school discipline not so long ago. The carefully documented references may serve as a bibliography.

MARKLE, SUSAN MEYER, "Inside the Teaching Machine," *Saturday Review,* pp. 58–60, November 18, 1961. Explains in detail the problem of programing instructional materials.

MICHELS, WALTER C., "The Teaching of Elementary Physics," *Scientific Monthly,* 298: 56–64, April, 1958. A new approach that emphasizes the understanding of basic principles. "The history of physics and mathematics supports the amalgamation of the two subjects."

MILLER, HARRY L., and ROGER R. WOOCK, *Social Foundations of Urban Education.* New York: Holt, Rinehart, and Winston, Inc., 1973. An excellent volume on contemporary urban education and a good source for commmentary on research relevant to this field of study.

MIZER, JEAN E., "Dear JM," *Today's Education,* 57 (No. 7): 18–25, October, 1968. Sage advice to beginning teachers is given in an informal and friendly way.

MUELLER, THEODORE, "Psychology and the Language Arts," *School and Society,* 87: 420, 422, 427, October 24, 1959. Shows why effective language training must center in audio-oral work.

MUSGRAVE, MARTHA L., "Seeing Double at Vero Beach," *American Education,* 4 (No. 8): 17–19, September, 1968. Numerous helpful ways closed-circuit television can be used in the school are explained. "Its versatility makes it suitable for use in many subject areas. . . ."

MUSS, ROF E., and others, "Discipline," *NEA Journal,* 52: 9–22, September, 1963. A series of discussions on the problem of discipline in the school.

NATIONAL EDUCATION ASSOCIATION, Research Division, *Ability Grouping,* Research Summary 1968–S3. Of special interest are the pros and cons of ability grouping (p. 5) and the summary and conclusions (pp. 42–44). "The majority of teachers—close to three-fifths of the elementary-school teachers and nearly 9 of every 10 secondary-school teachers—favor the grouping of pupils for instruction according to ability." "Despite its increasing popularity, there is a notable lack of empirical evidence to support the use of ability grouping as an instructional arrangement in the public schools."

NEA Journal, "Denver's Home Teaching Program," 56 (No. 2): 14–16, January, 1967. A description of the program of the Boettcher School of Denver, organized for the education of the handicapped child. The program combines instruction in school, hospital, and home.

NEA Journal, "Teacher Opinion Poll," 53 (No. 6): 25, September, 1964. Maintaining pupil discipline remains one of the most persistent problems teachers face. It appears that keeping order in the classroom has become a more difficult problem than it was in past years.

NEA Journal, "How the Professional Feels About Teacher Aides," 56 (No. 8): 15–16, November, 1967. Report of NEA Research Division poll on teacher opinion. Most teachers—80 percent—do not have teacher aides. Those who do, find them of substantial assistance, and prefer that the duties of the aides be confined to noninstructional activities such as clerical work. The survey reveals that aides perform a wide variety of services.

NOYES, KATHRYN JOHNSTON, and GORDON L. MC ANDREW, "Is This What Schools Are For?" *Saturday Review,* pp. 58–59, 65, December 21, 1968. The authors explain why "In sum, we run our schools almost totally without reference to the needs of the children who attend them."

OETTINGER, ANTHONY G., "The Myths of Educational Technology," *Saturday Review,* pp. 76–77, 91, May 18, 1968. A professor of linguistics and applied mathematics, after completing extensive research on problems connected with the application of technology (especially computers), warns of concluding that some teaching practices are much better than others. "Choice among existing practices cannot be made from data demonstrating the greater effectiveness of one over another. . . . We should plan for the encouragement of pluralism and diversity, at least in technique."

PATTERSON, C. H., *Humanistic Education.* Englewood Cliffs, N.J.: Prentice-Hall, Inc., 1973. An excellent book on the conditions and processes of more humane ways of educating persons.

PETROQUIN, GAYNOR, *Individualizing Learning Through Modular-Flexible Programming.* New York: McGraw-Hill Book Company, 1968, chap. 1. This chapter, entitled "A Computer-Generated, Teacher-Developed, Modular-Flexible Schedule," explains what modular scheduling is and how it has evolved. A beginning student entering his professional preparation will do well to become acquainted with some of "the straws in the wind" that foreshadow future change.

Phi Delta Kappan, "Programed Instruction," 54 (No. 6), March, 1963. This issue is devoted entirely to the subject of programed instruction; 20 specialists write on the contributions such instruction can make to learning.

POSTMAN, NEIL, ed., *Television and the Teaching of English.* Englewood Cliffs, N.J.: Prentice-Hall, Inc., 1961, 138 pp. A report made by the Committee on the Study of Television of the National Council of Teachers of English. Part I deals with the educational significance of television. Part II deals with classroom study through television.

RATHS, LOUIS E., MERRILL HARMIN, and SIDNEY B. SIMON, *Values and Teaching* Columbus, Ohio: Charles E. Merrill Publishing Co., 1966. This is a basic book on various methods of conducting values clarification exercises in classroom settings. It has been used by tens of thousands of American teachers since 1966.

REED, JERRY E., and JOHN L. HAYMAN, JR., "An Experiment Involving Use of English 2600, an Automated Instruction Text," *Journal of Educational Research,* 55: 476–484, June, 1962. From this, one gets an idea of what an automated textbook is like.

REID, JAMES M., "An Adventure in Programming Literature," *The English Journal,* 52 (No. 9): 659–673, December, 1963. A veteran book editor explains the programing of poetry after what he calls his "two-year adventure" in programing literature.

ROSENTHAL, ROBERT, and LENORE JACOBSON, *Pygmalion in the Classroom: Teacher Expectation and Pupils' Intellectual Development.* New York: Holt, Rinehart and Winston, Inc., 1968. A report on a study showing that children whose teachers were led to believe they would improve in their school work *did* significantly improve. The authors describe in detail their careful scientific methods, their results, and their conclusions. Readable and thought-provoking.

ROWLAND, HOWARD S., "Using the TV Western," *The English Journal,* 52 (No. 9): 693–696, December, 1963. Shows how a teacher may use television "Westerns" to build a foundation for critical viewing.

SAVA, SAMUEL G., "When Learning Comes Easy," *Saturday Review,* pp. 102–104, 119, November 16, 1968. This is a strong argument for what the author refers to as "a massive investment in early childhood education."

School Science and Mathematics, 68 (No. 2): 148–153, 154–158, February, 1968. Perusal of these pages will illustrate the extensive efforts the federal government is making through grants to colleges and universities, private and public, to improve instruction in science and mathematics in the public schools. Note that grants are to help pupils as well as teachers. Official publications in other fields—English, social studies, and so on—are just as extensive. These particular grants are through the National Science Foundation. Other extensive grants are under the National Defense Education Act.

SCHULTZ, FREDERICK MARSHALL, *Social-Philosophical Foundations of Education.* Dubuque, Iowa: Kendall/Hunt Publishing Company, 1974. This is a basic introductory study in social philosophy of education and educational policy studies. There is an emphasis on decision making and development of the reader's own social philosophy of education.

SCHMUCK, RICHARD A., and PATRICIA A. SCHMUCK, *A Humanistic Psychology of Education: Making the School Everybody's House.* Palo Alto, Calif.: National Press Books, 1974. This is a very interesting overview of goals and processes relating to humane change in education and human relationships in education.

SCOLLON, KENNETH M., "Why Art in Education?" *Saturday Review,* 70–72, 80. February 15, 1964. States many reasons why it is important to emphasize the fine arts in the schools.

SHANE, HAROLD G., and JUNE GRANT SHANE, "Forecast for the Seventies," *Today's Education,* January 1969. In this article the Shanes discuss their perceptions of what educational priorities seem to be called for in the 1970s.

SHAPLIN, JUDSON T., and HENRY F. OLDS, eds., *Team Teaching.* New York: Harper & Row, Publishers, 1964. Gives an overview of the team teaching approach in classroom teaching as furnished by a number of writers who have studied the movement.

SHARP, EVELYN, "The New Math: You Don't Count on Your Fingers Anymore," *Saturday Review,* pp. 65–67, January 19, 1963. Describes the new mathematics being introduced into the modern school curriculum.

SIMON, SIDNEY B., LELAND W. HOWE, and HOWARD KIRSCHENBAUM, *Values Clarification: A Handbook of Practical Strategies for Teachers and Students.* New York: Hart Publishing Company, 1972. A very useful compilation of 79 value clarification strategies with many different classroom applications. The authors have included instructions in the use of these strategies.

SKINNER, B. F., "Teaching Machines," *Scientific American,* 205 (No. 5): 90–102. November, 1961. Explains how teaching machines promote effective learning by enabling "the student to learn in small but rigorous steps, each of which is rewarding," and how they may introduce a new element to methods of teaching.

SKINNER, B. F., "Why Teachers Fail," *Saturday Review,* pp. 80–81, 98–102, October 16, 1965. An eminent psychologist analyzes the problem of teaching method. "Any special knowledge of pedagogy as a basic science of teaching is felt to be unnecessary. The attitude is regrettable. No enterprise can improve itself . . . without examining its basic processes." The author presents a strong case for the application of intensive study to methods of teaching.

Social Education, "Black Americans and Social Studies: Minority Groups in American Society," 33 (No. 4): April, 1969. The entire issue is devoted to the problem of adjusting education to the needs of various minority groups and ghetto children, including American Indians, Orientals, Spanish, and blacks.

STEVENS, MARTIN, and WILLIAM R. ELKINS, "Designs for Team Teaching in English," *The English Journal,* 53 (No. 3): 170–176, March, 1964. Description of team teaching in a high school in which experiments have been conducted with different methods.

STONE, JAMES C., and DONALD P. DE NEVI, eds., *Teaching Multi-Cultural Populations: Five Heritages.* New York: Van Nostrand Reinhold Company, 1971. This is a very informative collection of essays on the education and culture of Mexican, Puerto Rican, black, Indian, and Asian American populations in the United States.

STONE, JAMES C., and FREDERICK W. SCHNEIDER, eds., *Teaching in the Inner City: A Book of Readings.* New York: Thomas Y. Crowell Company, 1970. This is a truly exceptional book of readings on inner-city education. It represents a good sample of the best thought on this subject at the end of the 1960s and the beginning of the 1970s. It is a good source for basic information in this area.

STREHLER, ALLEN, F., "What's New About the New Math?" *Saturday Review,* pp. 68–69, 84, March 21, 1964. Explains why mathematics as taught in the schools is being revised· and explains why there is some confusion among educators as to what directions the revisions should take.

SUPPES, PATRICK, "The Teacher and Computer-Assisted Instruction," *NEA Journal,* 56 (No. 2): 15–17, February, 1967. Explains how computers can assist teachers in their instructional activities and answers some of the questions teachers commonly raise about the future of computers in the classroom.

THORNDIKE, EDWARD LEE, *Man and His Works.* Cambridge, Mass.: Harvard University Press, 1943. Chapter 8, "The Psychology of Punishment," analyzes the psychological effects of the use of coercion.

TINCHER, ETHEL, "The Detroit Public Schools Present English on Television," *English Journal,* 56 (No. 4): 596–602, April, 1967. Explains how television can be used effectively to strengthen classroom teaching.

UNDERWOOD, BENTON J., "Forgetting," *Scientific American,* 210 (No. 3): 91–99, March, 1964. An experimental study of forgetting. "Summing up these observations in the form of a general theory, we can say that all forgetting results basically from interference between the associations a man carries in his memory storage system."

VOYAT, GILBERT, "IQ: God-Given or Man-Made?" *Saturday Review,* pp. 73–75, 86–87, May 17, 1969. This is a critique of a research study by Dr. Arthur R. Jensen, University of California at Berkeley, which concluded that heredity is a more powerful determinant than environment and that the IQ is a valid indication of inherited potential. Highly controversial.

WATSON, GOODWIN, "What Do We Know About Learning?" *NEA Journal,* 52 (No. 3): 20–22, March, 1963. A brief, readable summary of what psychologists believe to be true about learning.

WEINSTEIN, GERALD, and MARIO FANTINI, " 'Phony' Literature," *English Journal,,* 84 (No. 4): 259–264, April, 1965. Finds most of the materials in English unsuitable for children from disadvantaged homes. Discusses how a teacher may develop his own materials.

WOODRING, PAUL, "Are Intelligence Tests Unfair?" *Saturday Review,* pp. 79–80, April 16, 1966. An eminent psychologist in a scholarly analysis sets the record straight on the right and wrong uses of standardized intelligence tests.

Index

76 77 78 79   9 8 7 6 5 4 3 2 1